THE RIGHTS CF NATURE
AND THE TESTIMONY OF THINGS

The Rights of Nature and the Testimony of Things

Literature and Environmental Ethics from Latin America

MARK ANDERSON

VANDERBILT UNIVERSITY PRESS

Nashville, Tennessee

Library of Congress Cataloging-in-Publication Data

Names: Anderson, Mark, 1974- author.
Title: The rights of nature and the testimony of things : literature and
  environmental ethics from Latin America / Mark Anderson.
Description: Nashville : Vanderbilt University Press, 2024. | Includes
  bibliographical references and index.
Identifiers: LCCN 2024011358 (print) | LCCN 2024011359 (ebook) | ISBN
  9780826506771 (paperback) | ISBN 9780826506788 (hardcover) | ISBN
  9780826506795 (epub) | ISBN 9780826506801 (pdf)
Subjects: LCSH: Latin American literature--History and criticism. | Ecology
  in literature. | Ethics in literature. | Ecocriticism--Latin America.
Classification: LCC PN849.L29 A53 2024 (print) | LCC PN849.L29 (ebook) |
  DDC 860.9/98--dc23/eng/20240319
LC record available at https://lccn.loc.gov/2024011358
LC ebook record available at https://lccn.loc.gov/2024011359

Front cover photograph by Mario A. Villeda, via Pexels

To my parents, David and Sandy, who taught
me to nurture the world as it nurtures us.

CONTENTS

ACKNOWLEDGMENTS

I would to thank the many, many people who, directly or indirectly, made this book possible. I am particularly grateful for the conversations, camaraderie, critiques, and suggestions provided over the years by Katarzyna Beilin, Dana Bultman, Cristóbal Cardemil-Krause, Sharae Deckard, Roberto Forns-Broggi, Carlos Fonseca, Carolyn Fornoff, Jennifer L. French, Juan Carlos Galeano, Iñaki García-Prádanos, Kevin Guerrieri, Gisela Heffes, Jonathan Krell, Serenella Iovino, Jorge Marcone, Ana María Mutis, Felipe Martínez Pinzón, Alejandro Quin, Kerstin Oloff, Elizabeth Pettinaroli, Charlotte Rogers, Victoria Saramago, Víctor Vich, Patrícia Vieira, Raymond Lesley Williams, Lesley Wylie, the participants of the 2018 Instituto SARAS workshop on sustainability (and Instituto SARAS for organizing it), and the UGA Green Leaves ecocriticism discussion group organized by Ron Balthazor. I deeply appreciate my colleague and climbing partner Rohan Sikri for his indispensable guidance regarding the philosophy of ethics (and rock and ice climbing techniques), as well as the many undergraduate and graduate students at the University of Georgia who allowed me to bounce my ideas off them in my courses on Latin American literature and environmental ethics, providing both insight and critique. Kate Bundy, Ida Day, Louisiana Lightsey, and Marcela Reales were particularly helpful interlocutors and encouraged me greatly with their shared interest in these topics. This project benefitted greatly from the support of the Willson Center for Humanities and Arts at the University of Georgia. I am also deeply indebted to all the compañeros and guides who provided invaluable knowledge about plants, animals, and local cultural practices in my excursions in Latin American environments, especially Mario Mar in Veracruz, Mexico; Gladys Jiménez in the Sierra Blanca in

Perú; and Miguel at the Heliconia Lodge on the Yavarí River in Amazonia. In the same vein, I would like to show my appreciation for all the philosophers and writers who, although I have not had the opportunity to meet them in person, have deeply impacted my thinking and worldview. I am particularly grateful to Davi Kopenawa for sharing his life and incomparable knowledge about Yanomami ontologies and cultural practices in *The Falling Sky*. Reading that book was truly epiphanic, opening my eyes to what was, for me, a completely new way of conceiving of both representation and politics. Finally, I would also like to acknowledge the great impact that Anthony Carrigan's passion for the field has had on my work despite his untimely passing. May he rest in peace.

Introduction

Representing "Nature"

The rights of nature legislation approved in the 2008 Ecuadorian Constitution and in Bolivian environmental laws in 2010 revolutionized ecological discourse and catalyzed popular ecology and indigenous rights movements worldwide, even when the implementation of these laws has been less than ideal due to entrenched interests and those nations' reliance on extractive industries to finance social programs. Although such legislation had been debated since US law professor Christopher Stone's seminal essay "Should Trees Have Standing?" (1972) and a municipal rights of nature ordinance was passed in 2005 in the Tamaqua Burrough in Pennsylvania, the 2008 Ecuadorian Constitution was the first in the world to grant nature legal personhood at the national level. This scaling is particularly significant because national constitutions always supersede state and municipal ordinances as the "highest law of the land"; no laws may be passed that contradict constitutional principles. Nonetheless, simply granting nature specific rights with the attendant legal standing to claim those rights does not ensure that they can be put into practice. The problem of juridical speech becomes particularly fraught when dealing with nonhuman entities, as they are considered incapable of representing their own interests in either lawmaking or the judicial system. They must always be represented by human politicians or lawyers.

As I discuss throughout this book, this problem is not limited to legal representation; it in fact lies at the heart of every discourse and political practice relating to nonhumans. Indeed, the problem of representation is intricately bound up with the central concern of environmental ethics, which is the revaluation of nonhuman beings as possessing intrinsic worth and interests of their own.[1] While this issue is often downplayed by deferring to their instrumental value for humans, whether economic or aesthetic, a truly ethical approach to nonhumans as something more than the straightforward projection of human interests, needs, and desires over nonhuman bodies requires acknowledging not only their heterogeneous autonomy or singularity with respect to linguistic constructs such as "nature," "environment," "animal," "plant," and similar categories, but also their ability to represent themselves through expressive modalities that are not restricted to language, that is, symbolic representation. The question then becomes: in what ways do nonhumans communicate their intrinsic values and interests, defined by their own specific, systematic relations with the world, to us, the humans? And how might those values simultaneously exceed and pervade symbolic representation in language, reordering our concepts of the social and the political?

This book explores the relations between writing, the philosophy of ethics, and legal discourse in the conceptualization of human and nonhuman personhood through different representational regimes. I am particularly interested in how Latin American Indigenous and non-Indigenous authors, intellectuals, and politicians have conceived of speech and political subjectivities in ways that provide an opening for nonhumans to testify on their own behalf and to participate affectively in politics as part of the multispecies community that not only comprises, but also produces what we usually call environments. Drawing on posthumanist thought, ecological studies, and a variety of Indigenous Latin American relational ontologies, I argue that these forms of cosmopolitical discourse—in which political subjectivities are viewed not as static, representative positions, but rather as intra-active assemblages of human and nonhuman bodies—reconstitute the polis as more-than-human multitudes and politics as a sympoetic reshaping of the world.[2] And it is only in such a conceptualization of politics in which nonhumans can truly be considered capable of claiming both ethical standing and the legal rights afforded in rights of nature legislation.

While many Indigenous societies conceptualize nonhumans as part of their communities and therefore multispecies governance, my objective is not only to draw attention to Indigenous cosmopolitical practices (a project that has already been carried out by a wide variety of Indigenous intellectuals and non-Indigenous anthropologists), but also to place these Indigenous cosmopolitical frameworks into dialogue with the Euro-American traditions of constitutional liberalism and the philosophy of ethics in order to develop a route toward the practical implementation of the rights of nature in liberal democracies. Since this question ultimately hinges on the question of representation, literature plays a key role in my analysis in at least three main ways. On the one hand, aesthetics—that is, the relations between artistic representations and the real—has been the central topic of artistic and literary theory since the foundations of the Euro-American humanistic tradition in ancient Greek thought. This tradition of aesthetic theory is useful not only for understanding how specific representational regimes and their attendant concepts function to order realities into ideologically inflected worlds or ontologies, but also for drawing attention to the arbitrariness of that relation and its contingency on sociohistorical context, even when some discourses make claims to absolute, ahistorical truth, that is, total correspondence between discourse and the real. In that sense, literature opens language up to forms of expression that are foreclosed by rigid classificatory logics, allowing us to imagine representation as something more than the symbolic overwriting of the other's singular affectivity, that is, its ability to transform us in encounter. Finally, literature has long served as an important space for the exploration of the social practice and limits of rights and human rights discourse in particular, beyond the meticulously delimited bounds of juridical discourse.

Literature, Representation, and Rights

As Jacques Derrida argued in *Literature in Secret*, the "secret" that literature reveals is the fictionality and self-referentiality of all representation, that is, the ultimately arbitrary, if analogical relation between words and things: "every text that is consigned to public space, that is relatively legible or intelligible, but whose content, sense, referent, signatory, and addressee are not fully determinable *realities*—realities that are at the same time *non-fictive* or *immune from all fiction*, realities that are delivered as such, by some intuition, to a determinate judgment—can become a literary object."[3] And since difference (that is, irreducible singularity) is always indeterminate and untranslatable, it can only be approximated through the symbol, never fully apprehended. In that sense, there are no "fully determinable *realities*," only approximation through different representational strategies (thus the italics). The secret of literature is that of representation itself: that even the most explicitly mimetic forms of representation such as scientific discourse are always partial, equivocal, and ultimately fictive. As Brazilian literary theorist Luiz Costa Lima brilliantly contended, the role of mimetic representation has never been to represent reality empirically, but rather to testify to the truthfulness of the ideologies underpinning representational systems.[4] The textual reference to an external object (the "mimetic product," as he calls it) serves as the evidence upholding the text's interpretation of reality.

All representation nevertheless relates directly to the real. As Derrida has long argued, the traces of concrete, material others intervene in the play between the signifier and the signified (that is, the sign as the relation between a sound-image and its conceptual referent), ordering the relation and producing meaning.[5] However, it is only in literary representation that this relation becomes readily visible, since the literary object can never be taken as the real thing; it is explicitly fictional, literary. Literature thus always serves as a forum for interrogating the relations between representations and ontologies. As Costa Lima drives home, "through the practice of mimesis [in literature], language loses its usual identity—something is said that has no immediate implications for the world—just as the producer divests himself of it—he speaks or writes to enliven ghosts which are not reducible to mere projections of his empirical self."[6] These "ghosts" are those of Derrida's hauntology; the traces of materialities that are not physically present in the text, but that are invoked or enacted by it as singularities (bundles of differences) that will always exceed the categories to which they are assigned in the representation.

In other words, when Venezuelan poet Andrés Bello describes the felling of a majestic Ceiba tree in his "Silva a la agricultura de la zona tórrida" (1826; Agriculture in the Torrid Zone), the tree species can only have meaning through its relation in the author's and readers' minds of concrete experiences with individuals of that species.[7] Even if the author or reader has never come into direct contact with that particular species, they must necessarily establish an analogical relation or chain of associations between the description and another tree with which they have had direct contact for it to have any meaning to them. It is the prior experience of that tree, a series of similar trees, or even non-linguistic images of trees that intervene to grant meaning to the sign. And the affective experience of those prior trees will necessarily have marked the reading subject with associations that exceed the reductivity of the written symbol and its abstract position in the system of language. In that sense, mimesis may be understood not as the mere reduction of bodies to symbols, but rather as the response to the human or nonhuman other's affectivity (their presence as apprehended by the subject) and the ongoing enactment of their traces in the production of one's own signs, always in economic and ecological relation, in exchange.

While this would be the case in all forms of representation, fictional or otherwise, literature's artistic freedom—its disregard for the imperative of "truth-telling" or claiming a 1:1 equivalence between the symbol and the thing it represents—allows for greater technical experimentation with respect to methodologies for drawing out and responding to the affective agencies of others within representation. As Gary Snyder argues in "Language Goes Two Ways," literature is often inflected with what he calls "wild" language, that is, grammatical structures and poetic turns of phrase that break with linguistic and ideological conventions. According to Snyder, the literary disruption within the normal order of language occurs when nature's self-ordering systems—including our own biology—manifest themselves during the writing process, reordering both language and the logic of representation:

> "Wild" alludes to a process of self-organization that generates systems and organisms, all of which are within the constraints of—and constitute components of—larger systems that again are wild, such as major ecosystems or the water cycle in the biosphere. Wildness can be said to be the essential nature of nature. As reflected in consciousness, it can be seen as a kind of open awareness—full of imagination but also the source of alert survival intelligence. The workings of the human mind at its very richest reflect this self-organizing wildness. So language does not impose order on a chaotic universe, but reflects its own wildness back.[8]

Furthermore, one could argue that reading also consists in a "wilding" or reordering of the text's own internal logic, since readers' experiences, inflected by the self-organization of life experiences and meanings within the brain, will necessarily intervene and transform the text's meanings. These life experiences—garnered through affective encounters with human and nonhuman others—invoke their traces in the process of generating meaning, populating the text with absent presences that lie beyond the purview of either the text or the author's own experiences. In this interplay, literary characters, whether human or nonhuman, come "alive," having their own perspectives, which may or may not coincide with the author's or readers' perspectives and their respective worldviews.

It is in this sense in which Marília Librandi Rocha, dialoguing with anthropologist Eduardo Viveiros de Castro's discussion of Native Amazonian perspectivism, proposes an "Amerindian theory of literature" in which "the ontology of the fictional" is understood as a "world of latent presences."[9] Creative writing and creative reading thus become ways of enacting not only the traces of singular others that exceed symbolic representation, but also the self-ordering systems or relational matrix to which those others belong. In this way, literature potentializes a reconceptualization of representation as a process of co-creation involving a multiplicity of agencies of differing degrees, which necessarily has profound implications for both the ethical revalorization of nonhuman beings as having inherent values and interests of their own and for political practice as multispecies collaboration. The accretive nature of mimetic representation, the enactment of a multiplicity of others in trace form, thus reveals that discourse is never simply a case of sovereign authorship, but always an invocation of the irreducible powers of its others, even when it subordinates them to an overarching ideology or worldview. The literary works in which I am interested in this book develop representational strategies that draw attention to and maintain fidelity to the affective agency of others through the conscientious, performative enactment of their traces.

Finally, the relationships between literature, justice, and rights discourse trace back to the origins of modern law in classical Greek and Roman texts, since when both fictional and biographical narratives have been used to illustrate moral and legal principles. With the advent of modern democracies in the nineteenth century in particular, literature served key roles in promoting human rights, both in the sense of problematizing political discourse that denied rights to historically excluded classes such as enslaved peoples, women, and other minoritized groups and in that of drawing attention to human rights abuses and their psychological and social effects.[10] In post-Independence Latin America, literature became a key public forum for debating and proposing solutions to the persistence of the colonial legacy of racialized economic, social, and political exclusions of Black and Indigenous peoples from the exercise of modern democratic citizenship. With the advent of fascistic dictatorial regimes in many Latin American nations in the 1930s and again in the 1970s, the juridical roles of literature became even more pronounced, drawing attention to human rights abuses that were censored by the regimes in question as well as experimenting with a variety of techniques for representing the psychological trauma caused by political repression, torture, and genocide. Crucially, many of these techniques searched for ways to represent what cannot be fully processed as representation, that is, the experience of trauma.

While I will not go as far as to speculate in this book regarding how nonhumans may experience and express trauma (which is clearly the case with at least some animals but becomes much more polemical with regards to plants and other "faceless' species], the representation of nonhumans' mental and social lives shares with human psychological trauma this fundamental problem of representing what cannot be represented directly through symbolization. Furthermore, the ethics of representation clearly come to the forefront in portrayals of human rights abuses and psychological trauma, particularly when the representation in question is not autobiographical, as it never can be in the case of nonhumans, at least in the conventional sense. It is by no means coincidental that since at least Argentinean writer Esteban Echeverría's *El matadero* (1871; *The Slaughterhouse*), animal rights abuses have been used in Latin American literature both to stand in for human rights abuses and to problematize class and even species exclusions.[11] In this novella, Echeverría uses the torture and slaughter of a bull to represent metaphorically but also metonymically the human rights abuses committed against political opponents during Juan Manuel de Rosas's dictatorial regime (1845–1852). On the one hand, the slaughter scene appears to appropriate animal suffering to symbolize the brutality of the regime, but, at the same time, the humiliation and torture inflicted upon the *Unitario* (Centralist) at the slaughterhouse reflects upon the treatment of the bull. Through parallelism (rather than pure symbolization, in that species differences are maintained), the inhumane treatment of a human person also frames animal slaughter as unethical, at least in the way in which it was carried out in the novella. In this manner, a text about human rights abuses simultaneously brings into play the question of animal suffering and its attendant ethical ramifications. It thus comes as no surprise that one of Rosas's key detractors and political opponents, Domingo Faustino Sarmiento, would also become a founding member of the Sociedad Argentina Protectora de Animales (Argentinean Animal Protection Society) in 1879. As this case illustrates, approaching rights through an ethics rooted in affectivity inevitably exceeds the bounds of the human-animal divide despite the roots of human rights discourse in that same conceptual division.

Finally, I have argued elsewhere that performative strategies used by popular movements to activate the affective traces of forcibly disappeared persons in the public sphere effectively redefine politics.[12] Rejecting the demographic construction of institutionalized polities, these popular movements construct an open demos through the enactment of an economy of indebtedness, whereby the living are compelled to respond to those who are not present, to defer to their traces above and beyond their own interests. As I will argue throughout this book, a similar economy of indebtedness arises from affective encounters with nonhumans; even when living, animals and other nonhumans' political agency is suppressed as if they were dead or inert presences. Disappeared or erased from the political sphere through categorization as nonhumans, they nonetheless place an ethical demand for representation that involves evoking and maintaining fidelity to their traces as singularities rather than mere apolitical objects or interchangeable examples of their species, Nature, or the nonhuman category. In this sense, literature often responds to and contests juridical representations of rights as contingent on the human-animal divide, problematizing the categorization of nonhumans as mere objects or property through a form of anthropomorphization that, rather than projecting exclusively human characteristics and interests over nonhumans, draws out instead the singularity or "personhood" of individual animals in relation to humans. These literary representations tend to frame nonhuman individuality in terms of common differences with humans, interrogating how and to what degree animals and even plants may be said to engage in conscious behavior and intersubjective relations, thereby implicating morality (altruism and the sense of justice), sociality, and, ultimately, politics.

Literary Ecologies and Environmental History in Latin America

Literature and environmental history have always been intricately entwined, as literary production emerges from, responds to, and acts from within specific economic regimes that simultaneously institute social orders and reorder environments, transforming their meanings to support distinct forms of economic and cultural production. As Michael Niblett perceptively argues, "world literature will necessarily register ecological regimes and revolutions (again, even if only negatively) since these organize in fundamental ways the material conditions, social modalities, and areas of experience upon which literary form works."[13] While Niblett refers specifically to literary forms such as the novel that were exported abroad during successive waves of European colonization and capitalistic globalization, Indigenous American peoples' poetry, song, and storytelling also necessarily foreground their own "world-ecologies," that, is their ways of viewing the inspirited land and its nonhuman inhabitants, as well as the systems of value that regulate appropriate ways of interacting with them. Embedded within these traditionally oral literary forms are ethical principles such as the sense of belonging and "beholden-ness" to the territory, respect and reciprocal care for the living land, affiliative or genealogical relationships with the environment and other species, and the privileging of embodied, contextual knowledges.[14]

In turn, these principles are ritually re-enacted and put into practice through the art of storytelling, thereby serving as both template and part of the process of world-making, that is, the co-creation of meaningful environments. As Darren Ranco and Jamie Haverkamp summarize, "Indigenous storytelling operates across relational, epistemological, and ontological planes as a meaning-making and world-making practice that informs culturally specific ways of being, surviving, and thriving."[15] World-making here does not allude simply to the symbolic overwriting of the unmediated real with meaning or to the abstract inference of the world beyond the limits of one's own sensorial apparatuses, but to the actual co-creation of environments through culturally specific, intra-active regimes that include but are not limited to language. Indeed, as I discuss in Chapters 5 and 6 of this book, Indigenous cultures tend to view environments as multispecies societies, all of whose members tell stories about themselves (thereby serving as the owners of their own epistemologies) and all of whom contribute to the communal labor of building and maintaining environments.[16]

Writing and literature also played central roles in the colonial European appraisal and transformation of Latin American environments, if in very different ways. The arrival in Latin America of European literary genres such as the *relato* or report, historical *crónica*, European poetic and theatrical forms, and eventually the novel accompanied and most often justified discursively the colonial and postcolonial reordering of environments and human labor for intensive mineral extraction, monocultures, and meat production using imported European species. As is well known, Cristopher Columbus's letters detailing his encounters with Caribbean environments focused heavily on descriptions of potential commodity production; developing each of these commodities would necessarily entail specific forms of environmental transformations and labor exploitation. From the earliest moments of colonization, then, European representations of American environments tended toward a Eurocentric discourse of appropriation whereby the Americas in their entirety came to be viewed as sites of extraction. This would be the case even in ostensibly more empirical works such as José de Acosta's *Historia natural y moral de las Indias* (1589; Natural and Moral History of the Indies), which looked to reconcile prior Greco-Roman geographical knowledge with the observations on nature made by early Spanish colonizers, and the nascent naturalist tradition kicked off by Rafael Landívar in his epic poem

Rusticatio Mexicana (1781). As Lesley Wylie points out, citing Anthony Higgins, these works looked not only to catalogue Latin American environments, but to order colonial space for future economic exploitation.[17] Following the wars for independence, similar representations of natural environments appeared in works such as Bello's "Silva a la agricultura de la zona tórrida," which promoted deforestation and the implementation of large-scale mono-cultures as the basis for reconstructing the economies of the nascent Latin American nations.

In subsequent years, Romantic landscapes in literature and painting depicted Latin American nature as the source of national idiosyncrasy, as what rooted national identities. During a period in which Latin American elites usually looked to imitate European cultural and political models, environments came to be seen as what distinguished *criollo* (European descendants) and mixed-race *mestizo* patriots from their Spanish forebearers. At the same time, representations of natural grandeur looked to generate a sense of collective, transcendental destiny. The sublimity of epic landscapes served simultaneously to cultivate a sense of national pride and to over-write with shared territoriality the colonial economic and racial divisions impeding national unity.[18] Despite their celebration of national landscapes, however, these works did not by any means place themselves at odds with Bello's discourse of nationalistic development. In both literature and painting, Romantic landscapes' sweeping, impressionistic natural vistas almost always minimize biodiversity (species differences) and ecosystemic complexity, emphasizing instead the general allegory of natural abundance and the productive potential of the *madre patria* (homeland, with gendered connotations of passive maternal fertility and patriarchal political authority). In that sense, Romantic representations of environments as vast, uninhabited spaces spreading out before the entrepreneurial traveler complement fully Bello's neoclassical enumeration of tropical and trans-Atlantic agricultural species available for intensive monocultures.

The advent of the novel in Latin America, whose production had largely been prohibited by Spanish censors during the colonial period, closely mirrored booms in commodity production with their accompanying reorganization of labor regimes and terraforming practices. Despite idyllic descriptions of pastoral landscapes, Romantic novels like Cuban author Gertrudis Gómez de Avellaneda's *Sab* (1841) and Colombian Jorge Isaac's *María* (1867) were set on sugar plantations utilizing enslaved labor, marking not only continuity with colonial economic practices, but also the expansion of commodity frontiers into formerly undeveloped, tropical rainforest. As Jennifer L.

French points out. "rather than the 'escape' from the realities of industrial capitalism that Romanticism offered to European readers, Spanish American nature writing much more directly represents the continent's predominant economic forms and, as a result, its gradual incorporation into the international capitalist system."[19] While late nineteenth-century realist and naturalist novels most often focused on social problems in urban environments, those that were written with an eye to incorporating marginalized regions and ethnic groups into the national imaginary generally centered on the economic modernization of diverse environments, promoting homogenizing terraforming practices to implement intensive agricultural and cattle production, often using European species. Such is the case with Eugenio Cambaceres's *Sin rumbo* (1885; Without Direction), for example, which depicts the failure to modernize the Argentinean cattle industry as an obstacle to national progress. Likewise, novels like Mexican author Arcadio Zentella's *Perico* (1886; Parrot) and Peruvian Clorinda Matto de Turner's *Aves sin nido* (1889; *Birds Without a Nest*) depict the persistence of racialized, semi-feudal labor and political structures on rural haciendas, inefficient and politically unpalatable practices that would clearly be out of place in modern, capitalistic democracies.

This would be a common theme in the second wave of Brazilian regionalist novels as well. While regionalist works in Brazilian Romanticism tended to emphasize the grandeur of tropical landscapes and symbolize national unification through interracial love affairs, end-of-the-nineteenth century realist novels like Franklin Távora's banditry novel *O Cabeleira* (1876; Cabeleira) and José do Patrocínio's novel on drought in Northeastern Brazil *Os retirantes* (1879; The Refugees) engaged Hippolyte Taine's formulation of environmental determinism, a perspective shared by Euclides da Cunha in his famous nonfictional account of the War of Canudos in *Os Sertões* (1906; *Rebellion in the Backlands*). Interweaving meticulous descriptions of hostile landscapes and racialized human savagery and abjection, these works tacitly or explicitly promoted the nineteenth-century Positivist ideology that technological modernization, environmental terraforming, and forced acculturation were necessary to bring an end to the anarchic state of nature, "barbaric" behavior and cultural practices, and inefficient modes of production, which is to say, the failure to conform to the nation-building projects of national elites.

While turn-of-the-twentieth-century Spanish American Modernismo produced few direct representations of either nature or labor regimes, Colombian author José Asuncion Silva's novel *De sobremesa* (After-Dinner Conversation: Diary of a Decadent) directly links the Modernista aesthetic of refinement and

Eurocentric, if cosmopolitan, humanism with the nineteenth-century Positivist discourse of authoritarian development summarized concisely in the motto featured in the Brazilian flag designed by Raimundo Teixeira Mendes: "order and progress."[20] While Modernista texts such as Nicaraguan poet Rubén Darío's short story "El rey burgués" (1882; The Bourgeois King) and Uruguan author José Enrique Rodó's influential essay "Ariel" (1900) criticized what they viewed as capitalism's superficial telos of material satisfaction, their universalist emphasis on "aesthetic selection" following Eurocentric cultural values clearly reflects the Positivist ideology of human evolutionary progress toward perfection as defined by European ideals. Likewise, Silva's *De sobremesa* transparently reveals the extractive industries and labor exploitation that underpinned and made possible the Modernista elites' sense of humanistic refinement, particularly with respect to the purchase and enjoyment of imported luxury goods, not to mention their "grand tours" of Europe, which were exorbitantly expensive at that time.

This developmentalist imaginary—what Ericka Beckman refers to as "capital fictions"—continued to dominate Latin American literary representations up through the mid-twentieth century, most notably in the novelistic subgenre known variously as "regionalismo" (third-wave, in the case of Brazil), "telurismo," or "criollismo."[21] During this period, novels like Venezuelan author and politician Rómulo Gallegos's *Doña Bárbara* (1929), Colombian writer José Eustasio Rivera's *La vorágine* (1924; *The Vortex*), and Argentinean novelist Ricardo Güiraldes's *Don Segundo Sombra* (1926) depicted interior, economically marginalized regions as reserves of authentic national cultures (in contrast to Europeanized coastal and/or capital cities), unskilled labor, and untapped natural resources slated to be modernized for export commodity production. As Beckman argues, "during the Export Age, the jungles, forests, and plains depicted in regionalist novels were by no means outside modern capitalist social relations but rather at the very center of commodity export regimes. Rather than representing the negation of urban space, then, the rural-extractive sector represents its hidden complementary counterpart."[22] Indeed, Victoria Saramago links the resurgence of Latin American literary regionalism in different historical moments to boom-and-bust cycles in commodity production.[23] Furthermore, these commodification novels tacitly encode a political imaginary in which incorporation into the modern nation-state implies a transition from a Hobbesian state of nature to an "enlightened," patriarchal despotism enacted through the male protagonists' domination of both human and external nature, which is frequently symbolized by female characters.

While these works and others from the period such as Brazilian novelist Jorge Amado's cycle of novels dealing with commodity production, Peruvian author César Vallejo's *Tungsteno* (1931; *Tungsten*), and Colombian novelist César Uribe Piedrahita's *Mancha de aceite* (1940; Oil Spill) often deployed powerful critiques of the exploitation of workers in extractive industries, environmental degradation appears at most as a subtext, in its capacity to affect human health, and there is very rarely any concern for the ethical treatment of nonhumans (with the somewhat ambiguous exception of Rivera's *La vorágine*, as I discuss in Chapter 5). Similarly, Indigenista novels from the 1920s through the 1940s, generally authored by non-Indigenous writers, focused almost exclusively on the themes of discrimination, political and economic inequalities, and the exploitation of Indigenous peoples' labor, very rarely delving into either Indigenous ontologies or the environmental effects of the exploitative labor regimes they depicted. This is not to say, however, that these early Latin American representations of capitalistic socio-ecological revolutions have had no impact in raising environmental awareness or in promoting environmental justice. As Saramago points out, a "mimetic rift" emerges in the comparison between these novelistic descriptions of pristine natural environments, sustainable land management practices embedded in their ethnographies of rural customs (even if the novels themselves relegate them to disappear with modernization), and the radical socioecological transformations that they undergo with the implementation of modernizing projects, thereby strengthening public engagement.[24] Nonetheless, this mimetic rift emerges a posteriori, from the contemporary reader's knowledge of the historical degradation of those same or similar environments in the years following the publication of those novels.

It wasn't until the mid-twentieth century that the devastating socioecological effects of the expansion of commodity frontiers reached a scale wherein it became difficult or impossible to reconcile the traditional imaginary of Latin American nature as limitless and eternal with the rapid expansion of extractive industries, particularly with the intensification of global trade and neoliberal economic policies following World War II. This period of rapid, global economic expansion, technological modernization, and demographic growth, which environmental historians John McNeill and Peter Engelke denominated the "Great Acceleration," brought into common view what Jens Andermann has called the "horizon of postnature," that is, the impossibility of conceiving of a nature beyond human influence and of human and environmental history as discrete from one another.[25] This shift in perspective is quite clear in representations of natural landscapes in Latin American literary works. By the 1950s, for example, erosion caused by deforestation to implement monocultures and intensive cattle ranching became widespread across Latin America, a phenomenon that is reflected in works such Pablo Neruda's poem "Ode to Erosion in Malleco Province" (in *Nuevas odas elementales*, 1956) and the overgrazed, denuded landscapes in Juan Rulfo's *El llano en llamas* (1953; *The Burning Plain and Other Stories*) and *Pedro Páramo* (1955). Nonetheless, few works from this period can truly be considered either biocentric or ecocentric; they were generally most preoccupied with how environmental degradation lowered the productivity of land and increased poverty, on the one hand, and the loss of aesthetic pleasure and/or the national iconography of nature on the other. Overall, there is little explicit discussion of the ethical standing or wellbeing of nonhuman species, although Neruda does describe "Mother Nature" as having been wounded by her own children.[26]

As environmental activism became more mainstream from the 1960s on, however, many Latin American writers began to represent environmental themes explicitly in their works. Prominent among them, one finds authors such as Homero Aridjis (Mexico), Giaconda Belli (Nicaragua), Ignácio de Loyola Brandão (Brazil), Mayra Montero (Cuba), Ana Cristina Rossi (Costa Rica), and Marie Vieux-Chauvet (Haiti), who wrote works focusing explicitly on environmental degradation and justice. At the same time, these works coincided with a rise in Indigenous rights movements throughout the Americas, and with them, the hard-fought recognition of Indigenous literatures, much of which represents relational ontologies that do not uphold the Euro-American human-nature divide. As is evident in works by authors such as Briceida Cuevas Cob (Maya, Mexico), Jaime Huenún (Mapuche, Chile), Davi Kopenawa (Yanomami, Brazil), and Celerina Sánchez (Zapotec, Mexico), a large part of this literature is dedicated to revalidating Indigenous conceptualizations of territoriality, but in its broadest sense of multispecies community. These works portray environmental degradation caused by extractive industries as a form of colonialism and environmental justice as inseparable from indigenous territorial rights.

Due to the thematic focus on development and modernization in the majority of Latin American literary works written up through at least the 1980s, most literary criticism has centered on reappraising representations of nature through the analysis of the social and environmental impacts of modernization and the expansion of commodity frontiers into formerly isolated areas. There exists a sizable body of ecocritical approaches to Latin American literature within this modality by scholars such as Jens Andermann,

Laura Barbas Rhoden, Ericka Beckman, Scott Devries, Jennifer L. French, Gisela Heffes, Adrian Kane, Jorge Marcone, Malcolm McNee, Kerstin Oloff, Lizabeth Paravisini-Gebert, Victoria Saramago, Steven F. White, and Lesley Wylie, among others.[27] However, the majority of this work focuses primarily on social injustices and labor exploitation related to extractive practices rather than the ethical standing of nonhumans or multispecies sociality and wellbeing. With the exception of a few scholarly works drawing on critical animal studies such as those of Scott Devries, Gabriel Giorgi, and Maria Esther Maciel; Patrícia Vieira's work on "zoophytographia"; Carolyn Fornoff's recent book on the "subjunctive aesthetics" of environmental possibility in Mexican cultural production; and Vera Coleman's doctoral dissertation on multispecies encounters, there has been scant in-depth critical attention paid to the question of the representation of nonhumans in Latin American literature, particularly as it relates to cosmopolitical agency and the practice of rights.[28] Furthermore, very little of the work that has been done in this area engages with Indigenous ontologies, which is absolutely necessary to understand and, I argue, put into practice the provisions relating to the rights of nature in the 2008 Ecuadorian constitution.

Rather than adding to the sizable body of critical work scrutinizing and historicizing representations of the socio-ecological impacts of the expansion of commodity frontiers, this book examines literary discourse related to environmental ethics that looks to disrupt development-oriented nature imaginaries relying on the human/nature divide, thereby potentializing the actual practice of nonhuman legal rights such as those enshrined in the 2008 Ecuadorian constitution. I approach environmental ethics in its broadest sense as the concern for the fragility and vulnerability of nonhuman beings as others deserving of personal concern, not objects or interchangeable examples of their species or simple placeholders within environments as a whole. While one might argue that ethics lie at the heart of most literature, whether in a positive or negative sense (as absence), in that most literature deals with the treatment of the other in one capacity or another, there is not a linear genealogy between Latin American literary representations of nature, environmental ethics, and the rights of nature. Rather, what emerges are a series of chronologically discontinuous literary works, written by Indigenous and non-Indigenous authors, that reflect on human encounters and relations with individuals of different species or with environments as multispecies societies, as well as on how to maintain ethical fidelity within the act of representation. For this reason, my book is not organized chronologically, but rather thematically, tracing what I believe to be the logical sequence or trajectory linking together human-nonhuman encounters, ethical engagement and representation, multispecies sociality, and cosmopolitical practice.

In that sense, the corpus of works I have chosen was not based on the criteria of representative samplings of historical texts, novelty, or demographic diversity, but rather on the degree to which the authors problematize these central themes. Nonetheless, the bulk of Chapter 3 and all of Chapter 4 are dedicated to one of Brazil's most renowned women writers, Clarice Lispector, while most of Chapters 5 and 6 focus on to the analysis of Yanomami shaman and indigenous activist Davi Kopenawa's testimonio *The Falling Sky*. At the same time, I follow Lucia Sá's methodology in *Rainforest Literatures* in re-reading texts written by non-Indigenous authors for Indigenous tropes and ontologies, showing how modernity can be inflected and transformed by Indigenous thought, as well as Fornoff and others' proposal to recover the traces of nonhuman others' agency even in texts in which it does not appear to hold a central thematic position.[29] Likewise, I engage with the object-oriented ontology inflected approach taken by Héctor Hoyos in *Things with a History*, in which he argues that materias primas (raw, but also primary materials) possess political agency, ordering social relations, environments in the broad sense, and, therefore, politics.[30] However, I take Hoyos's thesis a step further, since I will be arguing that nonhumans are capable not only of affecting social and political structures, but also of political expression and a degree of linguistic self-representation through the organization of discourse itself. I look to draw out and amplify the ways in which nonhuman affectivity persists in trace form in literary representation and to rethink representation itself as something more than the symbolic overwriting of singular others' presences.

Chapter Summaries

The first chapter of this book provides a critical assessment of the 2008 Ecuadorian Constitution's rights of nature provisions. I argue that the constitution's strategy of using co-terms, specifically nature/Pacha Mama and buen vivir (good living)/sumak kawsay, implies much more than a simple multicultural nod to Ecuador's sizable Indigenous population. The ontological ambivalence opened up by the usage of co-terms that cannot be directly translated in fact constitutes a decolonial strategy of ontological pluralism, whereby it becomes possible to conceive of nonhumans from beyond the bounds of the objectifying lens of Euro-American categories such as "nature," "animal," and "plant" that serve primarily to abstract humans from their affective relations with other species. In framing nonhuman bodies as emerging simultaneously, horizontally, and ambivalently within the fundamentally incompatible ontologies of science and Andean *tirakuna* or earth beings, the Ecuadorian constitution explicitly disavows a univocal phenomenal reading of bodies and their relationships to rights, making possible the recognition of the affective agency of nonhumans as individuals or persons, and thus opening jurisprudence to cosmopolitical practice.

The following chapter, "Rights, Ethics, and the Testimony of Things," lays out a theoretical framework for the problems of nonhuman political agency and speech, interrogating the division within liberal juridical discourse between *persona* and *res* (thing or property) in the construction of political subjectivities. I draw together deconstructive thought regarding the relationships between speech and subjectivities, new materialist "intra-active" phenomenology, and Indigenous American relational ontologies to argue in favor of a view of politics as the action of more-than-human multitudes and of political speech as an inter- and intra-subjective phenomenon in which nonhuman entities speak to and through the "human" via processes of ontological diplomacy.

Animal rights are often seen as the gateway for nonhuman rights due to animals' biological and affective proximity to the human, while the ethics of animality have historically played a central role in Euro-American conceptualizations of the human and human rights as well as in Indigenous American stories that form the cosmological basis for these communities' environmental ethics and cosmopolitical practices. However, in both political practice and everyday life in Euro-American societies, the ethical orientation toward singular animal others that emerge during human-animal encounters are circumscribed discursively through the deployment of what Derrida calls the "animot," that is, the animal discursive category. Furthermore, this circumscription—which, as Derrida reiterates throughout *The Animal that Therefore I Am*, potentializes the construction of the human through the categorical negation of a series of capacities to the "animal"—forms the basis for conceiving of politics as human governance (Aristotle's bios) and of human rights as what are denied to the animal as well as animalized humans. Within this context, the ethical demands placed by singular animals in encounter are deferred to the institutionality of the human/animal divide, whereby the law substitutes for the sense of justice. Nonetheless, these ethics of encounter always exceed the bounds of both discourse and institutionality, continually drawing into question the exclusion of the animal from ethical and, ultimately, political standing.

The third chapter of this book, "Humanistic Institutions, Animal Affectivity, and Passive Decision," analyzes the emergence of this double bind in representations of domesticity in short stories by two Latin American authors. In the first part, I engage in a close reading of Argentinean writer Julio Cortázar's short story "Axolotl," arguing that even as the ethical orientation toward the titular animal as a singularity is circumscribed by the spatial institutions of the aquarium and the zoo, the ethics of encounter re-emerge through the axolotls' affective demand for representation in the story the fictionalized, autobiographical main character writes about their encounter. Rather than a straight-forward personification of an animal other (both the human narrator and the axolotl narrate in first person), what emerges is a complex, hybrid narrative structure whereby the axolotl's affective traces interpellate the reader not because of, but despite analogy with the human. Rather than overwriting the axolotl's singularity with either the human or the animot, the interplay between the axolotl's personification as narrator and their anatomical and perspectival differences draws their ambiguous singularity to the forefront, demanding a response to it that cannot be fully circumscribed by the humanistic institution of literature. Like the protagonist, the reader is thus compelled to re-present the axolotl, that is, to evoke their traces.

The second part of the chapter focuses on Brazilian writer Clarice Lispector's story "The Buffalo," in which the protagonist enters a zoo with the express purpose of finding a caged animal seething with hatred, hoping to internalize the animal's anger toward humans in order to motivate herself to commit an act of self-harm. I read this story through Derrida's theorization of passive decision, whereby the traces of the other are what in fact make decision—the rupture of sameness or continuity—possible. In this story and the texts that I analyze in the following chapter, Lispector develops a theory of representation akin to that exemplified in Cortázar's "Axolotl," whereby writing becomes an act of passive decision through what Eduardo Viveiros de Castro calls "equivocation"—that is, the conceptualization of translation not as the act of establishing equivalences, but rather of drawing out differences. Lispector develops a series of representational strategies designed to leave the text incomplete or open, whereby the animal other's absent presence becomes not only visible but demands ongoing enactment. This form of writing, which I call "going astray," thus potentializes ethical relations beyond the moment of encounter.

Chapter 4, "The Familiar Animal and the Aesthetics of the Stray," traces the passage from Lispector's ethics of representation toward her reconceptualization of polity. The chapter begins by discussing Lispector's problematization of the ethics of representation in her iconic novel *The Passion According to G. H.* Written in a flow-of-consciousness narrative style, this novel interrogates the ethical problems that emerge in the protagonist's encounter with a cockroach that she irreflexively crushes in a cabinet door. Ensnared between her irrational hatred of cockroaches and the sense of guilt that she feels watching the still-living cockroach struggle to survive, the protagonist undergoes a process whereby the passive decision to kill the cockroach to end its suffering enters into conflict with the desire for redemption or absolution, which requires identification with it. Through this unresolvable contradiction, she theorizes a form of irredemptive justice, whereby the encounter with the singular animal opens the human to what Derrida calls "infinite hospitality." However, this process occurs not through the violence of the initial encounter itself, but rather through the act of representation, in the secondary event of writing. The ethical imperative placed by the cockroach during the encounter demands fidelity to its traces in the act of representation, but that fidelity is always doomed to failure, since writing is always the subjective act of overwriting the traces of the other. In this way, "desistance" becomes the only way of maintaining fidelity to the truth of the event, to the openness of encounter, which is how Badiou defines ethics.

In the second part of the chapter, I analyze three of Lispector's stories that link the ethics of encounter—that is, what Derrida calls the "law of infinite hospitality"—with forms of affiliation that problematize political discourses relying on the family as the metonymical basis for polity. The first, "Family Ties" deconstructs biological filiation as the basis for familiar relationality, displacing it onto the discursive and performative enactment of affective "family ties." This reconstitution of the family on the basis of affective relations becomes particularly poignant in the "The Crime of the Mathematics Teacher" and "A Chicken," two stories in which animals come to be viewed as members of the family, but are subsequently exiled from the family relation through the deployment of the animot. In the case of the first story, the family dog becomes subjected to variable substitution, whereby the species stands in for the singularity of the individual in relation to the other family members. Nevertheless, the mathematics professor is unable to achieve redemption for the crime of abandoning the dog through an act of compassion to another stray dog, thereby reinforcing Lispector's perspective that ethics consist in maintaining fidelity to the encounter with the singular other.

"A Chicken," in contrast, narrates the trajectory whereby a food species (a "Sunday chicken") becomes integrated into the family structure through the performance of both an ambiguous singularity and gender: the hen demonstrates a degree of voluntaristic agency and therefore individuality upon escaping from the family's house and she comes to be considered a "mother" when she lays an egg following her recapture. Nonetheless, in the end she is devoured without a second thought, as she fails to demonstrate over time the proper affirmation of the "family ties" that the father and daughter project over her. Despite this ironic ending, however, the problem of human-animal affiliations is drawn to the forefront, which necessarily has powerful implications for theories of politics that rely on the metonym of the family as the basis for polity. In both stories, the ethical orientation that arose through iterative encounters with singular animals persists, even after the dog has been abandoned and the hen has been eaten. In this sense, I argue that Lispector's thinking regarding affiliation provides another way of conceiving of the relationships between ethics and polity, reimaging communities as multispecies, self-governing collectives founded on a law of infinite hospitality and the practice of equivocation, that is, the ethical injunction requiring a representational praxis that approximates the irreducible other through expropriation (integrative difference) rather than appropriation (assimilation).

The fifth chapter, entitled "Biosemiotics, the Arche of the Forest, and the Politics of Multispecies Representation," follows this line of thinking in proposing a reading of environments as agential biosemiotic networks that potentialize specific cosmopolitical forms. Taking the narrator's description in José Eustasio Rivera's *La vorágine* of the Amazonian rainforest as a "powerful vegetal family that never betrays itself" as the point of departure, I analyze the forms of affiliation that arise through the apprehension of the forest as a multispecies biosemiotic matrix relying primarily on iconic and indexical signs, which, unlike symbolic representation, do not allow for the "betrayal" of open affectivity through nominalization (that is, in the way in which Lispector portrayed the trope in "The Crime of the Mathematics Teacher"). Drawing on biosemiotician Jesper Hoffmeyer's and anthropologist Eduardo Kohn's expansion of the semiotic theories of Charles S. Pierce into nonhuman communications and philosopher Karen Barad's materialist conceptualization of relational agency or distributed intra-activity, I argue that the rainforest exists as an ambiguous collectivity or social assemblage that both emerges through and reiterates specific forms of cosmopolitical order—what I call the arche of the forest—that are potentialized by biosemiotic intra-actions among and between all species, not only humans.

I then contrast this cosmopolitical arche with what Thomas Hobbes called the "state of nature," arguing that understanding Indigenous Amazonian political forms requires a radical deconstruction of the concept of state as the meticulously coordinated movement between constitutional law, institutional biopolitics, and individual (human) rights rooted in the person/res distinction. To this end, I engage in a close reading of Indigenous activist and shaman Davi Kopenawa's descriptions of Yanomami cosmopolitical practices in *The Falling Sky*, in which political discourse is distinguished from daily speech precisely in that it is viewed as being incapable of deception. This perspective relies on the fact that politics are not viewed as the negotiation of interests, but rather as the establishment of friendship ties through incorporating the other's *õno* or traces into one's own being. In Yanomami culture, hospitality and diplomacy thus emerge as the principal political institutions.

Furthermore, diplomacy with human and nonhuman others is carried out primarily in song form, whereby the songs themselves are viewed as carrying the traces of multiple others that are then internalized by the listeners. In this example of what anthropologist Ellen Basso calls a "musical view of the universe," these songs are not viewed as human (and therefore subjective) creations, but rather are traced back to primordial *amoa hi* trees that function as the archive of political speech, and they are transmitted to humans by primordial beings called *xapiri*. These songs, bearing the traces of multiple human and nonhuman others, are incorporated into the listener's bodies, becoming part of them and thereby establishing political decision-making as passive decision, that is, as the enactment of multiple others' traces. In Yanomami thought, then, politics consist in the actualization of internalized traces of the other through the arche of the forest in order to create working friendship relations that foster ecosystemic continuity and abundance for all species in the co-production of the *Urihi-a*, the forest-world.

Chapter 6, "The State of Plants and the Cosmopolitics of Friendship," draws into dialogue the Yanomami conceptualization of political agency as the enactment of the arche of the forest through the institutions of hospitality and diplomacy with philosopher Michael Marder's theorization of plant being as the biological foundation of all orientation toward the other, and thus both ethics and politics, as well as Derrida's proposal in *The Politics of Friendship* for a "democracy-to-come" that, rather than the ultimately exclusionary figure of democratic fraternity, relies on the openness of friendship to configure the demos. I argue that the Yanomami essentially view politics as a "state of plants," whereby political agency is conceived of in terms of constitutive openness to others that is both potentialized and mediated by plants. In this context, representation is not seen as the abstraction of images or essences of either objects or demographics; rather, material bodies are viewed as the enactment of specific relational potentials that arise in intra-action. Political representation would thus consist in the enactment and mobilization of the traces of others in the co-production of the world through collaborative work relations rather than the negotiation of consensus among competing interest claims. In turn, polity is conceived of not through genealogical ties of sameness, as fraternity, but rather through difference, in the establishment of friendship relations that conceptualize affiliation through the figure of the potential in-law, that is, one who is exogenous to the family.

I then return to Derrida's discussion of the trope of "welcoming" or what he calls "infinite hospitality" in Levinas's ethics, in which all sociality is made possible by a fundamental openness to the other that is rooted in perception and is inseparable from and prior to both subjectivity (speech) and socialization. In this perspective, hospitality denotes not only the affirmative response to the demand placed by the other in encounter, but also, simultaneously, the awareness that a third person, a present-absence, may at any moment interrupt the face-to-face relation and make the same demand. The ethical demand for responsibility toward the other becomes generalized as justice, since the third will always demand equality within the relation. Levinas's first ethics thus gives rise to the "law of hospitality," extending itself "gradually from one person to the next, from neighbor to neighbor" and thereby heralding the State as such.[31]

At the same time, hospitality consists in offering one's home to the other; in this way, the state as a territorial formation emerges through the gifting or entrusting of one's own home to the state, which in turn gifts it back as property rights. This conceptualization of hospitality becomes particularly poignant in the Yanomami relational ontology, since the Yanomami believe that the body houses the traces of the other in the same way that visitors hang their hammocks in the communal roundhouses. The state of plants thus emerges through the ethics of responsibility in encounter extended as the law of hospitality toward human and nonhuman others in diplomatic rapprochement, as well as through this figure of territoriality in which one is always a guest in one's own home at the same time that one plays host to the other. In Yanomami political practice, governance is not conceived of in terms of the emergence of monarchical or popular sovereignty from some primordial, anarchistic state of nature, but rather as the amplification of plant being and biosemiotic intra-activity into a multispecies cosmopolitics of friendship. Clearly, this is a radically different kind of state when compared to the constitutional state as conceived of in Euro-American political history, but it is nevertheless a state in that it consists of a political structure that maintains itself from generation to generation through the enactment of law (the law of hospitality or incalculable justice) upheld by specific institutions (hospitality and diplomacy), and it constitutes citizenship through a system of reciprocal rights and obligations as well as communal territoriality (the ecosystem as what is proper, but not property, to the polis).

In the concluding chapter, "Indigenous Posthumanisms: Rethinking Modernity for Cosmopolitical Practice," I examine the potential for rapprochement between this Yanomami cosmopolitics of friendship and the posthumanist ethical and political proposals of Donna Haraway, Bruno Latour, and Isabelle Stengers, with an eye to assessing how cosmopolitics might be put into practice in modern political systems. Building on Latour's and Stengers's thought in particular, I examine recent Indigenous thought and activism that works to re-modernize social and political practice within and beyond their communities in ways that are compatible with relational ontologies. Following in the footsteps of recent anthropological work by scholars such as Mario Blaser, Marisol de la Cadena, Eduardo Kohn, Marilyn Strathern, and Eduardo Viveiros de Castro, I approach Indigenous philosophies and cultural practices not as some remnant of primitive humanism from prehistoric times, but rather as complex intercultural systems that have interfaced with Euro-American modernity at every step of its development.

Without minimizing in any sense the historical realities of conquest and the ensuing slow violence of colonialism and acculturation into modern political and economic regimes, I scrutinize Indigenous adaptations, reformulations, and creative inversions of specific modern forms. I argue that the Pachakutik movement and the 2008 Ecuadorean constitution represent powerful examples of transformative Indigenous responses to the often violent challenges posed to relational ontologies by Euro-American humanism and its epistemological machinery, carried out in multiple fronts from religious to economic, political, and scientific discourse. When modernization has nearly always been taken as synonymous with acculturation, in what ways have Indigenous peoples forced a reconceptualization of meanings and practices associated with modernity? What are the decolonial strategies that current Indigenous activists, artists, and intellectuals are using to deauthorize human exceptionalism and reaffirm relational ontologies in the Anthropocene? How do they contest the intensification of human exceptionalism present in transhumanism? Finally, what alternative modernities compatible with their relational ontologies do they propose?

In this somewhat cursory exploration of the topic, I focus on two specific cases of Indigenous re-modernization: the Ecuadorean Sarayaku community's

Kawsak Sacha (Living Forest) project and the Sin Maíz No Hay País and Red en Defensa del Maíz Nativo food sovereignty movements in Mexico. Kawsak Sacha is a sustainable agroforestry project that relies on deep, embedded ancestral knowledge of the communicative intra-actions among the rainforest species in the Pastaza region of Ecuadorian Amazonia. The Runa Sarayaku community, under the leadership of the Gualinga family and in alliance with multiple local, national, and international NGOs, has engaged in a legal and political campaign—appealing to the UN among other political powers—to reinscribe territories as multispecies communities rather than private property or storehouses of commodities. On the one hand, the technological intervention consists in the use of legal, social media, and internet technology frameworks that draw simultaneously on Kichwa ontologies and scientific discourse. On the other, this reconceptualization of territoriality is posited as the model for humanity's future in the Anthropocene, while the Sarayaku Runa ancestral relational modes for interspecies communications are represented as multispecies technological interventions oriented toward the facilitation and maintenance of more-than-human social networks. In a biofeedback loop, these communicative networks effectively enact the forest as a multispecies community, thereby configuring material space in that form. Kawsak Sacha is thus presented as an alternative social construction of space using building technologies that rather than creating comparatively lifeless, uniform business environments (as in monoculture and extraction zones), nourish and strengthen the multispecies societies that are environments.

The food sovereignty movement in Mexico arises specifically in resistance to the transhumanist underpinnings of the GMO movement and corporate monoculture's anthropocentric terraforming practices. While both sides of the debate cite the millenary history of human-facilitated genetic recombination of food species as their source of ethical legitimacy, the Indigenous activists involved in the Red en Defensa del Maíz Nativo movement portray their relationship to the corn genome as a form of technological intervention rooted in an ethics of reciprocal care—a sympoetic, mutual becoming of people and corn that propitiates the quality of life of both species and the environment as a whole. I contend that this conceptualization of the recombinatory modification of corn and of polyculture as sympoetic technologies designed to facilitate biodiversity and sustainable production consists in a form of cyborg intra-activity that is not generally recognized as such by Euro-American posthumanism due to the anthropological relegation of Indigenous technologies to the traditional, if not the primitive or pre-modern. In this sense, both the Mexican food sovereignty movement and the Sarayaku

Kawsak Sacha comprise Indigenous cosmopolitical projects to remake the world according to Indigenous ethics of reciprocal care and "good living"—a view of modernization in which technologies are envisioned as emerging from, sustaining, and intensifying multispecies intra-actions rather than radically reducing them to a single commodity or form of production, as technology is most often conceived in Euro-American modernity.

Taken together, these chapters foreground the diverse ways in which Indigenous and non-Indigenous writers, intellectuals, and activists from Latin America are reconceiving ethics as a form of multispecies diplomacy in which humans and nonhumans forge worlds sympoetically, that is, as a biological and biosemiotic mutual becoming oriented toward fostering the conditions for collective life and sociality in the more-than-human communities that are environments. This is necessarily a cosmopolitical project entwined with the complete reformulation of the terms of political subjectivities, polities, representation, governance, and accountability. When society can no longer be conceived of as solely and uniquely human, a radical reevaluation of what it means to have rights, legal personhood, and moral standing will inevitably follow.

CHAPTER 1

The Rights of Nature from Latin America

Rights have to be able to tell a good story—factual knowledge
is not enough to convince anyone of the rightness of a relation.

—MIHNEA TANASESCU

In 2008, Ecuador approved a new constitution that granted "nature" legal standing and assigned specific rights to it, a move that was hailed by environmentalists worldwide as a groundbreaking step toward reestablishing a sustainable relationship with our environments and remediating the global ecological catastrophe brought about by modern economic practices. As the preamble makes clear, the new constitution was conceived explicitly as the juridical base for "a new form of public coexistence, in diversity and in harmony with nature, to achieve the good way of living [buen vivir], the sumak kawsay."[1] In this sense, the rights of nature and the human rights outlined in Title II of the new constitution are meant to be sustained by a restructuring of the hegemonic way of life away from modern consumerism and hyperproductivity toward a high quality of life based on principles of collective physical and mental well-being; pluriculturalism; juridical equality; equal access to food, education and healthcare; environmental sustainability; and respect toward human and more-than-human nature. In an overt conceptual and linguistic reframing of the consumerist "good life," the use of the verb rather than the noun in "buen vivir/sumak kawsay" (living well) implies sustainable continuity and ethical engagement with both human and nonhuman others.[2]

Although most of the principles of buen vivir/sumak kawsay are encoded to some degree in a variety of constitutions, laws, and policies throughout Europe and the Americas, the explicit designation of nature and nonhuman beings as subjects of rights entails a drastic shift in direction in modern jurisprudence, much of which defines human rights explicitly or implicitly through the Euro-American human/animal or human/nature divide. Indeed, if the possibility of granting nature legal rights or at least moral standing had been debated as early as the nineteenth century in Europe and the United States as the socioenvironmental effects of industrialization and urbanization became increasingly clear, these projects remained largely hypothetical or partial, such as the protections afforded certain animals, endangered species, conservation areas, or sites sacred to particular Indigenous groups.[3] Within liberal constitutionalism, most environmental legislation appears as a corollary to property rights (such as conservation easements), water rights, and public health policy.[4] To date, only Ecuador, Bolivia, and a handful of local and state governments in the Americas have approved blanket rights of nature statutes, although legislation has been debated in Argentina, Brazil, the European Union, and Nepal, and the rights of nature have been argued with differing degrees of success in court cases in several other nations.[5]

Many scholars view the Ecuadorian constitution's radical departure from traditional liberalism's doctrine of individual, corporative, and property rights as a decolonial strategy that emerges directly from the tactical resistance of Indigenous and popular movements to the effects of the neoliberal economy of extraction on local communities.[6] The decolonial thrust of the new constitution is evident from the outset, since the principles of collective sovereignty laid out in the first lines of the preamble dismantle one by one the bases of the patriarchal, racialized, extractive colonial and neocolonial orders that had structured and governed Ecuadorian society since Spanish colonization in the sixteenth century.[7] Indeed, the 2008 constitutional assembly was the culmination of more than two decades of popular and Indigenous political mobilization in the nation. These movements largely arose in response to three interconnected issues: the ongoing cultural, economic, and political marginalization of the nation's sizeable Indigenous and Afro-Ecuadorian racial minorities, particularly in relation to the oil-fueled development boom that began in the late 1960s; the neoliberalization of the extractive economy that was initiated with the 1976 military coup against the populist government of General Guillermo Rodríguez Lara and intensified with the currency crises of the 1990s and the dollarization of the economy in 2000; and the environmental and public health legacies of oil spills in the Amazonian province of Oriente, which resulted in three decades of litigation against transnational corporation Texaco-Chevron and a powerful shift in public sentiment against the neoliberal policies of the Ecuadorian state during the 1990s and early 2000s.[8]

At the same time, however, Ecuadorian Indigenous movements clearly form part of a continental decolonial project that emerged into public view as governments throughout the Americas were preparing to celebrate the fifth centenary of Columbus's arrival in the Caribbean. Indigenous peoples largely perceived this celebration as a reaffirmation of European colonialism and its legacy of white supremacy, and they reacted by declaring 1992 the "Year of Indigenous Peoples of the Americas." In July of 1990, representatives of Indigenous groups throughout the Americas converged on the Ecuadorian capital Quito for the first Continental Congress of Indigenous Peoples, producing the *Declaration of Quito* that laid out a series of key demands centering on the recognition of Indigenous peoples as sovereign nations (within their respective nation-states) with the rights of self-determination and territorial sovereignty. While this document does not focus explicitly on the rights of nature, the sixth point states that: "We Indigenous peoples consider the defense and conservation of natural resources, currently under attack by transnational corporations, of vital importance. We are convinced that this defense will be real if Indigenous peoples are the ones who control and administer the territories we inhabit, under our own organizational principles and communal ways of life."[9] As much as a cultural conflict over the legacies of European colonialism, then, these movements must also be seen as arising in response to the economic crises of the 1980s and the implementation of neoliberal policies and extractive practices throughout the hemisphere, which had the effect of the rapid, large-scale economic expansion into Indigenous territories that had formerly existed on the margins of industrialized economic activity, as well as the dismantling or privatization of social and public services, which many Indigenous communities were still lacking.[10] The hemispheric solidarity of Indigenous movements and adoption of the toponym Abya Yala, a term originally used by the Kuna people of Panama to refer to their territory in the Darien gap uniting North and South America, to replace the European "America" were thus designed as strategies for countering the hegemony of the neoliberal economic policies pushed by the US and local elites as models for continental development during and after the Cold War.[11] In practice, these movements used time-honored tactics to reaffirm their territorial claims and political agency, including marches, blockades, and occupying extraction sites and public spaces as well as pioneering new forms of social activism in the nascent new media.

These acts of Indigenous resistance have frequently led to confrontation with transnational extractive corporations, their private guards and/or paramilitary forces, and state and national security forces. Due to the rise of digital media and the widespread availability of digital photography and videomaking, however, governments have been unable to respond effectively to these Indigenous and popular movements through the common twentieth-century strategy of combining coercion with media spin, in which governments pressured or collaborated with media conglomerates to label Indigenous activists "terrorists" or "delinquents" bent on the destruction of the nation. With the rise of social media, file sharing, and alternative media sources, state-mass media alliances are no longer successful in exercising a monopoly over the public narrative of events, and governments have been forced to answer to evidences of human rights abuses against their own citizens. In keeping with the neoliberal playbook, most nation states have responded by importing the US doctrine of multiculturalism, which provides a framework for more inclusive cultural citizenship (and niche marketing) but does not address Indigenous people's demands for political autonomy, communal land rights, control over economic development in their traditional territories, redress for environmental harm, and the sustainability of Indigenous languages and traditional cultural practices.

Rights of Nature Provisions in Context

It is within this complex, dynamic matrix of local and international social, political, and environmental interactions that the Ecuadorian constitution emerged as a novel framework for renegotiating the antagonism between Indigenous thought and cultural practices and the Euro-American liberalism that, since the nineteenth century, has underpinned constitutional law and economic policy in Latin America.[12] The articles dealing with the rights of nature in particular respond to specific effects on both human populations and the environment of the neoliberalization of the Ecuadorian economy between the 1970s and the 1990s.[13] As Cletus Gregor Barié notes, the specificity with which Ecuador's constitution deals with the rights of nature differs from the somewhat vague language of the similar constitution that Bolivia ratified in 2009, which although it also refers to the rights of nature and *suma qamaña* (a parallel concept to buen vivir/sumak kawsay), emphasizes the spiritual importance of Pacha Mama for Bolivia's Indigenous cultures without delineating clearly the state's responsibilities for protecting those rights.[14] In contrast, the language in Articles 14 and 15 in Title II of Ecuador's constitution addresses concrete experiences of environmental and public health catastrophes caused by the lax regulation and enforcement of environmental laws with respect to both transnational corporations' and state-run industries' extractive practices. When Article 15 states that "the State shall promote, in the public and private sectors, the use of environmentally clean technologies and nonpolluting and low-impact alternative sources of energy. Energy sovereignty shall not be achieved to the detriment of food sovereignty nor shall it affect the right to water," it is clearly responding to situations such as the legacy of toxic contamination left in Oriente by both Texaco-Chevron and the state-run oil company Petroecuador.[15] Likewise, the prohibition of "the development, production, ownership, marketing, import, transport, storage and use of chemical, biological and nuclear weapons, highly toxic persistent organic pollutants, internationally prohibited agrochemicals, and experimental biological technologies and agents and genetically modified organisms that are harmful to human health or that jeopardize food sovereignty or ecosystems, as well as the introduction of nuclear residues and toxic waste into the country's territory" in the following paragraph constitutes a clear rejection of specific neocolonial economic practices that have affected Ecuador and other Latin American nations, among them that of outsourcing toxic waste and dangerous work to "developing" nations and the proliferation of Monsanto's Round-up Ready GMOs and the massive use of agrochemicals in industrial export monoculture, many of which have been outlawed in Europe and the US, as well as widespread fumigation with broad-spectrum herbicides in the US-sponsored drug war, which activists have compared to the devastating use of agent orange during the Vietnam war.[16]

Besides these injunctions, Article 72 stipulates that "nature has the right to be restored. This restoration shall be apart from the obligation of the State and natural persons or legal entities to compensate individuals and communities that depend on affected natural systems."[17] This section is clearly intended to disrupt the mechanisms by which transnational corporations such as Texaco-Chevron have attempted to escape remediation for decades of environmental damages with severe consequences for human health by paying token reparations with little real impact.[18] Of course, this article applies to national corporations (particularly Petroecuador and its spin-off

Petroamazonas) and the tourism industry as well, responding to problems such as widespread pollution in the Galapagos Marine Reserve.

Despite these specific legal responses to the history of environmental abuses and human health disasters in Ecuador, many observers nevertheless read this and similar rights of nature legislation in Bolivia and, at the state level, the Federal District of Mexico, as multicultural gestures designed primarily to incorporate these nations' marginalized Indigenous communities and popular movements into the national polity without providing an effective legal apparatus for enforcing those rights in a court of law. Erin Fitz-Henry exemplifies this point of view when she writes that,

> at a time when the natural world is increasingly being talked about at the United Nations and elsewhere not as a "rights-holder," but as an "ecosystem services provider," I suggest that while the discourse of "rights" signals promising shifts in how Andean governments are conceptualizing agency and responsibility in ways that productively break with the trend toward marketization, it also runs the risk of providing the administration with symbolic cover for its intensifying commitment to what Eduardo Gudynas has called a "new extractivism."[19]

Gudynas's and Fitz-Henry's warnings are germane given the open-pit mining agreements in the Corriente Copper Belt into which Rafael Correa's government (2007–2017) entered with US and Chinese transnational mining corporations, megaprojects that are staunchly opposed by the majority of the region's Indigenous inhabitants, as well as when the Ecuadorian government mobilized military force against multiethnic protestors against oil pollution in Dayuma in 2008, labelling them terrorists and saboteurs. This coercive strategy was reinforced when Correa signed Executive Decree 16 in 2013, effectively allowing the state to dissolve any civil society organization involved in political activities that it deems inimical to national interests. Tellingly, the first organization to be shut down was the Fundación Pacha Mama, which had been working for Indigenous rights and environmental protections since 1997 and had mobilized Indigenous protestors in November 2013 in opposition to the government's plan to open 2.6 million hectares in the Ecuadorian Amazon to oil drilling following the collapse of the Yasuní-ITT initiative.[20] Declaring the initiative unsuccessful and voiding a 2014 petition signed by more than 750,000 Ecuadorian citizens to bring the issue to voters in a referendum, Correa's administration approved permits to Petroamazonas for oil extraction in Yasuní National Park and drilling began in 2016.

Similarly, in Bolivia, Evo Morales's administration (2006–2019) ordered the violent repression of Amazonian Indigenous activists protesting the construction of a highway connecting Bolivia with Brazil through Isiboro Sécure National Park and Indigenous Territory in 2011, scarcely more than a year after legislation protecting Indigenous communities' right to consultation and final say about development projects affecting their territory was approved in the 2009 constitution, leading to the deaths of four Indigenous activists. As Jorge Marcone notes, Correa's and Morales's initial justifications for the use of state force differed little from the discourse employed alike by neoliberal military juntas and New Left regimes whose social programs rely on environmentally unsustainable natural resource extraction: claiming that the protestors were "enemies of the nation" acting as puppets of foreign powers.[21] Eventually, Bolivian Defense Minister María Chacón Rendón resigned in protest of the police actions, and the Minister of the Interior in charge of the project was forced to abdicate after massive popular protests. Giving in to popular pressure, Evo Morales announced the suspension of the project on October 21, 2011, but it was resurrected in a 2017 law annulling the area's protected status. Ironically, in a speech promoting this law, Morales referred to the largely Indigenous protestors as beholden to "colonial environmentalism."[22] Clearly, Morales's government's commitment to protect Indigenous human and territorial rights as well as the rights of nature came deeply into question, which likely influenced the popular rejection of the 2016 referendum for a constitutional amendment to allow him a fourth term in office as well as lending ammo to his critics, who forced him to resign in 2019 following unsubstantiated accusations of electoral fraud.

Bolivia approved more binding definitions of the rights of nature in two statutes approved respectively in 2010 and 2012: La Ley de los Derechos de la Madre Tierra (Law of the Rights of Mother Earth) and La Ley Marco de la Madre Tierra y el Desarrollo Integral para Vivir Bien (The Framework Law of Mother Earth and Integral Development for Living Well). These laws arose out of negotiations between the Bolivian state and the Pacto de Unidad (Unity Pact), a political alliance between various Indigenous and agrarian organizations, following the World People's Conference on Climate Change and the Rights of Mother Earth, held in Cochabamba, Bolivia in 2010.[23] The first of these laws enumerates the specific rights to which nature is entitled, which are summarized in Article 7 as the rights to life, biodiversity, water, air, ecological balance, restoration, and pollution-free living, as well as the state's obligations and duties of citizens with respect to maintaining those rights.[24] While this law does not specify the legal mechanisms by which Mother Earth's rights will be protected, Article 10 mandates the creation of a "Defensoría de la Madre Tierra" (Mother Earth Ombudsman), whose mission consists in "ensuring the enforcement, promotion, diffusion, and compliance with the rights of Mother Earth." The second law creates the operational framework for enforcing those rights as well as laying out a series of definitions and policies promoting "Integral Development in Harmony and Balance with Mother Nature," as they relate to the conservation of cultural and ecosystemic biodiversity (Article 23); agriculture, fishing, and cattle ranching (Article 24); forestry (Article 25); mining and hydrocarbon extraction (Article 26); water (Article 27); land use and Indigenous and agrarian territorial rights (Article 28); air quality and environmental health (Article 29); energy (Article 30); waste disposal (Article 31); climate change (Article 32); and inter- and intracultural education (Article 33).[25] This law also mandates the creation of a "Consejo Plurinacional para Vivir Bien en Armonía y Equilibrio con la Madre Tierra" (Plurinational Council for Living Well in Harmony and Balance with Mother Earth) to oversee compliance with these legal dispositions and promote a cultural shift toward sustainable development.

Although a law to create and fund the Defensoría de la Madre Tierra was finally proposed in 2021 with the backing of President Luis Arce, as of 2023, neither the Defensoría de la Madre Tierra nor the Consejo Plurinacional para Vivir Bien en Armonía y Equilibrio con la Madre Tierra have been formally instituted. This lapse led Villavicencio Calzadilla and Kotzé to a diagnosis similar to that of Fitz-Henry; namely, that until now, at least, these laws constitute mere "window-dressing" that serves to promote the Bolivian government's "ethno-ecologist" image and occlude its neoextractivist agenda, which it views as necessary to support its social programs.[26] Indeed, these authors point out that both of these laws are subordinated to the Bolivian constitution, which in Title II states that "the industrialization and sale of natural resources shall be a priority of the State."[27] Furthermore, they have also been superseded by posterior legislation such as the 2014 Law 533 on Mining and Metallurgy that authorizes mineral extraction in protected areas and revalidates retroactively existing contracts and mineral rights.[28] In this sense, Villavicencio Calzadilla and Kotzé coincide with Eduardo Gudynas's contention that the Framework Law "restores the idea of development, legitimating it as a political norm and placing it as a necessary element for vivir bien. In other words, among the varieties of development, the law selects one, 'integral development,' and then places it as a necessary measure for achieving the vivir bien of the future. This turnaround should not be understated, because it minimizes vivir bien and robs it of its vocation as a radical break with development and the transcendence of modernity."[29]

Perhaps due to this suspicious delay in founding the mandated penal institutions to oversee the enforcement of the rights of Mother Earth, there have been no punitive cases related to the rights of nature legislation in Bolivia through 2023, at least as far as I was able to ascertain. The Defensoría del Pueblo (Human Rights Ombudsman) makes periodic reference to the two laws described above in its annual reports since 2012, but there is no mention of any concrete court cases brought against offenders against the rights of Mother Earth, nor is there any record of such cases in newspapers or academic studies from the last decade. The newly founded International Tribunal on the Rights of Nature, which was established in 2015 to uphold the Universal Declaration on the Rights of Nature that had been approved in the 2010 Cochabamba assembly, visited Isiboro Secure National Park and Indigenous Territory in 2018 to assess the socio-ecological impacts of the highway construction through the park, but having no legal jurisdiction, they were unsuccessful in their attempts to negotiate with the Bolivian government and were in fact detained illegally by coca producers for several hours.[30] In a penal sense, then, the rights of Mother Nature in Bolivia remain "letra muerta," that is, inactive legislation. Nevertheless, Indigenous and popular environmental activists continue to pressure the government to fulfill its legal obligations.

Despite similar ongoing tensions between legislation and political practice in Ecuador, hundreds of cases have in fact come before courts in which state governments and the national government as well as national and multinational corporations have been arraigned on charges of violating the rights of nature. While many of these cases are still in litigation, some have been resolved in favor of the plaintiffs. The first such judgment was decided in 2011, when the Criminal Court of Loja Province ruled that the Provincial Government had infringed on the rights of the Vilcabamba River when it widened the Vilcabamba-Quinara highway without conducting an environmental impact assessment, thereby damaging water quality and the riverine environment.[31] According to statistics cited by Nathalie Cely, "between 2008 and 2013, the National Judicial Council recorded 1,164 cases filed in connection with crimes against nature, of which 550 have been settled and 614 are pending settlement. The latest 2013 figures show 570 cases, of which 278 have been resolved."[32] Indeed, court cases dealing with infractions against the rights of nature have become common enough to appear regularly not only in "Ecology" or "Nature" sections and opinion columns but also in the "Crime" pages of Ecuadorian newspapers like *El Universo*, *El Comercio*, and *El Telégrafo*. In this sense, it appears that the Ecuadorian rights of nature legislation has had a measurable impact in reformulating constitutional liberal rights to include the legal rights of at least some nonhuman entities, even when rulings are only selectively enforced.[33]

Rights, Pluralism, and the Question of Multicultural Appropriation

As Fitz-Henry and others have rightly pointed out, these nonhuman rights are indisputably entwined with the human rights of Ecuador's ethnic minorities, particularly with regards to public health and environmental justice, on the one hand, and territorial and cultural rights on the other. However, I will make the argument that they do not appear solely as an extension of the liberal rights of the individual to the nation's Indigenous communities or even as a corollary to the social rights of Ecuadorian citizens to live in freedom from toxicity, but rather that they exist in a somewhat juridically unstable yet unambivalent textual shared space that presents liberal human rights, social rights, and the rights of nature in such a way that none are subordinated to or contingent upon the others. This constitutive instability—unstable in that it purposefully does not support a hierarchy of either precedent or precedence—is captured in the constitutive co-terminology of nature/Pacha Mama in the constitutional language regarding the rights of nature. While the term "nature" appears frequently in the constitution without reference to Pacha Mama, it is always framed in the initial article of each section dealing with the rights of nature as a co-term, either separated by a comma, "nature, Pacha Mama," or as "nature or Pacha Mama." As in the case of the Bolivian constitution, the deployment of the Andean deity Pacha Mama, or world-mother, could appear in this context to appeal to the neoliberal doctrine of democratic multiculturalism, which recognizes Indigenous peoples' right to equal cultural representation, but does not grant any kind of common property rights to Indigenous communities and much less to environments themselves. Yet, in the Ecuadorian constitution (unlike the homologous Bolivian laws), Pacha Mama is purposefully not translated as Mother Nature or Nature capitalized; the co-term nature and the specific use of scientific language throughout the constitution instead invoke the Euro-American epistemological tradition of the natural sciences, but in their systemic aspect as ecology. And, as is well known, ecology emerged in tandem with its political aspect environmentalism in the mid-twentieth century as an academic discipline oriented specifically to disrupt from within the instrumentalist, biopolitical, and ontological project that had dominated Euro-American science since the seventeenth century—that is, the collective technological domination and harnessing of human and nonhuman nature for the economic ends of capital accumulation. In the discursive co-presence of ecological nature and Pachamama in the Ecuadoran constitution, neither term can be conflated with, interpreted through, or subsumed to the other; they simply share legal standing. It is from within this space of unresolvable, permanent ontological tension that new, biocentric political ecologies can be negotiated and put into practice.[34]

A similar dynamic is at work in the co-terminousness of buen vivir/sumak kawsay. As Javier Cuestas-Caza notes perceptively, these terms are not precisely translatable or equivalent, since they arise from three distinct, if sometimes affiliated epistemic communities: an Andean "Indigenous-culturalist" one arising from the lived experience of collective cultural and political practices and resistance to the cultural and environmental effects of neoliberal development; a more international, environmentalist "postdevelopment" one that has approached the Kichwa philosophy of sumak kawsay primarily from the academic standpoint of the European degrowth movement; and lastly, a "socialist-statist" one related to "pink-tide" Latin American political movements, which are generally more interested in promoting egalitarian development than addressing environmental degradation.[35] Citing a variety of ethnographic studies, Cuestas-Caza contests the equivalence that the buen vivir movement establishes with sumak kawsay, arguing that buen vivir arises out of Euro-American notions of well-being that have their origin in a philosophical genealogy that, following Alberto Fierro, he traces back to Aristotle through Epicurus, Spinoza, Kant, and Schopenhauer.[36] Similarly, Whitten and Scott Whitten affirm that the basic tenets of buen vivir are "based on capitalist wealth accumulation, albeit for common good."[37] In contrast, sumak kawsay denotes a specifically Kichwa ontology that Whitten and Scott Whitten describe as "something like 'beautiful life' or 'beautiful life force,' and it incorporates such concepts as deep knowledge, especially as revealed in male shamanic gnosis and performance, and the strong visionary creativity of female master potters. The Canelos Quichua concepts of community, conviviality, kinship, integration with nature and supernature, and a shunning of capitalist wealth accumulation are all subsumed under the rubric of sumaj causai."[38] For Cuestas-Caza, the somewhat forced equivalence between buen vivir and sumak kawsay would constitute a neocolonial decontextualization of Kichwa epistemologies and ontologies for a project that is fundamentally underpinned by Euro-American environmentalist and socialist ideologies. Although he notes that all three epistemic communities offer valuable alternatives to neoliberal development, he appears to argue that, due to these fundamental epistemological and ontological differences, they cannot find a common linguistic ground from which to construct a shared political platform.[39] Gómez Barris presents a similar perspective in *The Extractive Zone*, arguing that "the management state's incorporative logic of el buen vivir, or good living practices, . . . has become the institutional reduction of Indigenous knowledge formations."[40]

The question of cultural appropriation cannot be swept under the rug, particularly given that the majority of lawmakers who participated in the Ecuadorian constitutional assembly as well as the administrators of the official Buen Vivir project do not consider themselves ethnically Kichwa. Nonetheless, Cuestas-Caza's laborious preservation of ontological distinctions and epistemic traditions downplays the intercultural realities of history, global geopolitics, and the amorphous inter-ethnic alliances without which democratic politics in postcolonial societies are unthinkable. In short, upon insisting on the impossibility of ontological rapprochement between these epistemic communities, he falls into the trap of imagining "Indigenous authenticity" as static and apart from Euro-American influence and modernity itself, a position that is particularly untenable in the Andes following centuries of Spanish colonization and the ongoing expansion of globalized capitalism. Likewise, it would imply that the Kichwa in Ecuador and Indigenous cultures in general have made no substantial contributions to either Ecuadorian political discourse or Euro-American environmentalist or social thought, an assertion that is patently inaccurate.[41] Unfortunately, Cuestas-Caza's negation of any cross-over of Indigenous epistemologies and ontologies into the discourse of buen vivir and his implicit disavowal of interethnic consensus-building has the possibly unintentional effect of reasserting Europe as the foundational site of epistemic production and reinscribing Euro-American control over what is an explicitly decolonial discourse.

In contrast, anthropologists like the Whittens and Quick and Spartz present an ethnographically grounded perspective in which they argue that Kichwa intellectuals such as Inés Bonilla, César Cerda, Luis Macas, Juan César Umajinga, and Carlos Viteri Gualinga successfully interpellated the Euro-American discourse of well-being, transforming it for their own decolonial political project. As Quick and Spartz frame it, "the discourse of sumak kawsay seeks a hegemonic inversion that subverts dominant development narratives by proposing that fulfilling lives may only be achieved by reaffirming and enacting Indigenous ancestral principles."[42] In the biography on his website, Sarayaku Kichwa politician and scholar Carlos Viteri Gualinga claims that he himself proposed the sumak kawsay-buen vivir equivalency as a political project in 1993, and in the same year he presented a series of conferences on the topic throughout the Pastaza region as well as circulating a paper entitled "Visión indígena del desarrollo en la Amazonía" (An Indigenous Perspective on Development in Amazonia) that was later published in *Polis* in 2002.[43] Furthermore, Quick and Spartz emphasize that the buen vivir/sumak kawsay covalence encoded in the constitution was first presented at the national level in documents written by Indigenous intellectuals, notable among them the 2007 proposal to the constitutional assembly prepared by the Confederación de las Nacionalidades y Pueblos Indígenas del Ecuador (CONAIE, Confederation of Indigenous Nationalities and Peoples of Ecuador).[44]

In fact, some researchers have argued that sumak kawsay is not an ancestral philosophical tradition at all, but rather an intervention of Indigenous intellectuals responding to cultural loss and environmental degradation related to modernization, one that consolidates a variety of concepts, principles, and practices that had not always been articulated under a single term.[45] As a case in point, Quick and Spartz note that the term sumak kawsay is not commonly used outside of political discourse: "The Kichwa people with whom the first author of this paper (Joe Quick) has conducted ethnographic and oral history research in highland Ecuador rarely talk about sumak kawsay. The phrase makes sense to them, but the intellectual work of consciously elaborating a named set of ancestral principles and practices is not part of the everyday lives of most Kichwa people."[46] Likewise, Tanasescu states that the Indigenous leaders she interviewed admitted that the notion of rights was not present in traditional thought, which tends to frame ethics more directly in terms of reciprocal duties, but that they had adapted their discourse in order to interpellate the state's legal apparatus.[47] In this sense, the discourse of buen vivir/sumak kawsay constitutes a utopian Indigenous political intervention that seeks to transform Ecuadorian political culture and construct an alternate modernity that is compatible with Indigenous epistemologies and ontologies, but that is also explicitly intercultural in its engagement with non-Indigenous epistemic and political communities.[48]

In this context, it must be recognized that the covalence of Kichwa and Euro-American terminology in the constitution is not a straightforward multiculturalist appropriation of Indigenous culture, but rather a conscientious discursive strategy designed to disrupt the hegemony of Euro-American thought in Ecuadorian juridical discourse. As Whitten and Scott Whitten argue, the dissonance in political discourse between Euro-American notions of buen vivir and the Kichwa philosophy of sumak kawsay is a productive one;

it generates a fundamental ontological aporia that negates the imperative and the possibility of assimilation—that is, direct translation, which would in the end entail the subsumption of Indigenous ontologies to the hegemony of Euro-American forms.[49] In this sense, the strategy of co-terminousness underpins the constitution's discourse of plurality, drawing on the contestatory, disruptive power of *Kichwa* thought as a "minor literature," to borrow Deleuze and Guattari's terminology, that disavows the very legitimacy of the category "minority" as configured within the biopolitical, demographic machinery of the liberal state.[50] In this way, it opens the discursive field to new ways of becoming—a decolonial procedure that is crucial not only to Indigenous political and cultural agency but also to the rights of nature.

Discursive Heterogeneity and the Pluriverse as an Alternative Modernity

In contrast with both the transcultural discourse of mestizaje that dominated the construction of national identities in Latin American nations with sizeable ethnic pluralities in the twentieth century and the more recent advent of US-style multiculturalism, the Ecuadorian constitution deploys the concept of plurinationalism to delegitimize the epistemic hierarchies that maintain ethnic minorities in a subaltern position with respect to both cultural hegemony and democratic governance. Article 1 leaves no room for doubt on this score: "Ecuador is a constitutional State of rights and justice, a social, democratic, sovereign, independent, unitary, intercultural, plurinational, and secular State. It is organized as a republic and is governed using a decentralized approach."[51] In this sense, plurinationalism consists not only in the acknowledgment of the federated structure of polities within the state, in which Indigenous peoples are recognized as "nations" with at least a degree of local political autonomy (the decentralization), but also in this specifically "intercultural" (a term that contests both acculturation and transcultural hybridization or synthesis) gesture that deterritorializes the demographic structures of governance in the postcolonial liberal state. A plurinational, intercultural formation can never become a static or stable multicultural synthesis; it must always exist in permanent tension.[52] As Article 6 emphasizes: "Ecuadorian nationality is a political and legal bond between individuals and the State, without detriment to their belonging to any of the other Indigenous nations that coexist in plurinational Ecuador."[53] The heterogeneity of the national state is thus both codified and put into practice through the use of co-terms in the constitution.

In describing this approach as the discursive practice of heterogeneity, I draw on Peruvian literary critic Antonio Cornejo Polar's terminology for discussing Indigenista literature (that is, literature depicting Indigenous peoples, cultural practices, and sociopolitical themes, but usually written by non-Indigenous authors) such as that of Ciro Alegría and José María Arguedas. Cornejo Polar's conceptualization of heterogeneity was elaborated in response to Uruguayan literary scholar Ángel Rama's formulation of "narrative transculturation" that sought to theorize the specificity of Latin American writing in relation to the novel as a literary form originating in Europe and the technical advances associated with the rise of avant-garde literary modernism in Europe and the United States. Cornejo Polar contested the premise that narrative practice in Latin America consists primarily in the adaptation or reconciliation of local content with "universal" Euro-American forms through authorial genius, a process that would imply induction into a kind of hybrid cultural modernity associated with the expansion of globalized capitalism, the subjectivation of the educated or "enlightened" author, and, in the realm of literature, the consolidation of the world literature market.[54] In contrast, he sought to foreground the complexity and instability of textual negotiations between ethnicities, political orientations, and oral and literary cultural practices on the "edges of dissonant cultural systems, at times incompatible with each other."[55] For Cornejo Polar, Indigenista novels like Arguedas's *Los ríos profundos* (Deep Rivers; 1958) cannot be viewed simply as hybrid, multicultural forms designed to incorporate Indigenous differences into national culture and the international literary marketplace; like Whitten and Scott Whitten, he views the work of heterogeneous literature as thrusting into the midst of the homogenizing discourses of mestizo nationalism and Euro-American modernity the permanent tensions—that is, the incompatibility and irreducibility—between these "dissonant cultural systems."

In fact, I would venture to argue that Cornejo Polar's usage of "edges" (bordes in Spanish) in this quote is somewhat misleading; there are no definitive borders or parameters that delimit a cultural "contact zone." All cultures are, in the most fundamental sense and in their entirety, contact zones in constant flux, extending even beyond the territorial boundaries that the geopolitical practice of mapping assigns them. As a somewhat coarse example, even Indigenous peoples who never had direct contact with European colonization during the colonial period were touched by it through the indirect transmission of pathogens and the second-hand commerce in trade items, vocabulary, and stories. Clearly, this reality is much more the case in today's world, where the few remaining "uncontacted" Indigenous groups live in "voluntary isolation," which is precisely that—a cultural transformation arising from the omnipresent horizon of contact that has altered every aspect of their lives, from where they live and hunt to how they speak and interact with neighboring Indigenous communities. In this sense, it would be much more accurate to speak not of cultural borders but rather of nodes of intensified heterogeneity, which may or may not coincide with territorial boundaries. The 2008 Ecuadorian Constitution embodies just such a heterogeneous space of intensified contact.

As tangential as it may appear to a discussion of rights of nature legislation in Ecuador, this debate over the cultural politics of identity in Latin American literature is highly germane to it, and not only because much of this book focuses on literary representations of others (mainly nonhuman rather than ethnic others). The polemic between Rama and Cornejo Polar brought to the forefront many of the issues that arise in the Ecuadorian constitution's incorporation of Kichwa terminology, particularly with regards to the questions of degrees of agency/authorship within intercultural discourse, the possibilities for epistemological and ontological rapprochement within a shared textual space, and the racialized distribution of power arising from political speech in texts that were not written by ethnically Indigenous people but nevertheless attempted to incorporate (some authors with greater success than others) Indigenous vocabulary and/or syntax, cultural and political practices, and cosmologies. Indeed, Indigenista literature is fraught with ethical, discursive, and methodological problems similar to those that arise with the constitution's incorporation of Pacha Mama and sumak kawsay. In this sense, the textual practice of heterogeneity allows us to conceive how plurinationalism might work outside the text, problematizing binaristic thinking and foregrounding the broad, complex spectrum and potentiality of interactions, transmutations, and synchronous negotiations that occur at every scale of communication, identity building, and cultural and political practice.

While I have relied on two concepts drawn from literary studies (Deleuze and Guattari's "minor literature" and Cornejo Polar's "heterogeneity") to describe the functioning of co-terms in the Ecuadorian constitution, Whitten and Scott Whitten describe a homologous "duality of patterning" in contemporary Kichwa ceramic design, which often incorporates Euro-American motifs: "To conjoin the concepts is to be part of a palpable structure of conjuncture . . . of dynamic Indigenous desirable life and life in a vortex of modern capitalist transformation."[56] In this sense, the practice of heterogeneity functions in all symbolic media, not only the written word. Upon evoking "dissonant" or unassimilable, if not static cultural systems and their associated ontologies and epistemic practices, heterogeneous discourse underpins the discursive construction of plurinationalism with an ontological one of pluriverses; that is, the inescapable conclusion that the phenomenal worlds construed by incompatible ontologies can never subsume each other in a single world, a topic I address in detail in the next chapter. Untranslatable terms like sumak kawsay and Pacha Mama function in a literal sense as linguistic portals to another, irreducible world(view).

In this context, it becomes clear that the constitutional language regarding Pacha Mama and sumak kawsay does not ascribe to them a purely multicultural value as symbols of Andean religious beliefs and thereby the religious freedom of the individual in liberal human rights discourse. That value would not necessarily extend to all of Ecuador's ethnic minorities in any case, since neither figure translates directly into Afro-Ecuadorian or non-Kichwa speaking Amazonian cosmologies. In the most general of terms, Afro-Ecuadorian religious practices engage natural forces through syncretic rituals somewhat akin to Caribbean Santería or Brazilian Candomblé, while Amazonian cultures, also syncretic in most cases, tend to ascribe "ownership" of the natural world to various spiritual "earth beings" such as forest and water "masters" or "mothers" rather than the Andean deity Pacha Mama.[57] There is a homologous sense that natural forces are also spiritual forces, but there is no consensus or direct equivalence across cultures regarding which natural forces are aligned with specific earth beings.

It is therefore paramount that Article 71 of the Ecuadorian constitution defines "nature or Pacha Mama" not as a deity, but rather as a vital, multispecies community "en donde se reproduce y realiza la vida" (in which life is reproduced and lived/fulfilled).[58] In fact, even the term multispecies falls short, since Indigenous perspectives are unequivocal in including what Euro-American cultures view as inanimate beings within this community; the "land" is not the mere stage upon which collective life transpires, but an integral part of the vital community itself. It is for this reason that many earth beings are not what scientific discourse would consider "organic" or carbon-based lifeforms, but may include inanimate (but not so for Indigenous peoples) bodies composed of minerals, water, or air. Mountains, stone outcroppings, rivers, lakes, the wind, and celestial bodies are all considered vital and active members of the community of life. In this sense, the concept of Pacha denotes not an empty, ahistorical space (as is the case in abstract Euro-American concepts such as "the land," "the globe," or even "the environment"), but an apprehension of space-time as a community of inter-relations that is embedded simultaneously within ecological cycles and the transformative progression of geohistorical time.[59]

The Bolivian Ley de los Derechos de la Madre Tierra, although it does not preserve this key co-valence between nature and Pacha Mama (since it trans-lates Pacha Mama directly as Mother Earth), provides a similar, if expanded definition in Article 3: "Mother Earth is the dynamic living system emerging from the indivisible community of all interrelated, interdependent, and com-plementary life systems and living beings, which share a common destiny."[60] However, it ascribes a relativistic spiritual aspect to Mother Earth, which ends up subsuming it, at least partially, to the liberal doctrines of multiculturalism and religious freedom: "Mother Earth *is considered sacred from* the worldviews of native Indigenous agrarian nations and communities."[61] The recognition of Indigenous and agrarian spirituality is nevertheless embedded within a more materialist, ecological perspective in the following article defining "life systems" as "complex and dynamic communities of plants, animals, microorganisms and other beings, and their environments, in which human communities and the rest of nature interact as a functional unit, under the influence of climatological, physiographic, and geological factors as well as the productive practices and cultural diversity of the Bolivianas and Bolivia-nos and the worldviews of intercultural and Afro-Bolivian communities and native Indigenous agrarian nations and communities."[62]

In both these formulations, then, Pacha Mama exceeds the bounds of lib-eral multiculturalism; it constitutes a legal recognition of a different, non-Euro-American order of materiality that is at once complementary and trans-formative in relation to the Euro-American science of ecology, since it forces ecology to account for the social fact that the sustainability of life is insepa-rable from that of culture and economy itself. There are no humans beyond the environment, and, in the Anthropocene, there are no environments beyond the human. Pacha Mama thus embodies the indivisibility of the cul-ture/nature complex, that is, of the lived environment; it is fundamentally a socioecological figure or collectivity that, in this constitutional discourse at least, stands in or opens a space for all socioecological assemblages—that is, ecosystemic communities.[63] By postulating the collective conditions for life as an absolute value across species, the constitution seeks to lay to rest the fraught, humanistic question of cultural relativism. In this way, it addresses Gudynas's critique of Euro-American ecological sciences, which coincides with those of thinkers such as Ramachandra Guha and Enrique Leff: "the new concepts relating to the environment, including that of the ecosystem, also internalize a perspective of fragmentation, control, and manipulation of nature, and therefore may be appropriated by ideas that conceive our relations with our surroundings as arising purely from the necessity of securing access to resources with actual or potential economic value."[64] In that sense, the covalence of nature and Pacha Mama represents a specifically decolonial form of social ecology that looks both to reinstate the sociality of the environment as such and to transform that sociality away from extractivism and development at any cost toward long term socioecological and pluricultural sustainability.

Interculturality and Scaling the Rights of Nature

Clearly, there are several aspects of the Ecuadorian rights of nature legislation that resonate with or even incorporate aspects of Euro-American ecological discourses such as Aldo Leopold's land ethic, Thomas Berry's proposal for "earth jurisprudence," and the deep ecology promoted by Arne Naess and Gary Snyder, among others. Indeed, along with Christopher Stone's seminal essay "Should Trees Have Standing?", Aldo Leopold and deep ecology are cited and discussed frequently by Latin American environmental ethicists, among them Alberto Acosta, Eduardo Gudynas, Godofredo Stutzin, and Eugenio Zaffaroni, to mention only a few of the most prominent proponents of the rights of nature.[65] Despite this awareness of seminal Euro-American thought on environmental ethics and ecology in Latin American discourse on the topic, however, the Ecuadorian rights of nature laws could not be said to be derivative of either Aldo Leopold's land ethic or deep ecology; if anything, they share roots in Indigenous environmental perspectives.[66] As I hope to have demonstrated above, the Ecuadorian constitution responds specifically to local cultural context and historical experiences, if inflected by broader ecological and environmentalist discourse. The discursive refusal to conflate/translate nature and Pacha Mama constitutes a rejection of transcultural hybridity as a postcolonial methodology for resolving differences by recognizing an Indigenous component to political discourse and identity yet subsuming it implicitly or explicitly to a Euro-American one, in this case, ecology. As Jorge Marcone argues:

> It would be an even worse irony if the theoretical debate reduced BV [buen vivir] and other popular environmentalisms to just ontologies, and thus made us fall into an old mistake: a new version of the "ecological Indian." BV shows

that the epistemologies and ontologies being developed among the indige-neities of the twenty-first century are not merely non-Western or non-modern discourses available to those elaborating the new political ontologies inspired by and responding to the environmental issues of our times. Instead, they are "new" political ontologies that are already intervening in national and inter-national public spheres, not only by resisting very influential powers and in-terests, but also by imagining sustainable and resilient alternatives that are built on unearthing traditions and on alliances and interculturalism beyond their frontiers.[67]

As Marcone implies, these kinds of Indigenous and pluriethnic environ-mentalisms are explicitly decolonial in refusing to recognize the primacy of Euro-American cultural constructs, including modern science, yet in not dis-avowing them out of hand either. Instead, they expropriate what they judge useful for their own projects from language and concepts taken from Euro-American discourse, much of which is also inflected by non-Euro-American thought, environments, and cultural practices in complex feedback loops, but they reject those that are extraneous or contradictory to their projects of autonomy and sustainability. The Sarayaku Runa exemplify this decolonial strategy in their *El libro de la vida de Sarayaku para defender nuestro futuro* (Book of Life of the Sarayaku for the Defense of Our Future): "We look for answers that are in accordance and compatible with our reality, and that are the result of our own inquiry, and our full and integral participation in the adoption of models of knowledge, production, and resource management. We are open to that which makes us stronger and teaches us. We reject that which annihilates us and that which serves the interests of money and capi-tal."[68] This position is possible because they explicitly disown the overarching ideological supremacy that the West claims through its purported ownership of scientific theory and disciplinarity, but without disputing scientific knowl-edge about nature as such. In the Ecuadorian constitution, this knowledge simply exists plurally, equally immanent to both worldviews. In this way, it disavows the colonial argument of authority and the debt economy of intel-lectual property, while simultaneously instituting Pacha Mama as a figure of systemic socioecological relationality, a figure that occupies the place of the universal but that can never be considered universal due to its roots in a specifically Andean Indigenous ontology.

Thus far, I have focused exclusively on Ecuadorian and Bolivian rights of nature legislation, which, through its nexus with Indigenous rights and ontologies, provides a legal edifice for the personhood of nonhuman beings that cannot be articulated adequately through Euro-American frameworks due to constitutional liberalism's foundational doctrine positing the human/nature, subject/object divide as the basis for the rights of the individual and therefore of legal personhood. As many legal scholars have pointed out, even when considered a legal person within the liberal rights framework, nature cannot truly be conceived of as a moral subject; as the grounds on which rights are instituted, it may only have an ancillary status as a corollary to the private property rights embodied in the conservation model, the right of the individual to live in an environment that does not cause them harm, or as an "ecosystem services" provider.[69] In this context, the intercultural rapprochement between Indigenous and Euro-American ontologies would appear to be an absolutely necessary step for constituting the moral personhood of nature as a subject of rights.

This is not to say that this novel legal framework has no relevance for nations in Latin America and beyond that do not have sizable Indigenous populations. The Ecuadorian constitution in particular proposes a posthegemonic model for ontological rapprochement between different epistemic communities, irrespective of whether ethnicity is the foundational distinction between them.[70] Tellingly, the foundational Andean rights of nature legislation has had worldwide repercussions, catalyzing proposals for similar legislation at every scale of governance, including in Europe and the United States.[71] At the international level, the formulation of the "Universal Declaration on the Rights of Mother Nature" proclaimed at the 2010 World People's Conference on Climate Change and the Rights of Mother Earth at Cochabamba, Bolivia was submitted to the United Nation's General Assembly in response to the lack of a binding agreement to extend or replace the Kyoto Protocol at the United Nations Framework Convention on Climate Change held at Copenhagen in 2009.[72] This document transparently took the "Universal Declaration of Human Rights" ratified by the United Nations in 1948 as its model, and although its backers were unsuccessful in their petition for approval by the UN General Assembly, it altered the discourse on sustainable development and forced debate on the rights of nature at the highest levels of international governance.

Indeed, despite not adopting the declaration, the General Assembly approved a 2009 resolution on "Harmony with Nature" that designated April 22 "International Mother Earth Day" and instituted a yearly series of "Interactive Dialogues on Harmony with Nature" as well as reports on the global progress of sustainable development. Even though this resolution and the ongoing "Harmony with Nature" initiative could be viewed as concessions typical of greenwashing in the neoliberal multicultural model, the language it uses immediately places it at odds with the basic premises of liberal ideology: "the Harmony with Nature initiative speaks to the need to move away from a human-centered worldview – or 'anthropocentrism' – and establish a non-anthropocentric, or Earth-centered, relationship with the planet. Under this new paradigm, nature is recognized as an equal partner with humankind."[73] On the other hand, international non-governmental organizations founded after the 2010 Cochabamba conference such as the Global Alliance for the Rights of Mother Nature and the International Rights of Nature Tribunal continue to promote implementation of the rights of nature beyond Ecuador and Bolivia.

Clearly, the Andean conceptualization of Pacha Mama is unlikely to be adopted beyond the nations in which that particular ontology originated, at least in a meaningful way. Nonetheless, the abstract, transcultural figure of Mother Nature, even when it downplays the ontological specificities that I have argued are fundamental in opening the Ecuadorian legal framework to the personhood of nonhuman beings, forces a reconsideration of Euro-American liberalism's compartmentalization of its own indigeneity as folklore during the cultural, political, and economic processes of modernization, as evidenced in the questionable distinctions between "high" and "folk" art, literature and storytelling, poetry and song, and so on. The nullification of pre-modern and alternative Euro-American ontologies is drawn to the forefront in this process, and it becomes possible to conceive of modernity not as a teleological process of human evolution toward full emancipation from nature, but rather as a colonial and self-colonizing ideology that has led to worldwide socioecological crisis. In that sense, despite or perhaps because of its ontological homelessness in modern Euro-American culture, Mother Earth can still function in legal discourse in a sense akin to Pacha Mama in the Ecuadorian constitution, opening seemingly foreclosed classifications of rights and personhood to redefinition.

Pacha Mama provides one conceptual framework for recognizing the legal speech of nonhuman beings as subjects of rights, one that draws much of its power from its geographical and cultural specificity. However, many other ways of envisioning the personhood and concomitant rights of nonhuman beings have been proposed throughout Latin America, not all of which draw explicitly on Indigenous ontologies. Furthermore, while legal and philosophical discourse relies heavily on the expository form of the essay to make its arguments, there are many other ways of approaching and addressing ethical relationality. After all, the Indigenous ontologies that were so influential in Ecuadorian and Bolivian rights of nature legislation are not traditionally communicated in essay form, but rather through oral mythology, storytelling, song, and presential or "embedded" knowledge transmission. Indeed, recent decolonial trends within anthropology advocate for the recognition of Indigenous systems of thought as such.[74] This seems obvious at face value, but anthropology's roots in eighteenth and nineteenth century European colonialism imposed a hierarchy of cultural value that posited Indigenous peoples' thought and cultural practices as "primitive," "savage," and "prehistorical" with respect to the history of philosophy as well as Euro-American modernity and its teleological discourse of human progress. Confronted not only with the blatant coloniality of this perspective, but also the catastrophic material realities that the cultural hegemony of Euro-American development discourse has brought into being, the task has become to recognize other ontologies as systems of thought that correspond to alternative logics ordering the relationships between the material, politics, and cultural discourse.

This book follows in the footsteps of this anthropological project, but I am also interested in intercultural ethical thought that does not always incorporate directly Indigenous ontologies. When ethics is approached from the way in which French philosopher Alain Badiou frames it, as a bringing into the world of multiplicities that disrupt pre-determined ideological value systems, any proposal that disturbs the classificatory accounting that upholds modern biopolitics and geoontologies necessarily implies an ethical orientation in its own right. Indeed, the systematicity that we normally associate with Euro-American ethical formulations can only be viewed as coherent from within that ontology; from an other ontology, it is likely to appear arbitrary or even irrational in the extreme, particularly when collated with material evidences that disclose its internal contradictions.

In this sense, literary and artistic work that steps outside hegemonic ethical systems can provide valuable openings into other worlds, perhaps even bringing them into existence. It is for this reason that Marília Librandi Rocha argues for a perspectival "becoming native of literature" akin to the native Amazonian perspectivism laid out by Eduardo Viveiros de Castro (discussed in depth in the next chapter), in which the text is viewed as a "relational body," a "world of latent presences" rather than purely abstract representations.[75] As Vera Coleman argues, "multispecies communities are constructed and maintained through stories embedded with the ethical terms of encounter."[76] Therefore, I am interested in recovering texts that have imagined the rights of nonhuman beings in forms that are not usually taken into account in environmental ethics discourse, among them storytelling, literature, and multispecies ethnography, as well as a variety of other artistic genres. Indeed, while the essay notoriously relies on linear rationality and the argument of authority to make its case, many other art forms take more open, collaborative approaches to the production of meaning, opening the possibilities for less species-centric forms of communication. And, as I discuss in the next chapter, the question of nonhuman speech is ultimately inextricable from the rights of nature, since legal persons endowed with rights must be able to claim those rights and demand justice when they are infringed upon. In that sense, the first step toward the real implementation of the rights of nature requires reconceiving representation as something other than the subjective projection of language over human and nonhuman bodies and of rethinking rights themselves through the lens of heterogeneity rather than equivalence or "equality under the law." When equality is taken as the measure of justice, anyone/thing who is denied membership from a given community (humanity in this case) will necessarily be excluded from the practice of rights.

Finally, I would like to comment briefly on the urgency of this matter, given not only the likely irreversible environmental harm that neoliberal capitalism is wreaking on a planetary scale, of which global anthropogenic climate change is but one facet, but also the continent-wide criminalization, repression, and assassinations of environmental activists and journalists reporting on environmental abuses. Due to the prevalence of the "development at any cost" paradigm, right- and left-leaning governments alike have engaged in coercive behavior with respect to environmental and human rights abuses, at the least turning a blind eye and thereby tacitly condoning them and at worst repressing violently any dissent. Indeed, the recent history of Latin America is replete with high-profile murders of environmental activists from the 1988 killing of Brazilian sustainable forestry pioneer Chico Mendes to the 2016 assassination of Honduran Indigenous and environmental activist Berta Cáceres, many of which have never been prosecuted, while governments throughout the Americas have used military and police force against dissenters, including the US (in the case of the Dakota Access Pipeline protests, for example) and Canada (the Transmountain Pipeline and oil sands protests). In recent years, right-wing administrations such as those of former US president Donald Trump and former Brazilian president Jair Bolsonaro, who defended the use of death squads and promised a return to the 1960 and 1970s military dictatorship's scorched-earth environmental policies, have attempted to roll back or forestall every environmental protection they can.[77] In this context, the rights of nature seem more pressing than ever.

CHAPTER 2

Rights, Ethics, and the Testimony of Things

A Theoretical Framework

And yet a "reading" can make or break a life.

—ALAIN POTTAGE

One of the most pressing issues in both environmental ethics and the practical implementation of rights of nature legislation is how to resolve the problem of representing nonhumans as something other than the objects of human discursive forms. When it is assumed that only humans can speak for nature, it becomes nearly impossible to imagine how nonhuman beings might represent their own interests and thereby enact legal rights. Nonetheless, I argued in the first chapter that the 2008 Ecuadoran Constitution offers a way beyond this apparent aporia within the entwined logics of the philosophy of ethics and liberal constitutionalism. Through the decolonial strategy of coterminousness that links Euro-American rights discourse with Andean notions of nonhuman moral personhood without subsuming one to the other, the Ecuadoran Constitution places into question the hegemony of the modern culture/nature divide, instead framing bodies as existing and intra-acting simultaneously in multiple, incompatible ontologies. In this way, it opens the doors for understanding bodies as polyvalent and agentic, always exceeding the parameters of a single mode of representation, whether that of liberal constitutionalism, modern science, or Indigenous systems of thought. Intercultural discourse thus prepares the ground for rethinking representation as something more than the humanistic projection of static terms over fixed objects.

In this chapter, I examine the relations between ethics and rights through the lens of representation in its broadest sense, as how language and materiality intra-act in the co-creation or becoming of phenomena. I begin by problematizing the legal division between person and property in the liberal tradition, which necessarily places all nonhuman entities into the category of thing or property. Within this tradition, even if a nonhuman entity may be granted certain legal rights, it is not assumed to have moral personhood akin to that of human rights holders; it is seen as incapable of expressing a claim for justice as well as socialization in the sense of adhering to a collective moral code. I problematize the question of nonhuman expression through philosopher Karan Barad's theorization of "agential realism" or universal semiotics, in which she argues that all material phenomena emerge through semiotic intra-actions between bodies of all kinds. Within this framework, the abstract symbols that compose human languages are shown to be only one kind of sign among many, all of which come into play in the intra-active, mutual becoming of bodies in encounter. I draw on Derrida's theorization of the trace as the evocation of the other's presence (always apprehended through their signs) that intervenes in all acts of subjective interpretation and speech, endowing symbols with meaning, to argue that even ostensibly abstract, symbolic language maintains a direct connection to the materiality of both human and nonhuman others. Every act of re-presentation invokes the other, irrespective of whether one chooses to subordinate them through objectifying discourse or to recognize them as constituents of one's own subjectivity and therefore maintain an ethical relation of co-responsibility toward them. In this way, representation becomes not only a question of expression itself—that is, subjectivity—but also of the discursive parameters or conditions that constrain specific modes of expression. Since the philosophy of ethics, law, and literature are by definition anthropocentric (writing is necessarily produced by and oriented toward the human), the question thus becomes: in what ways can nonhumans influence the humanistic modes of representation whereby we construct notions of ethical standing and rights?

I then return to Indigenous Andean and Amazonian perspectives to contend that, for the rights of nature to be put into practice, both the social and the political must be reframed to account for and facilitate nonhuman semiotic, social, and political agencies. The first step in this process requires recognizing nonhuman beings not as objects, but as others capable of influencing us through semiotic intra-activity. This in turn requires a rethinking of subjectivity as an ongoing relational matrix in constant flux rather than a self-contained, sovereign, and static position within discourse. I argue that the Native Amazonian perspectives that anthropologist Eduardo Viveiros de Castro groups together under the term "cannibal metaphysics" can serve as a guide for understanding subjectivity as always multiple and impermanent, a becoming through the "eating" or integration of others' traces in face-to-face encounter. Every act of representation necessarily evokes and invokes the traces of human and nonhuman others; however, it is only by explicitly acknowledging this indebtedness that representation can be considered ethical. Through this ethics of encounter, politics can become something other than a demographic accounting and distribution of rights through institutional classifications, since encounters between individuals require ongoing diplomatic negotiations in which interests are never fully convergent.

Person versus Thing

The relations between rights and personhood have a long and convoluted history in Euro-American legal discourse, one that has generally relied on the distinction between *res* (thing) and *persona* inherited from Roman law.[1] In the broadest of terms, the juridical *persona* was defined as the one who could hold property and therefore claim rights in relation to it (that is, initiate legal *actiones*), while *res* was synonymous with property or potential property, and therefore the lack of rights.[2] These classifications generally functioned on the basis of what was considered "natural law," that is the presupposition of a hierarchical, natural order of persons and things as postulated in early Greek philosophical texts such as Aristotle's *Rhetoric*. In this framework, the nature/culture distinction served to sort bodies between the two legal categories, with nature as the domain of things subject to the rights of persons.[3] Clearly, the constitutive role of the nature category in this foundational distinction at the heart of the Euro-American conceptualizations of rights makes it very difficult to conceive of how nature could be said to have rights of its own.

In practice, however, the distinction between *res* and *persona* has always been contested and contingent on political forms and social practice. This was particularly the case with human beings who could be owned through the institution of slavery as well as those classified as wards of others, as was often the case with women, children, and people with cognitive disabilities or mental illness. At the same time, one might argue that modern biopolitical institutions in general place all people partially within the realm of things in that these institutions are oriented toward the technocratic control of bodies with little regard for subjective differences. Biopolitics thus consist in the obligatory relinquishment of specific bodily freedoms in exchange for the guarantee of abstract rights through the process of institutional subjectivation, that is, the construction of the governable citizen.[4] In modern institutionality, the body is inscribed as thing precisely within the allocation of rights to the individual; the *persona* is constructed first and foremost as the owner of its sole inalienable property, its own body. Claiming a right thus always passes through the originary claim that the persona makes on its own body as a condition of assuming the position of rights holder. These claims are necessarily made through political and juridical speech; indeed, it might be said that claiming the right to speak for oneself is coextensive with claiming ownership of one's body, although that speech may be delegated (also an act of speech) through legal and political representation. For those not afforded institutional rights through citizenship, however, the body remains partially or entirely within the realm of things and therefore with no juridical speech of its own, while those whose speech is delegated (whether by their own agency or through institutional intervention) to legal representatives suffer a dilution of their agency and thus fall into a gray space between persona and res. They become the objects of institutional policy.

Furthermore, the expansion of legal personhood and rights to some people who formerly fell into the *res* category as well as the subjectivation of the individual within biopolitical institutions has drawn attention to the fact that rights are not grounded in any universal natural order, but rather "fabricated" through legal techniques of personification and reification supported by complex, historical repertoires of "modes of action which are lodged in rich, culturally-specific layers of texts, practices, instruments, technical devices, aesthetic forms, stylized gestures, semantic artefacts, and bodily dispositions."[5] At the same time, the fragile and yet resilient hegemony of human rights discourse in the juridical sphere in the post-World War II period, in which it is considered that no human may be treated as a thing (in legal terms, at least), has become increasingly murky with the expansion of biotechnologies that place human body parts, genetic coding, and fetuses in a fraught and contested space between personhood and property. Within this latter domain,

> persons become indistinguishable from things: gene sequences are at once part of the genetic programme of the person and chemical templates from which drugs are manufactured; embryos are related to their parents by means of the commodifying forms of contract and property, and yet they are *also* persons; depending on the uses to which they are put, the cells of embryos produced by *in vitro* fertilisation might be seen as having either the "natural" development potential of the human person or the technical "pluripotentiality"

that makes them such a valuable resource for research into gene therapies. In each of these cases, the categorisation of an entity as a person or a thing is dependent upon a contingent distinction rather than an embedded division.[6]

As Pottage summarizes, "now the problem is that humans are neither person nor thing, or simultaneously person and thing, so that law quite literally makes the difference."[7] In this context, legal personhood exists primarily as juridical potentiality within a legal code, one that is actualized through the discursive procedure of claims-making. The multiplicity of actual and potential relations that characterize an individual's social life must be constrained to a single relation, which corresponds to the right that is claimed (through personification) or denied (through reification). As Tanasescu frames it, claims-making "confers a certain coherence, a semblance of unity, onto the irreducibly multiple"; the "semblance of unity" that emerges within a claim simultaneously inaugurates and formalizes the identity of the political subject.[8] In short, the legal status of both persona and res consist in the reduction of the inherent multiplicity of bodily relations to a single position with respect to a right, in which all other potential attachments are discounted as irrelevant to the case in question. The body thus appears in legal discourse as a reified institutional form rather than a heterogeneous locus of social relations and material practices.

In this sense, legal personhood never coincides fully with the social status of person, since social being necessarily entails a multiplicity of relations within a collectivity. As Pottage drives home, "the legal person has no necessary correspondence to social, psychological, or biological individuality."[9] This aporia is what leads Tanasescu to question the efficacy of the recognition of nature as a legal person, since in modern Euro-American cultures nonhuman beings are not generally afforded the social status of persons with moral standing.[10] While legal personhood and specific rights may be extended to nonhuman entities on the basis of protecting their interests (following Christopher Stone, Tanasescu cites the examples of ships, corporations, trusts, and monuments), she notes that this does not extend *de facto* moral standing to them:

> To become a person in law, one need not be recognized as morally significant, or as partaking in the universality of a class, or as being owed strict justice. All that is needed is that the law state the existence of a legal right for there to be an attendant legal person. In this sense, the legal person, just like a legal right, is an act of linguistic creation—another kind of proclamation, one which immediately institutes what it proclaims.[11]

Furthermore, in this construction of legal personhood based on protectable interests, the debt owed the rights holder is always mediated through its representative's own interests, since the representative effectively defines the interests of the rights holder as well as their relation to the right itself. In other words, nonhuman legal personas are effectively voiceless; it is always up to a representative to make a juridical claim on their behalf. And since claims-making constitutes the political subject, the agency lies with the claimant rather than the rights holder. Lawmakers and claimants define the interests and the corresponding rights in a process that, appearing as an apolitical moral decision, nevertheless lies at the center of institutional politics—that is, making a claim for a collectivity in which the politician and the claimant may or may not have membership.

Due to this lack of social standing, nonhuman beings cannot bear testimony on their own behalf within the framework of institutional law. As Tanasescu argues, in rights of nature legislation, nature stands in for a class of unrepresented beings who are brought into representation and therefore legal standing through claims made by others. More than any other criteria, this class is defined precisely through its members' inability to represent themselves. It may seem somewhat paradoxical, then, that rights of nature legislation appeals to the international legal framework set in place by eighteenth- and nineteenth-century "rights of man" discourse and twentieth-century human rights law. However, as a universalized ideal, nature functions in a way akin to the abstract "human" of human rights, and thus suffers a similar disjunction between the law and legal practice when an entity's rights come into question. As is well known, rights framed as universal and inalienable for all humans are nevertheless routinely withheld from noncitizens or those disenfranchised by law (for instance, those categorized as criminal, terrorist, or mentally ill). For this reason, Tanasescu diagnoses the rights of nature as a form of "moral progressivism" that is both ineffective and subject to abuse, since nature may never make a claim or testify on its own behalf, always relying on the contested and contradictory political interests of those who claim to represent it.

The Problem of Nonhuman Moral Personhood

In contrast to the personhood afforded by interest rights, "the legal-person constructed by moral rights counts as a subject, or a person in the existential sense, because it is seen as a rightful recipient of justice. The argument from moral rights, therefore, will always center around the creation of such subjectivities."[12] As Tanasescu points out, rights formulated through moral or social personhood rely almost entirely on a process of homologization in which unrepresented individuals or classes of people are portrayed as sharing specific fundamental capabilities with those who hold rights at a given historical moment: 'Inasmuch as an entity is recognized as mattering, it has to also be similar enough to the ideal type proposed by the universality and abstractness of rights in order to have access to their protection."[13] Nineteenth-century Euro-American abolition movements and women's rights proponents, for instance, relied on homologizing rightless people to male citizens through demonstrating that they shared the capabilities that endowed those white men with rights. Animal rights movements have typically deployed this same line of argumentation, contending that animals share with humans some or all of the capabilities that endow humans with rights, if to differing degrees.[14] As "fellow creatures," they have a certain moral standing within society.

Nevertheless, animal rights always run up against the fundamental problem of legal, political, and social representation. Even when animals clearly demonstrate communicative capabilities, whether through body language, species-specific speech, or even the ability to respond to and/or use human language in some capacity, they are never viewed as speaking subjects inhabiting the same legal ground as humans. This in turn places them in a precarious position with respect to moral subjectivity, since they are unable to articulate in an unambiguous way the specific needs or desires to which society would be morally obligated to respond. Furthermore, they can only very ambiguously be said to have the capability for acting morally toward the other members of society, and as such, are usually viewed as unable to fulfill the social obligations that a human community demands of moral subjects. In this sense, despite holding a certain moral standing, animals cannot exercise full membership within the community; they can never "count" in political demographics as more than an exclusionary class of nonhumans, at least in Euro-American rights-based democracies. This does not mean that they have no political agency, however. The animal (as well as animalized humans) holds a permanently disruptive position with respect to biopolitics and its demographic logic; in that sense, the animal class forces a constant renegotiation of the scope of political and juridical rights. If one subscribes to Rancière's and Badiou's definitions of politics, at least, animals are political subjects in that in their very heterogeneity with respect to the human, they continuously disrupt the count-as-one logic of biopolitical institutionality.[15] Their exclusion is forever unconscionable and yet inevitable, since they must always remain the foil against which the human and human rights are constructed.

Clearly, the problem of the moral subjectivity of nonhuman beings is exacerbated with respect to the abstract category of nature, which in material terms can never be pinned down as anything other than a fluid, amorphous multiplicity.[16] Referencing James Loveluck's Gaia hypothesis and New Age conceptualizations of planetary consciousness, Tanasescu diagnoses as theological the notion that nature in itself has any teleological self-interest or the ability to articulate itself with any fidelity within some kind of nebulous human-nature intersubjective formation.[17] For this reason, she downplays the viability of the Andean rights of nature legislation's appeal to the intercultural formulation of nature/Pacha Mama as a procedure for bridging the gap between legal personhood and moral subjectivity. In similar fashion to Cuestas-Caza's questioning of the buen vivir/sumak kawsay equivalence that I discussed in the first chapter, Tanasescu views nature and Pacha Mama as unbridgeable terms pertaining to two distinct epistemic communities, the former associated with Euro-American interest rights and the latter with Indigenous Andean notions of nonhuman moral subjectivity. In support of this argument, she notes that the Kichwa informants she interviewed did not subscribe to the notion that Pacha Mama existed within a framework of rights, but rather adhered to the position that Pacha Mama and humans co-exist through reciprocal relations of mutual care in a localized material rather than legal sense.[18] At the same time, Euro-American perspectives encounter a great deal of difficulty in viewing the Andean deity Pacha Mama as more than a symbol for universal nature, and therefore inscribe it with at most an abstract, distributed subjectivity drawn from pre-existing Euro-American metaphysical formulations such as Gaia or Mother Nature.

For Tanasescu, then, there is no possible rapprochement between the legal rights of nature and the moral subjectivity of Pacha Mama; granting nature/Pacha Mama rights cannot effectively endow it with moral subjectivity in social practice beyond that which it already holds in Andean communities. As she summarizes, "if nature will become a subject for us, it will not be as a subject of rights."[19] For this reason, she argues in her conclusions for an approach based on Bruno Latour's proposal in *Politics of Nature* to dismantle the conceptual nature/culture divide through the practice of a cosmopolitics of livability, in which more-than-human assemblages work to assure mutual well-being in local places, rather than in the abstract, universal spaces of legal discourse.[20] Following Latour and other proponents of reframing "nature" as a political ecology, Tanasescu contends that "the focus of representing nature should not be on nature at all, but rather on what kinds of things we want to make possible through our political claims; what kinds of things we want to do, where 'we' refers to neither humans nor nature, but to naturalized humans and humanized nature."[21] In the end, the moral standing of nature and nonhuman beings in general would thus amount to a question of cultural hegemony in which the notion of the social as the domain of human political action must be replaced by that of a social ecology recognizing that all political action necessarily runs through assemblages that encompass at some level all the members of an ecosystemic community, not only humans.

In this perspective, a cultural revolution would have to precede the political one in order for nonhuman rights to be supported by a moral framework. Since international rights of nature legislation enacted by political elites typically lacks broad or at least full popular support, she views it as fundamentally "anti-democratic."[22] This is a somewhat misleading statement, however, considering that the 2008 Ecuadorean constitution was ratified by 69 percent of voters in a nation-wide constitutional referendum. In any case, for the attribution of rights to nonhuman beings to become a democratic practice, a majority of humans need to acknowledge the moral standing of nonhuman entities as an integral part of their own lives; a political ecology would thus consist in the recognition that human political subjectivities are constituted through their relations with nonhuman others, and that we therefore owe them a moral debt. Clearly, this proposal runs up against the same problems that any proposal for utopian social change confronts; that is, finding the means to carry out a truly democratic social transformation rooted in popular practice.

However, another issue arises in the practice of political ecology that neither Latour nor Tanasescu address with the attention it deserves. If one takes seriously the materialist position that politics never exist abstractly, but are always enacted relationally, through and on concrete bodies, and that these bodies are not exclusively human, it necessarily follows that any formulation of a social ecology must address the political potentialities of both human and nonhuman bodies in a manner that does not rely on the persona/res distinction, that is, the subordination of the body to political speech. Despite acknowledging the intersubjective formations that constitute political practice, Tanasescu stops short of attributing any political speech to nonhuman others. For her, in line with Latour's formulation of actor-network theory and the "parliament of things," it is always the concerned human that acknowledges and speaks for the nonhuman other: "claims on behalf of nature are always to be treated as statements about our entanglements and metaphysical convictions. When speaking for nature, we are in fact presenting the hybrid beings that we are, and hybridizing and constructing further in the act of 'speaking for.' There is no solid ontological basis for representing nature—all we can have recourse to are the various claims in play."[23] In this perspective, nonhuman agency can only exist as a postulate or corollary to human subjectivity; while nonhumans may influence in political mobilization as informants or even "actants," the political potentialities of nonhuman bodies must be silenced as the condition for political speech itself, which arises through the claims made on behalf of the other.[24] In this context, what Tanasescu describes as intersubjectivity is in fact subjectivity at its purest, that is, the arrogating power of the unitary one over the heterogeneity of the other that is ostensibly immanent to the process of representation.

Rethinking Representation through the Materiality of Language

This fundamentally constructivist point of view disallows as its point of departure what cosmopolitical thought should, in my opinion, bring to the forefront: namely, the material basis for all political action. From a materialist point of view, all semiotic expression (and, in fact, meaning and subjectivity itself) must be viewed as existing not on some abstract symbolic plane, but rather as specific material effects that are generated, transmitted, received, and interpreted by concrete physical bodies. Despite comprising a complex, collective symbolic system, language does not exist metaphysically, at least when the metaphysical is defined as existing beyond the material, but must always be enacted performatively by bodies in social context.[25] As is often pointed out, even in his foundational formulation of the sign as comprised of signifier and signified, Ferdinand de Saussure insisted on the materiality of the signifier as "sound-image."[26] Psychoanalyst Jacques Lacan, who obstinately insisted that subjects cannot access the Real once they have been inducted into the symbolic order of language, went even further, acknowledging that "speech is in fact a gift of language, and language is not immaterial. It is a subtle body, but body it is."[27] Likewise, American philosopher and semiotician Charles S. Pierce's typological division of signs into the categories of icon, index, and symbol posited the inextricable relationality of indexical signs to their material objects as the grounds for semiosis.[28] In recent years, this position has been revisited by biosemioticians such as Thomas Sebeok, Jesper Hoffmeyer, Kalevi Kull, and Eduardo Kohn, who postulate that environments are themselves fundamentally indexical semiotic systems.[29] Even at the level of the symbol, which Pierce, following the Aristotelian hierarchy, posits as the most complex and therefore highest form of semiosis, recent advances in the cognitive sciences and the philosophy of language have made clear that meaning (the conceptual signified and its position in the symbolic order) itself is generated materially through the brain's association of word-effects with memories of prior speech, grammatical usage, and encoded physical encounters; what Jacques Derrida described as the traces of the other that inhabit and in fact produce meaning. As a case in point, people with brain damage or dementia often suffer from aphasia, that is, the loss of at least some capability for using and understanding speech, as well as identity dissociation, or disruptions in the ability to (re)construct the subjective narrative of their own identity.[30] Clearly, this would not be a possibility if the system of symbols and subjectivity itself existed in some abstract space beyond material bodies.

Despite Derrida's emphasis on the constructed nature of subjectivity—he famously stated in *Of Grammatology* that "there is no beyond-text" ("il n'y a pas de hors-texte")—his work on hauntology and, particularly, the animal, reveals that these traces are not strictly linguistic, at least in a purely symbolic sense.[31] In *The Animal That Therefore I Am*, he writes of the "mute traces of the animal"; they are what is interiorized of the other, the primordial (that is, intra- and intersubjective) visual, olfactory, auditory, and tactile traces of our encounters with others' bodies that must be overwritten by speech through the objectifying movement of subjectivity (for instance, by the "animot" or animal category). In that sense, traces are "the intimate relationship of the living present [the subjective sense of being in the now, which must be inferred continuously in relationship to projections of the past and the future] with its outside."[32]

Derrida developed his theory of the trace largely in response to Husserl's phenomenology of perception, looking to address the seemingly aporetic transcendence of bodily affect to subjectivity that necessarily occurs in the apprehension of the world (what the subject perceives as exterior to itself, which paradoxically and problematically includes its own material body, or at least its visible body-parts, since the wholeness of the body must also be inferred subjectively). In this framework, empirical objectivity must have a semiotic basis, since subjectivity would emerge precisely in the cognitive objectification of the affects that are generated in the body through encounters with other bodies. For this reason, he frames the trace in terms of erasure, in which affects are overwritten by the idealizing objectivity of language. At the same time, however, the system of signs is also prior and therefore ostensibly exterior to the subject, even when the subject reenacts, actualizes, and modifies it. It is "subject-less" in that it exists beyond any one subject and that its collective subjects (language cannot exist without users) have also effectively been erased and overwritten in the becoming of the subject in its present. This is why Derrida refers to the system of signs as "protowriting"; its subjects are "dead" (via Heidegger and Barthes) in that they are never present in the moment of enunciation, but must always be inferred and actualized by the subject in more or less idealized, disembodied, and de-individualized form. In appropriating language to name its objects, the subject undergoes a process of "auto-affection," in which the subject's speech act affirms its own presence (its sense of being in the present) through the erasure of both the affectivity of the other and the abstraction of the external system of language.[33] It is for this reason that Derrida insists that apprehension—and therefore perception itself—is fundamentally a semiotic process.

Nevertheless, he frames this process in terms of "auto-affection" rather than self-referentiality. His theory of the trace explicitly dismantles the Euro-American metaphysical tradition of positing subjectivity as an inalienable, timeless, and monadic state of being—the mind or soul that exists apart from and governs the body. In Derrida's reappraisal of Husserl's thought, the sense of being in the present arises not from the subject's absolute will to dominate the world through the objectification of external referents, but from the physical process of speech itself. It is the bodily experience of its own utterance—the "sound-image" to which Saussure refers—that affirms the presence of the subject to itself: "everything in my speech which is destined to manifest an experience to another must pass by the mediation of its physical side; this irreducible mediation involves every expression in an indicative operation."[34] In this sense, he dismantles the conceptual divide that Husserl established between expression as the ostensibly pure communication of the subject's consciousness—of ideal meaning, which would be "universal" in that it transcends the subject—and indication as the semiotic allusion to the presence of the other, which would by definition be devoid of ideal meaning other than indicating that extrinsic presence, since the other's subjectivity is never accessible beyond its traces.[35] Indeed, he argues that the distinction between indication as nonlinguistic sign and expression as a linguistic one cannot be sustained:

> Thus everything that constitutes the effectiveness of what is uttered, the physical incarnation of the meaning, the body of speech, which in its ideality belongs to an empirically determined language, is, if not outside discourse, at least foreign to the nature of expression as such, foreign to that pure intention

without which there could be no speech. The whole stratum of empirical effectiveness, that is, the factual totality of speech, thus belongs to indication,
which is still more extensive than we had realized. The effectiveness, the totality of the events of discourse, is indicative, not only because it is in the world,
but also because it retains in itself something of the nature of an involuntary
association.[36]

For Derrida, as for Lacan, the real world is never directly accessible to the
subject; nevertheless, material affectivity is always in play through the traces
of others and it is that refracted, indicative "self-affection" that in fact constitutes the subject as such.

Many of Derrida's critics view his theory of subjectivity as ultimately
nihilistic in that it appears to discount the possibilities for any nonlinguistic apprehension of the world or relation to others outside the rigid interiority of the monadic subject. However, a posthumanist reading—which would
perhaps be more in keeping with what Derrida says on the matter, since he
emphatically makes the case that traces are not only those of human others—allows quite a different interpretation. There is no convincing argument
that a subject can ever access directly (that is, without semiotic mediation)
the other's experience of being, irrespective of whether one speaks of other
humans, animals, plants, or even seemingly inert matter.[37] Furthermore,
with recent advances in organismic biology and ecology, it has become clear
that such monadic reductions of bodies to the singularity of the self and the
other are untenable: not only are living bodies always emplaced in symbiotic
relationships within ecosystems, they are nearly all multiorganismic (that, is,
they are composed of a variety of microbiomes and rely on them to function)
and, in fact, multispecies, since our genomes not only share most of their
sequences with other organisms, but actually incorporate others' DNA into
their own (through retroviral insertion, for example). As Anna Tsing notes
succinctly, "human nature is an interspecies relationship."[38]

In any case, according to Derrida's theory, any sense of presence (whether
that of the self or its others) must be inferred by the subject through its relations to the trace. The affectivity of the subject to its own use of language (that
"self-affection") and therefore its presence to itself implies that all extrinsic
presence—the apprehension of others, human or not—must necessarily be
inferred of as simultaneously and inseparably affective and semiotic. For
the subject, the ideal objects of language always allude back to their traces,
not to their objective ideality within discourse, which is erased by subjective
usage. In this sense, the subjective practice of speech inevitably attributes

the condition of being to that which it indicates. If affect and apprehension are fundamentally semiotic processes, it necessarily follows that all others, human or not, effectively communicate with the subject through their traces, and all are equally erased (but not annihilated, since trace indicates presence) by the subject in its self-presence.

In this context, the problem of whether or not nonhumans can speak in a legal or political sense transforms entirely. The question becomes not whether nonhuman entities can speak at all, but rather what constraints particular discursive systems—that is, forms of representation—place on the subjective overwriting of the trace and thereby the parameters of subject-object relations. It is in this sense in which Judith Butler approached the problem of the sexing of bodies in her seminal works *Gender Trouble* and *Bodies that Matter*; if bodies can only become present to the subject through the erasure of their traces, sexuation can never be apprehended in an unmediated, biological sense—that is, the body as it is in itself—only in a semiotic one. Like the animal, the sexes pertain to a discursive category that erases the traces of specific bodies, transforming them through the system of signs into gendered and sexed objects. The subjective performance of naming these bodies—and naming the subject's own body—constitutes them as sexed and gendered according to discursive norms. And those norms must be continually reenacted in the subject's ongoing present. In the same way, all objective categories—the animal, the plant, the mineral, and so on—are enacted continually in the subject's encounter with other bodies. These bodies may only be present to the subject as a kind through language and through the overwriting of their traces; for the subject, their bodies thus consist in specific enactments of language. It is only in this way in which bodies of any kind may matter in the double sense in which Butler uses the term: bodies are always placed within an ethics—a system of values—that is embedded within discourse; this system of values simultaneously dictates how they are apprehended and the kinds of relations they may hold with the subject. At the same time, nonetheless, all bodies that are named matter, if to very differing degrees.

Barad's Agential Realism and Universal Semiotics

New materialists such as Karen Barad have argued that Butler goes too far in discounting the affectivity of bodies, particularly with regards to their agentic capacity to shape both discourse and history.[39] Although Barad does not engage directly with Derrida's notion of the trace, preferring instead to draw on Deleuze and Guattari's theorization of bodily affects and Neils Bohr's phenomenology of scientific observation, her reformulation of subjectivity (a term she usually avoids for reasons I discuss further on) as fundamentally affective nevertheless converges with Derrida's thought. Like Derrida, Barad rejects the interior/exterior division that marks the subject/object distinction; however, for Derrida, all apprehension occurs within the becoming of the subject, while Barad implies that the concept (and enactment) of subjectivity itself upholds a solipsistic humanism that occludes the reality that all bodies, including human bodies, are phenomena, that is inter-agentic constellations that are present in and to the world through mutual, dynamic affectivity.[40] Rejecting the Heideggerian formulation of being as the subject's sense of self-presence that is actualized through the objectifying use of language, Barad eschews entirely the subject/object duality in proposing an "agential realism," in which being is viewed not as a teleological, conscious state, but as an event, that is, the conjunction of various "intra-active" agencies in the making/becoming of specific space-time coordinates. Following Bohr, she writes that, "phenomena do not merely mark the epistemological inseparability of 'observer' and 'observed'; rather, phenomena are the ontological inseparability of agentially intra-acting 'components.' That is, phenomena are ontologically primitive relations—relations without preexisting relata."[41] In this formulation, she simultaneously supersedes the primordiality of the trace in Derrida's theory of subjectivity and the primacy of the object in scientific empiricism, thrusting affective agency to the forefront: "the primary ontological units are not 'things' but phenomena—dynamic topological reconfigurings/entanglements/relationalities/(re)articulations. And the primary semantic units are not 'words' but material-discursive practices through which boundaries are constituted. This dynamism is agency. Agency is not an attribute but the ongoing reconfigurings of the world."[42]

In this account, subjectivity would consist in only one specific form of material intra-action among many that may come into play in the emergence of a phenomenon. Nevertheless, the Euro-American formulation of subjectivity itself would effectively be a mechanism for configuring the world, since she argues via Bohr, that "theoretical concepts (e.g., 'position' and 'momentum') are not ideational in character but rather are specific physical arrangements."[43] Likewise, she reframes linguistic discourse itself—that is, the matrix of potential subjectivities—as only one set of constraints among many that come into play in material intra-activity, carrying out the specific role of configuring meaning and positionality for language-users implicated in distinct phenomena. Furthermore, discourse is never static or singular, but always "a dynamic and contingent multiplicity."[44] As she summarizes, "discursive practices are ongoing agential intra-actions of the world through which local determinacy is enacted within the phenomena produced. Discursive practices are causal intra-actions—they enact local causal structures through which one 'component' (the 'effect') of the phenomenon is marked by another 'component' (the 'cause') in their differential articulation."[45] In a material sense, then, causality consists in this general process of marking or affecting bodies, which is in no way contingent on subjective intent. However, the discursive enactment or assignment of causality—which is fundamental to the subject/object divide as well as humanist notions of agency—is a subjective operation, one which generates a temporal and spatial hierarchy that is not immanent within the horizontal present of phenomena, but must always be performed by the subjective empiricist through the objectification of the nonhuman components of the phenomena.[46] In this sense, her notion of intra-activity both engages (if obliquely) and supplements Derrida's concept of the trace, dismantling the centrality that Derrida affords the subject as the interiority of all observable phenomena, but conserving subjectivity itself as a specific affective regime that relies on discourse to shape material phenomena (to the degree that it may) and to position itself within them.

In this regard, there is no direct conflict between Barad's and Derrida's perspectives. Barad never argues that humans are able to apprehend the world directly without semiotic mediation; her primary critique lies in how causality is both appraised and enacted through the subject/object dichotomy, opaquing and thereby constraining the complex, affective intra-activity of phenomena. In reality, Barad's theory of materiality is itself a discourse that looks to open the subject to alternative, non-solipsistic forms of engaging the traces of nonhuman others, which is to say that it points toward the creation of a new order of signs that is capable of recognizing and naming the intra-activity of phenomena. Clearly, as long as we engage in the use of language, we are subjects—or, as Donna Haraway reformulates it, adeptly weaving together the subjective inference of being in the present with the materiality of phenomena: "fleshly-material semiotic presences."[47] In disrupting the reduction of agency to subjectivity, then, Barad looks to expose language to the potentialities of nonhuman agencies, to force a reevaluation of the forms of speech the trace might make possible and the ways in which it may affect its own overwriting in the becoming of the subject as an intra-active material phenomenon. When the subject is viewed as one class of intra-active phenomena among a universe filled with other kinds of non-subjective phenomena, all relating through mutual affectivity, subjectivity itself must be reconceived of as a process of cowriting rather than a simple overwriting carried out by the subject. Meaning is thus generated not through the externality of an objective system of signs, but through the affective intra-activity of all the components that come to play in the becoming of any phenomenon, including the subject, in its present:

> This ongoing flow of agency through which "part" of the world makes itself differentially intelligible to another "part" of the world and through which local causal structures, boundaries, and properties are stabilized and destabilized does not take place in space and time but in the making of spacetime itself. The world is an ongoing open process of mattering through which "mattering" itself acquires meaning and form in the realization of different agential possibilities.[48]

The system of signs comprises only one of these potential components, even when it exercises a regulatory function in the relations between human and other bodies.

In this formulation, the trace might be rethought in the way in which Deleuze, drawing on Leibniz's conceptualization of the monad, frames apprehension in *The Fold*: as an involution of the affective properties of other bodies, all of which are present to each other differentially, in the form of effects.[49] Furthermore, if one accepts Hoffmeyer's thesis that processes like chemical bonding and selective cell receptor binding are in fact forms of indexical semiosis, these effects operate semiotically, as signs.[50] In tandem with biosemiotics, Derrida's theory of the trace thus reconciles the affectivity of these signs as something of the other that remains in or marks the body in ways that are not purely or only symbolic and yet persist in memory as an archive of indicative signs. Nonetheless, even in cases in which chemical molecules or physical markers of other bodies are not present in the subject's body or are present only second hand, through the chemical processes they trigger in the brain (that is, memory), those indicative signs are not precisely an absence (or erasure) in the sense in which the term is usually used; even in representation, the contours of the "absent" (non-present to the subject) material agent are delineated by the multiplicity of signs that coalesce around its position within the phenomenon, never fully accounting for its affectivity. As Derrida writes, "the lived experience of another is made known to me only insofar as it is mediately indicated by signs involving a physical side. The very idea of 'physical,' 'physical side,' is conceivable in its specific difference only on the basis of this movement of indication."[51] In other words, the indicative sign is always partial, its incompleteness indicating the affectivity to which it alludes but cannot name without ob-jecting it as exteriority.

When semiosis is viewed materially as physico-chemical processes that are the means by which all bodies inter- and intra-act in their becoming, there is no discrepancy between Barad's agential realism and Derrida's account of the trace beyond the primacy that he assigns the human subject in world-making. On this point, Barad states that: "if 'humans' refers to phenomena, not independent entities with inherent properties but rather beings in their differential becoming, particular material (re)configurings of the world with shifting boundaries and properties that stabilize and destabilize along with specific material changes in what it means to be human, then the notion of discursivity cannot be founded on an inherent distinction between humans and nonhumans."[52] Indeed, Derrida himself problematizes this question in his later work on the animal, not so much with regards to world-making (although that movement is necessarily implicated), but in a more specific dispute with Lacan's thesis that animals are incapable of "pretending to pretend," which Lacan posits as the uniquely human basis for symbolic representation. As Derrida queries in uncharacteristically straightforward language, "how could one distinguish, for example, in the most elementary sexual mating game, between a feint and a feint of a feint? If it here provides the criterion for such a distinction, one can conclude that every pretense of pretense remains a simple pretense (animal or imaginary, in Lacan's terms) or else, on the contrary, and just as likely, that every pretense, however simple it may be, gets repeated and reposited undecidably, in its possibility, as pretense of pretense (human or symbolic in Lacan's terms)."[53] "Moreover," he emphasizes, "even a simple pretense consists in rendering a sensible trace illegible or imperceptible," thereby implying that animals engage to at least some degree in what he views as the foundational movement of subjectivity, that is, the overwriting of the trace.[54] This indeterminacy leads him to the conclusion that "it is not just a matter of asking whether one has the right to refuse the animal such and such a power (speech, reason, experience of death, mourning, culture, institutions, technics, clothing, lying, pretense of pretense, covering of tracks, gift, laughter, crying, respect, etc.—the list is necessarily without limit, and the most powerful philosophical tradition with which we live has refused the 'animal' all of that). It also means asking whether what calls itself the human has the right rigorously to attribute to man, which means therefore to attribute to himself, what he refuses the animal, and whether he can ever possess the pure, rigorous, indivisible concept, as such, of that attribution."[55]

Recognizing that affect is fundamentally semiotic and that therefore anything that is apprehended by the subject has semiotic potential opens the doors to a complete reversal of foundational Euro-American notions of agency and of the human itself. If, as Barad argued, intent, or the expression of subjective willpower, no longer constitutes the arbiter of agency, but agency instead consists in the potential to affect other bodies and effect change in the becoming of the world, the circular logic that defined the will as the motivator of intentional action and intentional action/speech as the indicator of will falls apart. If all affect is fundamentally semiotic, there can be no assumption that symbolic expression indicates the presence of an exterior, immaterial form of agency (mind, soul, divinity, law) that orders the material. As a metaphysical, solipsistic formation with no empirical basis (in that it must always be inferred), the existence of the will becomes irrelevant. What differentiates the human, or constitutes the "human exception," then, is neither the use of signs nor the capacity to act, but the deployment of the "human sign," which orders an anthropocentric system of values rather than any kind of immanent "natural" order.[56]

Cosmopolitics: The Ontological Politics of Nonhuman Agencies

In this context, the distinction between interest rights and moral subjectivity in the debate over the rights of nature becomes a moot point. The foundational problem in political ecology is not whether nonhuman entities have being and therefore interests and moral standing of their own, but rather how a multiplicity of agencies converges in the ongoing becoming of bodies in the world and what specific constraints particular discursive regimes place on those agencies in the emergence of phenomenal meaning or "differential intelligibility," as Barad reframes it. When intent (that is, political subjectivity) is removed as the lens through which to view political action, it immediately becomes evident that all political action is the action of more-than-human multitudes. All politics are already cosmopolitical; the question thus becomes what specific constraints liberal humanism in its anthropocentric aspect places over phenomena in the construction of the polis (as comprised of only humans, and even then, not all humans), political subjectivities (that is, the subjects of rights), and political discourse. This is a somewhat circular question, since I have already argued that it carries out this process primarily through the persona/res distinction. When thinking of the rights of nonhumans, then, the task becomes to identify and/or create alternative forms of representational discourse that, rather than suppressing the political agency of nonhuman bodies, speak to it.[57]

Clearly, the orchestration of political causality (goals) through humanism results in a utilitarian politics in which humanity is necessarily the primary constituency of political action, while any nonhuman beneficiaries are always secondary at best. Even in Euro-American formulations of cosmopolitics, the human persists resolutely at the center of political discourse, with "actants" appearing within the political ecology as wards of human political subjects.[58] As Latour and Stengers have argued convincingly, this occurs because in Euro-American societies cosmopolitics may only be approached through the language of science due to the historical legacy of discursive modernity, which has always placed itself in a relation of enmity with respect to competing ontologies, aiming to "root them out," as it were.[59] Despite constituting a passionately subjective cultural practice—and one might add, one with quite a dose of cult of personality or hyper-subjectivity around the first author of scientific "discoveries"—science must appeal to the object of study itself as the "judge" of claims made on its behalf.[60] Nevertheless, Latour has shown that, discursively, science's aura of objectivity ultimately relies not on the speech of the object itself, but rather on the popular equivalence between science and legal discourse; the legal procedure of the case decided by a panel of experts imbues science with an aura of impartiality that is largely absent in its actual day-to-day practice.[61] In this formulation of political ecology, the agentic capacity of nonhuman bodies is fundamentally constrained by the speech of human experts, which frames them as objects of moral care.

In the first chapter of this book, I argued that the rights of nature legislation in Ecuador and, to a lesser degree, Bolivia, constitutes an intercultural formation that binds together Euro-American rights discourse and Andean notions of nonhuman moral subjectivity through the decolonial strategy of coterminousness. In framing nonhuman bodies as emerging simultaneously, horizontally, and ambivalently within the fundamentally incompatible ontologies of science (nature) and Andean *tirakuna* or earth beings (Pacha Mama), the Ecuadoran constitution explicitly disavows a univocal phenomenal reading of bodies and their relationships to rights. Eschewing the multicultural approach of incorporating and yet subordinating "minority" cultural beliefs and practices to the hegemony of Euro-American liberalism, which effectively posits the existence of a single, "true" but mute phenomenology with multiple cultural interpretations, intercultural discourse allows for the simultaneous emergence of co-phenomena, that is, of what Barad calls "differential patternings of mattering."[62] When ontologically incompatible discourses of causality come into play in the emergence of phenomena, they cannot be hybridized or reconciled through the hierarchical subordination of either of the discourses.

Not only are the traces of specific bodies signed in different ways, the traces that matter to different ontologies may not even be the same ones, even when they are enacted effectually from the same bodies. As Marisol de la Cadena notes in her discussion of Ausangate, in the most concrete of terms, the mountain that is described simultaneously by modern science using geo-surveying technologies as a geographical feature and by Andean inhabitants of the mountain's flanks as a living apu, or lord, is not the same mountain.[63] These are not two ways of representing the same mountain; both mountains come into existence in differentiated time and space coordinates as distinct phenomenal events. This occurs because all bodies are present to the world phenomenally as vast multiplicities of bundled effects, and no discourse is capable of totalizing all of them as a single, universal phenomenon.[64] For the geologist, the mountain in question is the objective summa of its measurable properties (its spatial coordinates within a cordillera, its topographical map, its geomorphology, and perhaps even its biomes); for the Andean inhabitant it is present relationally, as a force in everyday life that is demarcated by its causal intra-actions within its biotic community, which resolutely includes its human inhabitants. Both discourses largely disregard the traces that the other sees as mattering most. In this sense, discourse consists in the systematic reduction of bodily effects according to the constraints of legibility that it imposes as the conditions for its intra-action within a particular phenomenon. Each of those mountains precludes the other as its condition for existence, and yet they coexist simultaneously in a practical sense, in the contact between competing discourses. As de la Cadena points out: "sacred mountains, Andean shamanism, and Andean religiosity can accommodate the hegemonic distinction between nature and culture, in which the first exists objectively and the second is subjectively made by humans and therefore includes beliefs (sacred, spiritual, or profane) about nature."[65] However, this is not an ontological reconciliation (and therefore subjugation of Indigenous ontologies as relativistic "beliefs"), but rather a pragmatic, diplomatic procedure relying on "partial connections" within common differences. She argues that this occurs through a process of what Viveiros de Castro calls equivocation, in which it is recognized that the two concepts—and worlds—are fundamentally irreducible (untranslatable) to a single, common one: "in the case of earth-beings as sacred mountains, the equivocation may result from deploying the same word—Ausangate—across different worlds, in one of which the entity is nature and in another one of which it is an earth-being."[66] As Marilyn Strathern frames it in more general terms, "what look like semantic domains are not divisions of the same whole. Rather, what intersects at unpredictable junctures are worlds, each of which (an observer might say) recognizes its own environment."[67] In this context, the epistemic ambivalence of translation—its implicit recognition of inevitable misunderstanding or equivocation—demarcates the limits of one world and the beginnings of another

It is at this juncture that the notion of pluriverses, which is implicitly upheld by the interculturality of the Ecuadoran constitution and its emphasis on plurality, becomes so important. In recognition of the plurality of phenomena that arise through intra-actions with ontologically distinct discourses in their becoming, the notion of the pluriverse—"a world of many worlds" in the oft-cited language of the Ejército Zapatista de Liberación Nacional's *Fourth Declaration of the Lacandon Jungle*—rejects the epistemological possibility of a single universe that would be legible to all as an absolute, basal reality if only all humans would ascribe to the fundamental truths of modern science and biopolitics.[68] Clearly, this latter position, which characterizes much of scientific discourse and practice, disregards the reality that science itself is a constellation of subjective discourses and political practices that produces not only epistemological hierarchies, but also racialized and gendered geopolitical and economic power differentials.[69] As Mario Blaser and Marisol de la Cadena argue, the pluriverse comes into being as a result of "obstinate demands for existence presented by worlds whose disappearance was assumed at the outset of the Anthropocene."[70] Furthermore, science's veracity to itself is constantly under question, subject to revision as it strives to arrive closer and closer to its objects of study; as such, at most one could claim that scientific discourse has a greater degree of e/affectivity in the production of a broader range of phenomena than other ontological discourses. This itself reveals its anthropocentric (and, as ecofeminist scholars such as Val Plumwood have long pointed out, patriarchal) clingings, since the measure of that effectivity would be the ability of humans to dominate their environments progressively through the objectification and technological control of all of the elements comprising them.[71]

In contrast, relational ontologies, while not escaping objectification entirely (since there are no languages whose grammars eschew entirely subject-object positions), tend to privilege dynamic intra-activity and ongoing negotiation—or diplomacy, as Stengers calls it—over the fixity of form. In these ontologies, the measure of value is not the degree of objectification and/or commodification to which a body is subjected, but the overall health of the relations themselves. It is never assumed that there is a sole agent or representative—an acting subject—with absolute power over the object. Any action, any political event is fundamentally a reciprocal becoming, a mutual transformation. Relational ontologies thus emerge not from shared interests or goals, even ecological ones, but rather from a shared, irreducible difference—a dispute, an "uncommons" (in Blaser and de la Cadena's pithy formulation) that demands negotiation, which is fundamentally the way in which theorists such as Jacques Rancière and Alain Badiou define politics.[72] It is for this reason that Blaser and de la Cadena argue for a political ontology rooted in the simultaneity of diverse practices "negotiating their difficult being together in heterogeneity" as "heterogeneous worldings."[73] In this sense, any encounter of worlds necessarily entails an existential crisis and a historical conjuncture before which no world may remain impassive.

Diplomacy across Difference and Multispecies Sociality

Any diplomatic relationship between ontologies—any act of translation—is necessarily simultaneously semiotic and affective; it involves the recognition that the subject-object relationships (and therefore their positions within both discourse and perception) in the other's ontology are not directly equivalent to my own and therefore require negotiation. As Stengers notes, diplomacy is never a question of agreeing upon shared values, but rather of reconciling values that are fundamentally incompatible into a working relationship.[74] While Stenger's conceptualization of diplomacy focuses exclusively on political negotiations between human subjects coming from different ontologies, the reality that all political action is necessarily that of more-than-human multitudes means that diplomacy also implicates nonhuman actors. Indeed, the Amerindian, Andean, and Amazonian ontologies that came into play in the political negotiations of rights of nature legislation in Ecuador and Bolivia do not recognize the Euro-American human/nature divide. There is without exception no directly equivalent, abstract term to either the "human" or "nature" in Amerindian languages.[75] While these languages typically contain vocabulary alluding to "people" and/or "community," those words rarely apply exclusively to (and never all) *Homo sapiens*; they routinely name both human-nonhuman assemblages (as in totemic groups) and non-human species sociality.[76]

This occurs because, as Eduardo Viveiros de Castro famously pointed out, Amerindian ontologies tend to view "human" sociality as a universal form of relations across species, while species forms themselves are generally considered contingent on social practice, and therefore mutable (as in sha-manic transformations, spirits and animals that are able to assume human form, and the idea that the souls of the dead take the posthumous form of animals, meaning that animals are former humans). In his terms, most if not all species (as well as spirit beings and some geographic features) share a fundamental, reflexive "humanity" or personhood, whereas their bodily forms may change, leading him to speak of a "multinaturalism" that runs directly counter to the Euro-American notion of multiculturalism and its foundational premise that nature is universal while culture is relative. As Viveiros de Castro summarizes,

> animals, plants, and other Amazonian categories of beings never cease to be completely human; their post-mythic transformation into animals, etc., counter-effectuates an original humanity, which is the foundation of the ac-cess to the shamanic logopraxis enjoyed by their actual representatives. All of the dead continue to be somewhat beast, and every beast continues to be somewhat human. Humanity remains immanent by largely reabsorbing the pockets of transcendence that flicker on and off in the dense, teeming forest that is the Amazonian socius.[77]

In these ontologies, then, it can never be assumed that diplomacy is a uniquely human act; every interspecies and interpersonal encounter demands both parties engage in acts of diplomacy.

Furthermore, Isabelle Stengers points out that war is the horizon for all diplomacy.[78] Indeed, this notion is implicit in the Amazonian worldview that Viveiros de Castro takes as his point of departure for analyzing Indigenous thought as a "cannibal metaphysics."[79] For Stengers, however, it is the unde-clared war of modernity against other ontologies (and the more overt one against nature itself) that has created the conditions in which ontological diplomacy has become the only possible ethical response before moderni-ty's inexorable ethnocidal and ecocidal impulses. In contrast, the Amazonian ontologies Viveiros de Castro draws on view war in a very different light: as a form of universal sociality whose goal is not the eradication of difference, but its internalization through the metaphorical (ritual) and material ingestion of the other's perspective.

In the system of Amazonian ethical thought that Viveiros de Castro outlines, it is the subject who must struggle to inscribe itself as human in the eyes of the other, since the "human" perspective is not species-specific, but rather fundamentally predatory. If a jaguar or spirit, who views itself as human and may also be a deceased human, does not recognize a person as human, that person will become its prey.[80] Similarly, when a hunter encounters a prey animal in the forest, that prey animal may indicate through its behavior or a dream that it is in fact a former human known to the hunter, who can ritually release that human from its animal skin through certain rituals, which include its consumption (although it is often required that the hunter himself not participate in the eating of his own prey in order to avoid retribution from its spirit). In that sense, the horizon of predation is always present in bodily encounters, and the potentiality of those bodily encounters in turn configure the social network as more-than-human. The social body is constituted as such through these movements of integration or incorporation of the other's attributes or "symbolic resources," defining itself in opposition to its collective others (as in the human/animal divide), but in constitutive relation with them.[81] Thus the centrality of the cannibalism motif; one's own perspective emerges through incorporating that of the other, whether through symbolic or actual violence or shamanistic transformation.

Indeed, the logic governing both cannibalism and shamanistic diplomacy is the same, since engaging in shamanism requires "becoming other" by enacting the internalized traces of the other with whom one desires to communicate. Regarding this "transversal" shamanism, Viveiros de Castro posits that:

Amazonian shamanism, as is often remarked, is the continuation of war by other means. This has nothing to do, however, with violence as such, but with communication, a transversal communication between incommunicables, a dangerous, delicate comparison between perspectives in which the position of the human is constantly in dispute. And what, exactly, does that human position come down to? That is the question raised when an individual finds itself face to face with allogenic bundles of affections and agentivity, such as an animal or unknown being in the forest, a parent [kin] long absent from one's village, or a deceased person in a dream. The universal humanity of beings—the "cosmic background of humanity" that makes every species of being a reflexive genre of humanity—is subject to a principle of complementarity, given that it is defined by the fact that the two different species that are each necessarily human in their own eyes can never simultaneously be so in the other's.[82]

In that sense, shamanistic transformation is fundamentally an exteriorizing movement, a form of "cosmopolitical diplomacy," in which the shaman's body and therefore perspectival subjectivity becomes other in order to negotiate "diverse socionatural interests" with nonhuman beings on their own ground.[83] In contrast, the ethics of cannibalism consists in the internalization of the other's perspective within one's own body; it is the other's perspective of one as prey or enemy that is eaten, thereby conforming a conceptualization of the self as a multiplicity of perspectives, a becoming sustained through the other.

This is why Viveiros de Castro, in his study of Arawaté and Tupinambá ritual cannibalism, posits that it was not the enemy's body that was consumed for material sustenance, since only an insignificant (symbolic) fragment of the body itself was generally eaten, but rather a relation: "what was assimilated from the victim was the signs of his alterity, the aim being to reach his alterity as a point of view on the Self. Cannibalism and the peculiar form of war with which it is bound up involve a paradoxical movement of reciprocal self-determination through the point of view of the enemy."[84] At the same time, the violence of warfare or predation (which were roughly equivalent in Arawaté society) was expiated through rituals of filiation that included the incorporation of the captured warrior into the victor's family during a prescribed amount of time as well as the incorporative ritual of eating; the other's perspective—that is, his humanity—lived on through the perspective of the one who ate him. The relation was maintained intact, even when the body had been devoured. In that sense, warfare was never the elimination of difference, but rather a power differential relying on the assertion of humanity as a predatory perspective. In this predator-prey logic, what Viveiros de Castro calls perspectivity (rather than subjectivity) can only exist in function of its ability to eat other's perspectives of themselves as predators. If the prey did not view themselves as predator, that is, as human, there could be no validation, no sustenance.[85] This logic applies not only to eating human others, but also potent plant and animal others. In other words, the subject is never conceived of as a static being, but rather as a multiplicity in a constant flux of relational becoming. And this notion of the subject as defined by its relations to multiple human and nonhuman others implies an ecological focus on systematicity, on the health of the more-than-human society despite or even perhaps because of the violence of these relations.

Viewing one's relationship to nature through the lens of cannibalistic war will likely seem antithetical to the goals of most Westernized environmental ethicists (myself included), which are to arrive at a more harmonious or at least sustainable relationship with our environments. On the surface, the perspective that "every vital activity is a form of predatorial expansion"[86] seems problematic at best, particularly when many of us search for the creative freedom of "becoming-with" other species. Additionally, the so-called Enlightenment's emancipatory discourse consisted primarily in freeing Euro-American "Man" from his warlike relationship with nature (the tyranny of nature was a frequent trope in writings from this period) through the technological and institutional subordination of both nonhuman beings and animalistic "human nature" to human rational instrumentality.[87] Indeed, the Enlightenment notion of individual freedom is fundamentally dissociative; it is a liberation from contingency on others, human and nonhuman alike, a "freedom from" as Adorno points out in *Negative Dialectics*.[88] The humanistic objectification of nature allowed humans to live in perceived freedom from the fear of being harmed by beings outside our control. In this paradigm, any anomalous—and therefore, perverse—agency of nonhuman entities is seen as being due to incomplete knowledge and risk-control technologies. Modern anthropology worked largely within this project, not only mediating the threatening aspects of human others' difference (often exemplified in the trope of cannibalism) through classification, but also relegating "primitive' or "savage" societies to prior stages of human history or even evolution. In that sense, Viveiros de Castro's proposal to take seriously "cannibal metaphysics" as a formulation of ethics must contend with the baggage of nineteenth-century Spencerian social Darwinism and environmental determinism, which posited the fear of nonhuman entities as the province of primitive belief systems with insufficient technological domination over their environments. In the modern theology of human progress, "savage" is a name for a system of thought that does not have faith in technology's abilities to allay our fears and provide security.

Nevertheless, I think that most environmental ethicists would agree that it makes sense to examine seriously and respectfully the systems of thought that have upheld societies that have maintained sustainable relationships with their environments over centuries or even millennia. Furthermore, no one can possibly deny the fundamentally predatory nature of eating or any other form of consumption, particularly within Barad's agential realism; even the Fruitarian symbiotic ethic of eating only the fruits of certain plants and distributing their seeds to propitiate and renew their life cycle is nevertheless a somewhat violent intervention. And even within the heavily constrained species interactions of modernity, humans are routinely the "prey" of many species, particularly those that affect us at the microbial level. At some level, it is only through objectification of some members of an ecosystemic community that a pacific coexistence with certain species can be conceived of; which is to say that the lives of some species and all seemingly lifeless forms are viewed as existing outside the system of values.

Contra Immunitas: Ethics as Fright and Vulnerability in Encounter

The radical proposition embedded in native Amazonian metaphysics is that of an ethical relationship to nonhuman others not through the staticity of classification, but rather through the recognition of the fundamentally predatory and entropic basis for life itself. The power of predation—and, in a more general sense, affectivity—is the sign of subjectivity. External to the sacrificial logic that underpins the discourses of conservation and vegetarianism, cannibal metaphysics imply the constant negotiation of relations with all members of the biotic community. The default is therefore respect toward the other's fundamental humanity, that is, its ability to harm us but also its fundamental sociality within the life system sustaining all. Within this perspective, it is impossible to imagine systematically destructive relations with an ecosystem; modernity as an "undeclared war" against nature is inconceivable. As Viveiros de Castro points out, when it is assumed that all species see themselves as human, "it is impossible not to be a cannibal; but it is equally impossible to establish a consistently one-way active cannibal relationship with any other species—they are bound to strike back."[89] When the threat of war is the point of departure for sociality, diplomacy must be enacted continuously in all social interactions.[90] It is only when the species taken for consumption are done so with proper respect—that is, in agreement with the spirits that govern them—that war can be averted. The other's body can be eaten, but its perspective—its spirit—must be provided the proper treatment so that it does not take revenge through another body. Most often, this proper treatment implies establishing lines of communication and filial relationships with spirit beings—animal "masters"—that are nevertheless considered fully presential and therefore material. Multispecies alliances—what

Viveiros de Castro refers to as "disjunctive inclusion"—are formed through diplomatic relations arising from the fear of retribution (war), that is, of the other's response.[91] This logic of retribution is thus a causality of first order, an affective causality. Unlike the immunitary logic that Roberto Esposito detects at the heart of modern political thought and practice, in which fear is exorcized through objectification, the institutionalization of relations, and other sequestering technologies, cannibal metaphysics view contamination as the proper response to the demands placed by the other in its affectivity, as the "existential condition for the social form itself."[92]

In this context, I concur with Stengers that "fright," in its very excess with respect to instrumental rationality, is in fact the prime indicator that we have apprehended the other's ability to affect and transform us in ways we can never fully control.[93] While cognitive scientists often speak of objects of fear (thereby insisting that emotion is experienced rationally, as representation), enactive theories of affect posit that emotions are neither "objective" nor "response-dependent" features of the world, but rather bring new properties into existence through their imperative to act.[94] Indeed, this premise was fundamental to Jean Paul Sartre's early theorization of "emotional conscious-ness," in which he posited that emotional reactions to the other's affectivity fall beyond the bounds of the deterministic movement of rational subjectivity, even when those emotions are subsequently rationalized through discourse as "emotional states." In affective encounters, he argues, "the behavior which gives its meaning to the emotion is no longer our behavior; it is the expression of the face and the movements of the body of the other being."[95] In that sense, the representational content of specific fears would be an intra-active movement, a pragmatic apprehension of the other's affective agency that eludes to at least a degree the causal logic of discursive constraints.

Furthermore, the emotional response implies a transformation in the world, since it eludes the logic of causality whereby the subject assembles its worldview. As Anthony Hatzimoysis summarizes,

On the one hand, the "emotional apprehension" of the world hooks on to those qualities or aspects that carry affective meaning for the agent, while the "prag-matic intuition" focuses on features of the situation that make or not possi-ble the execution of a task, the realization of an objective, or the creation of a product. On the other hand, the agent's response in an emotional episode engages the overall stance and physiology of the body not so as to effect mate-rial changes in the world but so as to alter his or her perception of reality, and, through that, his or her relation to the world: "during emotion, it is the body which, directed by the consciousness, changes its relationship to the world so that the world should change its qualities" (STE 41). That change in qualities is called by Sartre "magical."[96]

For Sartre, this emotional form of relating to the object is "magical" due to its disruption of the rational logic of causality; however, given the history of dismissive associations in anthropology of magic with a primitive logic of irrational or at least ineffectual equivalences, I prefer to exchange the word for "indeterminate." The world that is opened up to the subject through the emotional apprehension of others' affectivity is indeterminate; it is a fleetingly open world, a world in which subjectivity itself becomes co-extensive with its affects. This is why Heidegger argues for "fearing," "as a slumbering possibility of the affectively found [befindlichen] being-in-the-world," which "has already disclosed the world, in that out of it something like the fearsome may come close [to us]."[97] It is this dangerous proximity to the world through the other, rather than its solipsistic overwriting, that gives meaning to the Dasein or being here-there.

On the other hand, discussing the phenomenon of fear-induced fainting, Sartre argues that "the real meaning of fear is now becoming apparent to us. It is a consciousness whose aim is to negate something in the external world by means of magical behavior, and will go so far as to annihilate itself in order to annihilate the object also."[98] This impulse toward annihilation of the other cannot be discounted in fearful apprehension, and it clearly often takes much more violent forms than fainting. Nevertheless, the cannibal metaphysics analyzed by Viveiros de Castro posit a substantially different relationship to that violent impulse: fear invokes not annihilation, but ingestion. Rather than annihilating the object of fear, whether through actually destruction or discursive neutralization within the sameness of the subject, it is the subject-object distinction that is annihilated. As Viveiros de Castro summarizes, "this is a form of fear that, far from demanding the exclusion or disappearance of the other in order for the peace of self-identity to be recuperated, necessarily implies the inclusion or incorporation *of* the other or *by* the other (*by* also in the sense of 'through'), as a form of perpetuation of the becoming-other that is the process of desire in Amazonian socialities."[99] The subject and the object of fear become relationally, differentially one, if not the same.

In more abstract and perhaps more comforting terms for the thinker for whom cannibalism is not part of social life, power differentials can never be avoided in relations; indeed, they are what form relations and make them possible. These are the powers of affect, the power to act upon and transform the other. In the moment of encounter, we are simultaneously captured by and capturers of the other; we are always the potential victim and victimizer of the other. Even if the differentials that come into play (whether those of mass, velocity, reactivity, formal stability, or sociopolitical power) do not necessarily or intentionally enact violence in and of themselves, they always bring about asymmetrical transformations in which one body's retentive or inertial capacities (that is, its resistance to change) are altered to a greater degree than the other, up to and including full absorption, as in the case of ingestion. In this context, an ethical stance toward the other implies recognizing its agentic capacities within those unavoidable differentials, its ability to transform us through affects, and therefore behaving respectfully toward them. Indeed, the relationship that is proper to fear—that is, fear-in-encounter—is respect. And, as Emmanuel Levinas argued, fear of the other also entails fear for the other, that is, an apprehension of the self as discontinuous and therefore multiple in relation with the other. "Subjectivity is being hostage," he writes; hostage not to the other as interlocutor in a semiotic exchange, but to the affectivity of "the nakedness and destitution of the expression as such."[100] For Levinas, this fear for the other, this dual, rending sense of vulnerability and defenselessness during the face-to-face encounter, emerges within the primordial imperative to respond to an absolutely incommunicable presence, which he posits as the expressionless face of the absolutely Other. While Badiou criticized this recourse to the absolute Other as theological rather than ethical, Derrida took a somewhat more subtle route, transposing it onto the semiotic by substituting the face with the trace.[101] In that sense, one might read Levinas's accounting of the fundamental incommunicability of presence as the unrealized, unidealized potentiality of affect itself. What one primordially fears in the encounter with the other is the otherness of the self before inscrutable difference, of the becoming multiple of the self before the unceasing demand for response in the affective encounter: "The more I return to myself, the more I divest myself, under the traumatic effect of persecution [referring here to the unceasing demand for response), the more I discover myself to be responsible; the more just I am, the more guilty I am. I am 'in myself' through the others. The psyche is the other in the same, without alienating the same."[102] Suddenly, Levinas's first ethics approximates cannibal metaphysics.

In this context, it hardly seems coincidental that many aspects of Derrida's thinking on the trace run align to at least a degree with the native Amazonian systems of thought Viveiros de Castro studies, since they all interrogate the transubstantiation of affect to the metaphysics of the self through material processes. Indeed, Derrida frequently acknowledged the violence implicit in the erasure of the trace and the constitution of the subject, which implies the silencing of the other as nonpresence. The parallels run far deeper than this, however. I would argue that Derrida's conceptualization of subjectivity is essentially cannibalistic, even if he usually prefers less fraught descriptors: if the trace of the other is all we may know of its body and therefore perspective, subjectivity effectively consists in an eating of the traces of the other.[103] Tellingly, Derrida's discussion of animation comes very close to the shamanistic conceptualization of becoming with and through the other: "what in effect happens in communication? Sensible phenomena (audible or visible, etc.) are animated through the sense-giving acts of a subject, whose intention is to be simultaneously understood by another subject. But the 'animation' cannot be pure and complete, for it must traverse, and to some degree lose itself in, the opaqueness of a body."[104] And if one takes seriously his problematization of animal traces and animal pretense as a form of ideal repetition akin to the movement of subjectivity (that is, the animal's erasure of its own traces as a performance or enactment of and for an other), he comes very close to Amazonian perspectivism and its imperative to become human in the eyes of the other. The divergence between these distinct philosophical traditions, of course, lies in exactly which ways the body is opaque in its difference. Derrida addresses the mutability of the body only from within the temporality of the subject and its world. The self would becomes present to itself as a bodily form in its nonidentity with the ideality of its body's inferred past and future: "for the ideality of the form (Form) of presence itself implies that it be infinitely re-peatable, that its re-turn, as a return of the same, is necessary ad infinitum and is inscribed in presence itself. It implies that the re-turn is the return of a present which will be retained in a finite movement or retention and that primordial truth, in the phenomenological sense of the term, is only to be found rooted in the finitude of this retention."[105] In other words, the form of the self as presence can only be conceived of through the idealization of its body as form and the projected disappearance of that form in death (finitude).

Amazonian perspectivism is yet more radical in claiming that the subject is itself fundamentally, essentially multiple in its present; its self-presence is always marked by its body's own potential difference (rather than sameness or continuity) to itself in relation to its past and future otherness. In a cannibalistic conceptualization of the subject, the self is never only itself, it is a crowd, always bearing multiple traces due to its fundamentally ingestive, predatory nature.[106] At the very least, it is always simultaneously potential predator and prey. This is what makes possible its mutations into forms that are not human; in cannibal metaphysics, the potentiality of repetition that Derrida views as presence may effectively be the repetition not of one's own form, but of the form (bodily perspective) of the other without ceasing to be oneself. The subject is fundamentally an archive of perspectival forms, any of which may be enacted in the now as human, whether the body is that of a human or that of a jaguar, for instance. Furthermore, this power of mutability is simultaneously contingent on the horizon of one's own death (viewing oneself as potential prey) and the death of the other (oneself as potential predator).

In turn, this modifies in interesting ways Derrida's proposition that the sign itself becomes possible through conceiving of being as a non-presence that is repeatable and therefore a universal (transcendental) or ideal form that will necessarily persist beyond my own death, since my death is itself an inference of the absence of my form, which can only be envisioned through the death of the other.[107] If, as Viveiros de Castro posited, cannibalism effectively consists in an eating of relations, what is eaten is effectively the finitude of the other's form (in death), which is then assimilated into one's own self as a multiplicity of potential forms. Logically, the ideality of language would itself be dependent on the form that the self takes in any given future; thus the sign becomes proper to the kind of body that the self displays. This is the nexus between cannibalistic and shamanistic practices; the shaman is able to speak the languages of many bodies because the self is already multiple and mutable. Self-affection—the basis for subjectivity according to Derrida—is fundamentally different when many forms speak through the self in response to and relation with multiple traces. A shaman hears himself speak as other and becomes other.

Clearly, the concept of eating one's relation to the other can only be metaphorical in a broader context than the native Amazonian perspectives that Viveiros describes. In general terms, however, it coincides not only with Derrida's notion of the trace but also with Karen Barad's new materialist perspective in the recognition of the phenomenality of one's own body as an intraactive multiplicity, which is certainly the case in biological terms, given the sympoetic biological processes that Haraway underscores as making possible all organismic life. In all cases, subjectivity is recognized as a fundamentally sympoetic and yet asymmetric process, and the recognition of that reality implies an internalization of relationality akin to Viveiros's cannibal metaphysics. In this context, an ethics capable of respecting the other's difference through its affectivity necessarily entails opening diplomatic channels to both relational ontologies and nonhuman forms of semiosis. In order for the rights of nature to become social praxis, political speech must become capable of acknowledging and enacting the traces of nonhuman others and accounting for their testimonies as subjects within the universal sociality of ecosystemic communities. Given the unlikelihood that non-Indigenous cultures will suddenly adopt Indigenous relational ontologies and the languages that embody them in practice, the task becomes how to make relational ontologies available to hegemonic languages in such a way as to open their worlds to the multiphenomenality of the pluriverse.

This is not as tall an order as it may seem. As my discussion of fear showed, the traces of others inherently affect subjectivity in unexpected ways, generating new causal relations with the subject and transforming its world. Even when the regulatory function of discourse always comes into play between the erasure of traces and the auto-affection of self-presence, those traces do not always trigger the same categorical chains of signs. If they did, poetry, art, and perhaps creativity itself could not exist. The subjective overwriting of the trace is always primordially ambivalent or even polyvalent due to the multiple partially formed meanings that inhabit signs in their relation to phenomena. In its potential to produce multiple phenomena, this ambivalence or indeterminacy is itself the grounds for diplomacy and, in a broader sense, the pluriverse.

If traces (whether those of human or nonhuman others), writing, and the system of signs all share the condition of erasure in the becoming of the subject, it is clear that writing is no less immediate to the inference of being of nonhuman entities than any other form of representation. All representation consists in this overwriting of the trace through different sign regimes. In the chapters that follow, I examine some of the ways in which diverse writers from Latin America have approached representation and the system of signs to problematize the status of nonhumans with an eye to reformulating ethics and the cosmopolitical potentiality of bodies of all kinds.

While I do not extoll the practice of cannibalism in any form, I argue that the logic of predation—that is, the affectivity of fear in bodily encounter—must underpin any ethics that views nonhumans as active political participants and not simply moral objects of human care. Nonhuman agency necessarily entails its ability to affect us in uncontrollable ways. While modernity relies on the logics of management, containment, and eradication of difference, Indigenous ethical thought offers alternative ways of approaching the powers of affect. And, in the acknowledgment of the predatory violence of encounter, this ethics also places a diplomatic imperative to affiliate and form sympoetic alliances of mutual becoming and aid.

In the next two chapters, "Humanistic Institutions, Animal Affectivity, and Passive Decision" and ' The Familiar Animal and the Aesthetics of the Stray," I examine literary representations of domestic human-animal filiation and predation by non-Indigenous authors who nevertheless approximate the relational ontologies underpinning cannibal metaphysics. These works draw out the ethical complexities of living with and eating animals, exposing and criticuing the conceptual devices by which modern subjects distance themselves affectively from animals that nevertheless have become in one way or another part of the family. I argue that fear of and for the animal other disrupts these containment strategies, resulting in horroristic tropes of cannibalism and animal revenge. This horror is produced within the Westernized subject when it is realized that, in domestic animals, it is the relationship—that is, the latency of multispecies societies—that is eaten, thereby threatening the stability of the subject and that of the family as a sociopolitical structure. I conclude my discussion of the politics of animality by taking a somewhat different tack, examining the trope of going astray as a multispecies cosmopolitical tactic for eluding domestication. The rupture of the domestic family potentializes and politicizes interspecies encounters wherein intra-activity becomes visible and diplomacy is required.

CHAPTER 3

Humanistic Institutions, Animal Affectivity, and Passive Decision

I don't humanize beasts because it's offensive—one must respect their nature—it's I who animalize myself.

—CLARICE LISPECTOR

I have already entered into communication with you with such force that, being, I ceased existing. You became an I. It's so difficult to speak and say things that cannot be said.

—CLARICE LISPECTOR

The problem of the representation of nonhuman agencies runs through questions of affectivity, semiotics, personhood, and ontological diplomacy, when ontology is viewed not as an exclusively human worldview, but rather as a particular logic emerging from within relational intra-actions between diverse bodies. In the interplay between Karen Barad's theory of "agential realism," biosemiotics, and Eduardo Viveiros de Castro's description of Native Amazonian "cannibal metaphysics," it becomes clear that every living being has its own logic of being proper to its body and its intra-active relations—that is, its own way of reading its relations to the world. In that sense, any act of communication, any exchange of signs not only between species but also between human cultures is necessarily an act of diplomacy across difference. However, according to most theories of language, symbolic representation involves the violent erasure or at least subordination of the other's signs to a specific symbolic order's grammatical parameters and archive of meanings.

The question then becomes: how can nonhuman semiotic agency influence human representational systems designed to impose their own symbolic order over their objects?

Literature, in its explicitly disruptive relation to both the conventions of the real and the "common sense" or practicality of instrumental language, offers a powerful tool for exploring the complexity of the relations between affectivity and representation. In this chapter, I examine two short stories that rethink affective encounters between humans and animals within the institutional context of the zoo: Julio Cortázar's "Axolotl" (1964) and Clarice Lispector's "The Buffalo" (1960). Rather than representing these encounters with animals as mere spectacle or the straightforward enactment of the human/animal divide, both stories problematize how animals engage the human protagonists affectively, transforming their perspectives and placing them in a state of constitutive indebtedness. The affective demands placed by these animals have both ethical and political ramifications through what Derrida calls "passive decision," in that every subjective decision invokes the traces of the other; it is difference that makes decision possible.

In both stories, passive decision relates to how nonhumans are represented in writing, to the persistence of the traces of their singularity between the lines of the text despite being overwritten by symbolization (animal and species categories), literary conventions, and the authors' personal styles. In the final lines of Cortázar's "Axolotl," the titular animal places a demand on the human writer to maintain fidelity both to its own subjectival perspective and to its constitutive relation with the human protagonist through reenactment, that is, writing and reading as ritual invocations that actualize its traces in the text's present. Similarly Clarice Lispector develops a methodology of "objective" or "neutral" representation akin to the Surrealist technique of automatic writing designed to suppress subjectivity to a certain degree. However, rather than access the Freudian subconscious as in Surrealism, Clarice's technique of "desistance" looks to enable and enact the traces of the nonhuman other. Through the process of de-subjectivation, which she equates to a becoming-animal, the traces of her own body but also animal traces—the memory of biosemiotic, nonlinguistic signs—operate within the literary text, re-ordering language from within to reflect their autonomy from the symbolic order. For Lispector, a text's meaning thus becomes dependent not on the erasure of the other through symbolization, but rather on the ambivalence of the symbol and of silence as modes of intra-activity that invoke relations rather than objects. Through techniques designed to accentuate rather than occlude passive decision in the writing process, the literary text transforms into a multiplicity, an intra-active, self-ordering system of which the author is not the sole proprietor. Others' traces thus emerge and participate in the writing process not against, but within the author's subjectivity as the enactment of a multiplicity of affective demands placed on the author by human and nonhuman others. In that sense, writing as envisioned by Lispector becomes a cannibalistic process akin to that proposed by Brazilian modernist Oswald de Andrade in "Cannibalist Manifesto," but one that is not appropriative in that it does not homogenize the other's difference into the sameness of the authorial self, but rather renders the author's (and the reader's) subjectivity multiple or other to itself. Lispector's writing is thus integrative or cannibalistic, but it is also an act of diplomacy, of opening oneself to the signs of nonhuman others.

While my approach to the representations of animals in Cortázar's and Lispector's stories relies to a certain degree on the Native Amazonian theories of representation summarized by Viveiros de Castro, I purposefully choose not to focus on Indigenous texts in this chapter and the following for two main reasons. First, I want to emphasize that the ethics of encounter that emerge in these stories is not culturally relativistic, but rather indivisible from intra-activity itself. It is the logic of relation to the other that emerges in the instant of contact and can only later—with physical and temporal distance— be overwritten through moral codes, rational ethical systems, and ultimately law. Second, I want to show the potential and relevance of both biosemiotics and Indigenous thought for re-reading critically representations of nonhumans in texts that are often located squarely within the Euro-American humanistic tradition, as far as one could get from Indigenous ontologies. In this way, I look to undermine the rigid disciplinary barriers that segregate Indigenous thought and concepts into the fields of anthropology and archeology, and thereby deny its potential for reconceptualizing a large number of other disciplines, among them literary theory and analysis, environmental philosophy, and even jurisprudence. As I argued in my first and second chapter, this approach will be central to reconceptualizing nonhumans not only as rights-holders, but also moral subjects and political agents.

Finally, I chose to begin my discussion of nonhuman agency and environmental ethics with animals simply on the basis that animals are nearly always considered both biologically and ontologically closer to humans than other nonhuman taxonomies. This proximity arises not only through mere analogy (the animal face, for example), but rather through the anthropomorphic recognition of forms of agency or personhood that may be parallel but not equivalent or reducible to human ones. In the representations of animals I analyze in this chapter, the authors eschew straightforward personification or allegory in favor of narrative strategies designed to draw out the ambivalence of animals with respect to concepts such as conscious individuality, perspectival subjectivities, intentionality, and social relations. At the same time, the biopolitical institutions that uphold the human/animal divide, sequestering animals from ethical and political standing, are often some of the most egregious and arbitrary, whether one refers to domesticity, wild animal conservation, animal slaughter, or, as in the stories in this chapter, zoos. As I will argue throughout this chapter, the encounter with animal others—simultaneously vulnerable and threatening—always exceed the institutional bounds of the human/animal divide, placing them into question.

Human-Animal Intra-Subjectivities in Cortázar's "Axolotl"

The ending of Argentinean author Julio Cortázar's iconic short story "Axolotl" (1952) has always struck me as particularly evocative in its treatment of the question of potential animal subjectivities, yet what is ostensibly the text's central theme is nearly always glossed over in critical readings. In this story, the first-person narrator happens upon the *Ambystoma mexicanum* at the aquarium at the Parisian Jardin des Plantes on a day in which he finds himself bored by the lions and panther he habitually visits. He immediately becomes entranced while viewing the axolotls in their aquarium and rather arbitrarily singles out one with whom he identifies, if in a poignantly ambivalent manner: "from the first minute I knew that we were linked, that something infinitely lost and distant kept pulling us together."[1] The reliance on the gaze—the only physical contact possible in the scopic regime of the zoo—in this initial identification simultaneously invokes and destabilizes the subject-object dichotomy, as is evident in the covalence of empirical and evolutionary distance, loss, and connection.[2] This visual ambivalence fugues into a complex play on human-animal intra-subjectivity. The narrator, returning obsessively to the axolotl exhibit on a daily basis, comes to refer to himself in first person from the subject positions of both human and axolotl, sometimes in the same sentence. Nevertheless, despite the many readings of this story that reference the Euro-American literary traditions of metamorphosis and monstrous human-animal hybridization, the bodies themselves never come into direct contact. They remain separated materially by the aquarium's glass, which also functions as a metaphor for the species divide. Nor does the narrator's human body transform in any way; it is his perspective that splits into two, part of which transmigrates from human to axolotl, without ceasing to be human. The ending drives home this unsettling state of affairs, narrating from the perspective of the axolotl:

> He returned many times, but he comes less often now. Weeks pass without his showing up. I saw him yesterday, he looked at me for a long time and left briskly. It seemed to me that he was not so much interested in us any more, that he was coming out of habit. Since the only thing I do is think, I could think about him a lot. It occurs to me that at the beginning we continued to communicate, that he felt more than ever one with the mystery which was claiming him. But the bridges were broken between him and me, because what was his obsession is now an axolotl, alien to his human life. I think that at the beginning, I was capable of returning to him in a certain way—ah only in a certain way—and of keeping awake his desire to know us better. I am an axolotl for good now, and if I think like a man it's only because every axolotl thinks like a man inside his rosy stone semblance. I believe that all this suceeded in communicating something to him in those first days, when I was still he. And in this final solitude to which he no longer comes, I console myself by thinking that perhaps he is going to write a story about us, that, believing that he is making up a story, he's going to write all this about axolotls.[3]

It is quite revealing that this story is rarely read as a serious philosophical reflection on the ethics of approaching animal subjectivities; at most, it is viewed as an exoticized projection of human desire, alienation, and consciousness into an animal body.[4] More commonly still, the human-animal encounter is dismissed entirely as an aesthetic ploy in keeping with the conventions of fantastic literature, surrealism, or Latin American magic realist aesthetics. It is routinely relegated to the metaphorical as a humanistic reflection on the construction of sovereign subjectivity through the other, in which the animal other's being is ultimately tangential, or even purely oppositional to the human.[5] The axolotl's image behind the aquarium's glass becomes that of a mere mirror, reflecting the human back to himself. Another strain of criticism focuses on the existential conditions of postcolonial alienation and exile, given that the axolotls and the autobiographical narrator share the experience of geographical displacement as Latin American others "exiled" in Paris.[6] Despite the story's explicit framing as an interspecies encounter, it is in nearly every case read as a humanist allegory, with critics sometimes going to excruciating lengths to downplay the phenomenology of encounter and maintain intact the sovereignty of the human exception.

Without a doubt, the story emanates a certain aura of fantastical exoticism. Nevertheless, I contend that this exoticism arises not so much from the passing association of the axolotl with an "Aztec face" and statuesque immobility or the story's geographic setting in a Parisian zoo, but rather from the ultimately honest ambivalence that emerges in the recognition that one can never know in absolute terms what any human or nonhuman other is thinking or feeling beyond what their body displays. What appears exotic and contrived to the humanist critic is that the axolotls are presented as having a "human" mental life of their own, which contradicts the foundational premise of human exceptionalism. Nonetheless, Cortázar's exercise in imagining animal subjectivities maintains meticulously the biological bounds of species differences, following a methodology akin to that employed in Jacob von Uexküll's seminal *A Foray into the Worlds of Animals and Humans* for inferring the umwelt of animals through the specificity of their sensory organs; thus, the story's extensive focus on the axolotls' anatomy (especially their eyes, hands, and skin), perspective of the aquarium environment, and sociality.[7] Beyond the axolotl's description of its species as human in the quote above, there are only two clear instances within the story in which the axolotl narrates thoughts that could be considered to lie beyond the purview of its species, at least as long as one takes into account the incontrovertible evidences provided by the cognitive sciences and ethology that humans and a wide range of animals share to at least some degree all of the neurological capacities that make cognition possible.[8] The first of these exceptions relates to the question of transmigration; the second, to the axolotl's parting hope that the narrator will consign the encounter to writing. All of the other, more suppositional forms of thought are contained within the human narrator's perspective. Thus, statements such as: "perhaps their eyes could see in the dead of night, and for them the day continued indefinitely," always appear as philosophically charged reflections of the human narrator, if usually based on empirical, anatomical observations: "the eyes of axolotls have no lids."[9]

In the Euro-American tradition, the concept of transmigration is generally traced back to ancient Greek philosophy, particularly the Pythagorean school of thought, but it gained widespread cultural currency in the nineteenth-century practices of spiritism and spiritualism as well as in writings by Romantic authors such as Fourier, Hugo, Maistre, Reynaud, Poe, and Schopenhauer. It continued to appear as a key trope in turn of the twentieth-century works by Joyce, Nietzsche, and Kafka, among many others. Clearly, the weight of this cultural tradition cannot be downplayed in Cortázar's story, particularly given its recourse to gothic aesthetics in the sections describing the transmigration. Despite this widespread interest in metempsychosis and some debate in nineteenth-century animal rights discourse as to whether or not animals had souls, however, Euro-American concepts of transmigration were nearly always envisioned as an exclusively human phenomenon—that is, as human souls reincarnating in *Homo sapiens* bodies.[10] Indeed, it is closely bound up with anxieties surrounding the discourse of human exceptionalism at a moment in which it found itself in question due to the emergence of the biological sciences and theories of species evolution. At the same time, these theories of transmigration–and the spiritist fascination with haunting in general—unquestionably bear the marks of deep historical anxieties stemming from the nineteenth century's rapid technosocial transformations, which gave rise to modernity's characteristic dread of outmoded subjectivities as well as the increasing marginalization of animals from daily life, particularly with respect to their formerly central roles in transportation and agricultural production.[11]

For a reader of Viveiros de Castro, in contrast, the interspecies shift in perspectives in Cortázar's story immediately calls to mind the kind of cosmological perspectivism that he finds common to Amerindian shamanistic ontologies, in which it is assumed that most if not all species view themselves as human: "if I think like a man it's only because every axolotl thinks like a man inside his rosy stone semblance."[12] Indeed, there are multiple, if nebulous points of contact with Indigenous ontologies, perhaps beginning with the frequent trope in Indigenous storytelling positing initial eye contact as the moment in which a nonhuman being may capture a human's spirit self, leading to an ontological transformation in which the human involuntarily becomes a nonhuman other: "and then I discovered its eyes, its face, two orifices like pin heads, letting themselves be penetrated by my gaze that seemed to pass through the golden point and lose itself in a diaphanous internal mystery."[13] In the Indigenous mythologies cited by Viveiros de Castro, this occurs due to a shift in perspective in which the human participant in the encounter comes to view the spirit or animal other as the real human to the exclusion of the humanity of *Homo sapiens*.[14] In the story, the human narrator is not fully dehumanized or othered; nevertheless, the human/animal binomial falls apart, implicitly placing the meaning of the Euro-American discourse of humanity into question: "That looked and knew. That claimed. They were not *animals*."[15]

Threatening Affectivities and the Cannibalistic Gaze

As much as the effect of gothic aesthetics, the horror Cortázar's human narrator experiences when he confronts this involuntary transmutation of perspectives places the encounter squarely within the fearful affectivity inspired by powerful nonhuman others in Indigenous ontologies. In the narrator's case, this affect arises from the specter of the dissolution of the humanist subject and entrapment within another biology, as well as his aporetic position with respect to the dehumanizing category of animality itself: "only one thing was strange: to go on thinking as usual, to know. To realize that was, for the first moment, like the horror of a man buried alive awaking to his fate."[16] The horror is produced within the ambivalence resulting from the incompatibility of the humanist symbolic projection of subjectivity over the axolotl and the realization through affective encounter that the axolotl's anatomical and environmental differences, specifically its eyes and confinement within the aquarium environment, reject encompassment within the narrator's humanist notions of what constitutes subjectivity. The absence of the possibility of speech, which is generally viewed within humanistic discourse as the indicator of free will or intentionality, would be equally troublesome.

The sense of horror thus emerges in this interplay between clarity and opacity, between the anatomical parallels that would clearly produce common affects across species—such as anxiety from entrapment—and the reification that the human perspective itself suffers as a result of the recognition of the potential yet unknowably alien subjectivity of the axolotls. At the same time, while fear-in-encounter may be primordially affective in the spontaneity of the instant, the subjective experience of horror, consigned here in writing, is effectively a deferral to discourse—an abdication of responsible action that is itself a form of violence against the other. Horror denotes the paralysis that occurs in the realization of the impossibility of assuming an ethical stance toward an other subjectivity that is systematically and institutionally reified, that is, toward a potential subject that is condemned a priori, without any possibility of appeal, to silence, confinement, commodification, and, ultimately, a timelessness that is the immortal waiting room of death (as eternal day must logically, if not chronologically, conjure infinite night). And yet, as an aesthetic effect, horror simultaneously names and disempowers the perverse ambivalence resulting from the aporetic relationship between the abjection of the zoo animal and the ostensibly humanistic imperative of justice. As Derrida famously pointed out in the eloquent example of finding himself naked before his pet cat, this imperative arises because an animal's direct gaze demands a response to it as an individual. As an "unsubstitutable singularity," its role as constitutive witness to the subject's self-presence cannot be entirely dismissed through the subjective deployment of the "animot," or animal category. One never finds oneself naked before an object; the demand for a response is simultaneously a moral imperative that places the human in a state of ethical responsibility.[17]

In this sense, the axolotl's direct gaze operates against the institutionalized power differential of the zoo, whose function, according to John Berger's discussion in *About Looking* of the optical constraints through which modern social institutions shape subjectivities, is effectively to sequester and disempower the affectivity of the animal gaze through the framing function of the zoo's series of enclosures. This spatial framing transforms zoo animals into inert, if living representations of their species to the exclusion of their individuality, that is, their ability to act affectively through encounter. As Berger argues, "the public purpose of zoos is to offer visitors the opportunity of looking at animals. Yet nowhere in a zoo can a stranger encounter the look of an animal. At the most, the animal's gaze flickers and passes on. They look sideways. They look blindly beyond. They scan mechanically. They have been immunized to encounter, because nothing can any more occupy a central place in their attention."[18] Tellingly, this is itself the plot device that leads to the human narrator's encounter with the axolotls; he becomes disillusioned with the lions and panther precisely because they do not return his gaze. Permanently entrapped and apathetic to their surroundings, these predators do not afford him the response that he requires to affirm his institutional power over them as human subject. In Viveiros de Castro's terms, what he is ultimately searching for in the animal encounter is the recognition of his humanity, of his perspective as that of an apex predator or even that of humanity as a godlike meta-status that consists precisely in renouncing its predatorial position within its environments, thereby placing itself beyond the predator-prey dichotomy in logic, if not in fact. And yet, due to its sacrificial logic, this godlike renunciation of the powers of predation over the animal can only be achieved through the animal's tacit (even if passive, that is structural) acknowledgment of those powers; otherwise, it is a renunciation of nothing and there may be no separation from the animal.

In contrast, the ontological continuity between body and soul in the native Amazonian thought that Viveiros de Castro studies means that even divine "spirit masters" are both material (although of a different order) and predatory; they are predators of spirits and therefore of bodies. In that sense, there can be no gaze beyond the predatorial gaze; power is itself always rooted at the most primal level in the power over life and death.[19] The entire Euro-American framework of nonpredatory, biopolitical killing, that is, lawfully administering death (whether to humans or animals) for institutional ends, quite straightforwardly constitutes a displacement of the juridical and ethical burdens of predation onto the state and its institutions. Furthermore, even though it arises from a fundamentally distinct system of thought, this biopolitical form of predation is correlative to what Viveiros de Castro terms Amazonian "cannibal metaphysics" in that it does not necessarily connote in a literal sense the eating of bodies, but rather that of relations. Power is never immanent; it is the systematic (institutional) power differential between the eater and the eaten that constitutes the relation—a differential that relies on the ongoing presence of both bodies, even if the eaten one persists only in trace form—more than the actual consumption of bodies.[20] In a material sense, then, it could be said that the cannibal metaphor underpins all indirect political representation, since it relies on incorporating relations of enmity into a polity through the insumption of individual bodies, which nevertheless persist within the body politic in abstract or "spirit" form, that is, as others who maintain a haunting corporality but function in political discourse and administration primarily as statistics, as demographic symbols of an identitary class. The fundamental difference between Euro-American political thought and Native Amazonian ontologies would thus lie primarily in the nature of the state; in Native Amazonian thought, the state is the environment in its totality, the forest as body politic, while in Euro-American thought it is an elite governing body, distinct from both the demos and the nonhuman environment due to its status as representative.[21]

Unlike the more horizontal Amazonian conceptualization of the "state" of nature, in Euro-American institutionality the animal stands in metonymic relation to the human as the human stands in relation to the state. Through homologization, the objectification of animal bodies justifies the biopolitical power of the state over human bodies, that is, human nature. Humanity as a collective under institutionality can only be conceived of because every human holds a state-like power over every animal. In the institutionalized environment of the zoo, then, the predatorial gaze of Cortázar's human narrator is only tangentially related to the politics of eating, in the sense that it is linked to the visual consumption of animal images. More to the point, it correlates to a differential set of freedoms/unfreedoms that converge in the construction of the human/animal binomial in modern society: the human's freedom from becoming either prey or predator of the animals themselves (in a literal or figurative, if no less affective sense) and of the zoo itself, as a biopolitical institution oriented specifically to the control of animal bodies. As Berger intimates, the animals in a zoo are systematically relegated to the status of prey of human desires.[22]

Unlike lions and panthers, however, amphibians' eyes do not track motion or have involuntary saccadic movements. Axolotls cannot look away or evade the human gaze through inattention; they identify predators primarily by their forms and patterns of movement.[23] This focal openness allows the human narrator to establish the predator-prey relationship despite the axolotls' apparent impassivity within the zoo's system of enclosures: "'you eat them alive with your eyes, hey,' the guard said, laughing; he likely thought I was a little cracked."[24] Paradoxically, this visual link is ultimately the portal to the inversion of perspectives; since the axolotl's eyes are inexpressive in human terms, the narrator cannot read within them the fear with which one might expect a prey animal to react to the human form: "it was useless to tap with one finger on the glass directly in front of their faces; they never gave me the least reaction. The golden eyes continued burning with their soft, terrible light; they continued looking at me from an unfathomable depth which made me dizzy."[25] The visual link is established, but human subjectivity is destabilized in the ambivalence of its status as predator; ultimately, the institutional status of human is unsatisfying within the encounter with the individual animal's excessive gaze.

From one point of view, this is where the story takes a decidedly Kantian or even Heideggerian turn. On the one hand, the inscrutable gaze of the axolotl appears to lead to the sublimation of the subject, in which case it would play the role of disembodied nature in stimulating a purely internal, transcendental self-affectivity within the subject rather than attributing any kind of subjectivity to the axolotls themselves.[26] On the Heideggerian side, the story's frequent references to boredom as the condition from which conscious thought arises generate a paradox with the axolotl's seemingly immobile or even immortal state with respect to time (and thus history). The axolotls' ability to experience boredom would ostensibly indicate awareness of the passage of time and therefore of finitude itself, which, according to Heidegger, are the foundational movements of Dasein, or the sense of being in the world. However, Heidegger famously viewed animals as poor-in-world; this interpretation, then, would lend itself to the humanistic reading of the story in which the axolotls function as a metaphor for the otherness against which the subject must constitute itself.[27] The axolotls' immobility would thus be read in a purely symbolic register, as an allegory of openness itself, belying any kind of self-awareness of their own. In that vein, the representation of the axolotl's face as absolute in its inexpressivity recalls Levinas's arguments regarding the absoluteness of the face itself, as the pure imperative of response placed by the absolute Other that calls us into an ethical relationship and, indeed, makes ethics themselves possible.[28] In this case, the axolotls' faces would not communicate (and, in fact, do not communicate in the story) any legible expression of their own; in their invulnerability, they reflect the vulnerability and responsiveness of the human face back to itself.

However, a less anthropocentric (and Eurocentric) reading might take this and similar passages more at face value; what they capture is the opacity of cognition and expressivity themselves, which is what places them within a metaphysical register. In this reading, the self-affective sublimation of the subject is denied through the affective power of the returned but ultimately illegible gaze. Furthermore, in the event of encounter, the axolotls interpellate the narrator through their gaze in a way that competes with and disrupts the interpellation of the state in its institutionalization of the animal, which is ultimately what would have allowed the subject to experience it as inspirational object rather than another subject. In response to the state's representative presence in the story, the zoo guard, the narrator affirms that "what he didn't notice was that it was they devouring me slowly through their eyes, in a cannibalism of gold."[29] This word choice is not random or purely aesthetic; it coincides with the logic of cannibalism in the Amazonian cultures Viveiros de Castro studies. Rather than a process in which the subject is objectified as food, cannibalism in this context denotes Viveiros de Castro's "eating of relations" in which the other's perspective is incorporated into the eater's through the ritual of ingestion. This form of relationality is captured incisively in the story's transmigration of perspectives, by which the human narrator's perspective is integrated into that of the axolotl narrator. In this process, a different kind of state is potentialized, one that resembles the kind of multispecies sociality that Viveiros de Castro describes, in which affective diplomacy governs interactions between species, rather than modern institutions and epistemological categories such as what Derrida calls the animot (animal-word) or animal category.[30]

In the ending of Cortázar's story, however, the human-animal distinction is preserved precisely through the state's institutional intervention. The part of the human that was capable of recognizing the potential humanity or personhood of the animal and therefore behaving ethically toward it is deposited along with it in the aquarium, and the human goes his way, having relinquished his ultimately fleeting proximity to the animal perspective.

This relinquishment costs the human narrator nothing; it was pre-ordained in the ordering of the zoo as a sequestering technology and space of containment. Once he leaves the aquarium for the final time, the axolotl no longer captures his attention. The affectivity of the encounter and the emergent inter-agential subjective assemblage—the human-axolotl subject position—is dismantled through the spatiality of the zoo and its institutionalization of animality. The relationship is thus cut short; the distance between human and animal has been reestablished and all possibility of interspecies diplomacy has apparently been truncated.

Animal Tracks: Writing as Diplomacy rather than Erasure

The reference to writing in the last line of the story nevertheless problematizes this ostensible final curtain or curtailing of animal affects. In a strict sense, axolotls clearly could have no notion of writing as a cultural practice nor of the world of books, that is, of symbolic discourse. In this context, the axolotl's professed desire to see the encounter consigned to writing comes across as a transparent fallacy of humanistic personification. When approached through Derrida's theorization of the trace, however, this final sentence takes on somewhat distinct overtones. As I discussed at length in the preceding chapter, Derrida's theory of the trace implies that writing and animal "tracks" share the condition of communicating "mute traces," which is to say that they are fully mediated in the auto-affective, autobiographical process of reading, that is, of the becoming of the subject. Neither the written page nor the animal performs a speech act in an orthodoxically humanistic sense of the word. Nevertheless, no one would argue that, despite the physical absence of an authorial subject, writing conveys no meaning of its own; if interpreted by readers according to their own subjective experiences, written signs undeniably play a constitutive role in the construction of a text's meaning for the reader. In Hélène Cixous's playful idiom, the reader gleans like a chicken for meaning from the text's scattered grains through the intervention of discourse, always leaving some behind in the dust.[31]

In the same way that writing can never be fully recovered by and subordinated to discourse, the heterogeneous traces left by singular animals cannot be subsumed fully as quasi-mechanical manifestations of the animal discursive category. What the axolotl thus implores, beyond speech as such, is its affective legacy, its co-authorship in the event of phenomenal subjectivity-in-encounter and the inscription of that event in the written record: "I think that I succeeded in communicating some of this to him in the first days, when I was still he."[32] In short, it presents a twin demand: that its constitutive role within the human narrator's subjectivity be recognized as such and that its testimony be heard and responded to beyond the event of encounter.[33] The human author may believe that he is writing autobiographical fiction ("believing he's making up a story, he's going to write all this about axolotls"), but the axolotl knows better: any written record of the encounter is necessarily an ethology of multispecies relationality. What is ultimately at stake is the possibility of ontological rapprochement—that is, diplomacy—between species. The story is not a fiction at all, but a myth: that is, a ritualized interspecies encounter that is reenacted in every recounting. The reader is forced to confront not the materiality of the axolotl, mediated as it is by the aquarium-like "glass wall" of the written page, but rather the persistence of its traces within the text itself, and the fact that these traces have an afterlife, affecting the reader's own subjectivity. In this sense, the reader is beholden to the axolotl, if perhaps in a very ambiguous or minor way, particularly if we think of these animal traces in terms of Deleuze and Guattari's theorization of minor literature.[34]

Unlike the hygienic, taxidermied museum specimens that are the subjects of the essays in Alberti's edited collection *The Afterlives of Animals*, these textual axolotls appear to the reader as permanently alive or after life, never dead in the same way as one could think of the human writer (particularly if one is aware that Cortázar died in 1984) despite or perhaps because they are doubly absent from the enunciation in a material sense.[35] The axolotl's speech may never be read as autobiographical in the same way as the human narrator's; its absence is unequivocally, unashamedly the trace of a trace, which immediately places it within the untimeliness of discourse rather than the inferred chronology of subjectivity. Furthermore, this textual afterlife is quite distinct from that of the embalmed animal museum exhibit, in which, as Geoffrey Swinney argues, 'any guilt or concern about the animal's welfare—its confinement, its isolation from its own kind's social structures, and the enforced company of humans—troubles us no longer; the animal is 'at rest,' while simultaneously prepared to be continually at our behest. Modeled in glass, its eyes are incapable of any disturbingly accusatory stare."[36] It is precisely this disturbingly accusatory if ambivalent stare that persists in trace form in Cortázar's story, peering from the page into its readers' imaginations, interpellating them and demanding a response. At the very least, it insists the reader take the axolotl's perspectival subjectivity into consideration and make a judgment regarding its verisimilitude. The ethics that were foreclosed by the spatial regime of the zoo are thus re-potentialized in the act of reading. At the same time, however, one might surmise that this animal claim on the human reader's subjectivity is precisely what puts into motion hyperhumanistic machinery in critical readings of this text.

Cortázar's "Axolotl" provides a nuanced analysis of how the spatiality of the modern zoo interpellates humanist subjectivities, instituting the human/animal divide at a level that counteracts without addressing directly both the interspecies phenomenon of becoming-in-encounter and the biological proximity established by evolutionary theory and ethology. Beyond its historical roots in royal menageries and imperialist collections, the zoo is a modern form of biopolitical domestication, a mass virtualization of the animal when animals rarely share with humans transparently central roles in work, transportation, or the social construction of gender, as in hunting and slaughter.[37] Furthermore, at a time when wild animal populations are declining precipitously toward a sixth "Great Extinction" event, the zoo assuages to a degree the guilt associated with massive habitat loss caused by the expansion of neoliberal capitalism and its extractive frontiers into every corner of the globe.[38] In the domestication of ostensibly wild animals, zoos simultaneously render them objects of human desire and care.

In the Anthropocene, wildness cannot be conceived of as existing beyond domestication, that is, a specific set of ethical constraints and legal protections, if not rights; "wild" animals now exist as such almost exclusively on nature reserves, wildlife sanctuaries, or in captive breeding programs and zoos.[39] Indeed, given the managerial state of "natural" habitats, one might argue that more than any particular set of behaviors, wildness consists of a specific, idealized form of representation that has its maximum expression in carefully edited nature documentaries.[40] Outside of those bounds, living unprotected in human environments, wild animals become vermin or at most, weed-like, a tolerated but always secondary and invasive presence. And in both the case of the zoo and the nature reserve, carefully choreographed enactments of space render the affective encounter predictable and fleeting, disempowering the transformative power of fear that one may experience in the permanent possibility of encounter with wild animals on their own ground.

In other words, modernity makes elusive animals familiar to us, but at the cost of virtualizing them as entertaining images, mere theme park attractions or museum specimens in a natural history that leads inexorably to extinction in the "wild." The possibility of a shared becoming is progressively nullified, and ethics may be conceived of only within very strict limits relating to the physical and mental wellbeing of these animals as human wards. And yet there remains an excess, a primordial affective link in the experience of shared biopolitical confinement and alienation. As Cortázar's story hints on its reverse side, modernity's biopolitical structures are not oriented solely toward the control of animal bodies; if the axolotls are prey of the human gaze, the human individual is also the prey of an exterior gaze, that of the state and its panoptics. As Cary Wolfe frames it, "to live under biopolitics is to live in a situation in which we are all always already (potential) 'animals' before the law—not just nonhuman animals according to zoological classification, but any group of living beings that is so framed."[41] It is also in that sense in which part of the human narrator is entrapped along with the axolotl. The sense of exile and alienation as a shared human/animal condition thus forms a common basis for an interspecies ethics—a relational ontology—against the modern state and its social, epistemological, and economic institutions. These are the kinds of ethical ambivalences that I look to draw out in Latin American writings on the animal.

In Cortázar's story, it is the zoo's spatiality that allows or even obligates the human narrator to abandon his diplomatic rapprochement with the axolotls and abdicate the ethical responsibilities that they place on him through the affective encounter. The wild animal is thus domesticated as an object of human consumption. Other Latin American writers problematize the relationships between modern enclosures, domesticity, writing, and interspecies affectivity in quite different ways. Like many scholars of zoographies, I find Brazilian author Clarice Lispector's work particularly ground-breaking in this area. Interestingly, much of her writing centers on the domestic space of the home as the setting for human-animal encounters, sidestepping to a degree the rigid institutionality of the zoo's spatial regime in consolidating the human-animal divide and thereby drawing the question of intersubjective familiarity to the forefront. Nevertheless, when Lispector does engage zoos, cages, and gardens as settings or tropes in her works—and it has been argued that the house in *The Passion According to G. H.* (1964) serves a parallel function—similar interrogations of the roles and holes of spatial regimes in subjectivity and affective relationality arise.[42] As in Cortázar's story, Lispector's representations of institutionality almost always foreground the ways in which affective encounters exceed the disciplinary interpellation of these spatial regimes, transforming subjectivity and discourse itself in ways that the institutions themselves cannot fully police. In her writing, it is most often the affectivity of fear-in-encounter or fright that leads to a reconceptualization of subjectivity as an ongoing, becoming-with animal others arising through what Derrida calls "passive decision" rather than the consolidation of a sovereign or institutional humanistic discursive position. In turn, in her later works, writing itself is reconceived of as a form of going astray, of giving free rein to bodily expressivity—that is, of striving to maintain, impossibly, fidelity to the animal traces of one's own body as well as those of external animal others—through both deconstructive procedures and the performative materiality of language.

Becoming with the Animal Other

Tellingly, in Lispector's only story featuring the zoo as its primary setting, "The Buffalo" (1960), the zoo's enclosures are ultimately ineffective in containing the animals' potential to affect the human protagonist. In this story, a woman visits the zoo not for entertainment, but in search of a form to express an affect that eludes her: hate. As in Cortázar's story, the scopic regime features prominently; however, it is constantly supplemented for by the other senses. Furthermore, in "The Buffalo," it is not the animals whose gaze turns obliquely away from the human, but rather the human who turns away from a series of animal gazes precisely because they immerse her in a primordial sense of love that she wishes to abdicate:

> The woman looked away from the cage, where only the warm scent reminded her of the carnage she had come in search of in the zoological gardens. Then the lion passed, heavy-maned and tranquil, and the lioness, her head on her outstreched paws, slowly became a sphinx once more.
> "But this is love, this is love again," the woman said in rebellion, trying to find her own hatred, but it was spring and the two lions were in love. With her hands in her coat pockets, she looked around to find herself surrounded by cages, and caged by locked cages.[43]

In her search for affective freedom, it is the protagonist who feels entrapped not only in a metonymical sense by the zoo's series of enclosures ("the cage was always on the side where she was"), which symbolize her desire to liberate enigmatic animal affects within herself (thus the reference to the Sphinx), but also by a primordial affiliative drive.[44] The deep ambivalence within the term "próprio odio" (not fully captured in the translation as "her own hatred") simultaneously evokes the instinctual primacy that humanism associates with animal emotions—"hate itself," undiluted by rational, symbolic mediation—and, aporetically the reflexive "self-hate" that the woman requires to give form to her quasi-traumatic emotional pain upon being rejected in an amorous relation. Ironically, the primordial, predatory violence that she searches for in the zoo animal as the formal supplement to and materialization of her conscious "vontade de ódio" (will to hate) is belied by the bland, cage-like domesticity of the lions' relationship, pushing her onward to a series of animals (a giraffe, a hippopotamus, a troop of monkeys, an elephant, a camel, and a coati), all of whose seemingly passive conformity with subjection to imprisonment exacerbates her rage.

This will to hate—whose word choice simultaneously evokes and problematizes Nietzsche's will to power and his underlying distinction between *Kraft* (raw force) and *Macht* (power arising from sovereign decision)—is itself fundamentally ambivalent; it is at once a discursive proposition and a material state akin to predatory hunger: "In her stomach, the will to kill [vontade de matar] contracted in a colic of hunger."[45] This association of the "will to hate" with a more instinctual "will to kill" evokes a Freudian death drive, a correspondence that is nevertheless not founded on sameness—which in a Lacanian sense would refer to the drive to preserve the subject's desire and therefore the integrity of the symbolic order through killing the excessive other—but rather on difference or equivocation.[46] The confluence of the conscious will to hate and the subconscious drive to kill thus reverts to the subject herself in an impossible desire to reconstitute subjectivity as animal other (that is, as simultaneously pre-symbolic and expressive) through its own elimination. It is for this reason that the discursive enunciation of hate is insufficient, lacking the immanence of voluntaristic power in Nietzsche's thought: "'I hate you,' she said to a man whose only crime was not to love her. 'I hate you,' she gasped in haste. But she did not even know how to begin."[47] The humanistic prioritization of conscious intent (or, in Lacan, symbolic transference) over the immanent materiality of the performative act, which is fundamental in the discourse of human exceptionalism, thus comes into relief as an ultimately aporetic conjunction. Her drive to find the materiality of her emotion in and through the animal other posits hate as a being with, a relational becoming, rather than a conscious state preceding or following violent action.

At the same time, love is portrayed not as the recursive, symbolic projection of desire—which Lacan invokes as the foundational difference at the heart of the human-animal divide—but in a somewhat Levinasian sense as passive openness to the other.[48] The animals love passively because, despite their subjection, they are seemingly incapable of the conscious singularity of hate, of the "vontade de ódio," and its transferences to objects of affect. Lispector's zoo animals do not recognize subjection as such; they may only apprehend it spontaneously as pure, unmediated violence in the instant of conflict with a subjugating force, the event of entrapment. In contrast, permanent encagement comes to symbolize a Heideggerian timelessness or being-out-of-time that is in a literal sense "poor in world"; like Cortázar's axolotl, Clarice's zoo animals are imprisoned both by the limits on movement and lines of sight imposed by spatial boundaries and by the foreclosed passivity of living in the eternal instant. In this conceptualization, which she develops in greater depth in *The Passion According to G. H* and *Água viva* (somewhat problematically translated as *Stream of Life*) in terms of "neutral" or "oblique life," love refers to a basal, irreflexive state of responsivity to others, a primordial sociality whose openness is not necessarily to the other in and of itself (since that would imply a subjective movement in animals that Lispector does not address in most of her work; an ultimately honest evasion, as one can never know empirically what the animal may be thinking or feeling with respect to its encounters), but rather to the undifferentiated world itself, which is nevertheless limited to their immediate surroundings.[49]

In a somewhat gendered way, the protagonist establishes a parallel between herself and this ostensibly indiscriminate and primordial animal affective state, whose instinct is toward affiliation rather than the radical separation of singularity.[50] In contrast, her male love interest makes the conscious decision to reject her advances and therefore the possibility of union. This uncomfortable affective proximity to what she views as animal passivity leads the protagonist to underscore her difference as subject through a series of hyperhumanistic gestures, evoking angrily as she passes before each cage a chain of oppositional topoi that delineate the human exception: animals as scenery (passive nature), the inability to formulate thoughts, unconscious nudity, and long-suffering passivity. Nonetheless, these humanistic gestures are ultimately ineffective in reaffirming her subjectivity against the affiliative demand placed by the animal others, as they rely on the institutional powers of clichéd disciplinary topoi rather than the differential relationality that she requires to express her affect. Her will to hate cannot manifest itself fully as hatred, constituted as it is within and against the discursive category of the animot rather than any singular, responsive other. Entrapped within endless recursivity (the series of animals), her hatred exists only diffusely and fleetingly within the metonym of anger, that is, as a vector-less hatred, a hatred whose objects, as she is only too aware, are immaterial or partial products of symbolic transference. Anger is always with, never wholly against.

Always at its discursive limits, Lispector treats the problem of human exceptionalism with characteristic subtlety, drawing into view its aporetic suppositions: if the will to hate is the singularity that distinguishes the human subject from the animal, how is that, in the end, it is the buffalo who "teaches" her to hate, actualizing her singular hateful potential? And this does not occur, as one might logically expect, through the reification of the buffalo as supplemental object of her own projected hatred toward the lover that scorned her, as much as she forces this displacement, challenging the buffalo verbally and throwing rocks at it: "'I love you,' she said, out of hatred then for the man whose great and unpunishable crime was not loving her, 'I hate you,' she said, imploring love from the buffalo."[51] This passage captures the complex interplay between the symbolic projection and negation of desire over the buffalo through transference—in which hatred would emerge as the sovereignty of the subject over its passive drive to affiliate—and the affective internalization of the buffalo's intense, absolute otherness, which takes momentary possession of her: "The buffalo with its black back. In the luminous light of the approaching evening, his was a blackened shape of tranquil fury. The woman sighed softly. Something white had spread itself inside her, white as paper, fragile as paper, intense as whiteness. Death hummed in her ears. Another canter by the buffalo brought her back to her senses, and in another long sigh, she came back to the surface. She did not know where she had been."[52] The clean slate—intensely white paper—seemingly symbolizes at the same time a liberation from and a potential rewriting of subjectivity, while the reference to death both evokes and dismantles Heidegger's conceptualization of death as the horizon for Dasein. Here, finitude—that is, the singularity of a differentiated life—is not apprehended through the death of the other, but rather within the self-affectivity proper to subjectivity itself, as a prescient rupture within self-representation that is like an epileptic seizure (thus the intense whiteness and buzzing in her ears) or, as she intimates in *Água viva* and *The Passion*, an overwhelming sensorial orgasm.[53] Nevertheless, she returns to herself ("à tona") as subject precisely through the aural interpellation of the buffalo's footsteps (its animal tracks, as Derrida might say), that is, through the intervention of the other's indexical presence, a trace that supplements and thereby potentializes her own sense of self-presence.

As this passage hints, equivocation is the operative procedure in Lispector's approach to otherness rather than the consolidation of the human subject as the privileged reader of encounter, that is, as the uncontested translator/overwriter of the traces of the animal other. The buffalo simultaneously embodies and symbolizes hatred ("um corpo ennegrecido de raiva" [a body blackened by anger]), but the relationship between its material affectivity and the subjective apprehension of that affect is entirely aporetic, transparently suppositional. Indeed, the symbolism, inscribed in the chromatic opposition between black and white, that she attributes to its body is immediately disarmed by its gaze: "There stood the buffalo and the woman face to face. She looked neither at his face, nor his mouth, nor his horns. She looked at his eyes [olhou seus olhos—capturing phonetically the reciprocity of the act]."[54] The protagonist apprehends hatred not as a legible state transmitted by the buffalo's form or gestures, but as a perspectival form of relationality in which she sees herself through the focal point of the buffalo's hateful gaze: "The buffalo remained calm. The woman slowly shook her head, terrified by the hatred with which the buffalo, tranquil with hatred, watched her."[55] The irony that emerges in the differential between the buffalo's inscrutable calmness and its objectifying gaze posits the hateful relationship within the terrain of irreconcilable (and therefore threatening) ontological difference rather than epistemological translation.[56]

Perspectivism, Controlled Equivocation, and Passive Decision in Animal Encounters

This perspectival procedure for approaching animal affectivity breaks with the Euro-American literary tradition of personification, in which animal behavior is homologized to human emotions and thus acquires meaning within the sphere of human sociality. In that sense, it comes much closer to Viveiros de Castro's theorization of "controlled equivocation" in Amerindian perspectivism, which he contrasts to anthropology's traditional focus on comparative equivalence. As he argues,

> the aim of perspectivist translation—translation being one of shamanism's principal tasks, as we know (Carneiro da Cunha 1998)—is not that of finding a "synonym" (a co-referential representation) in our human conceptual language for the representations that other species of subject use to speak about one and the same thing. Rather, the aim is to avoid losing sight of the difference concealed within equivocal 'homonyms' between our language and that of other species, since we and they are never talking about the same things.[57]

In "The Buffalo" as well as in G. H.'s encounter with the cockroach in *The Passion*, Lispector delves into the inner workings of subjectivity on the basis not of signing the animal other as an object of knowledge through deciphering its performative representations of itself, but rather as an unknowable singularity that interpellates the subject through its threatening, untranslatable difference. In Lispector's writing on the animal, humans and animals are never equal (that is, equivalent), not because of the exceptionality of the human, but because of the exceptionality of the singular animal with respect to the humanistic animal category. Through the differentiating, nonlinguistic interpellation of the animal gaze, the entire scale of valorization within humanistic discourse comes into question. And when equivalence becomes untenable, equivocation remains as the only possible form of rapprochement. Indeed, Viveiros de Castro is careful to emphasize that "an equivocation is not an error."[58] An error in judgment, a mistranslation, would imply that there is at some depth an equivalence to be excavated, a common grounds for interpretation, as it were. In contrast, perspectival equivocation assumes the untranslatability of difference; the goal in this kind of communication cannot be arriving at a common understanding, but rather rapprochement and continual, ongoing negotiation, that is, diplomacy without the possibility of consensus. Indeed, this is precisely the form of intra-action that Lispector calls oblique life:

> Oblique life? I know full well that there's a slight discordance [desencontro] between things, they almost clash, there's a discordance between beings that lose [miss] each other between words that say virtually nothing more. But we almost understand each other in that casual discordance, in that almost that's the only way of bearing life at its fullest, since a blunt face-to-face encounter with it would frighten us, would stun its delicate spiderweb threads. We look at each other sideways [Nós somos de soslaio—which could also be translated as "we live sideways"] so as not to compromise what we sense as being infinitely other in that life I'm telling you of.[59]

Rather than equivalence, it is this "leve desencontro" (literally, an "unencounter," a just barely missing one another), this equivocal, "sideways" nature of encounter itself, that gives rise to an "almost understanding each other"; that is, the possibility and potentiality of ontological diplomacy.

In the story, the protagonist internalizes without understanding the buffalo's hateful perspective of herself, that is, its view of her as threatening other within its own "will to kill," which empowers her to actualize her will to hate through real or figurative self-harm:

> Innocent, inquisitive, entering ever more into those eyes that fixed her without haste, ingenuous, wearily sighing, without wishing or being able to escape,

she was caught in a mutual assassination. Caught as if her hand had fastened forever to the dagger that she herself had thrust. Caught, as she slipped spell-bound along the railings—overcome by such giddiness [vertigo] that, before her body toppled gently to the ground, the woman saw the entire sky and a buffalo.[60]

The protagonist's suicidal gesture (stabbing herself) is not presented as a sovereign decision, as a power exercised over her own life and, by extension, if one subscribes to Agamben's reading of the sovereign exemption, in a willful divesting of her status as subject that aporetically reaffirms her sovereignty by placing her own body within the realm of bare life. Since it is narrated in the imperfect subjunctive mode, it is not entirely clear whether this act is an actual suicide or a metaphorical one symbolizing the annihilation of subjectivity (the desire to lose herself, to feel no emotional pain). Nevertheless, this distinction is ultimately immaterial. In either case, she becomes the "prey" of a "mutual assassination," the object of a Derridean passive decision within a predatorial, multispecies socius that is both contiguous to and within her own body. I refer here to Derrida's theorization of decision as a response to the traces of the other:

> The passive decision, condition of the event, is always in me, structurally, an-other event, a rending decision as the decision of the other. Of the absolute other in me, the other as the absolute that decides on me in me. Absolutely singular in principle, according to its most traditional concept, the decision is not only always exceptional, it makes an exception for/of me. In me. I de-cide, I make up my mind in all sovereignty—this would mean: the other than myself, the me as other and other than myself, he makes or I make an excep-tion of the same.[61]

Tellingly, Derrida's insistence on the absoluteness of the other within reso-nates with Lispector's description of neutral life as objective or inexpressive; beyond interpretation, it is the illegible demand that the other places through its traces that makes it total in its difference, its "exception of the same." It is this absolute difference of the other in the self that in fact produces sovereign autonomy, as the subject is always contingent on its relations. Only the other can except the self from its own sameness, providing an alternative to continu-ity and thereby making decision or change possible. The other's demand for response takes the form of an unconditional gift, as the other cannot dictate to the subject how to respond to it. This unconditionality of the trace is itself the condition for the possibility for subjectivity: "This normal exception, the supposed norm of all decision, exonerates from no responsibility. Responsible for myself before the other, I am first of all and also responsible *for the other before the other*. This heteronomy, which is undoubtedly rebellious against the decisionist conception of sovereignty or of the exception (Schmitt), does not contradict; it opens autonomy on to itself, it is a figure of its heartbeat. It matches the decision to the gift, if there is one, as the other's gift."[62]

In the story, the buffalo's gift to the human protagonist—its call to the protagonist, its unspoken demand for a response—is hatred itself and of itself, that "próprio odio.' It is the internalized specter of the buffalo's perspective on her own threatening difference deciding, hauntingly, for her and within her to act against the tyranny of the humanistic subject, a passive decision that nevertheless coincides with both her conscious "will to hate" and her quasi-instinctual "will to kill." This is the common difference—the coincidental yet not equivalent intent to kill—for which she searched in the zoo's animals, the rapprochement that would allow her to actualize her intent. And yet, the actualization of this hateful intrasubjectivity, rooted in mutual threat, is also an act against the trace, against the other's demand on the self for affiliation, an annihilation of the self and of the other in the self. In this way, Lispector foregrounds the aporetic relationship at the heart of subjectivity; even in the ultimate sovereign decision, suicide, one acts at once for and against oneself and the other.

Hyperhumanism versus the Ethics of Encounter

As in the case of Cortázar's "Axolotl," many of Clarice Lispector's readers recur to humanistic allegories to recover the primacy of human subjectivity in her animal encounters. The most egregious of these readings view Lispector's human-animal encounters purely as allegories of gender relations and/or of the gendered constitution of subjectivity through the other.[63] Famously, Hélène Cixous viewed Lispector's writing as exemplary of *écriture feminine* (emphasizing, for example, the gyno-allusive visual impact of the article O in Portuguese), ultimately dissociating the embodiedness of Lispector's writing from her deep engagement with animal others despite acknowledging it explicitly. In Cixous's reading, Lispector's animals stand in metonymically for the materiality of the body itself; the concern is finding a language that expresses more fully the (feminine) body, not necessarily maintaining fidelity to the traces of singular animals and thus to the multiplicity of the subject as an intra-active phenomenon.[64] Cixous's move to downplay this aspect of

Lispector's writing is certainly understandable, given the long-standing patri-archal association of the female body with domestic animality and species reproduction; nevertheless, it also minimizes the more radically deconstruc-tive aspects of Lispector's treatment of that association, as I will discuss in the next chapter regarding her story "A Chicken." In short, gender relations are transparently a central concern in all of Lispector's writing, even that deal-ing most explicitly with animals; however, as I have argued, the relationship between her representations of gender and those of animals is not one of symbolic equivalence, but rather of parallelism and equivocation, in which the social structures of the family and the state interpellate women's bodies and animal bodies in ways that are sometimes similar and others completely different, depending on their range of positions within the male-female and human-animal discursive axes.[65]

Other critics draw out the complexity of Clarice's thought regarding the human-animal encounter, but nevertheless frame them entirely through the lens of discursivity; somewhat along the lines of Cixous's reading, the encounter itself is taken as reenacting the relations between materiality and language within the realm of subjectivity.[66] Ittner exemplifies this approach when she writes about "The Buffalo" that, "it seems hardly necessary to emphasize that in this powerful story about the gaze of the >Other< the buf-falo's role is entirely assigned by the human viewer. In her passionate inqui-ries into the human condition and breathtaking journeys into a deeper under-standing of the self, Lispector does not reflect on the constructedness of these encounters, directly or indirectly."[67] This rather orthodox constructivist reading is convincing if one views hatred as a legible emotion rather than as untranslatable, threatening affectivity; however, I would respectfully submit that it can only seem "hardly necessary to emphasize" due to its assumptions regarding the absolute sovereignty of the subject with respect to the traces of the other, an assumption that Derrida rejects entirely with his theory of passive decision. In contrast, I would argue that Lispector sought precisely to draw out the powers of the trace, that is, the demand for response placed on the subject by the other.

In a similar vein, Piskorski argues that "Lispector's zoopoetics are focused on the arche-animal rather than animals, insofar as she portrays animal-ity as a procedure."[68] As he clarifies, "if Derrida coined the 'old name'—or paleonym— arche-writing in order to circle the condition of language that would emerge 'before' the distinction between speech and writing, I hope to show that Lispector's novel explores an arche-animality which, in fact, fur-nishes the traditional concepts of animality—and its other, humanity—as it confusingly works within competing ontological systems."[69] It may well be that Lispector's adaptation in several works of writing techniques pioneered by the Surrealists such as objective chance, dream objectivity, free association, and automatic writing implies a supplemental movement whereby a kind of proto body-writing takes the place of the Freudian unconscious in Surrealist poetics. I will return to and problematize this notion of non-human arche (that is, discursive archive and organizing principles) in the fifth chapter in greater detail. Here, I will simply note that the equivalence that Piskorski draws between arche-writing and arche-animality (as the grounds for the human/animal divide) is fundamentally problematic, even when Derrida himself described animal tracks as a kind of proto-writing. The problem consists in the dismantling of the arche-trace-subject triad. By collapsing the (animal) trace into the arche, Piskorski effectively eliminates the other's demand for a response, which for Derrida, is the movement at the heart of subjectivity. I would suggest that Lispector's writing labors through equivocation to set the stage for diplomacy between these heteronomic, "competing ontological systems," rather than the disciplinary movement implied in "furnishing the traditional concepts of animality—and its other, humanity."

Writing, Becoming Animal, and Neutrality

One could certainly make the argument, and in fact many critics have, that what Lispector represents in her animal encounters is a process of de-subjectivation, in which case it might be said that her zoopoetics consist in the systematic suppression of humanistic subjectivity with the aim of letting the trace speak for itself within this multispecies arche-animality—and here I look to reframe Piskorski's concept in terms of biosemiotics, or the signs of life, as Jesper Hoffmeyer calls them—what Goh describes as "leaving the other as is."[70] Indeed, there is a fundamental ambivalence regarding subjectivity in her most experimental texts that has to do precisely with the instability of the relationships between bodies, perception, expression, and discourse, in which bodily sensations in the instant always exceed language, rendering subjectivity and representation transparently suppositional—a projected future acting back on itself, striving impossibly to re-present the affectivity of the instant that has already passed. It is for this reason that, in these texts, she depends heavily on a procedure of automatic writing in which objective neutrality (what she calls the "it" in *Água viva*, that is, what is opaque to representation or symbolic mediation) is derived from the material animality of the body rather than a Freudian/Jungian collective (human) unconscious: "I don't know what I'm writing about: I am obscure [opaque] even to myself. Initially I had only a lunar, lucid vision, and then I clasped that instant to myself before it died and perpetually dies. I transmit to you not a message of ideas but rather an instinctive voluptuousness of what is hidden in nature and what I sense. And this is a feast of words. I write in signs that are more gesture than voice."[71] Her creative process thus aims to blur the ostensibly unbridgeable divide between this arche-animality, the biosemiotic system that is life itself, and arche-writing, that is, the system of human signs: "I'm writing to you an onomatopoeia, a convulsion of language. I'm transmitting to you not a story but only words which live off sound."[72] Lispector coincides with Lacan in positing the relationship between signifier and signified within the realm of repression, in which the desire to access the affect in itself, as objective truth (what is inexpressive), is always repressed by the signified. The onomatopoeia would thus embody the purest form of affectivity within language, the most proximate to the instant of encounter and the most distant from signification: "the world has no visible order, and I have only the order of my breathing. I let myself happen."[73] The onomatopoeia is (in)expressive precisely in its excess with respect to language itself; it expresses what cannot be said, what is untranslatable, and yet still communicates both presence and affective intention. In that sense, Lispector's zoopoetics aim to draw out the indexicality that Derrida sees at the heart of all communication and, indeed, subjectivity itself as responsivity. As she writes in *The Passion*: "For the thing can never really be touched. The vital core [knot, point of contact] is a finger pointing to it—and what is pointed to enlivens like a milligram of radium in the tranquil darkness."[74]

Lispector's explicit references to dehumanization and animalization as a creative process, as the refounding of writing itself, have led several critics to associate her zoopoetics with Deleuze and Guattari's theorization of becoming animal in *A Thousand Plateaus*, which extrapolates from Deleuze's rethinking of difference as anti-mimetic in *Difference and Repetition*. In developing his "transcendental empiricist" philosophy, Deleuze rejected the philosophical primacy of the concept as a generality that supersedes and orders the particular as well as the classical metaphysics of being as the self-representation of an essential and definable state, in which difference would consist in the oedipal dialectic between static, oppositional terms such as the self and the other. Instead, he proposed that difference always emerges as a differential not through subjective categorization or even phenomenological perception, but rather from the infinite excess of movement with respect to the staticity of representation, what he terms the "intensity" of encounter.[75] Otherness is absolute and unrepresentable because nothing can remain identical to itself in repetition; at a very minimum, its vector in time-space differentiates it from its prior forms—difference always manifests intensively, as individuation in the here-now. This would clearly be the case in material forms due to entropy and other physical forces, but also in conceptual forms, which can never conserve their original meanings, as Derrida also made clear in his theorization of the supplement. Even when the concept is "eternal" and "virtual," existing as infinite potentiality, its referents (including the terms used to define it) constantly shift and transform. In that sense, both things and concepts are actualized as singularities within series over time and space. Furthermore, Deleuze dismantles entirely the distinction between the material and the ideational; rejecting the notion of the concept as an abstract, general, and static relation between terms, he sees the "Idea" as the emergent, immanent differential that structures intensive processes that produce behavioral patterns and individuation within systems. Thus, metamorphic difference (rather than general sameness) is the inevitable product of the "eternal return," that is, of the actualization of repetitive forms as individuation. Furthermore, the fact that difference always emerges in a series, rather than in the opposition between static terms, implies that it manifests as a multiplicity—an actualizing differential that produces potentially infinite individuation—that is horizontal (no single position in the series can be said to subordinate empirically the other positions, nor can any element, including a concept, be conceived of as existing outside the series) rather than hierarchical; ergo the oft-cited figure of the rhizome in *A Thousand Plateaus*, as well as the distinction between molar (integrative, territorializing) and molecular (distributed, nomadic) systems and structures.

A Deleuzian perspective on difference is particularly apt for approaching the becoming animal of Lispector's protagonists, since it is never a simple question of the symbolic substitution of the fixed human form for a fixed animal one, but rather a process by which the individual is constituted not as a singular, human exception to the continuum of life forms that includes animals, but rather as a product of that relational multiplicity of intensive attachments, which Lispector refers to indiscriminately as "love" or "neutral life." In Lispector, the body is never its representation, since it inhabits the intensity of individuation (again, always the actualization of a multiplicity) in the instant, while representation is always retrospective, comparative, and generalizing. As Nascimento perceptively argues, in Clarice's writing, it is never about analogies, because the fictional and bi-ographical experience of animality is not done for mere comparison, but rather to question the limits of the human. It's not about how a human might feel in an animal's place, but rather the ways in which the human inevitably crosses into the becoming-animal of the human, with all the dangers that such an ex-perience carries with it. The radicalness of this experience lies in the estrange-ment of oneself that happens in an uncalculable way.[76]

Lispector's animal becomings engage in a Deleuzian "theater of repetition," in which the calculated generalities of the human and animal categories dis-integrate before the irruption of the multiplicity of the body to itself and to its representations, which are always predicated on insufficiency and belat-edness with respect to the "it" in the here-now. I should point out that the "it" in Lispector's usage is not strictly Freudian, although she coincides with Freud and Lacan in positing the "it" as simultaneously inexpressive and the source of the expressive drive. Nevertheless, for Lispector, rather than a sub-stratum of subjectivity, the "it" refers to the immanence of absolute mate-rial difference in its multiplicity; that multiplicity simultaneously demands expression and condemns it to representational failure.

As Tornos Urzainki notes regarding Lispector's procedure of "de-personalization" in *A paixão segundo G. H.*, the protagonist explicitly rejects her own name, as it serves as a concept that defines her identity in static terms, forcing her to abide by its institutionalizing, disciplinary parameters:

The process of depersonalization discounts all anthropological and meta-physical premises to maintain a naked relation to an undifferentiated being, which questions the borders that delimit the human and animal spheres, upon reclaiming the primacy of an insipid and neutral substance that can only be narrated using an impersonal voice. Therefore the construction of a neutral body, in the becoming-animal, carries with it the destruction of all subjective framing, which reveals the insufficiency of the proper name, which is incapa-ble of testifying to the exteriority of being that also configures the subject. All becoming, therefore, implies a becoming-dead, in which in the "I" discovers its own ending upon entering into contact with an irreducible otherness: "I experienced, for an instant, a vitalizing death," claims G. H. that becomes the rite of passage that announces the dimension of what is neutral.[77]

This de-subjectification implicates a de-territorialization that carries over to the house itself, placing into question the institutionality of the domestic and the dialectic of ownership in relation to subjectivity, but it does not imply a de-individuation; rather it opens the body to the infinite individuating potentialities of the encounter, that is, its differentiating multiplicity. This differentiating potential deconstructs humanity as a static concept (the object of positivistic anthropology), opening the specificity of the body to its full range of potentialities: "Being human should not be an ideal for humankind, which is human by fate [fatalmente, fatally], being human has to be the way I as a living thing obeying through freedom the path of living things, am human."[78] This is why the figure of "indifference" takes on such a prominent role in Lispector's thought regarding neutrality; it implies the disavowal of the static difference generated in the opposition of the terms human/man and animal/beast as well as a passive, inhumane immorality, a fundamental indifference to both "ethical" valuation as a palliative for hierarchical difference and to the concept of institutional rights as the ordering of bodies through the interpellation of the law, an issue I address in the following chapter in my discussion of "The Crime of the Mathematics Teacher."[79] She frequently recurs to the trope of "Hell" and the demoniac (a figure also used by Deleuze and Guattari) to describe this indeterminate state of passive immorality: "And there is no punishment! Hell is that: there is no punishment."[80] In the unconscious "nakedness" of encounter, there is only difference.

Given this seeming impasse regarding the (moral) status of the other, which is also the possibility of ethics and the law itself, how can we then relate Lispector's writing to the topic of this book, that is, environmental ethics and the rights of nature? In a Deleuzian world of unrepresentable, monadic difference, of bodies without organs in which subjectivity and alterity are intra-active effects rather than moral states, what ethics and what kind of politics could possibly emerge?[81] Indeed, this has been a frequent critique of Deleuze and Guattari's thought; their deconstruction of representation seemingly implies that any form of ethics and therefore political representation—that is, the existence of the state in and of itself—is fundamentally oedipal (filiative) and coercive. Their proposal for a nomadic politics of affect, of free, multiple, and impermanent affective attachments that are necessarily violent and disruptive to territoriality and identity (ergo the "war machine" and the description of affects as "weapons") is quite ambivalent; it can be read as a proposal for a radical, anarchic pragmatism in which all interactions must be negotiated continually through direct attachments, freed from the oedipal logic of substitution, but it equally lends itself to the idealization of individual freedoms, deregulation, and unlimited expansion (growth) in neoliberal capitalism.[82] Fortunately, it is rescued from the association with fascism and its glorification of violent, masculine force (as a reductive reading of the "war machine" might suggest) by the insistence on horizontality, anti-identitarian multiplicities, and minoritarian destabilization.[83]

Lispector comes quite close to Deleuze and Guattari's thought in her anti-moralizing or "neutral" empiricism, the recognition of the immanent onto-logical violence of affective encounter, the deconstruction of the relations between subjectivity and representation, and the perspective of writing and subjectivity as processes of individuation that emerge from multiplicities. Nevertheless, she strays from Deleuze's rather dogmatic monadism in her treatment of responsivity. In Deleuze, the other is a linguistic or ontological effect, while difference is wholly and absolutely untranslatable; there can be no response to difference other than attachment or detachment (which nevertheless implies prior attachment) between individuated bodies. Lispec-tor's differentiating affective encounters also generate subjects and others indiscriminately as effects, but the relations between these differentiated, partial subjects and their perspectival objects are neither fully mediated nor nomadic in the sense in which Deleuze and Guattari use the term. Her bodies are not truly bodies without organs, desiring machines across which intensities flow freely. They are asymmetrical, relational bodies, bodies in which others' traces organize subjectivity beyond the instant of encounter not exclusively through discursivity but also through the unconditional, illegible, and ongoing demands that they place within the subject, which are ultimately demands for actualization, that is, expression through the sub-ject in its present. This process occurs within the becoming of the subject itself; subjectivity effectively becomes as and through the expression of the other in the self in a fraught and excessive relationship to the arche and its constitutive interpellation of the subject, that is, the imperative to represent itself to itself (self-affection) as a repetitive form, the product of recursivity. As Derrida noted, what Husserl defined as the quality most proper to the subject, expression, thus becomes indexical and multiple; despite its appar-ently monadic self-referentiality, expression itself is the "finger pointing to it," as Lispector called it, where the "it" is the relational multiplicity that produces the other and the self in encounter. In this reframing of subjec-tivity, the subject itself is a trajectory, a "line of flight" or "plane of consis-tency" in Deleuze and Guattari's language, that extends in time and space beyond the instant of encounter, but nevertheless reproduces the encounter as an ongoing relation (multiplicity) within the subject, an attachment that persists through the trace, even when the bodies implicated are no longer in direct contact. This rethinking of subjectivity, writing, and the grounds for ethics has profound implications for political praxis, as I discuss in the next chapter.

CHAPTER 4

The Familiar Animal and the Aesthetics of the Stray

To me, dissonance is harmonious.

—CLARICE LISPECTOR

The last chapter focused on disentangling the ethical relations that emerge in human-nonhuman encounters and how those relations are re-enacted and actualized through writing, exceeding the circumscribing effects of symbolic representation and thereby reconceiving representation itself in terms of multiplicity and becoming-with others, whether human or nonhuman. Drawing on Clarice Lispector's *The Passion according to G. H.* (1964) and three stories from *Family Ties* (1960), this chapter delves into the political implications of the ethics of encounter and mutual responsibility, particularly in terms of the reconstitution of both society and the body politic. In Lispector's stories, what has traditionally been considered the basis for both the social and the state, the nuclear family, is reconfigured as an open formation relying on affective ties rather than the genealogic of patriarchal filiality and/or democratic fraternity. Furthermore, this reconceptualization of family ties also problematizes the anthropocentric conceptualization of polity, since animals are often drawn into the family structure, if in fraught and tenuous ways. The destabilization of the family institution also forces a rethinking of the ontological origins of law as something other than sovereignty and therefore of rights as more than the inheritance of the individual as sovereign subject. When ethics arise through passive decision rather than phallogocentric rationality, justice emerges in relation rather than through the hegemonic application of the rule of law. In this way, justice becomes something other than the ideal of equality, which can never adequately address differences among humans, and even less so other species such as the cockroach in *The Passion according to G. H.* And law emerges as process rather than dead letter through ongoing acts of representation, as what Lispector calls "desistance" or the deferral to the other's traces in writing.

The passive decision that actualized simultaneously the woman's suicidal "will to hate" and the buffalo's "will to kill" in Lispector's "The Buffalo" finds its parallel in many of her works featuring animal encounters, including her iconic novel *The Passion According to G. H.* This work strips the plotline to a bare minimum in order to draw out in minute detail the transformational ontology of encounter and its relations to both subjectivity and artistic representation. The novel's sole action is comprised of a sequence in which G. H. enters her absent domestic worker's room, glimpses a single cockroach, and, reacting almost instinctively, immediately crushes it in a cabinet door. This act of irreflexive violence precipitates a passive decision to eat the dying cockroach, an act that is ultimately frustrated when she vomits it out due to her deep-seated revulsion toward the insects. Not coincidentally, the protagonist is a plastic artist who nevertheless decides to represent the encounter in writing, which immediately draws attention to the materiality of representation. The novel's title refers to the painful, almost sacrificial trajectory that the character undergoes during the event of encounter with the insect other and its recounting to an unidentified, possibly divine "You," configuring the novel as a profound reflection on the ethical and ontological ramifications of both passive decision and representation for the humanist subject.

Despite the absence of a moralizing position toward the still-living cockroach G. H. has crushed in the cabinet door, that is, the lack of a conditional, empathetic response that would require her to atone for her violent act either by helping it in some way or putting an end to its suffering, she is nevertheless compelled to respond to it. Her sudden compulsion to eat it is not a moralistic response, the engaging of a corrective logic of justice. Nevertheless, it is an ethical one, since it implies the valorization of the cockroach as something other than mere object; it is more than a reified "bare life" that can be killed—or not even killed, merely eliminated—without repercussions. In Lispector's writing, there is no bare life; all life places the subject into a state of duty, that is, ineludible responsibility. G. H.'s thought (that is, virtualized passive decision) to eat the cockroach is a cannibalistic act, an eating of relations, in which the cockroach's constitutive otherness in her becoming animal will be formalized through ritual ingestion: "For redemption must be in the thing itself. And redemption in the thing itself would be putting into my own mouth the white paste from the cockroach."[1] Redemption for the violence of encounter through an incorporative movement is thus an ethical thought that is proper to the thing-in-itself, the "it," that, is a fidelity to the relationality of encounter: "I realized that by putting the cockroach mass in my mouth, I was not bereaving myself as saints bereave themselves, but rather I was seeking accretion. Accretion is easier to love."[2]

In this sense, Lispector's ethics resonate with Badiou's proposal that ethics consist in maintaining fidelity to the truth of an event, which he defines as the irruption of a multiplicity within the count-as-one demographic logic of biopolitics.[3] This "truth" is immanent to the event itself, not the product of ideological predisposition or logical conditionality, as Lispector makes clear: "I couldn't stop myself any longer, and I thought what I was actually already thinking."[4] The "already" thus indicates an emergent, Deleuzian idea that precedes and actualizes conscious thought, the "atrás do pensamento" as she calls it in *Água viva*.[5] In that sense, both Lispector and Badiou coincide with Deleueze's insistence that thought emerges in the affective encounter through the differential, rather than substituting for it retrospectively as conceptual interpretation and valorization. As Lispector writes, "true thought appears without an author."[6]

Lispector's protagonist initially views her now-conscious, that is, subjective ("I thought what I was already thinking") desire to ingest the cockroach's insides as the route to the actualization of the truth of the event (encounter as becoming in multiplicity), incorporating the instant of encounter within her own body, rendering it radically and serially multiple to itself. Given her deep-seated phobia of cockroaches, this gesture implies a sacrifice of subjectivity akin to the "mutual assassination" that the woman undergoes in "The Buffalo": "I arose and took a step forward, with the determination not of someone who is bent on suicide but of someone who is going to kill herself."[7] Nevertheless, it is interrupted in the end; the protagonist vomits, unable to stomach not only the cockroach's taste, but even the idea of eating it: "At just the idea I closed my eyes with the force of someone locking her jaws, and I clenched my teeth so tight that any more and they would break right inside my mouth. My insides said no, my mass [massa; body's substance] rejected the cockroach's mass [body]."[8] The sacrifice is disrupted and the protagonist questions whether she is capable of maintaining fidelity to the truth of the encounter, when her own body seems to reject it: "Shaken through and through by the violent vomiting, which had come without any warning nausea, disappointed with myself, frightened by my lack of strength to carry out an act that seemed to me to be the only thing that would bring my soul and body together again."[9]

Notwithstanding her failure to follow through, she paradoxically finds herself at peace with herself after vomiting: "Despite myself, after vomiting I had become serene, my head relieved, physically calm."[10] In a way very similar to Derrida's discussion of Abraham's sacrifice of his son Isaac in *The Gift of Death and Literature in Secret*, but with the telling twist that the sacrifice demanded by the other (not God, but a cockroach) is that of the self rather than the son, it turns out that self-sacrifice is not the response that is ultimately called for.[11] Rather, it is the contemplation of that sacrifice, that is, placing herself in a "here I am" relation of unconditional response or duty to the demand of the other, which is, in the end, entirely illegible and thus secret in an absolute sense. The passive decision in and of itself thus lies not in the act of sacrifice, but rather in the emergence of the relation of open responsibility to the other, which is to say, the idea—immanent to the encounter—that she has an ineludible duty to respond. This is itself the germinal point of conscious ethical thought, that is, the possibility of a relation to the other that transcends the instant of encounter: "For even in eating of the cockroach, I had acted by transcending the very act of eating. And now all I was left with was the vague recollection of a horror, I was left with only the idea."[12]

The redemptive act will always fall short, since it implies the absolution of guilt—that is, the fulfillment of the duty to respond and thereby the restoration of the sovereignty of the ethical subject, transcending the relation in a symbolic and ideological sense. The redemptive act would effectively consist in substituting for the relation a symbolic act, whose meaning relies on an equivalence between the subject and its object (i.e. do unto others as you would have them do unto you). In this way, the ethics that emerged in the encounter would be generalized as a norm or law within discourse, allowing for the symbolic transference of the desire to do justice to any other that fulfilled the categorical conditions that would classify it as the object of ethical treatment. The redemptive act thus implies the annulment of the particularity of the encounter, of the immanence of difference to it, and the symbolic subordination of the other to the transcendent, ethical subject, since the ethical equivalence is in reality asymmetrical; it is the subject that can read difference and decide to behave ethically.

However, the form of transcendence that emerges in *The Passion* does not rely on the symbolic projection of futurity, of the ethical subject into the future, with the other fixed as the object of memory and the relation substituted for by the law. The interruption of the ritual, redemptive act negates the potential for transcendence through symbolic representation, actualizing instead the "empirically" transcendental multiplicity of the idea as a differentiating form with an infinite potentiality for producing concrete relations ("I was left with only the idea"). It works to reproduce the potentiality of encounter in the ongoing flow of successive instants: "More than the instant, I want its flowing."[13] Nevertheless, this idea—this virtual multiplicity—does not conform an ethics in and of itself, as it remains dependent on the affectivity of concrete encounters to actualize itself. It is associated with the "vague remembrance of a horror," traces delineated by an abjection (in the sense in which Kristeva theorized the term in *Powers of Horror*): vomiting.[14] Unassimilable to the subject, it exceeds discourse, which is what would allow for the constitution of a just relation between subject and object.

Going Astray: Desistance and the Ethics of Representation

It is through this impasse that Lispector's ethics emerge. Unlike Abraham's obedience to the divine command, which ultimately requires the sacrifice of the animal to redeem the human, here it is the protagonist herself who comes to terms with the impossibility of redemption and is forced to desist. Desisting becomes the only viable, subjective response to the unconditional demand of the other, the only way of remaining loyal to both the truth of the encounter and subjectivity itself, as the becoming of the subject (or the human, as Lispector calls it) in relation to the arche of human language. Far from an abdication of duty, however, desisting implies the conscious decision to persist in a permanent, unresolved relation of responsibility; the disavowal of redemption is not a disavowal of the relation, but rather the possibility of its re-actualization, its repetition. Ethics thus emerge not as passive decision, but through passive decision actualized serially as subjective choice: "Insistence is our effort, desistance is the prize. One gets the prize when she has experienced the power of building and, in spite of the taste of power, prefers desistance. Desistance has to be a choice. To desist is life's most sacred choice. To desist is the true human moment."[15] In this way, Lispector bridges the gap between Derrida's Levinasian ethics of response and Badiou's ethics of fidelity to the truth of an event. The relationality has been established, the transcendental idea (responsibility and justice) has emerged as a new multiplicity potentialized to differentiate bodies (and therefore subjectivities) in altogether other ways: "desistance is a revelation," that is, a singular consciousness that is immanent not to the subject, but to the encounter itself.[16] As Deleuze writes, "by singularity, we mean not only something that opposes the universal, but also some element that can be extended close to another, so as to obtain a connection; it is a singularity in the mathematical sense."[17] This kind of singularity in becoming with the other is the neutral life, the "state of grace" in the flow of the instant that the protagonists of *The Passion* and *Água viva* inhabit: "The world looks at itself in me. Everything looks at everything, everything experiences the other; in this desert, things know things. Things know things so much that this . . . this something I shall call pardon, if I wish to save myself within the human plane. It is pardon in itself. Pardon is one of the attributes of living matter.'[18] Forgiveness, rather than redemption, is thus the product of an ethics of neutral life, a forgiveness that is unconditional in its openness to difference. And, as Derrida makes clear, "far from bringing it to an end, from dissolving or absolving it, forgiveness can then only extend the fault, it can only import into itself this self-contradiction, this unlivable dissidence within itself, and within the ipseity of the self itself, allowing it to survive in an interminable agony."[19]

Furthermore, despite its germination in affective encounter, this ethics can only actualize itself in the process of representation, since this is the differential by which subjects and others are produced, as relations. As Derrida argues, discussing Kafka's *Letter to His Father*, "one of the causes of this aporia of forgiveness is the fact that one cannot forgive, ask, or grant forgiveness without this specular identification, without speaking in the other's stead and with the other's voice."[20] If the physical and ontological violence of encounter must be preserved in order to maintain fidelity to the event beyond the instant, the sacrificial logic of the redemptive act, which effectively consists in the symbolic transference of the violence to the subject, cannot enter into play. Rather, it is the symbol itself that must be neutralized, de-personalized, detached from the sovereign propriety of the subject in order for the multiplicity to actualize itself in future encounters. This occurs in the process of representation itself, but not within the aural self-affection of subjectivity (hearing one's own voice), but rather within writing, and more specifically, in writing in "the other's stead and with the other's voice." This procedure brings to the forefront the aporia or open secret of literature itself: that it is fictional, that it always openly betrays the truth of what it represents.[21] Literariness consists in the acknowledgment of this secret; writing literature as such always consists in asking forgiveness for this transgression, that is, for fictionalizing the other, for attempting and necessarily failing to represent the other as such, in sustaining itself from the other's difference and speech in a parasitic but also symbiotic relation.[22]

Desisting becomes possible because of literature's relation to its secret, of its explicit refusal to filiate in an oedipal relationship with the arche or to say what it means, which reveals the arbitrariness of representation and therefore potentializes the multiplicity of the subject to itself. Thus, the singular ethical consciousness potentialized by the revelation of desistance is not itself the direct product of the affective encounter, but rather that of an other multiplicity, the encounter of the becoming-subject with the traces of the other in the event of re-presentation, of writing:

> Language is my human endeavor. I have fatefully to go seeking and fatefully I return with empty hands. But—I return with the unsayable. The unsayable can be given me only through the failure of my language. Only when the construct falters do I reach what it could not accomplish.
>
> And it is useless to try to take a shortcut and start right in, knowing already that the voice says little, starting already with depersonalization. For the trajectory exists, and the trajectory is more than just a way of proceeding. We ourselves *are* the trajectory. In living one can never arrive ahead of time. The *via crucis* isn't a wrong way, it is the only way, you get there only through it and with it.[23]

The repetition of encounter cannot occur within the becoming-subject when the other is absent; its traces are always already buried within the subject in its self-affection. As Derrida insists in the conclusions to *Speech and Phenomena*, "'the look' cannot 'abide.'"[24] The re-encounter can thus only occur within literature. The untranslatable encounter with the cockroach leads to an encounter with the arche, in which the first sacrifice, the self-assassination of the subject, which necessarily made ethics impossible, is substituted for by writing; writing is always already the sacrifice of the subject to its own traces: "And I give myself as an offering to the dead."[25]

It is in this second event, the event of writing, where ethics emerge as responsivity not to the other as such in affective encounter (an instant that has already passed, or is always already passing), but as responsivity to its traces, that is, the other in oneself expropriated as literature.[26] This demand for responsivity within writing eludes the arche's foreclosure of meaning, which is effectively the negation not only of the other's expression but also its expressivity, precisely through the process of representation itself, which is always already destined to failure: "I reach the height from which I can fall, I choose, I tremble, and I desist, and finally, devoting myself to my fall, depersonalized, without a voice of my own, in the last analysis without myself— behold everything I don't have is mine. I desist and the less I am, the more I am alive, the more I lose my name, the more I am called, my only secret mission is my condition, I desist and the more I am ignorant of the password the more I carry out the secret, the less I know the more the sweetness of the abyss is my destiny. And then I adore."[27] In this sense, ethics consists in desisting from redemptive acts—which would in the end be the salvation of the subject ("But it is first one's own salvation") —and following through with the representational process, even when she knows that it is destined to fail.[28] That failure gives expression to the other's traces in literature's silences, in its constitutive incompleteness (absent the subject as the origin of meaning), in the ambivalence of the virtuality of literature as multiplicity: "And miracles too can be sought and had, for continuity has its interstices that don't make it discontinuous, the miracle is the note that lies between two musical notes, the number that lies between the number one and the number two. Its just a question of seeking and having. Faith . . . is knowing that you can go consume the miracle. Hunger, that is what faith is in and of itself—and needing is my guarantee that it will always be given to me. Necessity is my guide."[29] While Lispector draws on theological terminology in this and many other passages, it is key to recognize her insistence that "for me, the divine is the real."[30] In this context, the "miracle" that is implored and given, the unconditional gift of the other and of the indifferent Real, is difference itself, that is, the differentiating power of literary language to produce what Deleuze calls "non-personal individuations."[31]

Permanent responsivity/responsibility without the possibility of response is the gift that literature gives the subject. One cannot maintain fidelity to the other-in-encounter, whose difference is absolute and whose demand for response is illegible, but one can maintain, precariously, fidelity to the other's traces within oneself by attempting and desisting from representing the other as such. For Lispector, fidelity to the event thus consists not in absolute passivity before the unconditional demand of the other, but in opting for an aesthetics of desistance. This is what I mean by going astray: opting to defer not to the representational power of discourse, but to the differentiating power of the trace with respect to language itself and following that "line of flight" to the limits of representation. Going astray in writing implies desisting from the humanistic faith in the expressivity of the subject, from the trajectory of the subject as the recursive form of itself and of the other as the object of its aesthetic decisions, and following the trajectory laid out in the encounter, in the becoming of the subject in multiplicity.

What then would be the political implications of going astray as an ethics of literary representation? Clearly, Lispector's rethinking of the human as a subject-in-becoming that emerges from intra-active encounter with animal others and who chooses to maintain fidelity to that encounter through an aesthetics of desistance, necessarily implies the disavowal of human exceptionalism and its construction of human rights in opposition to nonhuman others as those excluded from rights. Within this framework, the subject of politics is no longer the one who can arrogate rights to itself through its claims on the law (its demand for legal personhood), but rather the one who responds openly to the ethical demand for expression within and through the subject placed by the traces of both human and nonhuman others. In this context, the relationship between language and rights shifts drastically; rather than delineating the sovereign autonomy of the subject as rights-holder, this kind of literary language becomes a heteronomous "minor" language within language that is foreign to itself. Instead of empowering the subject as a member of the polis through the interpellation of the state, this minor, literary language functions as a multiplicity that potentializes the emergence of a different kind of demos, one that relies on the affective materiality of communication as a communal act, a living-with.[32] G. H. describes this communicativity in the following terms: "And I also have no name, and that is my name. And because I depersonalize to the point of not having a name, I shall answer every time someone says: me."[33]

As Gabriel Giorgi writes regarding Guimarães Rosa's "My Uncle the Jaguar" (but resonating equally with his reading of Lispector's *The Passion*):

> this narrator is the instantiation of a reinvention of the commons, of commonality beyond any recognizable community, or more specifically, of commonality as the axis of community, as this power or force that pulls community toward the reinvention of a commons so radical, so powerful, that it withdraws the human from their human fantasy—from the normative fantasy of humanism—and thrusts them into other ways of relating. Precisely where communication becomes rarified to the extreme, where even translation becomes improbable because we can't know if we find ourselves before a word or not: that is where the power of commonality emerges, because it disappropriates the monopoly of the human (or humanism) over meaning. Here meaning is exhibited as what occurs between bodies, this voice between

bodies that oscilates between the human and the animal, common space or spacing beyond all predefined community.[34]

Clearly, this form of representation relies on equivocation rather than translation (equivalence) as a procedure for relating through language. The multispecies community effectively comes into being through the common difference of expressivity itself, that is, an affectivity that is always already communicative, biosemiotic. Nevertheless, there can never be a common meaning—a law or system of rights and duties—other than responsivity itself; biosemiotic communications are always fundamentally untranslatable, as they rely on the indexicality of singular presence rather than common symbolic mediation. In this network of affective intra-relationality, which biosemioticians such as Kalevi Kull call environment, every body is a diplomatic body; it is never assumed that an abstract class (species) may circumscribe the relationality of individual bodies and their specific affective attachments. Representational politics thus become a question of maintaining fidelity to the truth of the multispecies encounter, to the event of diplomacy. And the law becomes the representational imperative to maintain fidelity to the traces of the demos that emerge in encounter, a biosemiotic law of relationality rather than a regulatory institution. This law is upheld not by the symbolic order, its classificatory apparati, and its oedipal or sacrificial logic, but by the minor language itself; a law of desistance rather than representative justice. This is a minor law, a processual law that invalidates from within the staticity of law as such. As Giorgi notes, it is only through the systematic dismantling of the animal form, the animot, that the singularity of relations between individuals of different species can emerge as common difference, that is, difference-in-community.[35]

Nonetheless, in Lispector's writing, the political community that emerges from this processual relationality is not strictly nomadic or "contagious"; it cannot be described accurately as a rhizomatic assemblage of bodies without organs.[36] The traces of the other carry out organ-like functions, ordering both language and political relations in ways that are not always detachable or impermanent, that is, entirely contingent on the instant of encounter. While Lispector coincides with Deleuze and Guattari in eschewing "arborescent" filiation as a form of social organization that produces oedipal subjectivities and epistemological practices (and therefore coercive political and representational forms), filiation itself nevertheless persists powerfully, even ineludibly, in nearly all her texts through figures of maternity and progeny, that is, through maternity as a differential that produces potential filiations.

Nevertheless, Lispector's portrayals of filiation break radically with heter-onormative notions of maternity.

Deferring to the Other and the Cosmopolitics of Intensive Filiation

In Lispector's writing, the relations between parenthood and progeny are not of genetic or archeological inheritance, but rather a question of productive affiliations in becoming, that is, of ongoing responsivity to others within emerging relational multiplicities. Lispector's progeny are formless and trans-formative potentialities that may be actualized in any relation; they are "eggs." "The egg is an exteriorization," she writes in "The Egg and the Chicken," that is, an ex-propriation in the Derridean sense of the word.[37] The egg is never an allusion to its mother (and even less so to its father), it is always "a suspended thing," a potentiality, a point of attachment, an expression of the traces of the other as relationality.[38] Rather than the projection of the subject into the future even beyond its own death, Lispector's eggs are an opening to what may follow the event, to the multiplicity of potential individuations that may emerge from it. It is in this sense in which Lispector speaks of giving birth to herself in *Água viva*.[39] And, in turn, this ambivalence of the egg places mater-nity in a position of permanently potential but undefinable affiliation and responsivity, that is, the becoming-mother to oneself and others.

In what follows, I discuss three stories from *Laços de família* (1960; Fam-ily Ties) that draw out in more concrete terms the political implications of Lispector's rethinking of filiation. The book's title quite clearly communicates the centrality of filiation as the overarching theme in the collection of stories. Since Aristotle, the family has appeared frequently in political theory as the basal unit of the polis in both literal and figurative senses, as the symbolic repository of the meaning of the polis and thus the grounds of legitimacy for institutional biopolitics. Yet the title's first word clearly communicates the insufficiency of the family as a self-producing, autonomous political unit in and of itself; these "laços" (ties) bear a supplemental and destabilizing rela-tionship to the family as both a genealogical lineage and a political form.

The story that gives its title to the book, "Family Ties," foregrounds this problem through a series of terse interactions when an elderly mother visits her daughter, son-in-law, and grandson at their apartment in Rio de Janeiro. Tellingly, the characters do not initially refer to each other by their relational pronouns, but rather, as a "modern family," by their names (Severina, Catarina, and Antônio; the child remains nameless), thus emphasizing monadic autonomy over the ostensibly inherent relationality of family. Nevertheless, there are three key events in the story that coalesce around the usage of relational pronouns. The first happens when the mother, Severina, insists that, despite their conflictive relationship, her son-in-law has become a son to her, to which Antônio responds only with a dissenting cough.[40] The second instance is when Catarina, following a dialogue in which her mother repeatedly asks if she has forgotten anything, calls out to Severina as she is leaving on the train: "Mama! the woman said," (where "woman" indicates an ambiguous relational potentiality that fails to actualize itself as either "daughter" or "wife"), a call to which Severina responds only with "Catarina," thereby rejecting the call to reaffirm the filial relationship.[41] This in turn leads Catarina to reframe Severina's preoccupation with forgotten possessions in terms of relationality: "What was it they'd forgotten to say to each other? And now it was too late. It struck her that one day they should have said something like: 'I am your mother, Catarina.' And she should have answered: 'And I am your daughter.'"[42]

The third and culminating moment is when Catarina's nameless four-year old son, whom the narrator describes as entrapped within his own incommunicative interiority ("the boy gazed indifferently into the air, communicating with himself"), calls her "mamãe" for the first time.[43] Moved, she promptly takes him for a walk outside, leaving Antônio behind in the apartment to ask himself: "Just when does a mother, holding a child tight, impart to him this prison of love that would forever fall heavily on the future man. . . . 'Catarina,' he thought enraged, 'that child is innocent!'"[44] Left out of the emerging relation, the father can only watch from the window as the two figures recede into the distance: "Seen from above, the two figures lost their familiar perspective."[45] Uncalled into the relation, the father is divested of the heteronormative position of the patriarch in ordering the family relation, and is left to mourn for the "innocent" (unresponsive, unbound by the duty placed by the call of the other) autonomy of the male child. In this story, then, filiation emerges as neither a natural biological state or discursive fact, but rather as a form of relationality that depends on affective response. The relational pronouns only indicate a potential relation, a calling to; they must be actualized by a response. Furthermore, inclusion in the relation relates directly to collective decision making; Severina cannot influence the grandchild's eating regime due to her exclusion, and Antônio is ultimately divested of his control over the patriarchal chronotopia of the home (it is explicitly patriarchal in this story despite the common association of the domestic sphere with the feminine) when Catarina and her son go astray, thereby potentializing other forms of social order.

Lispector's rethinking of filiation comes very close to Viveiros de Castro's discussion of affiliation in native Amazonian thought, which he proposes as a corrective to Deleuze and Guatarri's monadic nomadology. As Viveiros de Castro notes, "the common word for the relation, in Amazonian worlds, is the term translated by 'brother-in-law' or 'cross-cousin.' This is the term we call people we do not know what to call, those with whom we wish to establish a generic relation. In sum, 'cousin/brother-in-law' is the term that creates a relation where none existed. It is the form through which the unknown is made known."[46] Rather than relying on genealogical blood ties, then, affinity arises from proximity in difference: "here, the parties find themselves united by what divides them, linked by that which separates them."[47] Several key deconstructions emerge from this line of thought regarding the constitution of the familiar relationship: how can the family be a "natural" primordial unit if it relies on potential "ties," which may or may not be actualized through response, to hold it together? Furthermore, what exactly are these relational ties that will delineate the inside and outside of the family unit, of the state of the family as both a mode of governance and of social exteriorization/interiorization? And what relation does going astray (given Catarina and her son's flight from the patriarchal home) bear/bare to these exteriorizing and internalizing movements and to their projection of collective futurity? Finally, if responsivity is what effectively produces filiation rather than oedipal inheritance, what factors determine who or what may be considered a family member? Can nonhumans become affiliated with human families through responsivity, constituting a more-than-human demos? And, if so, how does this demos reconfigure the polis constituted in law? Can the polis be thought of as the community formed through a responsive practice of jurisprudence rather than identification with the law, that is, unquestioning fidelity to discursive categories?

These questions become particularly salient in two other stories from *Laços de família*, "The Crime of the Mathematics Teacher" and "A Chicken," both of which feature prominently animals who exist simultaneously within the family unit and without; they are nominal or aggregate family members who are also strays. As such, they simultaneously fall within and without the statutes regulating human sociality. Furthermore, they also problematize two forms of modern domestication upon which I have not yet touched: pet ownership and the social production of food species. "The Crime of the

Mathematics Teacher" problematizes the ethics that come into play in the protagonist's relationship with the quintessential human "companion species," the dog. In contrast, "A Chicken" engages in a nuanced critique of the categorization of species itself, drawing out the ultimately arbitrary discursive parameters by which individual animals fall into the categories of either reified food or affiliated companion species. In both stories, the animals become "part of the family," only to be cast out when the ethical implications of these family ties become onerous for the human protagonists, challenging the limits of the human exception and the reification of animals as either pets or food. As in my discussion of Cortázar's "Axolotl," I am interested in Lispector's representations of the specific institutional conditions that make possible the deferral or disavowal of an ethical relationship toward animals as nonhuman familiars despite the human characters' encounters with them as individuals or, to return to Derrida's words, "unsubstitutable singularities." At the same time, however, I examine the cosmopolitical ramifications of these familiar relationships and of the act of going astray, particularly with respect to the theorization of the family as a primordial political state. I will argue that going astray effectively potentializes the act of desistance and the emergence of multispecies polities, even when, in these two stories as in "Axolotl," those potentialities are ultimately subordinated to the institutionality of humanistic domesticity.

In keeping with Lispector's procedure of minimizing plot and therefore heroic protagonism, the only action that occurs in the main narrative moment of "The Crime of the Mathematics Teacher" is the protagonist's search for a spot on a nearly featureless plain (resonating with the desert of the neutral in *The Passion* as well as anticipating Deleuze and Guattari's plateaus) in which he seeks to bury a deceased stray dog that he has encountered on the street, followed by the acts of burying and then unburying this unknown dog. The majority of the text is occupied by rationalistic philosophical reflections on his relationship with a pet dog that he had formerly owned and then abandoned on the pretense of having to move his family to a new city. Through a series of flashbacks, it becomes clear that the math teacher conceives of burying this unknown dog as a calculated, redemptive act intended to atone for abandoning the first dog. Nevertheless, as in *The Passion*, the ritual act of redemption is ultimately unable to rectify the abandonment of the pet dog, José, since it disregards the singularity of the relation he had developed with him. This unknown stray dog is clearly not the same dog (José), who likely continues to survive on the streets of his former city, himself now a stray. The professor's mathematical ethos of variable substitution fails to establish an equivalence between the two dogs, and the professor must instead return to the differentiality of relation. In this sense, his final act of unburying the dead dog is represented within the same framework of desistance as that of the narrator's relationship with the cockroach in *The Passion*: it is only in leaving his "crime" of abandonment in an unresolved, virtual state of guilt that he can maintain fidelity to the singular truth of his relationship to his former dog, and it is this choice to desist from symbolic atonement, rather than the reification of the pet as disposable possession, that ultimately makes him human.

While *The Passion* dedicated some space to the cockroach's perspective, that is, its ability to "touch" or interpellate the protagonist affectively through its gaze, "The Crime" problematizes this question to a much greater degree, drawing out the specific modes of attachment that individuate the dog in relation to his family. Nevertheless, this trajectory of becoming "dog" within a human family places him in an ultimately aporetic position between the human and the animal. The dog is simultaneously property (an object of human agency), an adopted member of the family (to whom duty is owed), and an always potential stray: "'I remember when you were little,' he [the math teacher] thought amused, 'so small, cute, and weak, wagging your tail, looking at me, and I unexpectedly finding in you a new form of having my soul. But, from then on, every day you were already starting to be a dog one could abandon."[48] This potential abandonment is an emerging choice ("one could choose to"), but that choice is potentialized by a passive decision, that of affiliation itself ("a new form of having my soul"), and it emerges precisely through the demands for response that the dog places on the man: "By not asking anything of me, you asked too much. From yourself, you demanded that you be a dog. From me, you demanded that I be a man. And I, I pretended as best I could."[49] This passage captures the complexity of the intra-subjective relationships between humans and dogs. The dog cannot make specific demands in a clearly translatable "human" symbolic register, but its undeniable responsivity within human sociality (due in part to its co-evolution with humans and its millennial history as a companion species) places the human owner in an uncanny position of responsibility that exceeds that apportioned to the animal within discourse in Euro-American societies.

Dogs are always already demi-humans due to their enhanced ability to understand and communicate in a common, but always partial and insufficient symbolic register. It is this ambiguous position within discursivity itself that places the dog simultaneously within and without the family. Its presence within the family socius potentializes it as an almost human subject, but a subject that can never be fully actualized as such: "'While I was making you in my image, you were making me in yours,' he thought then with the aid of longing. 'I gave you the name José to give you a name that would also serve as your soul. And you—how can I ever know what name you gave me? How much more you loved me than I loved you,' he reflected curiously."[50] The dog receives a human name (and image, that is, projection of humanizing, family values), but the protagonist can never be sure what that name means to the dog, even when it responds to it. In turn, the dog's performative interpellation of the man through gaze and gesture leads him to the certainty that the dog has also named him, drawing him into an other symbolic register, one proper to the dog's body and species-specific sociality, to which he is only obliquely privy, through proximity and approximation: "We understood each other too well, you with the human name I gave you, I with the name you gave me that you never spoke except with your insistent gaze."[51]

Lispector thus problematizes interspecies communications in a very Derridian way: not only does the dog call to the human in an unequivocal way, but it places him in a state of responsibility that is proper to family relations. But that call is ambiguous on two fronts: it is an animal call, and therefore subjected to the humanistic animot (which negates conscious expressivity as such to the animal), and, although the human intuits that the animal names him, that name is illegible, unidentifiable in human terms. One might infer that it is an olfactory signature, a scent-trace, while humans are notoriously "poor-in-world" in terms of scent. The dog's call thus places the protagonist in a double bind: he is unequivocally placed into a state of responsibility, he acknowledges the call as such, receiving the dog's name for him, but the potential for individuation produced by the dog name is ambiguous and therefore always incomplete. Rather than producing another dog-subject, the dog-name for the human produces an undefinable relational multiplicity, a matrix of possible relations that ranges from incorporation to abandonment.

Furthermore, none of these potential relations can ever be fully actualized to the exclusion of the others; the equivocal nature of human-dog communications will always place the relation into doubt and therefore imbue it with an overtly virtual or suppositional indeterminacy. These two distinct ontological registers (patterns of becoming) cannot find common ground—a translation—outside the interspecies relation, that is, their bodily differences in differential encounter: "From yourself, you demanded that you be a dog. From me, you demanded that I be a man."[52] The relation, defined here as serial, virtual encounter (its defining parameter being the potential for the near infinite repetition of the encounter with the other's traces) is unequivocal and unconditional, but the subjective meaning of the relation is ambiguous, equivocal due to the untranslatability of these names to each other. Equivocation within partial symbolism thus becomes the mode for serial diplomatic rapprochement between the species, an indeterminate rapprochement that, despite its instability, nevertheless does not negate the familiar relationship (which is most often conceived on the basis of biological commonality), but rather marks it as one of affiliation rather than filiation. And yet, the pet-owner relationship is a form of affiliation that is uncanny in its resemblance to filiation; the pet is like a child, but can never become a child. In modern Euro-American notions of filiation, the animal can never truly, that is, consonantly or unambiguously, be a family member. Nevertheless, the owner is always indebted to the pet in a way that cannot be disavowed simply through the deployment of the animot; calling a pet dog "Dog" does not make it any less a member of the family.

As a math teacher, the protagonist finds himself entrapped within intolerable ambiguity; the family has been transformed from a clearly defined matrix of patriarchal power upheld by a strict genealogic and moral code (the father is the one who makes the collective decisions, decisions that are justified by rational thought but that do not bear a causal relationship to it) to an undefined state of responsibility, in which the dog places the father's sovereign power into question. On the one hand, the father's autonomy is circumscribed by the relation itself; despite owning the dog, he becomes bound by a kind of duty exterior to either the law of the family (that is, the discursive injunctions governing the human family socius) or an ethics of care for vulnerable dependents (animal rights). Indeed, the dog's own ambiguous autonomy within and without the family relation undermines the father's authority as the de-facto representative of his family's interests, that is, his position as the head of the household. The father can never be said to represent faithfully the dog:

> Because you were indomitable ["irredutível," which also evokes Derrida's theorization of what is irreducible to the symbol]. And, calmy wagging your tail, you seemed to reject silently the name I'd given you. Ah yes, you were indomitable: I didn't want you to eat meat so you wouldn't get ferocious, but one day you leaped onto the table and, as the children happily shouted, snatched the meat and, with a ferocity that doesn't come from what you eat, you stared at me mute and indomitable with the meat in your mouth. Because, though you were mine, you never yielded to me even a little of your past or your nature.[53]

In this act of rebellion, ambivalent with respect to intentionality and yet carried out within the symbolic center of the family, the dog reveals itself to be irreducible to its categorization as companion species and to the family as a patriarchal proto state. The ontology underpinning its sudden "anti-social" behavior is opaque, untranslatable to either psychological ("your past") or biological ("your nature") causality.

The dog is ultimately ungovernable through the family's biopolitical regime; not only does it fail to abide by the father's alimentary rules, but it fundamentally disrupts the coercive contract of nonviolence, in which the family members cede their capacity for violence to the law of the father in exchange for the father's gifts. It is the dog's failure to abide by the social contract of the patriarchal family that leads the father to consider abandonment, not because the dog has broken a form of sociality into which it could never enter fully of its own accord or otherwise, but precisely because its form of familiarity is unconditional, inimical to contractuality itself: "And, worried, I started to understand that you didn't demand that I give up anything of mine to love you, and this started to bother me."[54] "Love," the relationship proper to the family (that is, the relational matrix formed by "family ties"), threatens to become something altogether different than a social contract regulating respective rights and duties (rights and duties that are nevertheless produced and experienced as regimented affects, that is, as emotions delimited by relational pronouns). Rather than fidelity to hierarchical identitary categories (mother, father, child, pet), love emerges as the unconditional drive for affiliation that I discussed in the preceding chapter. The dog's insubordination—its simultaneous love for the family members and disarticulation of the law of the family—thus risks contaminating the entire social organization, transforming it into an ungovernable state: the children's illegible "happy shouts" threaten to become revolutionary dog-like animal calls. They potentialize another kind of state, a self-organizing one that emerges within the family but against the law of the father.

Furthermore, the persistence of the dog within the family despite its rejection of or inability to abide by the social contract (the father's rules), reveals that the law itself—as the discursive matrix regulating and producing family interactions and subjectivities—always maintains a certain exteriority with respect to the family structure. It does not apply equally as an interiorizing mechanism; as a symbolic order preceding encounter, it is always insufficient, arbitrary, rife with holes and exceptions. There are always cases that fall outside the law but within the family; and those cases delineate the excessive position of the individual's affective relationality with respect to its relational pronoun, its subjectivation as a family member. The law thus bears a supplemental relation to the family as a political unit; there is always a fundamental gap between the family as affective demos and the family as polity or proto polity, that is, the grounds of and for the law, the reason of and for governance. Confronted with this revelation, the discursivity of the law itself is transformed; the seemingly immutable law becomes situational, contingent, responsive to specific events or cases. Rather than an absolute form producing and regulating all social interactions, it is revealed transparently as a virtuality that must be actualized differentially by case, in practice. An ethics of responsibility—of ongoing fidelity to the serial event of encounter with the familiar other—thus supplements in turn the hard letter of the law, and the law is actualized through ethical practice rather than instituting ethics as a logical extension of itself, that is of rights that coincide with specific sets of relational pronouns, of subjects-before-the-law. The juridical form that emerges from the familiar relationship is thus a law of equivocation, an approximation to justice, that is, to rights and duties that emerge incompletely and excessively from the multispecies interlanguage of encounter.

It is this interplay between the conviviality of communications and the absolute difference of bodies that places justice in a permanently virtual state; these rights and duties can never be fulfilled, but they are nevertheless continually, infinitely called into being in every family relation. The professor's calculations (that is, his rational deliberations regarding how to do justice unto his pet dog) fail and yet he perseveres to the point of desistance; the familiar relation continually calls for an incalculable, that is, infinite justice. And, as in *The Passion*, the only way that this justice may emerge is through equivocal approximation; it is through a series of failed calculations that one may draw closer to it without ever reaching it. It is effectively Derrida's unpayable debt.

Ostensibly, the owner's abandonment of the dog would restore the patriarchal order and the law of the father. However, the possibility of restoration is already negated by the framing of the flashbacks detailing the owner's relationship with his pet within the narrative of the burial and unburial of the stray dog. The persistence of the irreducible pet dog's demand on the owner's subjectivity even when the dog himself is no longer present condemns the ritual atonement, the symbolic fulfillment of duty to a family member, to failure and with it the invalidation of systematic, calculable justice under the only law left to apply: family law.[55] The dog as stray, as ongoing absence within the family, instead potentializes the state of responsibility that the ritual sought to subordinate through symbolic transference. The owner can never absolve himself of the guilt of abandoning his obligations to a family member, and opting to maintain fidelity to that unpayable debt is what in fact makes him human in the sense in which the dog called for him to be "man" in relation to it. In this sense, the dog's absence reconstitutes the family as an open polity under the law of equivocal responsivity, a polity that can never return to the biologically enclosed, nuclear family, that is, the family without a dog. No longer a demographic accounting organized around father, mother, and children, the family is an excess to itself, a plus-one as Deleuze and Badiou would describe it. The dog's absence thus becomes transcendent, a virtuality in the Deleuzian sense (a multiplicity that is actualized in each encounter), but also juridical in its narrowness, in the restrictions that it places on the autonomy of the humanistic subject and in its demand for actualization as serial justice in difference, for calculations that approximate it to the incalculable: "I'm quite sure now I wasn't the one who had a dog. You were the one who had a person."[56]

Chicken Kin? The State of the Family and the Ethics of Eating

As "The Crime of the Mathematics Teacher" draws out, this kind of familiar relationality is always already present in encounters with species like the dog that are categorized, a priori, as potential human companions, as well as with other domestic animals that unambiguously respond to names assigned by human owners. However, Lispector does not limit herself to traditional companion species in exploring this state of familiar responsivity. In another story from *Family Ties*, "A Chicken," she delves into a more liminal form of domesticity: that of the food species. Tellingly, this story examines the problem not from the rigid institutionality of industrialized meat production, but from the ambiguous position of a "Sunday chicken" within a nuclear family structure. Initially, nonetheless, the story places the titular hen in a strictly reified position of food species; having no name of its own and its individuality being immediately subordinated to its species (it is simply "a hen"), its ability to demand a response from the family members is negated from the outset: "still alive because it wasn't yet nine in the morning."[57] Entirely bounded by its designation as a chicken destined to be eaten for the family's Sunday meal, its prescribed death is rendered meaningless, the simple product of a linguistic killing machine that circumscribes any ethical or political implications. Unaware of its impending death, as there are no immediately legible environmental cues that would lead it to feel threatened, the chicken awaits passively in a corner of the kitchen: "she looked at no one, no one looked at her. Even when they selected her, feeling up her intimate parts indifferently, they couldn't tell whether she was fat or skinny. No one would ever guess she had a yearning."[58] Nevertheless, the static configuration of the chicken as passive food object is suddenly disrupted when it spontaneously flees (again, without any evident causal stimulus), fluttering up onto the patio wall and leaping from rooftop to rooftop with the "man of the house" in hot pursuit. This act of going astray potentializes a series of transformations in the proprietary subject-object relationship; the "owner/head ["dono"] of the household" also spontaneously transforms into a predator, a "dormant hunter" whose ostensible primordial regression is humorously driven home by his near-naked state in "swimming trunks." The chicken's flight deterritori-alizes the institution of the house in relation to the family state formation and modern food production, placing both the hen and the father in an affective, nomadic relation of predator-prey. At the same time, the hen is thrust into the position of making decisions that cannot rely purely on instinct: "Ill-adapted to a wilder struggle for life, the chicken had to decide for herself which way to go, without any help from her race."[59] Within the instinctual fight-or-flight paradigm, violent resistance is discarded as an option (an option that is simultaneously potentialized and minimized in the words "pouco afeita" or "ill-adapted"); lost in an unfamiliar environment, the hen must neverthe-less choose her trajectory of escape, necessarily implying at least a minimal degree of voluntaristic agency within the instinctual drive. The instinct to flee itself becomes a plus-one, a passive decision before a predator that opens a multiplicity of potential lines of flight between which the hen must choose.

Despite intimating a certain degree of agency, however, the hen's sudden act of going astray is not enough to disrupt the family state in the same way as the stray dog's in "The Crime." She was never a family member to begin with. Individuated at least momentarily in flight, she is no longer strictly a passive object of serial, mechanistic killing, but she is nevertheless still prey, not a potential relative or companion. Furthermore, her flight appears not as a subjective exteriorization of willpower or concrete actualization of individuality, but rather as a fleeting intensity, a potential but ambiguous individuation or becoming individual: "Alone in the world, without father or mother, she ran, panting, mute, focused. At times, mid-escape, she'd flutter breathlessly on the eave of a roof and while the boy went stumbling across other roofs she'd have time to gather herself for a moment. And then she seemed so free."[60] Nevertheless, this spark of potentiality—the reflexive "time to gather herself"—is disarmed by her passivity when she is recaptured and returned to the domestic space of the kitchen, circumscribed concentrically by the animot (the chicken as food species), the institutional spatiality of the kitchen (as the place proper to food preparation), and her own biological limitations with respect to human sociality, that is, her inability to respond to or provoke a response within the family in an unambiguous way. Her demonstrated, if limited capacity for conscious decision-making—that "anseio" (yearning/desire) for freedom, which is in any case qualified by the ambivalence of the verb "parecia" (seemed), reverting the interpretation of the act to the narrator's perspective—is insufficient to inscribe her with personhood within the law of the family. In this subtle way, Lispector implies that the potential for individual freedom is never the determining condition for political personhood or ethical treatment within a polity. The humanistic family state remains intact; she may no longer be a straightforward Sunday chicken, but she is still delimited as animal prey in strictly dialectical opposition to the human

Tellingly, this compelling but ultimately truncated flight of the chicken is not the climactic event in the story, although it sets the stage by problematizing subject-object relations with respect to the domesticity of the food species. Marked by the phrase "That's when it happened," the event that places the state of the family into question is instead the advent of maternity. Immediately following her recapture, the hen lays an egg that, "Perhaps it was premature. But right after, born as she was for maternity, she looked like an old, experienced mother."[61] At the blurred limits of reproductive instinct and gendered identitary performance, the hen becomes mother before the eyes of the family, leading the daughter to exclaim excitedly: "Mama, Mama, don't kill the chicken anymore, she laid an egg! She cares about us!"[62] Upon invoking the maternal pronoun, the daughter calls the hen into a familiar relation, even if only in parallel. Nonetheless, the hen remains illegible due to her untranslatable bodily differences: "Warming her offspring, she was neither gentle nor standoffish, neither cheerful nor sad, she was nothing, she was a chicken. Which wouldn't suggest any special feeling."[63] While the laying of the egg could be read as the placing of an affective demand, a calling into being of an affiliative relation, the hen's seeming impassivity means that it is unable to actualize affectively the potentiality of the mother pronoun with respect to the family state. Her sudden status as mother is entirely one-sided, the product of a gendered, discursive circumscription of the event that forecloses its openness to a cosmopolitical reconfiguration of the family as more-than-human. For this reason, the encounter does not produce an ethical thought akin to that which emerged from the encounter with the cockroach in *The Passion* and the dog in "The Crime": "The father, the mother, and the daughter had been staring for some time, without thinking anything in particular."[64]

Nevertheless, the deployment of the mother pronoun calls the father into an other form of relationality, in which the consumption of the hen takes on shades of cannibalism: "If you have this chicken killed I'll never eat chicken again for the rest of my life!"[65] The passive enactment of maternity spontaneously invokes Levinas's ethical injunction "thou shalt not kill" through the affiliative potential of the maternal pronoun, rather than what Levinas postulates as the human face's absolute or divine legibility, that is, the face as the condition for legibility even prior to expression. The hen acquires a pronoun that is proper to the family through the (coerced) gift of maternity ("she cares about us!"), thereby potentializing an affiliative relationship in which the family members are open to responding to ethical demands by the animal other. But nameless, without speech or human-like face, she is unable to place this demand; her position within the family is always precarious, ambivalent, dependent on a relational pronoun she is incapable of actualizing in a legible way. Despite now being treated like the "queen of the house," she lives with but not within the family: "Unconscious of the life she had been granted, the chicken began living with the family."[66] The virtuality of the familiar relationship can never be actualized, circumscribed as it is by rigid discursive categories that proscribe any direct, diplomatic rapprochement.

The potential for individuation, however, persists in the memory of her flight and her desire to sing like a rooster—that is, to actualize her individuality through oral expression, a calling-out that would break her silence and potentially place a demand for responsive diplomacy: "Every once in a while, though increasingly rarely, the chicken would again recall the figure she had cut against the air on the edge of the roof, about to proclaim herself. That's when she'd fill her lungs with the kitchen's sullied air and, even if females were given to crowing, wouldn't crow but would feel much happier."[67] This eternally postponed call thus announces a potential future, a morning, the possibility of imagining serial repetition beyond the horizon of her death sentence. Nevertheless, this future is proscribed beforehand by both her gender (this is a subtle point, but hens also vocalize; the question thus resides in the gendered meanings associated with the rooster's call, which is popularly associated with masculine aggressivity and heralding the dawn) and the evolutionary specificity of her body: "Though not even then would the expression change on her empty head. Fleeing, resting, giving birth, or pecking corn—it was a chicken's head, the same one designed at the start of the centuries."[68] In this sense, the story appears to argue for a nuanced reappraisal of animal agency not as the becoming-human of the animal within the human family-state, as in the case of the dog, but as a becoming itself in a parallel but still relational engagement with the human family.

The fact that this becoming-chicken is in itself gendered speaks not to the "natural" dominance of the male over the female of the species, but rather to potentiality itself; the hen's ability to imagine herself crowing like a rooster implies a rethinking of sexuation as a fluid multiplicity rather than an ineludible biological property. While this passage doubtlessly comes across as contrived, humanistic personification to some readers (who would likely read this metaphorically with reference to the patriarchal subordination of human women's voices), one must take into account both the many documented cases of hens crowing (often in relation to hormonal changes) as well as the widespread phenomenon of animal mimicry within and across species.[69] The question that thus emerges is not whether or not a hen could conceivably imitate the crowing of a rooster, but rather whether a hen could "know" about this possibility in the sense of imagining it before it happens (an imagining that is nevertheless not spontaneous, but rather the actualization of the virtuality that emerged when she took flight; the memory itself *is* that virtual multiplicity), which would effectively imply voluntaristic or conscious imitation. And this is certainly not an impossibility, given the many documented cases of animal deception (which necessarily requires conceptualizing/imagining the negative of an act) as well as Derrida's fulminating critique of Lacan's assertion that animals cannot "pretend to pretend."

The cosmopolitical implications of the hen imagining herself performing male behavior are vast; this would imply that chickens' bodies too are inscribed by gendered performance in a way akin to that theorized by Judith Butler, if perhaps reliant on indexical gestural signs for gendering rather than abstract symbolic mediation. Furthermore, Lispector's story suggests that gendered performances function across species, if in equivocal rather than fully translatable ways. While in no way equivalent, women and hens are both gendered as female by parallel discourses that intersect in the event of maternity within the domestic environment of the family. And when human exceptionalism is removed as an organizing principle for critiquing gendered discourses (that is, the doctrine that gender is a cultural discourse, and that both culture and discourse are exclusive to *Homo sapiens*), justice for women may implicate females of other species as well, again through equivocation rather than equivalence. Unlike Lispector's dogs (in *A Breath of Life*, she reflects that "The dog hungers so much for people and to be a man. A dog's inability to speak is excruciating"), the hen may not be able to imagine herself human, but she can imagine herself other in a different way, within the possibilities of her body's evolutionary history and species-specific gender performance.[70] It is this capacity to imagine and imagine articulating another future that endows Lispector's chicken with cosmopolitical agency in a way that exceeds her frustrated inclusion in the family polis. The question that peers out between the lines is thus: what would have been the effects on the family if the hen had, in fact, articulated the rooster's revolutionary call? Or, as Henry Schwarz suggests in somewhat schematic terms, may the laying of the egg itself embody such an act of cosmopolitical defiance, given the death sentence placed on the hen?[71]

Yet, in the end, the cosmopolitical potential appears to be cut short; unable to affiliate effectively with the family, the relation defaults to the law of the family kitchen, and the story ends unceremoniously: "Until one day they killed her, ate her and years went by."[72] The food species designation overpowers the weak form of affiliation that emerged intensively from the event of maternity, while the subtly humorous tone of the story also plays a role in minimizing its cosmopolitical potential. Nonetheless, one cannot help but surmise that the meaning of eating chicken has been forever altered. Indeed, while the chronological reference "years went by" seemingly alludes to the reestablishment of the absolute, timeless (the hen is literally out of time and figuratively out of history: "it was a chicken's head, the same one designed at the start of the centuries [beginning of time]") hegemony of the human over the animal-as-food, implying that there are no ongoing ethical consequences that arise from eating the hen, it nevertheless projects that event into the future as an ongoing potentiality.

Ironically, it is precisely the hen's discursive subordination to her species ("A Chicken") that makes repetition, that is, the emergence of a series, possible. The individual bird in question has been killed and eaten, but hens in general live on in multiplicity, each individual hen always simultaneously and irreconcilably both potential food and mother. The cosmopolitical event could thus potentially be reenacted in every subsequent encounter between chickens and human families. In this sense, the daughter's acknowledgment of the egg as gift and therefore something that is given, not simply taken, implies a reappraisal of the eating of the food species as something other than purely mechanistic killing and consumption. Nevertheless, the girl's inferred complicity in killing and eating the hen ultimately implies acquiescence to the family law, to her becoming human subject within a patriarchal order that subordinates her as female (and future mother) and the female chicken as food (and mother). Nonetheless, while the family may not have entered into a fully actualized ethical and cosmopolitical relation with the chicken within the bounds of the story, the reader inevitably finds themself drawn into a more clearly defined ethical dilemma. Having confronted the hen's potential for desiring individual freedom within a strict biopolitical and discursive regime that condemns her a priori to meaningless death, the reader is necessarily forced to reconsider the implications of eating individual animals.

These ethical questions are deepened by the parallels between species within the story's problematization of gender and the functioning of the mother pronoun within the patriarchal family institution. Similarly to the allegorical readings of Cortázar's "Axolotl," Lispector's hens in this story as well as in "The Egg and the Chicken" are often read as symbolic representations of the dehumanization of women.[73] Nevertheless, like Cortázar, Lispector takes careful pains to preserve species differences; rather than presenting the chicken as a human personification, a "feathered woman" akin to the murderous hen in Mexican author Francisco Tario's darkly humorous "La noche de la gallina," the author foregrounds the institutional discourse of gender within the family, which inscribes human and nonhuman female bodies alike as sites of reproduction and sustenance. In the logic of patriarchy, females serve the ends of species reproduction; their individuality is sacrificed to their institutional role.[74] Furthermore, when speaking of women's bodies as a/the site of human sustenance (in the literal sense of breast milk as well as the figurative sense of the nonreciprocal consumption of nurture), cannibalistic overtones are unavoidable.

In this way, Lispector reveals common biopolitical constraints that the patriarchal family institution places on women's subjectivities and bodies and the hen's body and potential subjectivity through the construction of gender and animal categories. They become the prey of patriarchal institutions. Tellingly, roosters are only rarely eaten and do not produce eggs, a fact which itself genders the classification of the chicken as food species. At the same time, as I have argued, Lispector's cross-species critique of gendering discourses functions through equivocal parallelism rather than allegory, thereby extending, even if obliquely, concerns about justice for women to the chicken. Chickens may not have any claim on human rights, but, in Lispector's writing, the same repressive gender structures subordinate women and hens, if asymmetrically. Furthermore, the cannibalistic overtones of consuming the mother force a drastic rethinking of the political ontology of eating;

rather than reinforcing the hegemony of the subject over the food object, eating becomes a relational act, the "eating of relations" that Viveiros de Castro described in native Amazonian "cannibal metaphysics."

Lispector's take on the gendering of food species resonates with Derrida's proposal in "Eating Well" that the sacrificial logic underpinning the food species designation is itself fundamentally gendered, an enactment of subjectivity as "carnivorous virility."[75] In this "carno-phallogocentrism," which he associates in particular with psychoanalysis, subjectivity is always already oedipal, "the idealizing interiorization of the phallus and the necessity of its passage through the mouth, whether it's a matter of words or of things, of sentences, of daily bread or wine, of the tongue, the lips, or the breast of the other."[76] As he clarifies,

> authority and autonomy (for even if autonomy is subject to the law, this subjugation is freedom) are, through this schema, attributed to the man (homo and vir) rather than to the woman, and to the woman rather than to the animal. And of course to the adult rather than to the child. The virile strength of the adult male, the father, husband, or brother (the canon of friendship, I will show elsewhere, privileges the fraternal schema) belongs to the schema that dominates the concept of subject. The subject does not want just to master and possess nature actively. In our cultures, he accepts sacrifice and eats flesh.[77]

It is precisely this sacrificial logic that is dismantled in "A Chicken." At the least, the sacrifice has become visible, no longer deferred to the institution of animality. Read this way, the story's final lines imply something altogether different: eating the chicken is not a reaffirmation of a humanistic "natural" order of animal sacrifice, but rather a pragmatic eating of affects.

As Derrida makes clear, reconceptualizing subjectivity through its relations to the affective traces of others requires a shift from thinking of individuation as the institution of the monadic, sovereign "who" to a privileging of the relational "what," that is, becoming-with in ongoing, serial encounter. As I have already discussed at length, this process in turn reconfigures ethics as fidelity to the encounter itself; rather than responding to the logic of sacrifice, that is, the interpellation of the law and its interdictions regarding what may be killed and eaten without consequences, ethics become acknowledging the debt to the eaten other and maintaining fidelity to their traces: "the question is no longer one of knowing if it is 'good' to eat the other or if the other is 'good' to eat, nor of knowing which other. One eats him regardless and lets oneself be eaten by him."[78] This is what, following Viveiros de Castro, I have called affiliation, and Derrida calls "infinite hospitality."[79] As Derrida summarizes, "the infinitely metonymical question on the subject of 'one must eat well' must be nourishing not only for me, for a 'self,' which, given its limits, would thus eat badly, it must be shared, as you might put it, and not only in language. 'One must eat well' does not mean above all taking in and grasping in itself, but learning and giving to eat, learning-to-give-the-other-to-eat. One never eats entirely on one's own."[80] Eating well thus becomes the basal form of affiliation, the foundation of an ethics of responsivity toward the other. Furthermore this reappraisal of eating—quite literally the re-source of life—also implies a rethinking of life itself not as the simultaneous source of the humanistic autonomy of the subject and object(ive) of the state's biopolitical institutions, but rather as a relational, responsive multiplicity, that is, a collective more-than-human becoming through mutual sustenance.[81]

Affective Communities and the Law of Equivocation

The distinction in Roman law between persona and res falls apart in Lispector's writing, and with it, the rigid attribution of rights to the legally defined persona. In her families, rights are produced virtually within the relation as emergent ethical thoughts, and they are actualized through the interplay between ethical duty and discourse, that is, the practice of responsivity. This is what distinguishes Lispector's perspective on affiliation from Deleuze and Guattari's viral nomadology, in which governance is always a negative, what is deterritorialized by the intensity of materiality in encounter: "even in bands of animals, leadership is a complex mechanism that does not act to promote the strongest, but rather inhibits the installation of stable powers, in favor of a fabric of immanent relations."[82] Deleuze and Guattari's perspective on politics is ultimately reactive, the product of the overdetermination of modern biopolitics and overpowering consensus in neoliberal capitalism; recognizing that there has never truly been a lawless, nomadic society, they are forced to propose polity in purely idealistic terms, as a perpetually postponed, virtual demos, a counter-State always in becoming. Giorgi extended this perspective to Latin American writing on animality, in which animals in literature represent a deterritorialization of biopolitics and demographic representativity; for Giorgi, becoming-animal functions in purely deconstructive terms, as the non-subject that deterritorializes the state.

In these deconstructive exercises, however, the only way to move beyond anthropocentric politics is quite literally apocalypse, the end of a world; that is, the end of both the regulating functions of language and representative governance, in reality, that of communicative sociality and collective agency themselves, which in Deleuze and Guattari can only exist either as Statism (hierarchical territorialization or striation) or as the disruption of Statism (rhyzomatic deterritorialization). Taken to its theoretical limits, nomadology can never become a hegemonic "majority" or even posthegemonic (if one could somehow magically dispel the demographic majority-minority paradigm in political hegemony) practice; it cannot be the way of life of all, only that of the disruptive minority. This is quite obviously the case not only in the pragmatic sense of social history and competition over resources and state power, but also simply the parameters established by its own logic: it is a theoretical proposal that can only inhabit that which it disavows. At the same time, one might easily argue, as Peter Hallward and many other critics have, that capitalistic globalization is itself a form of nomadology, a deterritorialization of ethics, rights, states, and epistemologies in favor of impermanent (and extractive) attachments of all kinds.

Lispector's thinking regarding affiliation provides another way to move forward, to reimagine communities as multispecies, self-governing polities founded on a law of equivocation, that is, the injunction requiring a discursive practice that approaches the irreducible other through ex-propriation rather than appropriation. Despite the parallel's between Lispector's and Deleuze and Guattari's thought, Lispector's families do not exemplify a nomadic state-to-come, deferring instead to an always already present, latent affective state that simultaneously underpins all affiliation and yet is often suppressed by humanistic law through the personhood-res mechanism. Her characters' radical gestures thus consist not in conceiving of a new kind of politics, but rather in going astray from the rigid bounds of humanistic discursivity to create discourses that actualize this affective virtuality rather than repressing it. In that sense, Lispector's stray is not a nomad; it is an individual that becomes familiar, but is not produced fully by either the family state or the state-disrupting war machine. Rather than pure disruption, it produces ethics that are affiliative, familiar: it transforms the family into a state of relational responsivity, that is, an open polity that is produced by fidelity to the relation rather than the law of the father. And, as the conclusion of "Family Ties" hinted, this kind of family is not patriarchal even when the patriarch may persist within it. The father loses his privileged position as both repository and enforcer of the law; he is simply another affiliated member of the family living under the law of equivocation. In this state of responsivity, representational governance does not disappear altogether (since collective decisions must always be made and nonhuman beings and nonverbal humans cannot always articulate their interests in an unambiguous way), but it is always compelled to respond to the demands placed by the relations that compose it.

Lispector's lines of flight are always tandem, a flying or fleeing from and with the other and its threatening presence. The asymmetry of these relations are precisely what imbue encounters with powerful, if indeterminate ethical and political undercurrents. Nevertheless, these ethics should not be viewed as a negation of the Deleuzian principle of untranslatable, absolute difference; rather, her procedure of equivocation proposes a corrective to Deleuzian thought regarding politics, particularly in its ahistoricity. Equivocation makes it possible to think of politics not as an affective state always ensnared within its own status as potentiality in the now, that is, its political impossibility, but as an ethical procedure for approaching difference that can project a different future, a future toward which one can work rather than merely fleeing. As Adorno perceptively noted, a freedom is always a freedom from; and a "line of flight" carries within it the implication of fleeing from, even if it poses as pure, infinite potentiality. Even if one "follows" a line of flight traced not by the subject but by a differential, one nevertheless negates the other lines of flight; the multiple becomes the singular, a destiny or destination. Actualization (and individuation) implies that one can never linger or remain within the potential. Lispector's animal encounters restore to the encounter its condition as a political event with its own truth in the sense in which Badiou uses these terms, that is, as the irruption of a multiplicity to which one may make the ethical (if passive, in Derrida's theorization) decision to maintain fidelity.

Biosemiotics, the Arche of the Forest, and the Politics of Multispecies Representation

This is why I told the white people: "You often claim to love what you call **nature**. Then do not settle for making speeches, truly defend it! You must help us protect what still remains of the forest. All its inhabitants already speak to us with the fear of disappearing. You do not see their images dance and you do not hear their songs in your dreams. Yet we shamans, we know how to listen to the bees' distress, and they are asking us to speak to you so your people will stop eating the forest."

—DAVI KOPENAWA

The previous two chapters focused on the ways in which Julio Cortázar's and Clarice Lispector's writings draw to the forefront and problematize the institutional structures upholding the human/animal divide, thereby opening interspecies relations to an ethics of passive responsibility arising within affective encounters. Scrutinizing the relations between the subject, the arche or symbolic order of language, and the animal other's demand for response within the event of encounter, both authors place into question the validity of the Euro-American conceptualization of subjectivity as the basis for human exceptionalism, showing how animal others place humans into a state of ethical responsibility that cannot be eluded through the imposition of the animot or even deferral to the redemptive justice of rights discourse. In turn, Lispector's meticulous rethinking of affiliation and of the family as the proto-political institution par excellence not only calls for a reappraisal of the family itself as an open-ended multispecies socius, but also of the grounds for the social itself and therefore of politics and the law. Through the tropes of going astray and desistence, Lispector reframes the terms of political representation altogether, whereby the demos is constituted through affective relations in encounter and polity is delineated not through the persona/res distinction between rights holders and rightless entities, but instead coalesces around a law of equivocal or incalculable justice that emerges reiteratively in encounter.

This form of justice does not depend on shared interests, analogous values, or the ultimately unattainable ideal of equality under the rule of law, but rather on the actualization of mutual, collective responsibility through the reenactment of human and nonhuman others' traces in ongoing and future encounters.[1] Responsive justice thus emerges performatively as "discourse" in the materialist sense in which Karen Barad uses the term, as intra-active, boundary-making agential patterns within phenomena.[2] Responsibility becomes "law" in this sense, as a reiterative mode of configuring emerging collectivities that is oriented toward maintaining and expanding the relation itself, unlike the order of the sovereign subject that enacts an agential cut (such as the human/animal divide) embedded within the humanistic symbolic order (the law of language) to subordinate the other participants in the relation as its objects.[3] In this way, Lispector's thought charts a route toward a new kind of open, multispecies democracy akin to what Derrida refers to as the "democracy to come" and Jason W. Moore terms an "authentically multispecies politics of emancipation," that exceeds the bounds of both constitutional liberalism and Deleuze and Guattari's anarchistic nomadology.[4]

Given the biological similarities between *Homo sapiens* and other animals, the long history of human-animal domestic conviviality, the prevalence of animal rights discourse in the liberal tradition, and recent ethological and neurological studies showing that humans and animals share to at least some degree the biological substrates of "consciousness," it is not surprising that animals would open the way toward reconceiving the political as multispecies cosmopolitics. Indeed, proponents of human exceptionalism from Aristotle to Descartes, Heidegger, and Lacan have always felt obligated to address and foreclose this proximity in justification of the animal exclusion from ethical consideration and political standing. However, this question becomes much more fraught when dealing with plants and other beings whose radical biological differences from humans preclude straight-forward identification. As Michael Marder makes clear in his examination of the place of plants in the philosophies of being underpinning Euro-American humanism, plants rather than animals have most often served as the discursive foil and dialectical counterpart to the human.[5] Defining plants categorically as silent, immobile, passive, and unconscious (lacking a central nervous system and therefore sentience), Euro-American philosophers since the Socratic school have traditionally represented them as the primordial form of bare life, entrapped in biological teleology—that is, within the unconscious actualization of biologically encoded potentials—and absolute openness to their others, constitutionally unable to "return to themselves" as subjects.[6] In contrast, humans are inscribed as self-reflexive, living in a world of abstract projections or future possibilities rather than raw material potentials, which is ostensibly what allows them to make voluntaristic decisions and instrumentalize their others.[7] Within this humanistic hierarchy of being, animals typically occupy a middle ground, as constitutively lacking or defective humans, which is what allows them a certain claim on ethical treatment and political rights within the liberal tradition, without ever fully inhabiting those rights in the same ways as humans.

Nevertheless, a large corpus of Latin American literature and art has problematized such categorical distinctions with respect to the questions of human-plant mutual responsivity, the roles of plants in society, the multiplicity of forms of agency and intentionality, and cosmopolitical potentials and practices. As Lesley Wylie's seminal study *The Poetics of Plants in Spanish American Literature* demonstrates, representations of plants and what she calls "phytocentric" tropes have taken a central role in a wide range of literary texts dealing with colonial and postcolonial identity politics, land-use practices, and ontologies of ecological embodiedness.[8] Arguing against the grain of traditional literary criticism regarding plant imagery, Wylie contends that representations of plants in Spanish American literature do not simply reproduce humanistic processes of reification whereby plants become mere commodities, aesthetic objects in human cultural production, or symbolic personifications of human traits, but rather frequently intersect with Indigenous ontologies, in which it is often assumed that plants have being and personhood, thereby forming part of a multispecies socius. In this sense, much of Latin American literature prefigures what Marder calls "plant-thinking" and what Duchesne Winter terms "plant theory," that is, a reframing of the terms of subjectivity and the social through close attention to plant modalities of affiliation and human-plant affinities.[9]

Re-Encountering Plants through Aesthetic Excess

In Wylie's re-reading of many of the canonical texts of Spanish American literature, human-plant proximity emerges primarily through the co-production of

common space, as in the postcolonial cultural construction of national landscapes, or through shared suffering and economic exploitation in extractivist
enterprises. As in my prior chapters, I am interested in a somewhat distinct,
if not unrelated angle: human-plant encounters that lead to a fundamental
reconceptualization of representation itself and thus the grounds for both
the social and the political. Following in the steps of Wylie and several other
ecocritics, I return to an iconic text within the *novela de la selva* genre, Colombian writer José Eustasio Rivera's *La vorágine* (*The Vortex*; 1924), as my point
of departure.[10] As Jorge Marcone notes, the subgenre of travel fiction known
as the *novela de la selva* was characterized by a constitutive tension between
its authors' involvement in early-to-mid twentieth century projects to territo-
rialize Amazonia within nationalistic geopolitical and economic frameworks
and a reappraisal of extractivism as an unethical mode of relating to nature.[11]
He contends that these novels prefigure ecological critique in the forms in
which they represent relatively sustainable, local land-use practices as embedded within modern economic networks, while simultaneously resisting the
imposition of large-scale extractivism.[12] In this way, they suggest alternative
forms of modernization that respect cultural biodiversity and local environments, rather than reducing them to externalities in the calculus of large-
scale natural resource extraction and the construction of the liberal state.

Expanding on Marcone's seminal ecocritic reading of the *novela de la selva*
genre, I propose to bracket (but not disavow by any means) the well-versed
reading of Rivera's representation of Amazonia in *La vorágine* as what Margarita Serje has called "el revés de la nación" (the underside/reverse of the
nation), a space of exception in which the Colombian republic's institutions
are almost entirely absent, leaving the region in a Hobbesian "state of nature,"
whereby unregulated, predatory capitalism runs amok.[13] While many critical readings have been successful in drawing out *La vorágine*'s critique of the
simultaneous exploitation of human workers and nature in the turn-of-the-
twentieth century rubber boom, few have discussed the possibility that the
novel may offer insight into these more ecologically conscious, alternative
forms of modernization. This largely happens due to the critical focus on the
novel's plotline, which places nearly all the weight of thematic development
on the movements of its human protagonists within the labor structures of
first the cattle and then the rubber industries. Beyond a brief reference to
the sustainable harvesting of feathers to adorn metropolitan women's hats
in a *garcero* (heron rookery), the novel proffers few economic alternatives to
rubber extraction.[14] Despite the overbearing weight of the theme of economic
exploitation, however, I argue that these alternative forms of modernization

drawn out by Marcone do in fact emerge in the novel, but between the plot-lines, in its aesthetics, and that they relate to cosmopolitical potentials rather than economic sustainability.

In particular, some of Rivera's more enigmatic descriptions of Amazonian plant life create dissonance with the thematic focus on economic exploitation, even when coinciding in a general sense with the aesthetics of abjection and exploitation that characterizes the second part of the novel. These passages are frequently dismissed as either the product of a post-Romantic negative sublime (the protagonist, Arturo Cova, is a poet—a "sleep-deprived dandy," as Molloy calls him—from Bogotá and the first part of the novel reproduces many Romantic tropes) or as literary projections of Rivera's own mental states, including bouts of tropical illnesses and an unspecified neurological disorder.[15] While both these perspectives are certainly valid, they are often used in similar fashion to hyperhumanistic reappropriations of Cortázar's and Lispector's representations of human-animal encounters; that is, they are deployed to dismantle the ethical and political implications that emerge when these passages are taken at face value as representing transformative encounters with nonhumans.

I find several passages at the beginning of the second part of *La vorágine*, when Cova and his companions confront radical environmental differences upon descending from the Colombian Llanos Orientales (Eastern Plains) into the Amazonian rainforest, particularly evocative with respect to both what Marder calls "plant being" and cosmopolitical potentials. As a variety of critics have noted, the shift from the post-Romantic nationalistic imagery used to describe the savannah (featuring prominently the Romantic figure of the enterprising individual, liberated from social strictures and sublimated by nature's grandeur) to tropes of hyperbolic abjection and horror simultaneously prepares the way for the aesthetic shift toward the social realism that predominates in the second and third parts of the novel, depicting human rights abuses in the rubber boom, and captures the threatening excesses that Amazonian environments posed to the Regenerationist/post-Regenerationist project of regional integration and economic modernization.[16] While these readings do much to explain these passages' aesthetics in a general sense, few critics have discussed at any length the specificity of either their aesthetics or content. As I have argued elsewhere, a closer look reveals not simply a shift in narrative style, but a breakdown in the aesthetic conventions of nature writing and, in fact, the Euro-American conceptualization of nature itself. As Cova famously queries, "Where is the pastoral poetry here, where are the butterflies like translucent flowers, the enchanting birds, the singing brook? Impoverished fantasies of poets that know only domesticated wilds!"[17] The encounter with the Amazonian environment simultaneously deconstructs the premodern trope of nature as the benevolent, pastoral "mother" of human civilizations and inspiration for artistic mimetism, as well as the modern capitalistic framing of nature as the passive repository of what Moore calls "Nature's free gifts," that is, latent raw materials for commodity production.[18] The Amazonian environments' radical differences rendered the region opaque to modern theoretical frameworks and stylistic conventions, which were unable to account satisfactorily for the region's vast biodiversity and ecological complexity, leading to convoluted narrative textures that in a previous essay I called the "natural baroque."[19]

In what follows, I argue that it is precisely this breakdown in representation that opens the encounter with plants to affective responsivity, which in turn suggests an entirely different basis for the social and politics. Tellingly, the second section of *La vorágine* opens with an apostrophe in which Cova simultaneously genders the Amazonian rainforest as female (a gendering already present in the Spanish words "la naturaleza" y "la selva") and deconstructs the implied social roles of spouse and mother: "Oh jungle, wedded to silence, mother of solitude and mist! What malignant spirit left me to languish in your emerald prison?"[20] Jaramillo and most other critics dismiss this representation as a gothic trope of monstrous, anthropophagous maternity fusing *horror feminae* with what Simon Estok calls "ecophobia," in keeping with the Spanish colonial naming of the region for the mythical Greek Amazons.[21] However, a more nuanced interpretation becomes possible when one considers the aporia that emerges between the social roles of women in patriarchal society and the relatival clauses that Rivera associates with these roles, thereby undermining the traditional representations of "Mother Nature" in nationalistic humanist discourses relating to both agrarian production and the reproduction of the national citizen. Rather than "Man"'s consort and mother, the rainforest is married to silence (the absence of a symbolic order capable of nominalizing it and thereby recovering it for human instrumentalization) and engenders solitude and mist (the intangible, what is not commodifiable).

In that sense, what initially appears to be a straight-forward gothic inversion of the traditional Euro-American anthropomorphization of nature assumes quite a different form, disarticulating the human (in its overgendered aspect as Mankind) as the default point of reference. As I argued in my previous essay: "The face of Amazonia—which only appears when Cova is delirious with fever—is featureless, characterized solely by absence and abandonment. It signifies, yes, but what it signifies is the lack of humanity, the absence of culture, the collapse of the symbol into "soledad" (no culture, and thus no symbolic order), "silencio" (no signifier), and "niebla" (an immaterial signified). The face of Amazonia is thus no more nor less than the allegorical disintegration of the human face and its human(ist) features."[22] What persists in this maternal imaginary is thus not an idealized or even monstruous "Mother Nature," but rather something much closer to Lispector's theorization of maternity as an ambivalent position of permanently potential but undefinable responsivity and affiliation. The rainforest's somewhat anarchic (in the sense that the ordering principles of mother and father are characterized as silent, lacking, or absent), inhuman family is rooted in affective "family ties" rather than blood kinship, oedipality, and the patriarchal law of the father: "Your vegetation forms over the earth a powerful family that never betrays itself. Vines and lianas grant the embrace that your branches cannot give one another, and you feel empathy/solidarity with even the pain of a falling leaf. Your polyphonic voices form a single echo mourning for the falling trees, and in each gap new plants sprout and hasten their labor."[23] When humanist language/culture is silenced as the arbiter of intelligibility, the forest's sounds become meaningful, if ambiguous "multísonas voces" and an other mode of communicability—what I will call the "arche of the forest"—emerges as the ordering principle governing "solidarity" and affiliation, that is, the bases for sociality itself.

Biosemiotics and the Arche of the Forest

Rivera captures this forest arche or principle of order through figures of institutionality that evoke an inhuman biopolitics: the "green jail" in the earlier quote and a "cathedral." Continuing with the apostrophe, he writes: "You are the cathedral of sorrow, where unknown gods whisper in hushed voices, in the language of murmurs, promising longevity to the imposing trees as ancient as Paradise; they were already elders when the first tribes appeared and they await impassibly the sinking of future centuries."[24] Through these allusions to institutions, the personification of the forest expands into an altogether different figure: metonymy. Simultaneously itself and its others (a "tú" but not a "yo"), the rainforest draws into relief the constitutive tension in Euro-American ontology between subjectivity and distributed or social being. Rivera concedes personhood to the rainforest, but not subjectivity as such. Its singularity is always already an allusion to multiplicity, to its self-organizing systematicity as a collective locus of enunciation (those "polyphonic voices") that nevertheless can never fully inhabit a subject position. In other words, the rainforest emerges as an ambiguous collectivity or social assemblage that coalesces not merely around shared space (as in the Euro-American conceptualization of environment), but rather what Ursula Biemann, drawing on Eduardo Kohn's discussion of Amazonian Indigenous conceptualizations of biosemiotics in *How Forests Think*, calls "forest law," that is, a principle of cosmopolitical order—a systematization of multispecies relations—that emerges as a fundamentally semiotic infrastructure or discursive framework within ongoing, intra-active encounters.[25]

Given the historical functions of religion in social governance, the metaphor of the forest as cathedral immediately sequesters these multispecies intra-actions from the Hobbesian reductivism of viewing all interspecies encounters as actualizations of a single kind of relation—the only one that would be proper to nature in humanist political philosophy: predator-prey interactions between individual bodies, governed by the instinctual "law of nature," that is, the Spencerian "survival of the fittest." As the common space in which divine law is imparted, the cathedral is simultaneously a divine and a human institution, a space beyond the discursive strictures of daily sociality in which humans communicate with nonhumans. At the same time, nonetheless, divine law never exists by or for itself; it is always conceived of as the basis of and precursor for human law, as what invests human law with objective authority. Under divine law, humans are subjected equally to God's absolute sovereignty *in absentia*, which prefigures that of the state as the sole administrator of the coercive—in that one can never fully opt out—political contract of citizenship. As Foucault's analyses of biopolitical governmentality made clear, this is the case even in representative democracy: the state's ultimate monopoly on authority emerges precisely in the interplay between democratic political representation (popular sovereignty) and the law, in which elected lawmakers create institutions that supplant even those lawmakers' authorship, subjecting them and their constituents to (relative) equality under the law and the biopolitical institutions that, at the same time, uphold the law and re-enact the state through disciplinary procedures designed to create governable or "docile" bodies.[26]

Rivera's engagement of the cathedral trope in relation to the rainforest— and the reference to these "unknown gods" speaking a "language of murmurs"—thus extends far beyond the architectural metaphor comparing the forest's canopy to a cathedral's vaulted ceiling. The objective (divine) order of language is effectively displaced from the human ("Man" as the actualization of God's image on Earth) sphere of culture to these "unknown," ungendered vegetal gods who speak a hushed dialect that is unintelligible to humans and yet is apprehended as an "idioma" (language), in its dual connotation in Spanish of communal system of signs and communicative mode that is specific to a particular context. With the subtle expression "idioma de los murmullos" (language/idiom of murmurs) Rivera captures simultaneously the systematicity of nonhuman semiotic interactions within the rainforest and their uncanny or haunting quality for humans, since they transmit forms of meaning that are not mediated by the symbolic order of language—what Derrida frames as proto-writing or the arche, the objective set of discursive conventions regulating the systematic relations between signifiers and signifieds that is actualized and reenacted in each subjective speech act.[27] Rather, the arche of the forest emerges through what logician Charles S. Pierce calls indexicality and iconicity, that is, nested systems of signs that generate meaning (which Pierce reframes in materialist terms as "interpretants," or meaningful effects that put into motion acts of interpretation) through relations of perceptual likeness and/or direct material referentiality (a physical or existential relation to their "objects").[28]

These are concrete signs (versus the relative abstraction of the symbol) that are used and interpreted in different ways and to different degrees by all life forms, whether bacteria, insect, plant, or animal, yet these interpretative intra-actions always occur in a systematic way, defined by specific sets of constraints that can be understood in a broad, Derridean sense as iterative, that is, discursive. As biosemiotician Jesper Hoffmeyer argues, "it is not enough to sense: organisms must also create functional interpretations of the myriad of sensory stimulations so that these do not become isolated incoming impulses but are integrated into a form that the body understands and can act upon appropriately."[29] As he drives home, "life is composed of molecules, which manifest themselves as signs."[30] This is transparently the case with the relatively static or "digital" coding of DNA and RNA, but also in the active, selective permeability of cellular membranes and other forms of chemical recognition and signal transmission (as in the electric signals produced by ionic gradients in nerve and neuronal cells) that form the biological basis for what he calls "analog" or epigenetic codes involved in protein transcription and other modes of information transmission within cells, between cells within an organism, and between organisms.[31] In the latter case, the auditory, olfactory, visual, and tactile signs displayed by one organism are apprehended and internalized as meaning by another through the generation of molecular interpretants at the cellular level, which is what allows the organism to perceive and respond to them. It is in this sense that Hoffmeyer argues that biologists' standard usage of semiotic terminology to describe how cells function and communicate is not merely metaphorical, as those same biologists often claim: life in itself is fundamentally a semiosphere, that is a vast series of emergent (always in becoming), nested, dually coded digital and analog semiotic processes, which are what allow organisms to develop, metabolize, reproduce, and interact in other ways with the outside world.[32] As he summarizes: "in the biological world, signs incite the generation of interpretants in the form of actions which are future-oriented, inasmuch as living beings always seek signs for survival and for reproduction. That organisms react to signs necessarily implies that these signs are meaningful, and that they are directed toward latent activities, whether now or later."[33]

The circulation and transformation within material intra-actions of ontological meanings or, as Karen Barad sometimes reframes them, "matterings," underpins the entire system of ecological cycles, that is, collective life itself. I refer here to Barad's rethinking of meaning not as externally determined by a system of signs, that is, as the human inscription of matter within a series of nested abstract symbols, but rather as the mutually, but differentially intelligible systems of interpretants that emerge within the phenomenal intra-actions that constitute matter itself, which Barad insists is never a fixed substance or essence, but always an ongoing becoming or materialization within intra-action.[34] Furthermore, Barad extrapolates from physicist Neils Bohr's implication of the observer within quantum probabilities to contend that all chemical and physical phenomena (re-actions), even ones that do not involve living beings, are fundamentally semiotic intra-actions:

> I argue that phenomena are not the mere result of laboratory exercises engineered by human subjects; rather, *phenomena are differential patterns of mattering* ("diffraction patterns") produced through complex agential intra-actions of multiple material-discursive practices or apparatuses of bodily production, where *apparatuses are not mere observing instruments but boundary-drawing practices—specific material (re)configurings of the world—which come to matter.* These causal intra-actions need not involve humans. Indeed, it is through such practices that the differential boundaries between humans and nonhumans, culture and nature, science and the social, are constituted.[35]

In Barad's "agential-realist" perspective, meaning is thus not an abstraction inferred through the interplay between the subjective usage of signs and the external system of language, but rather a series of effects akin to Pierce's interpretants that emerges within these phenomenal intra-actions and simultaneously configures their possibilities through discursive patterns—that is, the range of potential ways of intra-acting that makes intra-action possible, but that are always only present as such within the intra-action itself. Separating conceptually this discursivity from the phenomenon in question would in fact consist in another kind of intra-action, since it would involve a human scientist acting within the intra-action as observer and enacting an "agential cut" that results in the abstract, epistemological ordering of these discursive patterns as "natural laws"—laws that in turn can never exist abstractly, external to the phenomenon, but only emerge in ongoing, serial intra-actions within phenomena.

Indeed, for Pierce, as for Barad, meaning always emerges from within intra-actions: "I define a sign as a thing that is so determined by something else, called its *object*, and so determines an effect upon a person, which effect I call an interpretant, that the latter is thereby mediated by the former."[36] By referring to the "person" as the object of a sign, he does not intend to subtract entirely the interpretative agency from the human; he simply means that the interpretant must always emerge in relation with the sign and its interpreter. Agency would thus consist in the recognition of the sign as such, in the production of and further response to interpretants, which necessarily occurs in relation to specific discursive patterns or possibilities that come into play within the intra-action in question. As Hoffmeyer drives home: "the process by which something gets recognized as something different is the root form of all *semiosis*."[37] It is effectively how, as Barad frames it, "parts of the world" become intelligible to each other in the sense that they become able to intra-act upon "recognizing," even if in seemingly mechanical ways (as in chemical signaling and reactivity), the signs of their material others.[38]

From the perspectives of both biosemiotics and Barad's "agential realism," agency thus consists not in conscious decision-making or interpretation, but in "knowing" how to intra-act with other bodies in an immanently practical sense, that is, in the enactment or reiteration of relational patterns or materialization of potentials within phenomena: "*agency is a matter of intra-acting; it is an enactment, not something that someone or something has.* It cannot be designated as an attribute of subjects or objects (as they do not preexist [the intra-action] as such). It is not an attribute whatsoever. *Agency is 'doing' or 'being' in its intra-activity. It is the enactment of iterative changes to particular practices—iterative reconfigurings of topological manifolds of spacetime-matter relations—through the dynamics of intra-activity.*"[39] Furthermore, Barad points out that this possibility of iteration necessarily marks these patterns as discursive, if not in an exclusively linguistic sense:

> Discourse is not a synonym for language. Discourse does not refer to linguistic or signifying systems, grammars, speech acts, or conversations. . . . Discourse is not what is said it is that which constrains and enables what can be said. Discursive practices define what counts as meaningful statements. Statements are not the mere utterances of the originating consciousness of a unified subject; rather, statements and subjects emerge from a field of possibilities. This field of possibilities is not static or singular but rather is a dynamic and contingent multiplicity.[40]

In other words, the range of possible iterative intra-actions effectively constitutes an arche not only or precisely in the Aristotelian sense of an originary "principle of being" that would be proper to a specific word or form, but even more so in that in which Derrida reframes the term, as the supplementary system of referentiality that emerges, actualized as meaning, in each semiotic act, always invoking and overwriting the traces of its prior iterations. In that sense, the arche of the forest would describe the full differential or range of possible intra-actions in which plants, viewed not as Linnaeus's taxonomical "Regnum Vegetabile" but instead as a specific way (set of formal constraints or "discursive" patterns) of intra-active being/becoming, of relating to other bodies as well as inflecting how animal and insect bodies relate to one another.[41]

This is certainly not to say that any given system of signs has no bearing in the emergence of the interpretant; it comes into play both in the constitution of the sign itself and in the associations it provokes in the one apprehending the sign. Nevertheless, this meaning can only arise materially from within the intra-action. As Barad argues, extrapolating from Bohr's theorization of the materiality of concepts as "apparati" working within phenomena and Foucault's insight that discursive practices produce, enact, and materialize specific forms of knowledge, "meaning is not a property of individual words or groups of words but an ongoing performance of the world in its differential dance of intelligibility and unintelligibility. In its causal intra-activity, part of the world becomes determinately bounded and propertied in its emergent intelligibility to another part of the world, while lively matterings, possibilities, and impossibilities are reconfigured."[42] Meaning is thus the network of differentially interpreted signs or signals that allow bodies to "recognize" (in a material, intra-active sense, rather than that of nominal identification), engage, and affect each other in mutual transformation. This becoming intelligible of bodies to other bodies in relation is necessarily a differential (that, is a series of different "values" or interpretations emerging within a continuum of possibilities delimited by the self-organizing parameters of the intra-action) rather than a unitary or universal process, since the interpretants that arise within phenomenal intra-actions necessarily "mean" different things (up to and including nothing) to different intra-actants within the relation, affecting them asymmetrically. For Barad, then, symbolic meaning—"language"—is only one form of semiotic intra-action that may come to play within a phenomenon, one that necessarily implicates humans; all intra-actions, whether involving language or not, produce interpretants that are simultaneously semiotic and material in that they are apprehended and acted upon in different ways and to different degrees by the participants implicated within the intra-action.

In this context, I argue that the tropes of horror and melancholy that Rivera associates with the rainforest in the second and third parts of *La vorágine* arise in large part from this intra-active, embodied encounter with an entirely other semiotic system, which is largely irreconcilable with the humanist conceptualization of nature as passive, silent, and ontologically subordinate to human interests. The displacement of humans as the sole producers and arbiters of meaning generates the melancholic sense of loss that Rivera captures in the trope of "pesadumbre" (the cathedral of sorrow), a sense of loss that indicates nostalgia not only for the constitutional order (given the absence of state institutions in Amazonia at the time Rivera was writing), but at a more primordial level, that of humanist exceptionalism itself, which, in this specific environment, is superseded by the law of the "powerful vegetal family," that is, forms of affiliation that are configured by a more-than-human grammar of intra-action.

Plant Familiarity, the Law of the Forest, and the Question of Betrayal

Rivera relates this more-than-human family (bound together by semiotic ties rather than genetic lineage) directly to a political order through the reference to the biopolitical institution par excellence, the prison (the "cárcel verde"). As in the figure of the cathedral, the "emerald jail" exceeds its allusive parameters as a metaphor designed to capture the curtailing of human perception by the rainforest's dense vegetal entanglements and the resulting loss of human agency, since the sense of entrapment within the Amazonian environment belies the modern subject's foundational claim of emancipation from nature's "tyranny" (that is, the individual's subjection to its own "human nature" or animal instincts as well as to external nature's "whims" such as food insecurity, disease, predation, and exposure to climate and weather), while the forest's ecological complexity negates humanist language's sense-making and instrumentalizing functions. The political institutionality of jails—their roles in the biopolitical disciplining of bodies—can never be excised from the word, even when used metaphorically, since a symbol can only function as such through the transference of bundled, if always fundamentally ambivalent connotations. What this green prison circumscribes or excludes from the forest's order is not the human species itself, since Cova and his companions are "entrapped" within the forest ecosystem—or semiosphere—and they encounter a variety of Indigenous human inhabitants of the forest, but rather the doctrine of human exceptionalism, that is, its ability to impose the hierarchical culture/nature divide by which the latter is subordinated to the former. Within the Amazonian rainforest, modern *Homo sapiens* qua Cova can no longer imagine himself as Mother Nature's favored son in an oedipal relation (the "father" being prior more primitive human generations), in which culture supplements nature through progressive technological instrumentalization, thereby claiming what Moore called Nature's free gifts (natural resources) as its inheritance. Here, the maternality of nature as the primordial basis for human sociality that must nevertheless always be dominated by culture is effectively subtracted from the equation in a way somewhat akin to Derrida's deconstruction of the ultimately exclusionary trope of democratic fraternity in *The Politics of Friendship*.[43] When nature can no longer be conceived of as humanity's mother, but rather as a cacophonous, multispecies family that emerges in the mother's silencing of the human symbolic order and haunting materiality ("esposa del silencio, madre de la soledad y de la neblina"), the very grounds for the social must necessarily be reconceived.

Cova and his companions become fully entangled within an entirely other form of (vegetal) sociality and an inhuman order ruled by an ambiguous law that comes into play not as prohibition (as in the Torahic "thou shalt not kill") or the prescription of citizenly duties, but as ineludible, systematic affectivity in encounters with other bodies within the rainforest environment. Enacted through silence (Lispector's desistence) rather than rights claims, the imperative imposed by forest law is to open oneself to the other, to the semiotic affectivity and heteronomous time of the nonhuman other:

"promising longevity to the imposing trees as ancient as Paradise; they were already elders when the first tribes appeared and they await impassibly the sinking of future centuries."[44] Plant time—the "promise" of ecosystemic longevity and renewal not despite, but through the iterative deaths of individuals—thus exceeds and destabilizes history, that is, the causal narrative explaining the emergence of human political institutions and the progressive technological instrumentalization and commodification of nature. As I discuss in greater depth in the next chapter in dialogue with Michael Marder's theorization of "plant being," apprehending this heterotemporality is what makes both ethics and cosmopolitics possible; it requires conceiving of time through the other rather than either the enclosed narrative trajectory of the subject or the metanarrative of human history. And clearly, it is what the Euro-American disciplinary division between human and natural/geological history is designed to circumscribe. The subordination of temporal multiplicity to human history potentializes the conceptualization of modernity as what Lenin famously called "uneven and combined development," that is, the paradoxical notion of universal human progress in which all other species and many, perhaps even the majority of humans, are left behind or sacrificed in the name of a purported species evolution toward perfection.[45]

Within this framework, Rivera's affirmation that the forest comprises a "powerful family that never betrays itself" poses a tantalizing problematization of both the Euro-American conceptualization of the human family as the social basis for polity and Lacan's famous affirmation in "The Subversion of the Subject and the Dialectic of Desire" that while animals (and by extension, all nonhumans) may mis-represent themselves in a variety of ways, they cannot "feign feigning" or "pretend to pretend," as Derrida's translator rewords it.[46] Indeed, Rivera's seemingly poetic statement becomes much more concrete when read through Lispector's profound exploration of betrayal in "The Crime of the Mathematics Teacher." As I argued in the last chapter, Lispector coincides with Derrida in deconstructing the key tropes underpinning humanist exceptionalism (that is, what ostensibly separates humans from other animals: consciousness, abstraction, language, clothing, cooking, culture, etc.), in effect placing into question the entire series of binomials that underpin the human/nature distinction, all of which are fundamentally rooted in conceptual negation rather than rigorous empirical observation, if such a procedure can be claimed to exist.[47] Indeed, recent scientific research has problematized all of these oppositions, reframing them not as questions of ontological difference, but rather as matters of degree, intensification, and multiplicities. For Lispector, in contrast, the quintessential human "freedom" is the possibility of betrayal within relation, a perspective that Rivera reinforces in his assessment of the forest as a "powerful family that never betrays itself."

This possibility of betrayal is not the capacity for "lying" per se, since Derrida notes it is a humanist projection to assume that animals are unable to "erase their own tracks," that is, represent themselves as something other than what their bodies indicate.[48] Lispector instead frames betrayal as the reversal of the passive decision of affiliation; that is, the conscious rejection of the demand the animal other places on the human, the disavowal of the traces with which it has marked the subject during encounter. And both Lispector and Derrida coincide in framing this betrayal as an act of representation, of the subjective overwriting of the traces of singular animals with the animal taxonomy, Derrida's animot. It is only by classifying the animal family member as "dog" in opposition to the human and by framing that dog as a variable (that is, one that may be substituted for by any other member of its species), thereby disavowing its singularity within the family relation, that the protagonist of "The Crime of the Mathematics Teacher" can abandon him. Needless to say, the mathematician would never say that one of his children could be substituted for by some other child taken from the streets. Betrayal thus consists not in trickery or even "lying" in the sense in which Lacan used the term—as "pretending to pretend"—but rather in substitution, in the conscious disavowal of the traces of the other, that is, of the advent of singularity in encounter.

Despite its reliance on displacing the singular with the categorical, this betrayal is not merely nominal or symbolic. It effectively implies removing the "animal" from the purview of ethical rationality (but not, as the ending of Lispector's story showed, from Levinas's "primary" or affective ethics) and thus exposing it to multiple forms of violence. The way in which this taxonomic betrayal of affective relations is carried out is proper only to the symbolic order, since iconic and indexical signs are always read as direct enactments of the traces of specific individuals, not species or classes of beings. For instance, when an animal senses a predator, it necessarily interprets that sign or series of signs (whether visual icons such as specific body shapes or patterns of movement or the indexicality of scent and sound) through an arche or systematic relation to prior meanings (some instinctually encoded, others inscribed in memory as learned behavior), but the interpretant that emerges within the encounter always actualizes the arche from within the intra-action as material presence, never as abstract, categorical meaning. In other words, the signs are interpreted as indicating the presence of a dangerous individual capable of producing certain bodily effects (in this case, harm) within the immediate relation. They would never allude to an abstract or indeterminate class of predatorial beings, any of whom could potentially cause harm at an unspecified moment in time. For the organisms within the relation, it is not a question of classification, but rather of potential effects.

Nonetheless, the affects provoked by the predator sign are not limited to the immediate present in a strict sense of the word; the interpretants that emerge in the relation are oriented toward the heterogeneous time of the singular other, to inferring its passage through shared space and projecting its future behavior. The other's past and future are thus the points of reference for the now of the interpreting agent, who is effectively living in the shadow of the other, fully oriented toward its traces. The other is not necessarily present bodily in that moment, but it is nevertheless fully present for the interpreting agent, if asynchronously, in a different, but proximal temporality. In short, the predator's traces or tracks are concretely present, even in its momentary absence as a totality or entity. In contrast, Derrida insists that the human symbolic order of language exists solely in the time of the subject, enacting and reproducing itself in each speech act (or act of reading). Substitution (or supplementation, as Derrida would say to highlight its systematic, accretive nature) is in fact its full material existence; the subject's enactment of the symbol in the speech act effectively overwrites the materiality of the traces of the other, erasing the other's presence. In other words, the symbol materializes as representation in the erasure of the other's materiality. It is in this sense in which the vegetal family can never betray itself, since its members do not engage in symbolic semiosis.[49] As an assemblage of singular individuals that emerges within heterotemporal iconic and indexical intra-actions, no one member can disavow another by overwriting it as a mere example of its timeless class, that is, as a variable substitution. All encounters are necessarily encounters between singular individuals, never between an individual and an institution in the humanist sense of the word.

From this point of view, the political order constituted by humanist law, itself potentialized by the pure abstraction of divine law (for which the absence of the author or absolute Other is always the precondition), can only be actualized through the betrayal of affective relations with nonhumans and, as Agamben and others have argued, human others as well, who are either overwritten through legal representation as idealized rights holders or animalized in justification of their exclusion from rights.[50] Nonetheless, the inevitable sense of guilt arising from this betrayal is always displaced from the subject to the humanist institution; the subject can never be seen as individually responsible in either a linguistic or a political sense for the violence inherent in the categorical erasure of the other's traces. As I pointed out in Chapter 3, the spatial regime of the zoo was what allowed Cortázar's protagonist in "Axolotl" to elide any sense of ethical failing in abandoning his relation with the axolotl. The question then arises: what forms of representation, and therefore sociality and politics, become possible in the absence of these humanist institutions, when the ethics of responsivity is not overwritten by the institutional enactment of the human/nature divide? What kind of "institutions" might emerge when the only law is that of open, ongoing responsibility to the other? While Rivera's allusion to the "powerful vegetal family that never betrays itself" hints at this other kind of sociality, neither the author nor his main character are equipped with the ontological tools necessary to theorize it. It can only manifest itself in the sense of loss and the gothic aesthetics of monstrosity, that is, abjection in the sense in which Kristeva defines the term in *Powers of Horror*.

The Politics of Indigenous Representation and the Colonial State of Nature

In what follows, I explore the cosmopolitical implications of Rivera's description of the rainforest as a plant family, amplifying and solidifying this admittedly ambivalent, poetic representation through the deconstruction of the colonial trope of the "state of nature" and a close look at Indigenous Amazonian thought regarding the politics of representation as rooted in what Viveiros de Castro calls "intensive filiation." I continue to draw on Lispector's theorization of desistance as well as Michael Marder's philosophy of plant being and ethical affectivity, although I will not address the latter's arguments explicitly until the next chapter. Given *La vorágine*'s denigrating, animalizing portrayal of native Amazonian cultures as hopelessly primitive and irrational, however, I am reading completely against the grain of the novel's deeply embedded, Eurocentric humanism. Relying almost entirely on nineteenth-century colonial, social Darwinist stereotypes about Indigenous cultures, Rivera depicts the only native Amazonian tribe with which Cova and his companions come into direct contact almost entirely in the negative: "the head of the family displayed a certain coldness toward me, which translated into a disrespectful silence. I attempted to ingratiate myself in several ways due to my desire that he instruct me about their traditions, their war songs, their legends; my courtesies were useless, because those rudimentary and nomadic tribes have no gods, no heroes, no homeland [patria], no past, nor any future."[51] In depicting native Amazonian cultures as socially, politically, and ontologically empty, Cova clearly engages in a hypereurocentric, taxonomical overwriting—a betrayal of the affective relations with his Indigenous hosts—that erases their presence and overwrites the encounter with the tropes of the Hobbesian state of nature.

Without a doubt, Rivera's portrayal of the Amazonian environment, its Indigenous inhabitants, and the rubber boom itself defers almost entirely to Thomas Hobbes's seventeenth-century theoretical formulation of the "state of nature" as one of permanent war, characterized by the struggle over resources between individuals who are free and sovereign in an absolute sense, owing no allegiance to any governing power and therefore living prior to or beyond the rule of law.[52] As many critics have noted, though universalist in its language, Hobbes largely formulated his theory in the negative, generating a binomial opposition between European states and Indigenous American "savages," a distinction necessary to justify European colonialism by positing the superiority of European political forms over what he frames as the anarchy of supposedly stateless (sovereign-less) Indigenous peoples.[53] In his formulation of international law, only modern nation-states could enter into diplomatic relation; these nationless Indigenous peoples would thus be incapable of collective political representation within the international order. Therefore, war could be waged against them without just cause (*casus belli*). In short, Indigenous peoples could not claim territorial sovereignty without being represented by a sovereign invested by the constitutional order of law in the European model.

While the language with which Hobbes frames his arguments is not usually explicitly colonialist, it follows closely the logic that had been simultaneously criticized and reproduced a century before by Spanish jurist Francisco de Vittoria during the mid sixteenth-century debate regarding the justice of the Spanish Empire's conquest of Indigenous American peoples. In the section of *Relectiones Theologicae* (1539) dedicated to the topic, Vittoria acknowledged that the land effectively belonged to the conquered Indigenous peoples, but he set the stage for the "civilizing the savages" argument that would predominate in colonialist discourse up through the twentieth century:

> although the aborigines in question are (as has been said above) not wholly unintelligent, yet they are unfit to found or administer a lawful State up to the standard required by human and civil claims. Accordingly, they have no proper laws or magistrates, and are not even capable of controlling their family affairs; they are without any literature or arts, not only the liberal arts, but the mechanical arts also; they have no careful agriculture and no artisans; and they lack many other conveniences, yea necessaries, of human life. It might,

therefore, be maintained that in their own interests the sovereigns of Spain might undertake the administration of their country, providing them with prefects and governors for their towns, and might even give them new lords, so long as this was clearly for their benefit.[54]

The overlap between the language that Rivera used in the quote above and Vittoria's justification of colonization cannot be understated. Indeed, Rivera's portrayal of the state of nature goes much further than either Hobbes or the even more explicitly colonialist John Locke, both of whom insisted that it was governed by the natural law of reason, which they essentially viewed as a proto-political, social drive toward peaceful coexistence and conflict resolution between individuals despite competition over resources.[55] In contrast, Cova systematically negates the existence of any "rational" structure in the Indigenous community: instrumental technologies ("rudimentary tribes"), private property and by extension territorial sovereignty ("nomadic"), religion ("no gods"), mythology and therefore culture and cultural history ("no heroes," "no past"), nor a nation state (no "patria") or any other political or protopolitical formation. Reproducing Vittoria's affirmation that Indigenous peoples "are not even capable of controlling their family affairs," the fictional Indigenous women in the novel engage in promiscuous sexual relations with any visiting male that can hunt them down like prey, thereby placing into question even the patriarchal, patrilineal family as proto-political social formation.[56]

Tellingly, this leads Cova to the conclusion not only that Indigenous people have no place in modernity (no "future"), conceptualized as the inevitable future of the human species, but it ironically places into question the validity of liberal humanism's universalizing idealism: "I felt incapable of any illusion/hope (ilusión)."[57] Nonetheless, as scholars such as Gabriela Nouzeilles have shown, this postcolonial paradox within humanistic universalism was a commonplace feature in post-Independence writing by Latin American political elites, almost exclusively of European or mixed-race descent, due to the tensions generated between the liberalistic political imperative to guarantee the individual rights and democratic political representation of all citizens and the hegemonic (at that time), Positivist doctrine of social Darwinism, which postulated that non-white races were biologically incapable of the rational thought and moral behavior necessary for civilized self-governance.[58] As many critics have noted, the counterpart to nineteenth and early twentieth-century Eurocentric humanism thus became either the political exclusion (despite economic integration as a source of cheap, unpaid, or enslaved labor) or genocidal elimination of societies that appeared unwilling or unable to acculturate into the political and economic superstructures of Euro-American modernity.

Rivera's disparaging representation of the Indigenous community has the effect of disassociating his own portrayal of the forest as a multispecies socius from its roots in those same native Amazonian ontologies, reappropriating it into humanistic representation as a post-Romantic, individualistic poetics of perception, which is ultimately what places it into the gothic paradigm of threatening, inhuman difference. Nevertheless, I have already argued that this fundamental representational betrayal fails in its attempt to overwrite the affective traces of both the Amazonian rainforest and its Indigenous inhabitants. Rather than resolving the fundamental tension between encounter and representation through the nature/culture dialectic, the narrative conventions of both nature and ethnographic travel writing enter into conflict with phenomenal perception, thereby revealing a fundamental instability or constitutive tension at the heart of the Euro-American conceptualization of representation itself. The glaring impossibility of a human collective existing without worldview, without culture, without memory, and without social or political structure effectively deauthorizes the narrator as its representative. In short, the Indigenous man's "derogatory silence" does not indicate his own culture's lack, but rather the narrator's failure to authorize himself as the Indigenous community's representative through ethnographic capture.[59] The geopolitics of language and universalist epistemology thus come into play in ways that further exacerbate Cova's inability to translate the forest's "idioma de murmullos."

Without a doubt, the eighteenth-century debate regarding the origins of rational governance in relation to this retroactively inferred, primordial "state of nature" weigh heavily even on current discourse regarding the nature of the modern state as such, which continues to frame Indigenous peoples in general and Amazonian peoples in particular as stateless or as living within the modern state, yet beyond or on the margins of its institutions. Far from a consensual basis for politics, however, the concept was as polemical as attractive for eighteenth- and nineteenth-century European political theorists, evoking and yet turning on its head Aristotle's foundational distinction between *bios* as the natural human tendency to form governments and *zoe* as the sphere of domestic (reproductive) life. Clearly, the rise of British colonialism—underscored by the founding of the East India Company in 1600—had much to do with Hobbes's and Locke's move to reappraise Aristotle's ambiguously species-wide perspective, as well as its polemical status in European thought. Given France's rivalry with Britain and the latter's aspirations to become a global empire, it is thus not surprising that Montesquieu and Rousseau argued against Hobbes and Locke in favor of the Aristotelian position, postulating the "state of nature" not as one of anarchical, warlike individualism, but rather as a primordial, self-organizing drive toward collective affiliation due to the fear of harm and greater efficiency in procuring nourishment. This primordial sociality would in turn have lead to the emergence of what Rousseau called a "general will" and Montesquieu framed as a guiding "spirit" or arche that underwrites the social contract and institutionalizes itself as law.[60]

Nonetheless, the French philosophers' arguments are not entirely opposed to Hobbes's and Locke's portrayal of the logic of rational self-preservation as the "natural law" that simultaneously generates the premised natural state of war and potentializes society formation. From either angle, the constitution of the political state as such is imagined in opposition to an inferred state of nature: in Hobbes and Locke as the sovereign imposition of the rule of law, and in Montesquieu and Rousseau, as the institutionalization of popular sovereignty that is potentialized by the natural drive toward affiliation, but that nevertheless is distinguished from it by its formal properties, that is, by the law, which places specific constraints limiting the full range of possible affiliative practices and structures. And, as I discussed in Chapter 2, the foundational constraint that Euro-American law imposes on affiliative practices and structures is the distinction between persona (rights holders) and res (property), with animals and all other nonhuman beings falling into the res category. In this sense, the state of nature performs the same work in each of these theories regarding the origins of political governance: it establishes retroactively a primordial state of indistinction between humans and nonhumans whose sole conceptual function is to implement that distinction (as the negative of the state of nature) in the construction of human sovereignty. In the end, it is precisely the persona/res distinction that enacts sovereignty as representational agency and therefore the ability to govern over/decide for others.

Rethinking the Grounds of the State from Indigenous Perspectives

It has become commonplace in anthropological studies since at least the 1980s to note that Indigenous languages and systems of thought do not articulate a clear-cut conceptual divide between humans and nature, at least in the same categorical and foundational sense in which these terms have developed in

Euro-American humanism.[61] In Indigenous languages, terms that are usually translated into European languages as "human" tend to be ethnonyms linked to specific communities and/or linguistic groups; they do not evoke a universal species or technocultural category. Furthermore, most Indigenous cosmologies ascribe to a familiar relation between humans and nonhumans, whether through totemic genealogies, the trope of interspecies marriage in mythology and storytelling, and/or broad, multispecies perspectives on what constitutes culture, community, and commonality. Given the non-existence of a clearly demarcated human-nature conceptual divide, it becomes a logical impossibility to speak of a political state in Indigenous societies through the premise of the state of nature as the primordial proto-political formation.

However, this conclusion transparently emerges from the aporetic status of colonialism in relation to individual freedoms within European political thought rather than from any empirical analysis of actual Indigenous political forms and practices. The vast archive of archeological, anthropological, and first-person testimonial evidence reveals highly complex, if diverse forms of political organization within even primary oral Indigenous societies that clearly do not possess "law" in the way it is usually thought of in Euro-American political theory—that is, as the "timeless," written legal code that supersedes intersubjective relations, generating the horizontality of citizenship through the impersonal or systematic authorization and actualization of political institutions.[62] Confronted with the aporia of organized societies without political institutions (state) as conceived of from within European cultural history, there can only be three possible approaches: 1) the Eurocentric, colonial dismissal of Indigenous cultures as stateless, which is clearly the route Rivera took; 2) the approach of more sympathetic and culturally informed authors such as Viveiros de Castro and Duchesne Winter, who refer to Indigenous Amazonian politics as decolonial "societies against the state"; or 3) a radical deconstruction of the concept of state that effectively disarticulates the state of nature as the foundational premise for governance, itself defined exclusively through the European model of the state as the meticulously coordinated movement between constitutional law, institutional biopolitics, and individual (human) rights rooted in the person/res distinction. I contend that only this latter option allows for an understanding of Indigenous governance and institutionality on their own grounds, as what I will call in the next chapter a "state of plants."

While the first perspective clearly follows Hobbes in framing Indigenous structures of governance as incompatible with modern geopolitics, the conceptualization of native Amazonian communities as "societies against the state" builds off Pierre Clastres's book of the same name and Deleuze and Guattari's expansion of Clastres's thought in their theorization of nomadology, locating Indigenous social structures as squarely oppositional or even deconstructive modes of resistance to modern biopolitics and geoontologies.[63] Through the lens of Euro-American political sciences, the structural case for this argument is persuasive in several senses, not the least being that many Indigenous communities continue to be marginalized from full political representation despite their legal status as citizens of modern nation states. One the one hand, this problem arises from the purposeful disempowerment of Indigenous communities from the political process through exclusionary mechanisms ranging from not providing civic education regarding constitutional rights or supplying accessible polling places or ballots in Indigenous languages to the gerrymandering of political districts and electoral fraud. On the other hand, Indigenous ontologies and political practices are often fundamentally untranslatable within the foundational premises of Euro-American notions of governance. To begin with, Indigenous cultures tend to conceive of territoriality as centripetal or nodal; a community's territory radiates outward from key habitational, resource, and sacred or mytho-historical sites toward relatively porous frontiers. These sites or nodes of multispecies intra-activity are enacted as such through emplaced cultural practices, rather than the cartographic delimitation of borders as in the modern state.[64] In that sense, Indigenous cultures tend to invert the Euro-American conceptualization of real estate (that is, land as sovereign possession).

In Indigenous thought, it is the individual that belongs to the land, while the land itself is conceived of not in a cartographic sense but rather in a holistic or communal one closer to "ecosystem." In other words, Indigenous terms that are (mis)translated as "land" in European languages include everything that is proper to it in an integral sense, not only its surface area and geographical coordinates.[65] As the Wixáritari people testified before the Mexican national senate, arguing against the granting of mining concessions in their territory:

> Territory, from an Indigenous perspective, constitutes the natural space of life, conceived of as a fundamental ecological unity, in which life develops in its multiple expressions and forms; this natural space is the source of knowledge and wisdom, culture, identity, tradition, and rights. In this sense, a territory integrates all of life's elements in its natural and spiritual diversity: the land with its diversity of soils, ecosystems, and forests, the diversity of plants and

animals, the rivers, lakes, and marshes. Natural ecosystems are considered by Indigenous peoples to be the habitat of gods that protect this diversity of life and who maintain the integrity and balance of the forest, rivers, and the lakes, as well as the soil's fertility, which allows the plants and animals to live and reproduce.[66]

Tellingly, the Amazonian Yanomami people, who will form the basis for my discussion of the arche of the forest in the following pages, do not have separate words for land and forest; the land is living forest, *Urihi-a*, which anthropologist Bruce Albert usually translates as "forest-world." For the Yanomami, deforested land is dead, a ghost of itself.[67]

Furthermore, since Amazonian Indigenous groups traditionally practice swidden agriculture, they frequently decamp and move to new areas every several years in order to allow the soil to recover its fertility and game animal populations to recover, a practice that from the point of view of Euro-American human geography could be considered "semi-nomadic."[68] And, as Deleuze and Guattari argued at length in *A Thousand Plateaus*, nomadism has long been viewed by settled/settler societies as antithetical to notions of "civilization" rooted in social stratification (labor specialization that gives rise to what Marx called "primitive accumulation" and thereby class divisions) and a political state that functions primarily as the guarantor of private property (the persona/res distinction) and the institutionalization and maintenance of the socioeconomic order. For "civilized" European colonizers, what Deleuze and Guattari call nomadic or "smooth" space is constitutively lacking precisely in that it does not display either clearly demarcated borders or the phallocentric, "arborescent" or "striated" symbolism of institutional architecture, which continually re-enacts public space as one anchored and presided over by the static, sovereign state, thereby making possible the oedipal transmission of political and economic power from generation to generation.

In terms of political structures, Indigenous Amazonian communities tend to rely on what Viveiros de Castro calls relations of "intensive filiation," rather than a sovereign governing power with absolute authority and/or the patrilineal transmission of power through prescriptive marriage alliances, both of which he frames as essentially oedipal modes of relationality aimed at assimilating difference into sameness.[69] While Euro-American political thought tends to frame tribal Indigenous societies as proto-monarchical "chiefdoms," that is, as patrilineal extended families headed up by a male leader who passes on his authority to a male heir, the reality is much more diverse and complex. What Viveiros de Castro refers to as "intensive filiation" embodies a specific mode of approaching relations as multiplicities, that is, of understanding them not through commonality (consanguinity), but rather through what Deleuze and Guattari call "disjunctive syntheses."[70] The seemingly subtle distinction between "filiation" and "affiliation" and is key: filiation denotes the centripetal movement of strategic marriage relations, that is, relations oriented toward maintaining the lineage of power, while affiliation denotes a more open form of relationality predicated on exogeneous difference rather than genealogical continuity (sameness). For Viveiros de Castro, this relational mode is exemplified by the Cashinua term *txai*, which he translates as brother-in-law or cross-cousin: "the common word for the relation, in Amazonian worlds, is the term translated by 'brother-in-law' or 'cross cousin.' This is the term we call people we do not know what to call, those with whom we wish to establish a generic relation. In sum, 'cousin/brother-in-law' is the term that creates a relation where none existed. It is the form through which the unknown is made known."[71] In other words, rather than the Euro-American atomistic view of the autocratic male/female couple at the heart of the social order, which is then amplified toward the paternalistic political order of the monarchy or the ostensibly horizontal brotherhood of democracy, both of which rely on the sameness of shared genealogy as the operative mode for conceiving of political relations, Amazonian Indigenous societies tend to view them in terms of diplomatic relations with people from outside the direct family relation.

In this sense, it is precisely the exogenous difference that potentializes the political relation: "if all men are brothers-in-law rather than brothers—that is, if the image of the social connection is not that of sharing something in common (a 'something in common' acting as foundation), but, on the contrary, is that of the difference between the terms of the relation, or better, of the difference between the differences that constitute the terms of the relation—then a relation can only exist between what differs and in so far as it differs."[72] Diplomacy, rather than sovereignty, thus becomes the primary mode of political agency. Interests can never be assumed to be shared, "family" interests, but rather common differences that must constantly be negotiated between actors in the relation. In that sense, the grounds for the political is not commonality, but what Marisol de la Cadena calls the "uncommons"—the terrain in dispute, the divergence that must be accommodated (not erased).[73] Therefore, this kind of political relationship cannot depend on the consensus/consent dialectic at the heart of the Euro-American "political contract" of citizenship, which in the end relies on the coercive discourses of paternalistic authority and self-sacrifice. As Locke himself noted, this form of authority is invested in the state not through free choice, but rather through "tacit" consent, which is necessarily both obligatory and enforced through punitive institutions.[74] However, if one ascribes to the possibility of a politics that does not emerge or enact itself through the nature/culture dialectic and the figure of the (human, male) sovereign, but draws different lines of inclusion and exclusion, one must reconsider the meanings of terms such as law, politics, and the state. The question thus becomes: in a form of politics in which the arche of power is diplomacy rather than sovereignty, what kind of institutions emerge to ensure the continuity of political relations? And what kind of "state" do they actualize, when the state is considered a "form" of governance in a material sense, that is, as the actualization of that arche in the present, through the enactment of institutions in relation to human and nonhuman bodies in the social construction of shared space or territory? This line of inquiry necessarily requires rethinking entirely the meanings of state, institutions, and the relations between ethics and law that underpin them. Furthermore, politics in Indigenous societies are never conceived of as a species-specific activity; they are always already cosmopolitical, not only taking into account the implications of political decisions for multiple species and the "land" itself, but envisioning governance itself as the domain of multiple species, all of whom collaborate in maintaining the conditions for the uncommons that is life itself.

Diplomacy as Foundational Institution in Yanomami Cosmopolitical Practice

Clearly, one cannot approach this kind of political difference through Euro-American political theories, which, when they address non-European political forms, have historically been biased toward justifying European colonialism. It is only through a close examination of Indigenous political forms and the recognition of Indigenous political thought as such that one can conceive of the possibility of a politics rooted in diplomacy rather than sovereign power. As a case study, the in-depth discussion of social organization and political practices in Yanomami communities in shaman and Indigenous rights activist Davi Kopenawa's *The Falling Sky: Words of a Yanomami Shaman* (2010; co-written with French anthropologist Bruce Albert) provides a great deal of insight into both the theoretical underpinnings and the actual practice of this kind of (cosmo)politics. Kopenawa's discussion of Yanomami politics underscores two key areas of dissonance with the chiefdom model as a proto-monarchy. First, there is no single leader invested with the authority to take decisions for others; if the decision making process is initiated by *pata tʰë pë* (translated by Albert as "great men," that is, male elders—although *tʰë* is not gendered, signifying "people," with *pë* indicating plurality), intra-community political decisions are made through a ritualized process of negotiation and partial consensus. *Pata tʰë pë* exercise an outsized influence on the decision-making process through the value assigned to their speech, but they rely on persuasion rather than coercion: "Our great men—those we call *pata tʰë pë*—usually address the people of their house a little before dawn or shortly after dark. They exhort them to hunt and work in their gardens. They tell about the beginning of time when our ancestors turned into game and they speak with wiscom. We call this *hereamuu*. Only the oldest men speak like this."[75] The legitimacy—that is, the persuasive power—of these speeches depends on two primary factors, both relating to the social standing of the speaker. Gender appears to be decisive (while Kopenawa states that some women become shamans, he makes no mention of them being allowed to speak in *hereamuu*), but the age criterion relates to the depth of the individual's ancestral knowledge and their position within family relations (specifically, the father-in-law's relations with his sons-in-law) more so than biological age. In other words, the authority to speak politically must be validated by the community as a whole not solely on the basis of the social standing of the individual, but also on that of discursive consonance with communal traditions and knowledge.[76]

Furthermore, it is evident in this case that the authority to speak is not the same as the sovereign authority to act in the collective interest. In the end, it is left up to individual community members whether or not to heed these *hereamuu* speeches and participate in collective action. There is no coercive enforcement; in Yanomami society, irresolvable disputes (including intracommunity political conflict) are ironed out through ritual, turn-based violence designed to expiate the emotion (anger) rather than impose a perspective or achieve dominance.[77] There is no winner in these bouts of ritualized violence, which are not fights in the sense in which the word is usually understood: the participants take turns punching each other's chests or hitting each other's heads with wooden clubs until both men agree not to continue. In this way, the emotions that could potentially escalate into a broader conflict threatening community relations are expiated in a way that does not subordinate differences to hegemonic sameness.

While everyday speech may discuss topics that undoubtedly have political import, it is not considered political as such until it is formalized during these intra-community evening *hereamuu* sessions. Similarly, political negotiations between communities are carried out through ritualized song-speech called *yãimuu* used exclusively in inter-community political meetings held during *reahu* funerary feasts, in which a hosting community invites another community to help lay a deceased person to rest. These meetings, held during the evening hours, follow clearly defined discursive procedures, in which speech is also regulated by gender and age. The session begins with a ritualized exchange of information:

> One young person from the hosts and one from the guests stand face to face and answer each other in song on the house's central plaza. One by one, the young people are replaced by others, forming new pairs. Then, once they have all finished, the older men gradually take their place and follow the same way, without stopping until the middle of the night. This is what we call *wayamuu*. The words of this talk are very long. They are like the news on the white people's radio. We use them to tell what we heard when visiting other people.[78]

Once *wayamuu* has concluded, the elders from both communities engage in *yãimuu*, a separate genre of song-talk used exclusively for political negotiations. As Albert explains, "the *yãimuu*, which involves the oldest men, is largely intended for negotiating economic and matrimonial exchanges (or disputes), as well as managing political and ceremonial relations. It is resumed on the last day of the *reahu*, just before the burial or ingestion of the funerary bone ashes of the dead celebrated in the feast."[79]

I should note that there is clearly a gendered sexual economy at play in these political negotiations regarding intercommunity marriages, in which the father offers the daughter (who must also agree) in marriage to a potential son-in-law in exchange for work obligations, at the same time forging political alliances with the son-in-law's community (most Yanomami marriages are exogamous). However, these Yanomami marriage arrangements differ from the oedipal logic of monarchical marriage alliances in two key respects. First, there is no single leader and no patrilineal transfer of political power, although Kopenawa does note that it is common for the children (including some women) of shamans to become shamans themselves, which in turn makes it more likely to gain the community's respect and become an elder.[80] However, this is not a precondition; anyone who shows aptitude for communing with the *xapiri* primordial beings (the translation of *xapiri* as spirit is problematic, as I discuss in the next chapter) may become a shaman following training and initiation. Second, the Yanomami do not engage in the patrilineal transmission of property; they do not conceive of land or the communal roundhouse as private property and, in fact, they destroy nearly all of a deceased person's possessions upon their death.[81] In this sense, the sexual economy associated with marriage in Yanomami society is clearly not oriented toward the accumulation and oedipal transmission of power and properties, but instead has to do with fostering collective work relations and establishing "friendship" alliances between communities, which essentially translate into pacts of non-aggression.[82]

As the case may be, Kopenawa explicitly frames these three genres of speech—*hereamuu*, *wayamuu*, and *yãimuu*—as political, in opposition to daily speech: "This is the heart of our talk. When we say things solely with our mouths, during the day, we do not truly understand each other. We do listen to the sound of the words addressed to us, but we easily forget them. But during the night, the *wayamuu* and the *yãimuu*'s words accumulate and enter deep into our thought. They reveal themselves in all their clarity and can truly be heard."[83] Tellingly, the content itself is not what marks speech as political; the same message may be transmitted during the day using normal speech, but it is not taken to heart by the listener. Furthermore, it is not the institutionalization of space as political (as in monarchical courts or congressional chambers in Euro-American political practice) that generates this difference, since these political forms of speech take place in the central plaza of the Yanomami roundhouses, which are also used for a wide range of purposes in daily life. Instead, it is the performative configuration of the bodies themselves that potentializes the political in a way that simultaneously evokes and deconstructs the figure of "congress" in Euro-American political thought. These particular forms of public speech, deployed in a specific social context and time of day, effectively "open" the congregated listeners' bodies ("enter our thought"), rendering them receptive to diplomatic rapprochement. Furthermore, despite the gender and age restrictions on political speech, the alternation of speakers assures that the process is not merely a form of indoctrination but rather an exchange of perspectives that is nevertheless distinct from a debate in the sense in which the term is usually conceived of in Euro-American political thought. The goal is not precisely to convince the other of the validity of one's arguments or of one's coercive power to impose hegemonic consensus, but rather to create a speech event as the collective production of intra-subjectivities in encounter.

Indeed, Kopenawa's references to the penetration and accumulation of words within the listeners' bodies during *yãimuu*, a trope he reiterates when discussing a variety of political and shamanic contexts, reveal a fundamentally different way of conceiving of both subjectivity and communicative intra-actions. Tellingly, Kopenawa uses similar language when explaining how he became an Indigenous activist: "these new words about protecting the forest came to me gradually, during my trips in the forest and among the white people. They settled inside me and increased little by little, linking up to each other, until they formed a long path in my mind. I used them to start speaking in the cities, even if in Portuguese my tongue still seemed as tangled as a ghost's!"[84] Diplomacy is thus not viewed primarily as the negotiation of interests, which become common through contractual agreements, but rather as the mutual incorporation of the other's words—that is, their irreducible perspective—into the body, which is conceived of as a multiplicity housing the traces of others, a topic I delve into in greater depth in the next chapter. This is why Kopenawa speaks of the other's words forming a path inside the listener's mind. More significant than the meanings of the words themselves (which could also be uttered in daily speech with little impact), the political act is defined by the incorporation of these traces of the other into the listeners' bodies, whereby the self is conceived of in relation to them.

In that sense, it is indicative that both *wayamuu* and *yãimuu* are song-speech; the asymbolic aspects of music (in that they do not evoke a direct relation between signifier and signified as determined by a symbolic order)— rhythm, melody, tonality—affect the listener's body in ways that exceed symbolic mediation. The sound of the other persists in the body in trace form, that is, as a memory that continuously evokes the singer in a way that words cannot, since, as Derrida made clear, words simultaneously defer to the arche of language (they gain meaning by deferring to the symbolic order) and are overwritten by the subject's self-affectivity (hearing themself speak, whether out loud or mentally) upon repeating them in the speech act. It is true that song can be imitated, but it is always a cover, an allusion to the other's song and an evocation of the way they sang it, that is, to their difference, their traces. In other words, the Yanomami conceptualization of diplomacy effectively requires a displacement from the symbolic order of daily language toward sensorial affectivity, which potentializes the understanding of the self as always existing in relation to the other.

The Arche of the Forest and the Origins of Cosmopolitical Speech

Furthermore, the Yanomami consider singing to be not only the political mode of speech between humans, but as always already cosmopolitical since song itself is learned from plants, animals, and their related *xapiri* primordial beings. Kopenawa states that, "Titiri, the night being [a Guan bird], taught our ancestors to use the *wayamuu* and the *yāimuu* in the beginning of time. He did it so we could warn each other about our thoughts and use that to avoid fighting too much."[85] Singing, the affective grounds for the political, is thus always an invocation of the nonhuman, who is nevertheless not seen as nonhuman, as the Yanomami believe that all *xapiri* and therefore their animal progeny view themselves as persons—that is, as human.[86] The truth value of song thus relies simultaneously on its affectivity (can music lie?) and its source of legitimacy in nonhuman beings, which, as I pointed out earlier in my discussion of biosemiotics, depend primarily on indexical and iconic signs that do not loan themselves to deception in the same ways as language. Ellen Basso captures this perspective concisely in her observations regarding the "musical view of the universe" of the Kalapalo Indigenous people of the Xingu river basin:

> Powerful beings are thus capable of inventing musical forms, whereas humans are capable only of copying those forms in their performances. Human beings can invent only through language, and their language should best be interpreted most broadly by understanding it as essentially figurative because of its main use in deception. Although humans are creative in contrast to other *ago* [beings/people], they are limited in their creative capacities in a way powerful beings are not because music is amenable to far more complex and highly varied, even idiosyncratic, interpretation than is language, and it subsumes or encompasses speech. In the myths, although powerful beings communicate with people by speaking to them, they are preeminently and essentially musical.[87]

Tellingly, Basso relates the Kalapalo perspective on interspecies communications to musicologist Victor Zuckerandl's affirmation that cultures that have a "musical view of the universe" intuit the biosemiotic relationality of ecosystems as a "science of the concrete," relying on sense perception and observation rather than the Euro-American deferral to the abstraction of faith and revelation.[88] It is in this sense in which Kopenawa downplayed the value of everyday speech for diplomacy; it is subject to misinterpretation and the possibility of outright deception, while song relies to a greater degree on the objectivity of affect (presentation over re-presentation) and the authority of these powerful beings, who could be angered if one misused their proprietary forms of speech.

While the *hereamuu* speeches given by roundhouse elders are not imparted in musical form, since their function is exhortation within existing community relations rather than diplomacy as such, they also acquire their authority from an animal *xapiri*, what Basso calls a "powerful being":

> To be able to make *hereamuu* speeches firmly, one must acquire the image of the *kãokãoma* loud-voiced falcon we call *Kãomari* [in Yanomami, the suffix -ri denotes this status of *xapiri* or powerful being]. It gives the words of our exhortations their strength. It comes down into us by itself, even if we aren't shamans. Then we let it settle into our chest, where it remains out of sight. It teaches our throat how to speak firmly. It makes the words rise out of it one after another, without getting tangled up or losing their strength. It allows us to deploy the words of a wise and alert thought in every direction.[89]

Once again, it is the integration of the animal *xapiri*'s *utupë* vital image into the speaker's chest that potentializes political speech, which adapts and trains the speaker's body to express an exogenous communicative form—one that does not emerge "organically" from the subject's own essence as self-expression, but rather actualizes nonhuman traces to access the universal biosemiotic arche of cosmopolitical speech. Like the musicality of the *yãi muu* speeches, *hereamuu* imitates the sounds of the "loud-voiced" falcon, drawing its authority from the falcon's affective modality, which both complements and exceeds the symbolic value—the meanings—of the words that are spoken.

Kopenawa describes a parallel process as part of shamanistic initiation, when under the influence of the hallucinogen *yãkoana* (the powdered bark of the *Virola elongata* tree) the *xapiri* who have "come down" to inhabit the shaman's chest reconstruct the shaman's vocal tract so that they may imitate their song and thereby be recognized as interlocutors.[90] This transformation—that is, the mimetic acquisition of an other experience of the body (the other's perspective on one's own body, which makes it other to itself) and exogenous forms of expression rather than a visible bodily metamorphosis—is thus the condition for engaging in diplomacy with the other. One may solely engage in political speech by ceding to the nonhuman other's traces and actualizing them within one's own speech as a distinctly nonhuman expressive form, that is, by effectively becoming other to oneself (the Yanomami use the verbs *nomãi*, to die, and *poremuu*, to "act/enter into a ghost state", to describe this process), to one's subjectivity as it relates to daily speech and sociality.[91] It is precisely this nonhuman difference that authorizes political speech as objective, that is, as indifferent to human deception and true to the arche of the forest.

Despite the association of political speech with animal *xapiri* like Titiri and Kãomari, these powerful animal beings are not themselves viewed as the source of these expressive forms, although they are their primary mode of communication; they learned them by imitating in turn the sounds of primordial *amoa hi* song trees planted by *Omama*, the creator deity: "all the spirit's songs come from these very old trees since the beginning of time. Their fathers, the shamans, merely imitate them, in order to let ordinary people hear their beauty. Do not believe the shamans sing at their own initiative, without a reason! They reproduce the *xapiri*'s songs, which follow each other into their ears like into **microphones**."[92] These *amoa hi* trees thus take on the function of the arche or archive of political speech; they potentialize both interspecies communications (between shamans and *xapiri*, for example) and political communications between humans, determining their iterative possibilities. For this reason, the singer is viewed not as the author of these songs, but rather as their actualizer or amplifier (thus the seemingly paradoxical image of ears as microphones); each act of singing is a reiteration and supplementation of this discourse in the Derridean sense. However, when the primacy of the symbol is subtracted as the essence of communication, supplementation takes a back seat to the trace itself; communication is about relations, about actualizing and maintaining fidelity to the other's traces more so than meaning itself, which is always in some sense deceptive—the product of an act of betrayal. The entire biosemiotic system comprising the forest thus relies on the actualization and amplification of this plant arche by all species, while political discourse itself coalesces around the fostering of what the Yanomami call *në ropë*, the forest's "value of growth."[93] From this point of view, the telos of diplomacy is to generate collective, multispecies work relations that foster ecosystemic continuity and abundance for all species. This is the relational ontology that lies at the heart of Rivera's ambiguous figure of the "powerful vegetal family that never betrays itself" and speaks an "idioma de murmullos."

As Lúcia Sá notes in her introduction to *Rainforest Literatures*, Indigenous aesthetics and cosmological concepts are ubiquitous in modern Latin American cultural production. However, these aesthetics are most often appropriated and decontextualized by non-Indigenous people for modernizing projects such as avant-garde art and literature, architectural and clothing design, touristic enterprises (including the visual tourism of ethnographic documentaries), and regional and national identity construction in which Indigenous authors, artists, intellectuals, and their communities rarely participate fully and whose benefits are most often not distributed equitably, if at all. Furthermore, as my reading of *La vorágine* draws out, this appropriation and commodification of Indigenous aesthetics necessarily requires the erasure of the ontologies through which those aesthetics emerged as meaningful cultural and political practices.

In concrete terms, this would imply a denaturing process by which those aspects of Indigenous aesthetics relating directly to the representation of "natural" entities are incorporated into the modern narrative of species progress as either primitive folklore superseded by modern ontologies or as modern proto-environmentalist tropes integrated into the pastoral or "nature writing" tradition of Euro-American humanism, while more abstract motifs become elements in modern design and mythological or social tropes are transformed into idealized historical symbols representing national pasts (in the case of heritage identitary narratives). The violence of this process of ontological erasure becomes quite clear when one recognizes that Indigenous cultures rarely if ever ascribe to the human culture/nature conceptual divide that upholds Euro-American concepts of representation, particularly in the humanist theorization of artistic mimesis and its negation in the avant-garde affirmation of aesthetic autonomy. Nonetheless, re-reading Latin American modern forms through Indigenous thought allows for both a critique of the colonialist procedures involved in the appropriation itself as well as the possibility of rapprochement between divergent ontologies, potentializing a cross-fertilization in which new forms of conceiving of the dynamics of cultural and political representation may emerge, particularly with respect to nonhumans.

Through a methodology of what Strathern calls "partial connections" and Viveiros de Castro calls "controlled equivocation," it becomes possible to arrive at an intercultural or "multinatural" (as per Viveiros de Castro) reconceptualization of the social as a multispecies social ecology and of politics as cosmopolitics. In this chapter, I have argued that Rivera apprehended the Amazonian environment as a multispecies, relational socius upheld by biosemiotic communications, even as his own hyperhumanistic machinery worked to overwrite affective experience with the tropes of nature writing and the Hobbesian state of nature. Reading *La vorágine* in tandem with Kopenawa and Albert's *The Falling Sky* reopens this humanistic foreclosure in a way that reveals that conceiving of environment as a multispecies socius is not exclusively the result of cultural difference (and therefore a question of multiculturalism), but rather a matter of acknowledging and responding to the signs of nonhuman others. The persona-res distinction becomes impossible to uphold as a rigorous ontological category once it has been acknowledged that that all relations, including human-nonhuman ones, are fundamentally semiotic and that perception itself is always already an act of intra-relation, in which one integrates the traces of both human and nonhuman others into one's own body and subjectivity. In turn, reconceiving of representation in this way necessarily leads to a reconceptualization of the relations between ethics, the law, polity, and the state as such. What remains, then, is to trace how this recognition can lead to a rethinking of ethics and politics, a topic I broach in the next chapter.

CHAPTER 6

The State of Plants and the Cosmopolitics of Friendship

We do not have laws on paper skins, and we do not know *Teosi*'s words. However, we have the image of *Omama* and that of his son, the first shaman. They are our laws and our government. Our elders did not have books. *Omama*'s words and those of the spirits enter into our thought with the *yãkoana* and dream. We have kept this law of ours deep inside us since the beginning of time by continuing to follow what *Omama* taught our ancestors. . . . It is thanks to his law that we do not mistreat the forest the way the white people do. We know very well that without trees nothing will grow on its hardened and blazing ground. Then what would we eat? Who will feed us if we do not have gardens or game?

—DAVI KOPENAWA

As this epigraph from Kopenawa's *The Falling Sky* makes clear, the Yanomami do not conceive of themselves in Pierre Clastres's terms, as a lawless "society against the state," despite being a primary oral culture without a written constitution or state institutions as they are usually conceived of from within Euro-American political history. This is not due to a lack of knowledge of either writing or Euro-American forms of governance; as Kopenawa's usage of terms such as "law" and "government" shows, the Yanomami have become familiar with modern political discourse since first contact with outsiders in the 1950s. This would particularly be the case for Kopenawa, who travelled extensively in his capacity as an Indigenous activist and agent of the Brazilian government's Fundação Nacional do Índio (National Indigenous Foundation), interacting with NGOs and Brazilian politicians to influence governmental policy regarding Yanomami territorial rights, health care, and police protection against the influx of artisanal gold miners known in Brazil as *garimpeiros*. In that sense, rather than a rejection of the concepts of governance and the state itself, what emerges throughout Kopenawa's testimonio is a fundamental reconceptualization (for his non-Indigenous readers) of both sociality and political representation, in which the forest is viewed not only as a multispecies socius in the sense in which Eduardo Kohn describes it in *How Forests Think*, but also a political form, a "government."

While the reference to the creator deity Omama and his son (the first shaman) may lead one to the inference that the Yanomami political structure is essentially theocratic, in which sovereign power is invested in the shaman as Omama's representative, this is not in fact the case. As I noted in the last chapter, Yanomami communal decision making is decentralized, relying on diplomacy across difference rather than political hegemony. Furthermore, the Yanomami concept of representation (the relation between form and meaning) and therefore political representation is diametrically opposed to that of Euro-American thought, a topic I deal with at length further on in this chapter. Since the Yanomami approach politics through common differences rather than consensus, a shaman would never claim to represent Omama's interests: 'Teosí [the Yanomami phonetization of *Deus*, the Christian god) is dead, as is *Omama*. All that remains of them is their name, their value of ghost."[1] Clearly, a theocratic chain of command requires the panoptic presence of a living (immortal) god, whose commands are executed by his human followers, invested with his authority. Here God is dead in the sense that he does not rule or act directly upon the world, but his traces persist in the form of his *utupë* vital image, which is not conceived of as immaterial spirit, but rather as the intra-active potential to produce specific material effects within relation.

Through shamanistic practice, Omama's and/or his *xapiri* representatives' *utupë* vital images are incorporated into the shaman's body, which makes it possible for the shaman to learn and re-iterate his words, which is to say, actualize his arche in the dual senses of law (as iterative pattern) and way of being or vital principle:

> I do not possess old books in which my ancestors' words have been drawn. The xapiri's words are set in my thought, in the deepest part of me. They are the words of Omama. They are very old, yet the shamans constantly renew them. They have always protected the forest and its inhabitants. Today it is my turn to possess them. Later they will penetrate the minds of my children and sons-in-law, then the minds of their children and sons-in-law. It will be up to them

to make them new. Then it will continue this way throughout time, again and again. This way these words will never disappear. They will always remain in our thought, even if the white people throw away the paper skins of this book in which they are drawn and even if the missionaries, who we call the people of *Teosí*, always call them lies. They can neither be watered down nor burned. They will not get old like those that stay stuck to image skins made from dead trees. When I am long gone, they will still be as new and strong as they are now.[2]

As I discussed in the last chapter, for the Yanomami, "law" is not enacted as objective discourse through writing, as in the Euro-American juridical tradition, but rather through desistance, that is, through communicative forms (whether speech or song) that defer to the other's traces. Non-deceptive words—the condition for speech to be considered political in Yanomami thought—are produced not through the truthful exteriorization of one's own perspective and interests, but by enacting traces of the other that have been incorporated into oneself by housing the other's *utupë* vital image in one's chest. They are nevertheless considered objective in the same way that the law is viewed as objective in Euro-American thought, as a discursive form that is egalitarian, directed to all, since its author is absent/dead (existing only in trace form) and therefore cannot form exclusive face-to-face relations with any one interlocutor. And traces can never lie; they do not encode any meaning in and of themselves, but simply mark the absence of an irreducible presence, that is, of difference, to which all meaning must nevertheless point. This is precisely why Derrida insists that the arche of language is always a form of proto-writing; meaning does not emanate as essence from the living subject that performs a speech act, but from the law of language, its constitutive, systematic relations between sign, speaker, and the traces of multiple others, including the interlocutor. Signs become deceptive through the subjective overwriting of the other's traces, but they can never be deceptive in and of themselves, as they lack intentionality.

For the Yanomami, the objectivity of the law emerges from the arche of the forest, that is, from the multispecies biosemiotic system potentialized by plants, wherein the other's traces are internalized as interpretants that, in turn, take on meaning as signs within the intra-action. As I discussed in the last chapter, the Yanomami believe that Omama planted *amoa hi* trees that serve as the archive of political speech, which is imparted primarily in song form during diplomatic encounters between humans and between shamans and *xapiri*, the *utupë* of powerful primordial beings. These songs are learned from the trees by the *xapiri*, who then teach them to human shamans in a transformative process whereby the shaman "becomes other" and sees the world from the *xapiri*'s perspective, a process that is also usually potentialized by a plant: the hallucinogenic powdered bark of the *yãkoana hi* tree. Within this framework, words are viewed metonymically, as imperfect translations of song; like the lyrics of any song, they bear a supplemental relation to the music itself, always referring back to it as much or even more than to the symbolic order of language and its arche of meanings, which, as I commented in the last chapter, the Yanomami view as clouded with deception (Kopenawa frequently uses the metaphor of the "mind filled with smoke").[3] In this sense, Omama is not viewed as some kind of primordial sovereign imparting law (moral order) from beyond the world, but rather as the absent source of the arche of the forest-world itself, which is effectively the re-enactment of his arche or vital principle. He does not manage or control the world directly, but he set the patterns of semiotic intra-activity that must be continually renewed in order to preserve the forest's health, that is, for the multispecies socius not to suffer hunger, disease, or even the return of the titular, primordial catastrophe (*The Falling Sky*), which always looms just over the horizon. It is for this reason that the Yanomami view the reiteration of Omama's words not as simple speech or induction into a moral compact, but as world-building.

Upon calling down Omama's *utupë* vital image (whether directly or in proxy, through the *xapiri*) and incorporating it into their bodies and "thought," the Yanomami actualize his way of being in their present, re-creating his modalities of intra-activity in their relations with the multispecies socius. Furthermore, this way of being was initially imparted to the forest's *xapiri*, who transmit it to humans (rather than Omama himself, who is generally "dead" or absent, although occasionally his *utupë* vital image may be called on directly by the most powerful shamans). The actualization of the arche of the forest thus becomes a kind of multispecies labor that relies on the institutions of hospitality and diplomacy to produce the forest not only as socius, but also as a state in its triple senses of ongoing state of being (or becoming), territorial form, and government. Following Omama through the actualization of his traces means re-creating the world, not only in the sense of the renewal of a culturally specific worldview, but also in the literal sense of producing material phenomena intra-actively in the sense in which Barad used the term: *"phenomena are differential patterns of mattering* ('diffraction patterns') produced through complex agential intra-actions of multiple material-discursive practices or apparatuses of bodily production, where *apparatuses are not mere observing instruments but boundary-drawing practices—specific material (re) configurings of the world—which come to matter."*[4] This process is considered

political in that it relies on the institution of multispecies diplomacy to establish, regulate, and maintain the collaborative relations that co-produce the
forest-world. As I will discuss toward the end of the chapter, the form of jurisprudence that regulates these intra-actions is what Derrida calls the "law of
hospitality" or "infinite justice."

In this sense, Kopenawa's discussion of Omama's words should be viewed
in similar terms to the relations between the Kichwa concept of *sumak kawsay* or buen vivir (living well) and the 2008 Ecuadoran constitution's rights of
nature and social well-being provisions, that is, as the nexus between social
praxis and law. However, while the Ecuadoran constitution aspires to transform Ecuadoran social praxis through the implementation of buen vivir as
an emergent cultural hegemony that looks to substitute multispecies well-
being for modernity's core value of development (extraction, production, and
consumption), in Yanomami society the arche of the forest is always already
hegemonic, as it is viewed as the source of life for all species. In that sense,
examining Yanomami political thought and social practice simultaneously
draws attention to the challenges that the buen vivir movement faces in transforming an embedded system of values and serves as a guide forward to what
Derrida called the "democracy-to-come" and Jason W. Moore referred to as
an "authentically multispecies politics of emancipation."[5]

However, it is extremely unlikely and ultimately undesirable that the
majority of non-Indigenous peoples would suddenly agree to reconfigure
entirely their systems of beliefs and values regarding governance and the
nature of the state to conform to the Yanomami worldview; in that sense, one
must engage at some level with the cultural history and political concepts
with which Euro-American readers are familiar in order to make "partial connections" that open the grounds for a rethinking of both systems. Indeed,
the Yanomami political system suffers from its own shortcomings, particularly regarding gender inequalities and the undemocratic exclusion of outsiders (*nape pë*) from political standing (although Kopenawa looks to address
this latter question precisely by framing his book as an act of diplomacy
aimed at engaging these same outsiders). In that sense, placing Yanomami
political thought into intercultural dialogue with recent Euro-American critiques of ethical and political relations will allow for both the deconstruction
and the rethinking of democracy, which, rather than a political system that
arises oppositionally from the anarchical free-for-all of the Hobbesian state
of nature vis-à-vis the sovereign (indeed, one must remember that Hobbes
was largely in favor of authoritarian governance), instead emerges from the
state of plants rooted in what, following Derrida, I will call the cosmopolitics of friendship.

Interestingly, the Yanomami perspective on plants as potentializing the orientation toward the other and therefore the basis for the cosmopolitics of multispecies diplomacy runs quite close to Euro-American philosopher Michael Marder's theorization in *Plant Thinking* of "plant-being" as the root of ethics. While Marder focuses primarily on exploring the nexus between plant-oriented phenomenology and the deconstruction of Euro-American ethical philosophy, reading his work in productive tension with Yanomami thought allows for the emergence of a broader cosmopolitical framework that can function across diverse cultural contexts without erasing the differences between them. Indeed, I contend that this kind of creative diplomatic rapprochement between seemingly incompatible ontologies is entirely necessary in order to imagine how the Ecuadoran constitution's rights of nature provisions and Pachamama/Nature covalence can function in practice, particularly with regards to the problem of nonhuman political and legal representation.

In this chapter, I draw Rivera's figure of the "vegetal family that never betrays itself" and Kopenawa's discussion of the arche of the forest into dialogue with Euro-American philosopher Michael Marder's theorization of "plant being" as the biological foundation for orientation toward the other, and therefore ethics, the social, and the political. Drawing on Levinas's formulation of the "first" ethics of encounter, Marder argues that plants' constitutive openness to their others underpins not only the metabolic food chain, but also the possibility of ethics itself, since he contends that all life forms participate to some degree in plant-like distributed being and heterotemporality. All living beings must necessarily be "open" to their others in order to interpret their traces as signs, that is, to understand the signals emitted or displayed by other bodies as interpretants relating simultaneously to their own body and that of the other, even if it is only to apprehend those traces as nutritional value or danger. I then draw on Derrida's re-reading of Levinas to draw out the cosmopolitical implications of this "first," vegetal ethics, particularly regarding what he calls the law of hospitality that prefigures justice (and therefore the written law itself), and thus the possibility of the state as the political form that imparts justice (some degree of equality) among its citizens.

Finally, I return to Kopenawa's discussion of subjectivity as an emerging, relational multiplicity housing the traces of the other, which underpins Yanomami cosmopolitical practice, to argue that Derrida's insistence in *The Politics of Friendship* that any form of governance that can be called democratic must maintain fidelity to the law of hospitality cannot exclude nonhumans, since it relies on the premise of a constitutive openness to the other prior to subjectivity or nominalization (the law). Although Derrida stops short of linking explicitly this "democracy to come" with his discussion of animal responsivity—and therefore ethical standing with respect to humans—in *The Animal that Therefore I Am*, the reconceptualization of politics as cosmopolitics is the logical consequence of this line of argumentation. Tellingly, Derrida extrapolates the origins of the state itself from Levinas's theorization of justice as what substitutes/supplements for the law of hospitality when the face-to-face encounter is interrupted by a "third" person (who demands equal hospitality); the state in its most primordial form is the superstructure that administers justice between citizens who may never encounter one another. Furthermore, he explicitly questions Levinas's exclusion of the animal as a potential third in this relation, noting that Levinas was forced to recur to the animot to deny the animal either ethical or political consideration. Finally, I argue that Yanomami political practice constitutes a real life example of how this kind of cosmopolitics might look, in which governance is not viewed as the primal emergence of monarchical or popular sovereignty from the anarchistic state of nature, but rather as the amplification of plant being and biosemiotic intra-activity into a multispecies democracy underpinned by the twin institutions of hospitality and diplomacy. It is in this sense in which I will refer to Yanomami politics as a state of plants underpinned by a cosmopolitics of friendship.

Plant Being as the Arche of the Social

In *Plant Thinking*, Marder contends that plants' excessive vitality and radical, absolute openness to their others (being without interiority) pose ongoing, irreconcilable challenges to the philosophy of ethics and political ideologies, perpetually deconstructing the Euro-American metaphysics of the sovereign subject that uphold modern political economies. He argues that the distributed vitality and "temporal heteronomy" of plants—in that their own parts sprout, grow, flower, disseminate, and decay at different rates, thereby undermining the concept of the unitary individual as a spatial and temporal totality—is not limited to vegetal life, but is in fact reflected in all living bodies, if one takes into account the differential biorhythms of apoptosis and cell regeneration in human and animal organs, for instance. This temporal heteronomy is thus proper to humans as well, who by privileging its materiality over the abstract metaphysics of the autonomous, sovereign subject, may engage in "plant thinking," that is a post-subjective reconceptualization of being as heteronomy or the proliferation of multiplicities.[6] In that sense, Marder's thought clearly parallels the Yanomami understanding of personhood as a relational becoming-with in multiplicity through the actu-alization of the traces of others, a process that both ontologies view as being potentialized through the affective arche of plant forms.

Tellingly, Marder frames this seemingly intentional act of deferring to "plant thinking" not as sovereign decision (which would ultimately subordi-nate it to self-identity or the unity of mind), but rather as a form of desistance akin to that proposed by Lispector. In order to apprehend a plant's temporal heteronomy, one must "turn one's back" on it, effectively renouncing the appropriation of the plant's time and therefore being:

> to turn one's back to the plant is to be no longer conscious of it, disrupting the intentional comportment that relentlessly and futilely projects human ex-pectations, rhythms, and durations onto vegetal and all other types of being. Distraction from the vegetal other dispenses its otherness back to the time of life qualitatively different from human existence. In the gap, formed as a re-sult of interrupting the relation between human and vegetal temporalities, the time of the plant finally discloses itself, albeit not as pure temporality but as a relative spatial increase.[7]

It is this encounter with the plant's differential temporality and distributed spatiality—that is, its seemingly imperceptible growth/movement—that makes it possible to conceive of our body's own heteronymy as an emerg-ing assemblage of multiplicities always in constitutive, ongoing relation to its own integrants and its external others. In this sense, Marder's focus on plant biology and temporality runs complementary to the Yanomami theo-rization of the role of plant affectivity in opening the subject to the traces of the other and thereby the self as multiplicity in heteronomous, intra-active correlation with its others.

In turn, Marder posits that "plant thinking" forces a reconceptualiza-tion of both ethics—in the sense of the formal system of moral judgements governing one's relation to the other—and politics, conceived of in the lib-eral tradition as either the sovereign or constitutional (in representative democracy) power to represent and make decisions for the other. Revisiting Kant and Levinas, Marder effectively argues that all orientation toward the other—the grounds for politics itself—is made possible by "plant-being." As I have already mentioned, the premise underpinning this affirmation is that humans partake in this plant-like mode of distributed being (which, refer-encing Aristotle's discussion of *arkhe ton zoon* as the "principle of animal being," he frequently calls "plant soul") through our own semi-autonomous, self-organizing cellular networks, despite not being coincident with plants due to the primacy afforded our central nervous system and our induction into the symbolic order of language as speaking subjects.[8] Without a subjective sense of self, vegetal life "throws itself toward its others" (everything that is external to its body—sunlight, water, nutrients, predators, etc.) in the movement of absolute exteriorization that Levinas posits at the heart of ethics, in that it disregards the sense of self-primacy and preservation and is "indifferent to the empirical demands of need and its satisfaction."[9] In its most primal, Levinasian sense, this "unconsciously intentional" movement toward the other lies at the heart of sociality itself, preceding even the ostensibly libidinal drive for affiliation. Furthermore, it poses one of the most vexing questions for both evolutionary biologists and political theorists such as Hobbes and Locke, who are generally unable to explain the excesses of altruism without recurring to the highly reductive supposition of increased chances of collective survival and therefore reproduction. As well known ethologists such as Frans de Waal have demonstrated convincingly, the telos of reproduction does not satisfactorily explain many aspects of even the most rudimentary social behavior among animals, including affective modes of relationality such as empathy, sympathy, and mourning, which sometimes cross even species boundaries.[10] For Marder, then, the possibility for ethics would arise in the simultaneity of these two modes of being or becoming, one consisting in a plant-like unconscious formal orientation entirely toward the other, the second in a reflexive, interiorizing movement toward the self, always already in constitutive relation with multiple others.

This reframing of the basis for ethics as plant-like absolute openness to the other becomes political in that plant being, in its excessive, heteronomous vitality—that is, its constant outward growth beyond what is necessary to sustain its own survival—deconstructs the political economy of appropriation at work in both representative democracy (the appropriation of others' interests) and economic extractivism, particularly with regards to the metabolic logic that capitalism claims for itself as rooted in "natural" (i.e. predatory and therefore evolutionary) competition over resources and social power. In its unending "gifting" of its parts, the wasteful overproduction and expenditure of seeds, fruits, flowers, and leaves toward the other, plants are simultaneously subjected to and exceed the commodification of others' labor (whether human or nonhuman) that underpins primitive accumulation.[11] In this way, what environmental historian Jason W. Moore referred to as "Nature's free gifts" or, in his more recent work, Nature's unpaid labor, constitutes through its very excess in relation to commodification (the social

production of exchange value through abstract labor equivalence) the underlying possibility of unalienated freedom itself, since what is freely gifted can
never be fully commodified as such.[12] Its value as gift is always relational at an
affective level, in that gifting generates an asymmetrical social debt between
individuals and/or collectivities, rather than transactional in the commercial
sense of exchange based on equivalent labor values. In other words, a gift
may be appropriated and commodified for exchange, but its prior status as
free gift always haunts its commodification in trace form, making visible the
arbitrariness (supplementarity) of the exchange value it has been assigned
and pointing back to the disrupted relation with the gifter as its primordial,
if "erased" and therefore unrecoverable value. In fact, as Moore's deployment of the term "Nature's free gifts" suggests, one might posit that the
Euro-American concept of Nature itself refers precisely to this aporetic relation with nonhuman beings (or bodies, if one includes all material forms,
not only living ones`, in that human agency is largely delimited through the
expropriation of what is always already "gifted" through its more or less passive or unintentional openness to its others.[13]

In turn, this gifting toward the undefined (if not abstract) other is what
makes possible collective life—life in society—as such: "the nascent teleology of vegetal life is malleable enough to blend with the ends of other
beings, for in plants the *teloi* are not 'elaborately articulated.'"[14] Indeed, evolutionary anthropology has long theorized that the domestication of plant
led to the emergence of complex human social orders, which, of course, were
never solely human. Following Marder's argumentation, this could only occur
because plant being is open to the human telos of food production, which
nevertheless is still not full instrumentalization (or later, commodification)
since it depends entirely on plant reproduction. At the same time, one must
necessarily acknowledge that by cultivating plants, humans also open themselves to plants' temporal heteronomy and their own implicit teloi, collabo-
rating in their growth and reproduction.

Rather than framing society as a collective, human project that coalesces
around the shared telos of more efficient instrumentalization of nonhuman
others through forceful objectification, then, collectivities of any kind would
be primordially potentialized precisely in the openness to "common differences"—that is, the multiplicity of teloi, distinct ontologies, and diverse forms
of agency that coproduce relationally what we usually call an environment
(whether "natural" or cultivated, if that distinction can honestly be made in
any environment inhabited or frequented by humans), but which more accurately would be described as a multispecies society. In its "unconsciously

intentional" orientation toward the other, free to at least some degree from the tyranny of the "empirical demands of need and its satisfaction" as well as the ideological strictures of subjectivity, that is, the subordination of the individuated self to the hierarchy of values embedded within the symbolic order of language, the plant prefigures the possibility of collective, multispecies collaboration toward the diverse, but nevertheless shared ends of maintaining life systems. From Marder's point of view, then, plants do not anchor ecosystems simply as the lowest living strata of the metabolic (food/energy) pyramid, but rather as the form of being that makes possible the complex web of reiterative interspecies intra-actions that are life-in-relation itself.[15]

This would be true in at least two senses. On the one hand, plants prefigure the ontological possibility of freedom, defined in the humanistic sense as the possibility of imagining or projecting one's future self as other (that is, the possibility of change as such). For Marder, the foundational potentializing movement of this kind of ontological freedom is carried out by plants in their processing of nutrients and solar energy, thereby making possible its iteration in other life-forms: "when [a plant] turns mineral substances into its own means of nourishment, for instance, it extricates them from their immediate existence, dispensing to them new ontological possibilities."[16] In a material process that underwrites the arche of all biosemiotic meaning (and therefore life itself), the plant's identification, processing, and internalization of seemingly inert, crystallized structures into material and energetic flows figures ontological freedom at its most primordial formal level, as the possibility of liberation from prior discursive strictures that emerges within phenomenal intra-actions due precisely to the transformative potential of encounter with others. In other words, through their metabolic processing of nutrients, water, and sunlight, plants potentialize the possibility of formal differentiation and therefore the system of signs, since the sign emerges precisely in the difference between the body and its meanings in relation with other beings.

Furthermore, as both Derrida and Hoffmeyer point out repeatedly, all semiotics are oriented toward the future; the speech act (or performative act in iconic and indexical signs) in the present is always superseded by the persistence of the sign toward the future interpretation of the other, even if this occurs only milliseconds later.[17] In other words, relations never emerge as such in the moment of encounter, but rather always point to the reiteration of the encounter in the undefined future through the ongoing interpretation of the signs of the other, which is what consolidates the encounter as an event (in the sense of the rupture of continuity, that is, change). In making possible cascading chains of semiotic associations and future relations, plants thus configure the arche of biological meanings (that is, the ever-expanding, entangled series of iconic, indexical, and symbolic signs) for all species, and with it the interpretative freedom that, according to Hoffmeyer, reaches its greatest complexity in human symbolic representation.[18] This freedom is not necessarily voluntaristic (the product of intentionality), but refers instead to the possibility of formal differentiation, that is, of becoming other to oneself through the relation with the other.

In this sense, the "free" association that we view as the essential property of human systems of signs does not except or excerpt the human from the multispecies socius, but instead always ultimately alludes back to it, whether through mimesis or anti-mimetic modes of representation. The ability to imagine oneself as other is fundamentally semiotic, one that emerges in the relation between the materiality of the body in its present and the future possibilities opened through the interpretant, that is, the encounter with the signs of the other. In other words, the arbitrariness that Saussure identified at the heart of the signifier/signified relation is not truly groundless or immaterial, as the symbolic order of language always bears a supplemental relationship (a following) to the plant-based arche of life itself. Indeed, as Hoffmeyer underscored, what we call "life" is an interconnected series of self-catalyzing metabolic systems, systems that are apprehended by individual organisms and the cells that comprise them as signs that must be interpreted in a self-referential way: "it is not enough to sense; organisms must also create functional interpretations of the myriad of sensory stimulations so that these do not become isolated incoming impulses but are integrated into a form that the body understands and can act upon appropriately."[19] While "meaning," which Pierce more accurately described as the "interpretant," properly emerges in the triadic relation between a sign, its interpreter, and the mediation of the semiotic system, the sign's concrete referent always haunts the relation in its very substitution by the sign. This is why Derrida insists that the trace inhabits the interval between signifier and signified. And clearly, the trace of the other, that is, difference itself, can never be mediated as such (it is always an unassimilable absence) and thus can never be considered truly arbitrary if one ascribes to the Latin etymology of *arbiter* as the act of judgement.

Indeed, the arbiter of language is clearly the arche itself, which, in Derrida's thought, effectively constitutes the other of the trace (the referent's absence in triadic relation with the subject's speech and the arche of language). In other words, the plant arche (again, composed of iconic and indexical signs) always haunts the symbolic order of language in trace form, as what language erases or overwrites; and it is that differential—generated in the act of erasure—that potentializes the symbol as such. Beginning with the encounters of the most primitive of plant forms, photosynthetic prokaryotes and eukaryotes, with their others (minerals, water, sunlight), cascading series of differentials form, all of which are potentialized by the plant's semiotic recognition of nutrients as such and subsequent transformation of them into its own body parts, which in turn become signs for other beings, all of whom in turn overwrite the plant's interpretants with their own meanings, but simultaneously evoking what they erase as their point of reference. Furthermore, semiotic complexity emerges from within the intra-actions between these cascading series of signs at different scales, as multicellular organisms acquire greater capacity for reading and processing signs.[20] The metabolic web anchored by plants is itself the semiosphere; life is semiotic intra-action potentialized by plants and supplemented and complexified by each species as it engages its multiple others phenomenologically, through their signs.

At the same time, the plant's integration of its others into its own heterogenous body while simultaneously proffering that body to others makes possible the very form of the assemblage, that is, of distributed being or becoming in collectivity. Plant being dismantles the social Darwinist conceptualization of eating (and therefore being) as a hierarchy of predation, that is, as the capture, objectification as food, and devouring of "lower-order" individual organisms by autonomous, more powerful individuals; here being in collectivity emerges simultaneously as a taking of nourishment from diverse others, thereby transforming its possible ontological "meanings," and returning it to others for whom its meanings will necessarily transform yet again according to their own biological imperatives and the context of the eating intra-action.[21] This is to say that what a particular nutrient that is searched out by a specific plant means to the plant for its own growth will necessarily be transfigured when a human, for instance, eats the fruit of that plant; the human would not find the particular nutrient meaningful in the form in which it is absorbed by the plant, but it becomes meaningful to the human through the assemblage of the fruit (a utility that also engenders meaning-producing epistemological practices such as agriculture and science that reinscribe the meaning of the nutrient in question). The fruit thus gains systematic meaning in potentializing the lives of others, the human, insects and animals that eat it, and the plant's own progeny, since the fruit's seeds may germinate and produce new plants, often disseminated by its eaters.

Furthermore, fruiting cannot be conceived of within the logic of sacrificial exchange, since it does not require the gifting or exchange of the plant's life or necessarily affect the plant's own growth adversely. This would largely be the case even with the consumption of the plant's leaves (as in grazing), since most plants are able to regrow them as long as the trunk or even only the roots remain intact. This excessive gifting to the other thus opens a pathway toward a politics that is not founded upon sacrifice, whether that of Agamben's "bare life" (the constitutive exclusion of the *Homo sacer*, which would necessarily always be prefaced and made possible by the foundational sacrifice of nonhumans to the human order of politics) or that of individual freedoms in order to gain rights within a social contract. Rather than the sacrifice of one form of materiality or practice to sustain or engender another, then, this cycle hinges on the ontological transformations of heteronomous meanings associated with particular bodies by its others in systematic relation.

Traces, Vital Images, and the Politics of Gifting in Yanomami Thought

This plant ethics—gifting one's traces to the other through openness and potentializing the heteronomy of the self through relational intra-actions—underpins the entire social ecology and representational economy in Yanomami thought. Unlike the Euro-American framing of exchange—and thus the basis for sociality—as rooted in the bartering of discrete meanings, goods, and services of equal value between sovereign subjects, the Yanomami view it as the intra-active enactment of a relation, in which the exchange or, more often, act of gifting forges a link between the participants that is not only emotional, but also fundamentally material, as it involves gifting part of oneself. In this sense, Yanomami exchange, including diplomatic speech and shamanistic practice, is oriented toward establishing friendship relations within affective encounter, in which all involved parties incorporate traces—whether words, sentiments, or aspects— of the other.

This is the case even in what Euro-American cultures would consider commercial exchange. For the Yanomami, trading with outsiders is not oriented primarily toward generating profit (that is, accumulation) or even the symmetrical exchange of goods of equal value, but rather gifting the traces of oneself to the other in order to establish relations of friendship: "we generously barter our goods in order to spread friendship among ourselves. If it were not so, we would be like the white people who constantly mistreat each other because of their merchandise. When visitors covet the goods we possess, we are sad to hear them complain about how they lack so much and to seem to desire them so strongly. So we quickly give away these things to gain their friendship."[22] Furthermore, the Yanomami believe that the gifted items bear the traces (õno) of the gifter, which endows the friendship relation with a materiality that is largely absent from Euro-American conceptualizations of relation: "we think that it is by acquiring a trace of another person that we become his friend."[23] This is not to say that the Yanomami do not view friendship as an emotional bond, but rather that the emotional connection is itself envisioned as fundamentally material, as a literal housing of part of the other. In the Yanomami materialist perspective, there is no clear division between the psychological, what in the Euro-American tradition would be viewed as the spiritual, and the physical realms; they are simply different modes of affectivity (that is, of being with) that converge in the coproduction of the real.

As a case in point, the Yanomami do not have a word that is equivalent to the Euro-American concept of "spirit," which Kopenawa deploys in Portuguese precisely to mark the equivocation of Albert's translation: "The *xapiri* are the images of the *yarori* ancestors who turned into animals at the beginning of time. This is their real name. You call them '**spirits**' but they are other."[24] Given Kopenawa's contact with Christian missionaries from a young age and his decades of national and international work and travel, he is clearly well aware of the meanings of the term "spirit" in common usage in Euro-American culture, which is why he rejects it as a translation for *xapiri*. Indeed, this difference hinges precisely on the nature of the spirit in Euro-American ontologies, which denotes simultaneously the immaterial or symbolic and the essential, whereby the abstract takes ontological precedence over the material. Kopenawa takes issue with the Portuguese word "espírito" in both these senses. For the Yanomami, the *utupë* vital image (of which *xapiri* are the kind specific to nonhuman beings) is neither immaterial nor essential, at least in the sense of an indivisible identity, since even species identities are mutable in the Yanomami ontology and the animal *xapiri* in particular are viewed as primordial humans who transformed into animals following a catastrophic event. Since the Yanomami conceive of identity as a continual becoming-with traces of others, the *utupë* cannot denote or symbolize the principle of immutable, sovereign identity in the same way as the soul in Euro-American humanist tradition.[25] In fact, Albert studiously avoids this translation, likely for this very reason. Instead, it alludes to a form of materiality that the traditional Euro-American conceptual division between the body/soul, symbol, or mind effectively occludes: the latency of both potential relations and unactualized material forms within all bodies.[26]

In Euro-American thought, these latent forms are typically viewed as immaterial since they exist as potentials until they are actualized in material form. However, from a strictly materialist or empiricist point of view, those potentials must necessarily be embedded within bodies themselves, not exist as abstractions beyond the material world that magically actualize themselves in material form. In other words, forms cannot antecede bodies, but instead must exist as possibilities within the bodies' own range of physical properties; when specific physical properties are activated through intra-actions with other bodies/energetic flows, they configure themselves as a series of cascading effects that converge in and maintain a particular form (which nevertheless can only be said to exist statically in the instant of observation).[27] In this sense, the *utupë* refers not to a generalized form or formal essence itself (since bodies are mutable), but rather to the potential for the emergence of a range of self-organizing patterns within specific intra-actions. From this point of view, the body is an actualization of the *utupë*'s formal possibilities within the parameters of specific relations with others. This is why the Yanomami word for body, *siki*, literally means "skin"; it denotes the superficiality of form (in a physical, non-moralistic sense) with respect to emergent potentials. Indeed, the Yanomami "change" skins and thereby form through body painting and donning *matihi* (in this usage, ritual adornments belonging to the *xapiri*), a process they view not as mere spectacle, but as activating the traces of other beings to become other themselves.[28]

Viveiros de Castro emphasizes that these different forms are viewed not as reified objects, but rather as distinctly subjectival or agential forms; changing forms is also changing perspective, that is, a subjectival shift whereby one assumes the perspective of an other without ceasing to be oneself, since one's *utupë* persists (again, not as an essence, but as the discursive possibility of continuity).[29] As Albert notes regarding shamanistic practice, "there is a change of perspective here: initially, the shaman 'calls' his spirit helpers (*xapiri*, plur. *pë*), 'brings them down,' and 'makes them dance.' Then, once they have carried away his image (*utupë*), he himself becomes a spirit person (*xapiri tʰë*), acting (*xapirimuu*) and moving (*xapiri huu*) as a spirit, seeing what the spirits see."[30] This is why the Yanomami use the term *në aipëi* (becoming other; assuming the value of other) or *poremuu* (act or enter a ghost state) when referring to any bodily change (including illness, pain, being under the influence of hallucinogens, and even indigestion) that affects how one perceives the world.[31] The same problem in translation that arose with the *xapiri*-spirit equivalence is present in that between *pore* and ghost (unless one reads it through Derrida's hauntology); *pore* does not refer in any way to immateriality, but simply to difference to oneself, to a change in perspective.

Poremuu is behaving in a way that is proper to another perspective, effectively enacting that body's properties. This is why the Yanomami refer to outsider's speech as "ghost talk," without viewing them as spirits or immaterial apparitions.[32] It is behavior that belongs to an other perspective, incomprehensible from the point of view of the Yanomami subject.[33]

In parallel fashion, the *xapiri* view Yanomami speech as "ghost talk" until shamans partake in *yãkoana* and learn to speak from their perspective, imitating their songs. Tellingly, Kopenawa describes this process in terms very similar to Lispector's "mutual suicide" in "O búfalo": one "dies" to oneself and becomes *xapiri*. As Albert summarizes, "by 'dying' (*nomãi*) under the effect of *yãkoana*, a shaman identifies with the *xapiri* image-beings ('spirits') he 'brings down,' and in doing so, incorporates their gaze. It is thus by becoming a spirit himself that he is able to see other spirits."[34] Needless to say, the shaman does not actually die nor does his body cease moving or speaking; he becomes other to himself, taking on the properties of the *xapiri*. It is in this sense that the shaman's body must be reconfigured to be able to produce the *xapiri*'s songs.[35] In summary, "becoming ghost" is a fully material phenomenon, alluding to a change in perspective and therefore behavior rather than immateriality.

This logic does not apply solely to humans or "powerful beings," but to any ontological change with respect to any body, including even the climate (as in climate change):

> What the white people call the **whole world** is being tainted because of the factories that make all their merchandise, their machines, their motors. Though the sky and the earth are vast, their fumes eventually spread in every direction, and all are affected: humans, game, and the forest. It is true. Even the trees are sick from it. Having become ghost, they lose their leaves, they dry up, and break all by themselves. The fish also die from it in the rivers' soiled waters. The white people will make the earth and the sky sick with the smoke from their minerals, oil, bombs, and atomic things. Then the winds and the storms will enter into a ghost state.[36]

Clearly, the trees, winds, and storms do not disappear or become immaterial; they become other with respect to their prior selves. In this context, *në pore* (the value of ghost) clearly indicates a conceptualization of otherness not as a becoming spirit, but rather as an other order of materiality that emerges intra-actively in encounter, as transformations that occur in relation with the traces of others.

In this sense, Albert's decision to translate *utupë* as "vital image" is much more effective in capturing the complexity of the concept than his translations of *xapiri* and *pore*; the seemingly contradictory terms, "vitality" usually associated with living bodies and the "image" with static symbolic representation, highlight its fundamental incompatibility with the Euro-American theorization of representation as essentially mimetic (even when it is anti-mimetic or abstract, in that it is viewed as re-presenting an artist's interiority or essence), that is, as an abstraction that supplants and reifies the real. Except perhaps in pop-culture misreadings of Richard Dawkin's polemical concept of the "meme" in *The Selfish Gene* (1976), in which he proposed that the body essentially functions as a vehicle for DNA to reproduce itself, the image or representational form can never be said to have a life (volition and therefore personhood) of its own in Euro-American thought; it is a symbolic re-presentation of an object or concept carried out by a human subject. Of course, DNA couldn't accurately be called a representation of the body in any case, despite encoding its materiality. The relation between a body's genetic code and its material form is clearly not a symbolic one, but rather emerges from within a series of highly complex, ongoing, multiscalar intra-actions between multiple levels of intra- and extra-cellular organization, including external "epigenetic" cues. In fact, genetic coding might be the closest concept in Euro-American thought to the way in which the Yanomami conceive of the *utupë*, which is neither an abstract re-presentation of the body (identity) nor an essential property (formal difference) that may be observed directly, but instead the virtual potentiality of form itself—that is, its potential for repetition as an actualized material form within certain discursive parameters that emerge intra-actively within the (epigenetic) relations in which it finds itself.

In that sense, the Yanomami conceptualization of the *utupë* comes quite close to what Gilles Deleuze, drawing on Liebnitz's calculus, frames as the differential. For Deleuze, difference does not emerge subjectively through observation and nominalization (that is, the comparative generation of abstracted conceptual oppositions), but rather through serial repetition; singularities emerge through the actualization of one of a "virtual" multiplicity's possibilities in the now, and it is the fact that it is not the same form as a preceding form in the series (even if it varies only temporally or spatially) that marks its difference or singularity.[37] It is imperative to underscore that, for Deleuze, the "virtual" denotes latent potentiality, not subjective abstraction; the virtual is inherently an unactualized multiplicity that generates specific, singular forms when actualized.[38] In this framework, difference is effectively the systematic variation between material forms within a series, whereby the relations between potential forms comprise the differential or series itself.

While this way of understanding formal differentiation can be difficult to visualize in the abstract terms Deleuze uses, Kopenawa provides a more concrete example of how it works in Yanomami thought in his discussion of the relations between game animals and their *xapiri* (the *utupë* of primordial human/animal ancestors):

> Every being of the forest has an *utupë* image. These are the images the sha-mans call and bring down. These are the images that become *xapiri* and do their presentation dance for us. They are like **photographs**. But only the sha-mans can see them. Ordinary people cannot. They are the real center, the real heart of the animals we hunt. These images are the real game! White people would say with their words that the animals of the forest we eat are only their **representatives**. And so, the *iro* howler monkey we arrow in the trees is other than its image *Irori*, the howler monkey spirit which the shaman calls.[39]

Interestingly, it is precisely Kopenawa's comparisons with the Euro-American conceptualization of representation ("photographs" and "repre-sentatives," both in Portuguese) that bring into relief the incompatibility of these divergent ontologies of the relations between form and materiality. What emerges is a fundamentally different way of viewing images; without waxing poetic, a Euro-American observer would never say that the photo-graphic image is more real ("the real center, the real heart") than the body; it is merely a lifeless image, a re-presentation of the body. In contrast, here it is the animal body that is a re-presentation (but a living one) or, more accu-rately, enactment or serial instantiation of a *xapiri*: "the animals exist, noth-ing more. They are food for humans. They are merely imitating their images [*utupë*]."[40] This apparent aporia can only be resolved through the recognition that for the Yanomami, images in general are not considered to be symbolic abstractions, but rather denote a distinct mode of materiality, which I have argued is that of formal potentials in repetition. The relation between the *xapiri* and its animal instantiations is thus not that between abstract form (determined by an observer from comparison between bodies' formal prop-erties) and living matter, but rather that between the material differential (virtual multiplicity of forms) and its actualizations as singular forms. In that sense, one might argue that the *utupë* refers to the principle of difference, that is, of singularity itself, but in repetition (that is, relation), not as essence.

The Self as Political Ecology: Accretion and the Eating of Others' Perspectives

Furthermore, the *utupë* can only be actualized as form, as *siki*, in intra-active relation with the traces of others. Since the Yanomami view bodies as multiplicities in relation, they are formed through accretive processes in intra-action with their others. As Albert notes, "the Yanomami think the flesh and blood of the fetus are gradually formed from the sperm of his genitors accumulated in the womb during successive acts of intercourse throughout the pregnancy."[41] Procreation—the birth of a singularity—is thus not viewed as a one-time event, but rather a process of ongoing, material accretion that may involve more than one progenitor, since Kopenawa affirms that a shaman's children are born not only of the father's sperm, but also that of the father's myriad *xapiri* allies.[42] Tellingly, eating figures prominently in this imaginary of the body as accretive; sustenance is not viewed merely as the appropriation of necessary nutrients, but as the incorporation (accretion) of the traces of plant and animal others into one's own body, which may have beneficial or detrimental effects depending on one's relation to the consumed being's *xapiri*. Furthermore the Yanomami also describe the incorporation of human others' traces in terms of eating; it is used as a synonym for sexual activity as well as acts of real or imputed lethal violence, which are generally framed as cannibalistic attempts to devour the *utupë* vital image of the victim.[43] In all cases, the body is conceived of in a literal sense as an accretive assemblage coproduced through the interactions between the *utupë* and the traces of human and nonhuman others.

It is for this reason that what the Yanomami view as the twin animating forces of the body, *wixia* (life breath) and *iyë* (blood), are simultaneously associated with the body's materiality and the traces of others' *utupë*: "these images [*utupë*] pass from a father to his son through his sperm, through the blood [*iyë*] of his sperm. They are invisible; they are deep inside us, in our thought, in our ghost, in our own image."[44] Nonetheless, this transmission of virtual potentials (linked to personality traits) is not limited to the father-son relation; while sperm is associated with *iyë*, the *wixia* of unrelated people may also pass on traces of their *utupë*: "the elder shamans are said to 'project their vital breath' (*wixia horamuu*) or 'give their vital breath' (*wixia hipiamuu*). It enters the initiate's nostrils and chest with the *yãkoana* and the *xapiri*, giving him his initiator's personal qualities (bravery, wisdom, courage at work, and so on)."[45] Clearly, if *utupë* were viewed as essential (monadic) or singular in and of themselves in a way akin to the soul in Euro-American tradition, they would not be capable of incorporating the properties of an other. Rather, relations with others expand the range of formal potentials of one's own *utupë*, potentials that then may be actualized in one's body. The body at any given moment is viewed as an instantiation of some of the *utupë*'s potentials, not as its full embodiment or manifestation. In that sense, one might affirm that, like the animals in the previous quote, the body is a representative (not representation) of the *utupë* in its difference from it, as a singular "minus-one" ex-propriated from the multiplicity. This view lies at the heart of the Yanomami conceptualization of personhood not as sovereign subjectivity (attained through the subject/object dialectic), but rather as the potential for relation. Being is thus never abstract or essential, but always relational, always a becoming-with multiple human and nonhuman others.

Clearly, the meanings of both the social and the political transform radically when the body is conceived of not through ownership (as one's most intimate property) but as an assemblage, as an instantiation co-produced within nested relations. As I have shown, these relations are not established at the level of bodies themselves, but rather at that of potentials, that is, of intra-actions between *utupë* that coproduce or instantiate bodies. This is why Kopenawa insisted that the *xapiri* are the "real game," while their animal instantiations are mere "food." Diplomatic relations cannot be established with the singular form, since the form itself is contingent on the relations that emerge at the level of potentials, co-producing the bodies in the relation. The same logic governs human political relations; everyday social interactions are not considered political in that they do not potentialize the relations themselves, but are only a manifestation or instantiation of them. It is only through engaging in *yãimuu* —viewed as the speech proper to *utupë*, learned from *xapiri*—that one may take the others' words to heart, that is, incorporate the other's traces into one's own *utupë*, thereby potentializing collaborative production.

This is why diplomacy is the primary mode of political engagement in Yanomami society. As Isabelle Stengers notes, there can be no rapport through identity or sameness, only across difference or what she calls "divergence."[46] And, for the Yanomami, the goal of diplomacy is not to establish common interests, but rather the friendship relation as the grounds for collaborative work. This explains why the Euro-American conceptualization of political representation is inadequate for understanding Yanomami politics. Logically, one cannot establish a working relation with the representative of a demographic class, only with a person with productive potential. For the

Yanomami, then, what we call political representation consists not in the re-presentation of a common identity through the negotiation of common interests, but in the enactment of the traces of the other in multiplicity, that is, the actualization of the relation through common differences with the goal of collaborative work.

In turn, this way of conceiving of the relations between sociality, politics, and the collaborative body—and therefore world-making—has profound implications for the meanings of both exchange and political representation in Yanomami society. Indeed, these terms would be indistinguishable for the Yanomami in any case, since all politics are conceived of as a matter of exchange. As I have already emphasized, Yanomami trade relations are not predicated on the exchange value of the objects in question, but rather on relation building, which is why Kopenawa insists that gifting is the primary mode of exchange in Yanomami society. This is the case even in symmetrical exchange, that is, when both parties contribute objects of seemingly equivalent value. From the Yanomami relational ontology, a gifted object can never be alienated from the one who gives it; using the object is both an evocation and an invocation of the other. Working with a gifted machete is effectively working alongside the gifter, or rather, the traces of the gifter work through and with the user. In Yanomami thought, then, what Marx would call the use value of an object is indivisible from its relational value to its owner/producer; in that sense, it is effectively an unalienated object, an object that always alludes to the work of its maker and its former owners.

This is one of the main reasons why capitalistic exchange value was initially incomprehensible to the Yanomami, and indeed Kopenawa continues to view it as inimical to Yanomami social forms.[47] Tellingly, the Yanomami word that Albert translates as "goods" or "merchandise," *matihi*, denotes any object bearing the traces of others, not only trade goods but also ritual adornments associated with *xapiri* and even the bones of deceased family members.[48] In this sense, it has no equivalence with the Euro-American conceptualization of commodity; its value lies in its traces, that is, its relation with its maker or prior owner: "our ancestors gave us this strong word [*matihi*] because the value that we give our bone ashes is higher even than the value the white people give the gold they covet so much."[49] Furthermore, the Yanomami believe that the manufactured merchandise brought by outsiders bears the traces of epidemic beings that sicken them and the forest: "merchandise has the value of *xawara* epidemic. This is why the diseases always follow it."[50] This perception may appear fetishistic to Euro-American readers, since it is clearly based on the Yanomami experience of epidemics caused by exposure to outsiders bearing diseases with which they had no prior immunity rather than any inherent property of the trade objects themselves. Nonetheless, it perhaps holds truer in both literal and metaphorical senses than a Euro-American reader would like to acknowledge, particularly if one takes the broad definition of epidemic proposed by the US Center for Disease Control to include disease caused not only by viral or bacterial pathogens, but also environmental toxins and pollution. In this sense, the Yanomami are perhaps more realistic than most Euro-Americans in viewing disease not as an externality to capitalistic production, but as a fundamental feature of modern extractivism, industrialization, and the global circulation of commodities and bodies: from plastic nanoparticles to chemical contaminants, we all bear toxic traces within our bodies, rendering us "other" or "ghostly" to our healthy selves.

Value as Coproductive Potential: The Cosmopolitics of Friendship and Predation

Within this framework, "value" is perceived not as an abstract symbolic equivalence between disparate goods that is determined by rendering labor abstract (hourly wages or salary) in the market economy, as in the "exchange value" that Marx finds at the heart of capitalism, but rather as the potential to produce specific effects on the bodies involved within a relation. Tellingly, the Yanomami word that Albert translates as value, "në" is a proclitic rather than a noun itself; it is always used in conjunction with an affective noun in a way similar to compound verbs in European languages, thereby denoting its status as an active operation rather than an abstract equivalence between different qualities and quantities.[51] These effects may be beneficial, as in *në rope* (the value of abundance or growth) or detrimental, as in *në ohi* (the value of hunger) or *në wari* (the value of disease). Tellingly, the Yanomami do not conceive of either hunger or sickness in terms of lack, that is, as the absence of food or health. Instead, they are effects produced materially by intra-actions with pernicious elements/beings, all of which are viewed as having intentionality. In this framework, relations that produce beneficial effects are conceived of as friendship relations, while relations that produce hunger or disease are framed as predation, as attempts to devour the body or the *utupë* vital image by hostile human or nonhuman beings.[52] Furthermore, these effects are not viewed precisely as the result of external actions by others, but rather as coproduced within the relation; the internalized marks or traces of others actualize the effect within the body.[53] In all cases, value is thought of as the potential for co-production in relation through the actualization of the other's traces. Gifting is thus viewed as producing beneficial effects, while taking forcefully is viewed as a predatory act producing illness or death.

The similarities between Kopenawa's language regarding *õno* (mark, trace) and Derrida's concept of the trace (which lies at the heart of his theorization of hauntology) is not mere coincidence; like Derrida, the Yanomami conceive of subjectivity in terms of multiplicity, as an ongoing becoming-with multiple others through their traces. From both perspectives, the other inhabits the subject through their traces, placing the subject in a state of primordial debt or responsibility to them. While there is some divergence in that Derrida views subjectivity primarily through the lens of language usage and the Yanomami focus to a greater degree on the enactment of relational potentials, this gap is bridged by the concept of performativity and Barad's recognition that all intra-actions are fundamentally semiotic. In other words, the apprehension and enactment of the other's traces always involve signs, whether "behavioral" or "linguistic" in the strict sense of the word. Indeed, when read through this lens, Derrida's polemical affirmation in *Of Grammatology* that "il n'y a pas de hors-texte" (there is no outside or beyond the text) takes on quite different connotations than those which critics usually associate with it: all interactions (not only speech) are fundamentally semiotic intra-actions when "text" is understood in its broadest sense as the discursivity underpinning the semiosphere that is environment. It is in this sense that the Yanomami conceive of selfhood as a form of sociality analogous to that of the forest itself as multispecies socius. This analogy functions at every scale: in the same way that the social economy of gifting leads to the establishment of "paths of friendship" between Yanomami communities, engaging in *yãi muu* is conceived of as the mutual gifting of words that establishes pathways of thought in the participants' minds, whereby perspectives are exchanged and not only understood, but actually housed within the self as a relational multiplicity. Rather than mutual interests, then, consensus is envisioned as the pathway itself, that is, as the relation between these different perspectives, which are not homologized.

Within this framework, the Yanomami conceptualization of the political runs very close to what Derrida calls "passive decision," that is a deciding for oneself and for the other through the traces of the other. As I discussed at length in Chapter 3, Derrida underscores that decisions cannot be made from sameness; indistinction cannot make possible a distinction, that is, a rupture within continuity, a choice. It is only internalized difference—that

is, the traces of the other—that makes decision both possible and imperative, since it presents a contradiction within the self that must be resolved to
assure the continuity of subjectivity and therefore identity:

> The passive decision, condition of the event, is always in me, structurally, an-
> other event, a rending decision as the decision of the other. Of the absolute
> other in me, the other as the absolute that decides on me in me. Absolutely
> singular in principle, according to its most traditional concept, the decision
> is not only always exceptional, it makes an exception for/of me. In me. I de-
> cide, I make up my mind in all sovereignty—this would mean: the other than
> myself, the me as other and other than myself, he makes or I make an excep-
> tion of the same.[54]

For the Yanomami, becoming other to the self (*në aipëi*, "to take the value
of/become other") is the precondition for diplomacy and thus political decision.[55] This process is simultaneously material and psychological; the body
becomes other to itself (how it is normally apprehended by the subject) both
through the performative aspects of the political ritual itself and through
altering states: in the case of the funerary *reahu* feasts during which *yãimuu*
is carried out, by gorging on plantain soup into which the deceased person's
ground bones have been mixed (for Kopenawa, indigestion is a "ghost state"),
and in the case of shamanistic diplomacy with nonhumans, through dreams
or the consumption of *yãkoana* (hallucinogenic snuff extracted from the bark
of the Virola tree).

Due to the Yanomami conceptualization of self as multiplicity—Kopenawa often describes one's torso as a communal roundhouse in which others' *utupë* hang their hammocks—it becomes possible to simultaneously be
oneself and other, that is, to identify with the other's perspective. Becoming
other to oneself—that is, not only opening oneself to the other's traces but
also seeing the world from the perspective of an other body—is thus the
precondition for political negotiations. Furthermore, since personhood is
not a quality associated exclusively with *Homo sapiens*, but rather with any
being possessing *utupë*, Yanomami politics are always already cosmopolitical;
friendship relations run across species and converge in the co-production
of the *në rope* value of growth that assures the continuity of the *Urihi-a*, the
forest-world. Additionally, since each *utupë* has its specific niche or role in this
network of ecosystemic production, relations are oriented toward preserving
and fostering these differences, that is, each being's well-being on their own
terms (rather than common interests). These friendship relations may also

be considered alliances in that they work together to combat common enemies: those beings that "devour the forest" and its protectors, producing *në
wari* (value of disease) and *në ohi* (value of hunger or scarcity).

For the Yanomami, then, ethics within diplomacy are not defined by maintaining fidelity solely to one's own community's or species' interests, but
rather to the common difference potentialized by the trace—that is, to the
relation itself. Ethical behavior within the friendship relation necessarily
implies maintaining fidelity to the other's traces—traces that are always
internalized as relation—rather than one's own, singular interests. Furthermore, since those traces are never fixed or reified, diplomacy must always be
ongoing. Although it may appear truistic to state in this way, relationships
can never exist on their own, as objects, states of being, or even contracts;
they must always be enacted through the actualization of the other's traces
in the subject's now. In that sense, it might be more accurate to speak of
friendship in broader terms, not as a specific kind of relation between individuals, but as a mode of being-with others in multiplicity. Indeed, Derrida
argues repeatedly in *The Politics of Friendship* that this is what Aristotle was
driving at with his famous affirmation that "oh my friends, there is no [sin-
gular] friend."[56] When friendship is conceived of on the basis of commonal-
ities, as analogous to brother (consanguinity, genetic sameness), there can
be no friend, since the other can never become one's blood sibling, which is
to say, equivalent to oneself.

Indeed, Derrida posits that this aporia simultaneously underpins and
undermines all Euro-American political discourse placing the brotherly
friendship/enmity dialectic at the heart of democratic political relations.
Deconstructing Carl Schmitt's theorization of enmity as the grounds for
politics in *The Concept of the Political*, Derrida finds an irreconcilable semantic instability between the conceptualization of enmity as an affective state
(between individuals) and hostility as a generalized mode of relating to
indefinite (undefined and therefore beyond temporality, that is, the event
of encounter) others:

> the antithesis of friendship in the political sphere is not, according to Schmitt,
> enmity but hostility. First consequence: the political enemy would not inevita-
> bly be inimical, he would not necessarily hold me in enmity, nor I him. More-
> over, sentiments would play no role; there would be neither passion nor affect
> in general. Here we have a totally pure experience of the friend-enemy in its
> political essence, purified of any affect—at least of all personal affect, suppos-
> ing that there could ever be any other kind. If the enemy is the stranger, the

war I would wage on him should remain essentially without hatred, without intrinsic xenophobia.[57]

In negating the affectivity of political relations—and thus, the possibility of hatred—Schmitt effectively displaces the political from individuals to states: the enemy can only exist as an objective category, as a "public enemy," while hostility between individuals would effectively be apolitical, a private affair. According to Derrida, this displacement is carried out in Euro-American political thought in general through genealogical discourse, through the appeal to the figure of the brother (as in the slogan of the French Revolution: *liberté, egalité, fraternité*) as the basis for democratic horizontality. The fellow citizen is a brother, while the public enemy is the generic/genetic foreigner, the one who can never be a brother (there is no "becoming brother"):

> As in every racism, every ethnocentrism—more precisely, in every one of the nationalisms throughout history—a discourse on birth and on nature, a *phúsis* of genealogy (more precisely, a discourse and a phantasm on the genealogical *phúsis*) regulates, in the final analysis, the movement of each opposition: repulsion and attraction, disagreement and accord, war and peace, hatred and friendship. From within and without. This *phúsis* comprises everything—language, law, politics, etc. Although it defines the alterity of the foreigner or the barbarian, it has no other.[58]

When mediated by the political discourse of fraternity, the encounter with the foreigner as a singularity is negated, overwritten by the political relation. The foreigner can never become a constitutive other in relation with the singular subject; they always exist outside the possibility of relation. A foreigner can never be known and yet remain foreign; neither brother nor enemy, they always inhabit the indefinite category of stranger.

At the same time, the brother can never become other; he is always already within the genealogical relation. Extending this logic to its limits, as Derrida does, there can be no encounter with the other, no diplomacy, and no negotiation of policy when democratic politics are conceptualized through the figure of fraternity. Politics would simply consist in defining and policing the boundaries of the family-state. This is one of the reasons that political theorists who used the brother metaphor frequently conflated it with friendship, looking to open the relation beyond the genealogical. In drawing this equivalence, however, they paradoxically subordinated the meaning (difference) of friend to that of the brother, that is, to sameness. Rather than an other-in-relation who is explicitly not a family member, the friend becomes one who is like a brother, thereby subjecting them to the same genealogic of exclusion by which the family is constituted. This is why Derrida, underscoring the exclusion of the "sister" from the conceptualization of democratic fraternity, characterizes the logic of democratic fraternity as phallogocentric or even carnophallogocentric.[59]

However, Derrida quickly finds the aporia within this formulation of the political upon deconstructing Schmitt's statements regarding internal political struggles. If, as Schmitt affirms, the horizon of warfare between states is effectively what constitutes the political, extending this logic to conflicts that are internal to the nation state—civil wars, revolutions—effectively places the opposition between brother and foreigner/enemy into question. The citizenly brother is always simultaneously a potential enemy. This aporia leads Derrida to two related conclusions. First, brotherhood cannot be the basis for a truly democratic politics, not only because it simultaneously posits confraternity as the grounds for the polis (thereby excluding anyone who cannot be viewed genetically or discursively as "brother," that is as one who is equivalent to oneself) and enmity as the grounds for the political (thereby negating the possibility of any political differences between "brothers"), but also because it conflates brotherhood and friendship, when these terms are in fact opposed inasmuch as the friend is always exogenous to the family. Second, while Schmitt ascribes in general terms to Hobbes's premise that politics arise from the need for mutual protection due to the primordially violent state of nature, whereby the unifying factors are simultaneously consanguinity and political enmity, Derrida clearly sides with his French precursors Rousseau and Montaigne in portraying friendship, that is, the drive for affiliation and mutual responsibility with the heteronomous other, as the basis for the political.

This other always exists in potential terms, simultaneously friend and enemy; politics, no longer the struggle for absolute power or sovereignty, but rather the ability to do justice, to make policies that necessarily respond to the self, the other, and, as I discuss further on, the third person that interrupts and generalizes the face-to-face relation, would thus consist in the recognition of the other as a political subject. From this point of view, hostility and therefore the possibility for politics becomes the product of discord—that is, difference in encounter—rather than categorical indifference to the other's singularity. If, as Derrida argues, this encounter with difference, with the singular other, is in reality the basis for politics, the conceptualization of the political cannot be based on tropes of genealogy, but rather must be predicated on difference-in-relation. This is why he refers to the "friend-enemy"; one can never encounter a brother as difference: "Has anyone ever met a brother? A uterine or consanguine (distantly related) brother? In nature?", wherein "met" refers to the encounter with the other's singular difference.[60] Likewise, he notes that "there is no friendship for the father, one is not the friend of the one who makes friendship possible. One can be grateful to him, since one is obliged to him. There is even reciprocal love with the father, but this reciprocal love (non-equal) is not friendship."[61] In this sense, a truly horizontal democracy cannot rely on the family as the conceptual basis for polity.

Diplomacy and Hospitality as Political Institutions

As I discussed in the last chapter, Amazonian Indigenous societies do not conceive of polity through the figure of the brother, but rather that of the in-law, that is, of potential affiliation with people who are exogenous to the family. Furthermore, as Viveiros de Castro noted in the case of the Cashinua, these in-law terms are often applied indiscriminately to anyone who one considers a potential friend: "the common word for the relation, in Amazonian worlds, is the term translated by 'brother-in-law' or 'cross cousin.' This is the term we call people we do not know what to call, those with whom we wish to establish a generic relation. In sum, 'cousin/brother-in-law' is the term that creates a relation where none existed. It is the form through which the unknown is made known."[62] Friendship (and by extension, all relations) can thus only be conceived of transversally, across difference. Furthermore, Derrida views friendship—a way of being that is always incomplete, always a becoming in relation with others—as the precondition for subjectivity itself; one always learns to speak from and with others, and even when one overwrites both the other's singular presence and their meanings upon appropriating and reusing their words (or name), the erasure always evokes what is erased, that is, the other's traces.

Extrapolating from Levinas's discussion of "welcoming" as the basis for sociality and therefore ethics, Derrida calls this primordial openness to others, rooted in perception and inseparable from and prior to both subjectivity (speech) and socialization, "unconditional" or "infinite" hospitality. Analyzing a passage from Levinas's *Totality and Infinity*, he writes that:

> The word "hospitality" here translates, brings to the fore, re-produces, the two
> words preceding it, "attention" and "welcome." An internal paraphrase, a sort

of periphrasis, a series of metonymies that bespeak hospitality, the face, welcome: tending toward the other, attentive intention, intentional attention, *yes* to the other. Intentionality, attention to speech, welcome of the face, hospitality—all these are the same, but the same as the welcoming of the other, there where the other withdraws from the theme. This movement without movement effaces itself in the welcoming of the other, and since it opens itself to the infinity of the other, an infinity that, as other, in some sense precedes it, the welcoming of the other (objective genitive) will already be a response: the *yes* to the other will already be responding to the welcoming of the other (subjective genitive), to the *yes* of the other.[63]

Reprising his affirmation in *The Gift of Death* that "tout autre est tout autre" (every other is entirely other), Derrida traces the basis for the concept of the infinite and therefore the multitude to difference itself; every other is singular in that its differences can never be known, that is, made the same through equivalence or analogy. Difference is absolute or infinite precisely in that it always exceeds categorization; identification through the nominalization of a difference can never be said to account even partially for the singularity of the other.

This is why the orientation toward the "other" is always already the orientation to all others: there is no singular friend (one the same as oneself), but there are infinite potential friends. In that sense, Levinas's unconditional "yes"—the response—is simply the recognition of difference, of the other as one who is not the self and to whom one must therefore respond, engage in relation, that is, in dialogue. Welcoming/friendship is thus a "movement without movement"; it is simultaneously an act of engagement—a decision to respond—that is nonetheless mandated structurally by the openness to all others, to the inevitability of encounter. This passivity relates to Derrida's extrapolation of Levinas's first ethics as unconditional responsibility/responsivity to the other, since it is the other who calls one's own subjectivity into being in the moment, in encounter, simultaneously acknowledging us (responding to our presence, calling out to us whether through words, gaze, or gesture) and demanding a response.[64] Intentionality (Levinas's "attention") thus comes into play as the passive decision to engage, to address (or actively ignore) the other.

In turn, this movement between passivity and decision, between infinite difference and the singular, underlies the passage or interplay between the ethics of encounter, politics, and the law. For Levinas, it is the irruption or specter of multiplicity—the "third" in his terms—in the encounter with the other that transmutes the "first ethics" of responsivity/responsibility into a question of justice and therefore politics. As Derrida reprises:

> The "birth of the question" is the third. Yes, the birth, for the third does not wait; it comes at the origin of the face and of the face to face. Yes, the birth of the question as question, for the face to face is immediately suspended, inter-rupted without being interrupted, as face to face, as the dual of two singulari-ties. The ineluctability of the third is the law of the question. The question of a question, as addressed to the other and from the other, the other of the other, the question of a question that is surely not first (it comes after the yes to the other and the yes of the other) though nothing precedes it. No thing, and es-pecially no one. The question, but also, as a result, justice, philosophical intel-ligibility, knowledge, and even, announcing itself gradually from one person to the next, from neighbor to neighbor, the figure of the State.[65]

In a concrete, linguistic sense, the "third" evokes the usage of the referen-tial third person (he/she/they) within the face-to-face encounter with the singular other (you), which would indicate a latent awareness that the face-to-face encounter can always be extended to an other who is not present in the moment (whether or not the third person pronoun is actually deployed), as well as the potential, presential interruption of the encounter by a third person. Whether physical or spectral (a distinction Derrida would disallow in any case, since for him, all presence-absence is apprehended through the trace), the presence of this third, of the other of my other, who is also my potential other, ad infinitum, demands "justice," that is, equality, equal standing within the relation that already exceeds the face-to-face encounter, becoming social or the grounds for the social. The "yes," the response to the other in singularity, thus enters into potential contradiction, as it always implies a possible infidelity, a sundering of the relation or the absoluteness of the relation to accommodate or prefer the third:

> Though Levinas never puts it in these terms, I will risk pointing out the neces-sity of this double bind in what follows from the axioms established or recalled by Levinas: if the face to face with the unique engages the infinite ethics of my responsibility for the other in a sort of oath before the letter, an unconditional respect or fidelity, then the ineluctable emergence of the third, and, with it, of justice, would signal an initial perjury [*parjure*]. Silent, passive, painful, but inevitable, such perjury is not accidental and secondary, but is as originary as the experience of the face. Justice would begin with this perjury. (Or at least

justice as law; even if justice remains transcendent or heterogeneous to law, these two concepts must not be dissociated: justice demands law, and law does not wait any more than does the illeity of the third in the face. When Levinas says "justice," we are also authorized to hear "law," it seems to me. Law [*droit*] would begin with such a perjury; it would betray ethical uprightness [*droiture*]).[66]

The origins of law—of justice and equal rights—would thus lie not in prohibition (the sacrifice of individual freedoms) per se, but rather in the imperative to open the face-to-face relation to the third, to multiplicity. This primordial injunction, the law of hospitality, prefigures the (written) law, as it extends from "one person to the next, from neighbor to neighbor," simultaneously potentializing and demanding the consolidation of the state as the formal relation of justice between citizens who may never enter into direct face-to-face encounter. "Perjury" is thus the condition for and of the law, in that it interrupts and substitutes for the call to and from the other, at once erasing its specificity in the face-to-face encounter and reaffirming it as a generality. In this way, politics (governance and governability) emerges directly through the law of hospitality, that is, friendship itself.

Homeland and Statehood

However, the state as political formation cannot be conceived of in the absence of either territoriality or exclusions (the foreigner, the non-citizen), whether territory is defined in centrifugal terms as radiating outward from a community toward frontiers or through the delimitation of borders, as in empire and the modern nation state. In either case, the territoriality of the state hinges on the figure of the home or homeland, which, as Derrida notes, derives not simply from the appropriation and delimitation of space as property—that is, what is proper to individual or state sovereignty—but once again emerges through the trope of hospitality. As he writes:

> As for the second direction referred to a moment ago, we must be reminded of this implacable law of hospitality: the hôte who receives (the host), the one who welcomes the invited or received hôte (the guest), the welcoming hôte who considers himself the owner of the place, is in truth a hôte received in his own home. He receives the hospitality that he offers in his own home; he receives it from his own home—which, in the end, does not belong to him. The hôte as host is a guest. The dwelling opens itself to itself, to its "essence"

without essence, as a "land of asylum or refuge." The one who welcomes is first welcomed in his own home. The one who invites is invited by the one whom he invites.[67]

Derrida's language recalls and amplifies the implications of that beloved and much clichéd Mexican expression of hospitality: "mi casa es su casa" (my home is your home). If offering hospitality means offering one's home to the other, as their home, it necessarily implies a renunciation of sovereign possession, that is, of absolute freedom to utilize and dispose of in singularity what now also belongs to the other. At the very least, one must ask permission—"con permiso"—to enter a bathroom or bedroom hosting the guest.

Furthermore, the home itself, as a spatial form, demands this hospitality. One cannot invite an other to one's home without offering hospitality; the invitation itself is a form of hospitality, a gifting of one's home, even if conditionally and temporarily. The home is thus the space proper to hospitality, effectively functioning as the foundational institution of hospitality as such. This is why Derrida says that within the welcoming space of the home, the host is also guest, accommodated by their invited guest/host. All who enter—even the "owner"—are equally welcomed within the home due to its primordial function as hospitable institution, as shelter or "refuge." Tellingly, the Spanish expression that is usually translated as home, "hogar," does not enter into play in the discourse of hospitality. No one says "bienvenido a mi hogar" (well-come to my home); "hogar" literally means "hearth"—having a more direct, intimate relation to habitation, to the use value of the structure. In that sense, "mi casa es su casa" captures this other, more institutional meaning of home as a welcoming space or refuge that is transitory in the sense that any admitted person, including the inhabitants, may enter or leave at will—thus the dichotomy casa/calle (street, public space).

This temporary and yet always latent transference or suspension of property—the passive decision to renounce property rights for the law of hospitality, to welcome not only the other but also the third—becomes much clearer in relation to the state's territory. As Derrida drives home, the state itself is founded upon an originary dispossession that is not Hobbes's renunciation of the absolute freedom of the nomadic individual living in the state of nature, but the opposite: renouncing one's sovereign claim to one's own home (that is, the possessive sense of territoriality) is the precondition for the constitution of the state as a political territory, as a homeland. As a citizen, one becomes a guest in one's own home(land), which in the end belongs first to the state and only secondarily to the citizen:

The one who receives is received, receiving hospitality in what he takes to be his own home, or indeed his own land, according to a law that Rosenzweig also recalled. For Rosenzweig emphasized this originary dispossession, this withdrawal by which the "owner" is expropriated from what is most his own, the ipse from its ipseity, thus making of one's home a place or location one is simply passing through:

> even when it has a home, this people [the eternal people], in recurrent contrast to all other peoples on earth, is not allowed full possession of that home. It is only "a stranger and a sojourner." God tells it: "This land is mine." The holiness of the land removed it from the people's spontaneous reach.[63]

Clearly, this passage from Rosenzweig's *The Star of Redemption* refers to the Judeo-Christian tradition in which humans (or, more specifically, Jews) are guests in God's creation (in this case, the Promised Land), which would nevertheless prefigure how private property is viewed as secondary in relation to the state's territory (e.g., powers of eminent domain, property seizure, etc.). Indeed, this expropriation precedes and underwrites all rights, including property rights, which can only exist as such when guaranteed by the state's territorial sovereignty, its constitutive ability to enforce its own laws equally throughout its territory.

Undoubtedly, this mandatory dispossession entails a coercive relation between the individual and the state, but where does this coercion originate? While many would argue that it is located in the tyranny of the sovereign state as such (the inheritance of feudalism), Derrida follows Montaigne and Rousseau in locating it in the foundations of sociality itself, in the law of hospitality and the passive (inescapable) orientation toward the other. From this perspective, the state of nature, if one continues to use that term, presupposes the political state as such not in opposition, through the figure of enmity, but rather through that of community, of communal hospitality. Within this framework, the exclusion of the non-citizen consists not in a primordial drive to eradicate difference, but rather in a calculated disavowal or negation of the law of hospitality through the deployment of the genealogical discourse of fraternity. The other as potential friend is disowned in order to generate inequalities, that is, a power differential, which is ultimately oriented toward the ends of economic accumulation through the appropriation of the other's properties (as in war over land and natural resources) and the devaluation of labor, whether in the repudiation of the sister as citizen, which limits her to unpaid domestic work, that of rightless enslaved or immigrant workers, or

that of "nature" itself as related to the multispecies work of renewing ecological cycles and making life possible for all.

Animal Thirds and the Path to Interspecies Justice

As I discussed earlier, Michael Marder and the Yanomami coincide in locating the passive orientation toward the other—and therefore the possibility
of hospitality itself—in plant being or what, in order to amplify its political
ramifications, I have called the state of plants. Clearly, in this ontology, the
individual's home—up to and including their body, which hosts the traces of
the other—is never fully their own sovereign possession, but always superseded by the state of plants through the law of hospitality. However, there
remains a key problem to which one must attend in order to justify the passage from Levinas and Derrida's theorization of the law of hospitality as the
origin of the (human) state to the state of plants as conceived of in Yanomami
thought. Regardless of whether or not one agrees with the postulate that plant
being makes possible the orientation toward the other (Marder), potentializing biosemiotic communications across species (Kopenawa), any theory of
cosmopolitics relying on Levinas's first ethics must address the political sta-
tus/stature of nonhumans. As I have already argued extensively, this question
hinges on two primary considerations: cross-species responsivity/responsi-
bility (the possibility of ethical orientation across species) and the problem
of political/legal representation (rights claims) for nonhumans, that is, the
possibility of a form of justice—what Derrida calls an "incalculable justice"—
that exceeds the bounds of human rights or rights themselves.

As David Clark notes, Levinas explicitly disavowed the animal and by
extension all nonhuman species (especially "faceless" ones), from the face-
to-face relation, a repudiation whose necessity immediately places its validity into question.[69] Indeed, both Clark and Derrida draw out the aporia that
emerges between Levinas's human-to-human first ethics and his description
in "The Name of a Dog, or Natural Rights" of how a stray dog living in the
concentration camp in which he and his fellow French Jewish captives were
imprisoned treated them with "human dignity," while their captors and local
German residents, imbued with Nazi ideology, treated them as subhuman
animals. As Clark notes, Levinas was forced to perform a series of rhetorical
maneuvers to elide the possibility that an animal in itself may place an ethical demand or "duty" on a human and vice-versa, ultimately claiming that
this can only occur through "sentimentalizing anthropomorphism" (that is,

an abstract analogy with the human face), not within the affective encounter itself.[70] As Levinas stated in an interview,

> One cannot entirely refuse the face of an animal. It is via the face that one understands, for example, a dog. Yet the priority here is not found in the animal, but in the human face. We understand the animal, the face of an animal, in accordance with Dasein. The phenomenon of the face is not in its purest form in the dog. In the dog, in the animal, there are other phenomena. For example, the force of nature is pure vitality. It is more this which characterizes the dog. But it also has a face.[71]

In the allusion to Dasein, Levinas tacitly defers to Heidegger's famous assertion in *Fundamental Concepts of Metaphysics* that animals are poor-in-world, that is, they lack a comprehensive worldview because they are attuned only to immediate objects, unable to extrapolate a broader network of relations between them.[72] For Heidegger, animals do not fully distinguish between their objects and themselves as singularities because, according to him, they are unable to conceive of finitude, that is, their own mortality (vis-á-vis that of the other) and therefore the temporality of being.

Returning to Levinas's quote, lacking language (logos and therefore the possibility of ethics), the animal calls to the human through the "force of nature" (shared biological vitality) and analogy, not through that of singularity/responsivity/responsibility (the "yes"), and therefore cannot place the human in a full state of indebtedness. Despite interpellating the concentration camp prisoners as humans and being called to by name (Bobby), Levinas's dog is poor-in-face, remaining always on the margins of hospitality and therefore sociality. As Clark summarizes:

> This transcendence would seem literally and even parodically to be the case with the dog, who involuntarily attests to the dignity of "man" without grasping the significance of what it has done. But where the lacuna between the witness and the witness's speech (or, we could say, between the performative and constative functions of the testimonial act) exposes the human to "the absolutely other," to whom it is held "hostage," in the animal this transcendent convocation serves the sole function of confirming the exemplarity of the human: it is the animal's privilege not only unwittingly to be held hostage by the human other but also never to be *autrui* for "man." According to an authoritarian logic that informs almost all of Levinas's essay, by which the animal has

in the mode of not-having, the dog is granted the power to be more than itself only insofar as it rigorously remains itself—*dans l'animal*—vis-á-vis "Man."[73]

As in the animal stories I analyzed in Chapters 3 and 4, the animal is thus excised from the social relation not because of any of its own properties or capacities, but through the deployment of the animot (animal category). Within the institution of the "human," humanist metaphysics or what Agamben called the "anthropological machine," the animal face can only represent the human face back to itself, but always imperfectly, always lacking human features.[74] According to Clark, this deployment becomes both necessary and highly problematic precisely due to the parallels and paradoxes that Levinas creates in the contrast between the Nazi animalization of Jews and Bobby's humanization; the dog can only be removed from ethical consideration by naming it a dog.

Levinas thus performs an animal sacrifice that Derrida is not prepared to make. Tellingly, Derrida opens *The Animal that Therefore I Am* with a long reflection on why he feels ashamed when meeting his pet cat's gaze while naked, which he associates with Levinas's concept of absolute vulnerability, that is, the naked face. Clearly, no one feels shame (or exhibitive exhilaration, its counterpart) while being naked before objects; it is only the other's gaze that can place one into that affective state of responsiveness—shame is always shame before others. This leads him to reflect on the meanings of response and erasure with respect to the animal, whereby he meticulously dismantles the long list of privations that institute the human/animal divide, what he calls the animot or animal category. As he summarizes:

> It is *not just* a matter of asking whether or not one has the right to refuse the animal such and such a power (speech, reason, experience of death, mourning, culture, institutions, technics, clothing, lying, pretense of a pretense, covering of tracks, gift, laughter, crying, respect, etc.—the list is necessarily without limit, and the most powerful philosophical tradition in which we live has refused the "animal" *all of that*). It *also* means asking whether what calls itself human has the right rigorously to attribute to man, which means therefore to attribute to himself, what he refuses to the animal, and whether he can ever possess the *pure, rigorous, indivisible* concept, as such, of that attribution.[75]

Scrutinizing in turn the thought of Descartes, Kant, Heidegger, Levinas, and Lacan, he argues that the problem of the relations between language and subjectivity—in the end, the dogma that there can be no form of self-awareness without symbolic language—lies at the heart of all these negations.

However, returning to his theorization of the trace as what animates or grants subjective meaning (the signified as apprehended by the subject) to the dead letter, the symbol (through the subject's erasure and overwriting), he reframes the problem of subjectivity in terms of self-reflexivity or self-erasure, that is, of responding to or "following" one's own traces or tracks (one's prior self) and those of the other. The subject is constituted in its present by actualizing the other's traces; it is that relation through which self-awareness emerges in relation to the symbolic order of language. Furthermore, this auto-referentiality would not be exclusive to the speaking subject, but rather a fundamental feature of life itself, of life as semiosphere (to use Juri Lottman's neologism) in the sense that all acts of semiotic interpretation, of reading one's environment (composed of infinite others), necessarily involve the erasure of the other's traces, if not necessarily through symbolic representation:

> Let me note very quickly in passing, concerning intellectual autobiography, that whereas the deconstruction of 'logocentrism' had, for necessary reasons, to be developed over the years as deconstruction of 'phallogocentrism,' then of 'carnophallogocentrism,' its very first substitution of the concept of trace or mark for those of speech, sign, or signifier was destined in advance, and quite deliberately, to cross the frontiers of anthropocentrism, the limits of language confined to human words and discourse. Mark, gramma, trace, and différance refer differentially to all living things, all the relations between living and nonliving.[76]

In that sense, self-awareness cannot be a purely linguistic and therefore exclusively human phenomenon, but rather a question of repetition and continuity in relation to difference, even when the difference is temporal, that is, existing in relation to one's past self, to the imagining or inference of one's past self: "no one denies the animal auto-affection or auto-motion, hence the self of that relation to the self. But what is in dispute—and it is here that the functioning and the structure of the 'I' count so much, even where the word *I* is lacking—is the power to make reference to the self in deictic or autodeictic terms, the capability to at least virtually turn a finger toward oneself in order to say 'this is I.'"[77]

Nevertheless, he argues that this question of self-referentiality—which is also the capacity to refer to the other as such—has always been defined exclusively through human language, whereas there are myriad biosemiotic examples of "virtual finger pointing," of both self-reference and of reference to the other in relation to the self. In the first case, he coincides with biosemioticians such as Jesper Hoffmeyer in viewing genetic transcription as a self-referential or "auto-deictic" system functioning at both the cellular and organismic levels.[78] In the second, he cites the example of "narcissistic" exhibition in sexual play and combat, in which animals not only represent/exhibit themselves to others in specific ways that are distinct from their normal behavior, but also frequently feign aggression or disinterest—effectively a performance rather than a mere, mechanical action or re-action (which would in any case necessarily entail response and iteration) driven by reproductive instinct.[79]

Therefore, the capacity of animals to refer to themselves and their others as such cannot be disputed without recurring to the "lack" of symbolic language. However, Derrida appears to coincide with Pierce and Hoffmeyer in locating the symbol not as an exception, but as existing in a continuum with iconic and indexical forms of semiosis, although he takes it in a somewhat different and possibly more radical direction given that Hoffmeyer and other biosemioticians generally follow Pierce in ascribing a hierarchy to the three classes of signs, with symbols assigned a higher degree of evolutionary complexity, since their referents are relations between indexical and/or iconic signs rather than objects themselves.[80] In contrast, Derrida rejects this hierarchization of sign types, arguing that all signs follow the same procedure of substitution, overwriting a perception (or more accurately the image of a perception, the trace) and emerging as concrete or meaningful abstractions precisely from within the triadic relations between trace, arche, and the interpreting/speaking/thinking subject. Deconstructing Lacan's denial of the animal's capacity to lie, to feint a feint or pretend to pretend, which Lacan takes to be the basis of psychic life (that is, the abstract self-image that emerges in the "mirror stage"), Derrida counters that,

> apart from the fact that, as I have tried to show elsewhere (and this is why I long ago substituted the concept of trace for that of signifier), the structure of the trace presupposes that *to trace* amounts to *erasing a trace* (always present-absent) as much as to imprinting it, all sorts of sometimes ritual animal practices—for example, in burial and mourning—associate the experience of the trace with that of the erasure of the trace. A pretense, moreover, even a simple pretense, consists in rendering a sensible trace illegible or imperceptible.[81]

Returning to the example of animal sexual mating games, he affirms that "pretense presupposes taking the other into account; it therefore supposes, simultaneously, the pretense of pretense, a simple supplementary move by the other within the strategy of the game."[82] In this way, he argues that animals not only interpellate human subjects, demanding a response and thereby becoming constitutive others, but that animals also apprehend their others as such, not as mere bundles of stimuli that provoke a reaction. On the same basis of iterability and response, he deconstructs the distinction between response and reaction, thereby placing the entire Cartesian logic of mechanistic reaction into question and coming very close to a biosemiotic understanding of species and multi-species intra-actions. From this perspective, the anthropomorphic gesture lies not in affirming that animals have a face and therefore ethics in a Levinasian sense, but rather in recognizing the denial itself, that is, the projection over singular animals of a categorical lack defined in linguistic terms, as oppositional concepts.

Finally, he argues in somewhat oblique fashion that animals cannot be exempted from ethical relation if they are indeed capable of pretense, which he ties in to Levinas's formulation of absolute vulnerability as the basis for relation and his own discussion of feeling shame/nakedness before the animal other:

> Yet if one takes into account seductive pursuit or predatoriness, a seduction that is tenderly or violently appropriative, one can no longer dissociate the moment of sexual parade from an exhibition, or exhibition from a simulation, or simulation from a dissimulation, or the dissimulative ruse from some experience of nakedness, or nakedness from some type of modesty. Hence some sort of modesty or shame, in the sense of some sensitivity to nakedness, would no longer be limited to the human and foreign to the *animot*.[83]

I will not belabor the point here for lack of space, but I would like to point out that many species of plants are known to "trick" pollinators as well as use defenses that mislead or misdirect predators to preserve their vital functions; in that sense, one cannot discount the possibility that plants, even if existing in a different temporality, also anticipate (the possibility of iteration) and respond to their others. Might one not also speak of plant pretense and modesty when considering how plants mimic insect shapes and pheromones and display or hide their sexual organs in response to certain signals? Could one consider fruit itself a "pretense" for reproduction in relation to the human or other animal that consumes it and distributes its seeds?

For Derrida, in any case, the question is not whether animals are aware that they are naked (and therefore demonstrate a sense of morality), but rather what nakedness as such means, why it generates feelings of shame and modesty. If, in gendered sexual exhibition, the female of a species does not accede immediately to the male's desire (and it must be desire rather than mere mechanistic reproductive instinct if it is projected toward the unrealized future, with reproduction as the potential but not guaranteed end result of the seductive performance), there is necessarily an element of choice, of passive decision, whereby the female decides to postpone the reproductive instinct, to withhold herself from the male, feigning indifference, always before the specter of sex. The question may not be one of morality as it is usually conceived of in human societies, as a generalized matter of conforming or not to socially defined norms of good or evil, but rather of whether or not the relation is desirable for her (although an ethologist might define morality itself in terms of the well being of a reproductive population, which would necessarily play out at the level of individual decision). Nonetheless, no one would deny that deciding what is proper, that is, what is contextually congruent or incongruent, is ultimately the purvey of the individual within the event of encounter and the social context. And competition over mating is clearly a question of sociality or what behavioral ecologists call social selection, since it has been demonstrated that, in many animal populations, desirability is defined collectively in relation to social rank, which is to say that individuals perceive a potential mate as more desirable when other individuals have shown interest in them.[84]

Either way, the female's feigned indifference, the deferral of decision, indicates awareness that the decision may be right or wrong for her. In short, it indicates self-doubt and doubt of the desirability of the male other (which both Heidegger and Levinas deny the animal). This is why Derrida states that, "every show of modesty is linked to a reserve of shame, to a reserve that attests to a virtual guilt."[85] There can be no deferral of decision without decision itself (the virtuality of multiple possibilities or choices) and without awareness that a decision may not be the proper one. From this perspective, natural selection itself becomes a passive decision, and there can be no clear dividing line between desire and reproductive instinct, between affiliative drives and ethics. This is not to say that there are no differences between humans and animals, but rather that human behavior exists on a continuum with animal behavior, not as an exception in any absolute sense of the word. For Derrida, then, the mistake lies not in associating animal sexual games with reproductive instinct, but rather in assuming that human pretense is ontologically distinct, that animals have no virtual life, no apprehension of the other as such, and therefore, no modesty (sense of vulnerability and therefore of death), no shame (no nakedness, no face), and, ultimately, no ethical standing. This is why Derrida follows his inquiry into animal modesty with a discussion of animal dreaming (which, as anyone who has lived with a dog who barks and twitches while sleeping is clearly the case), another form of virtuality that Descartes denied the animal. In other words, Derrida demonstrates that animals clearly exhibit the capacity for responding to the other as such, and therefore necessarily engage in an ethics of encounter even if it is not formalized as a symbolic code. This is why he states that, "it would not be a matter of 'giving speech back' to animals but perhaps acceding to a thinking however fabulous and chimerical it might be, that thinks the absence of the name and of the word otherwise, and as something other than a privation."[86]

Given the foundational status of the human-animal divide in Euro-American political thought, whereby the animal exclusion/sacrifice makes possible the conceptualization of the human polis, Derrida notes that the logical extension of Levinas's thought would be that the animal occupies the originary position of the third, who would later be substituted for by the human third upon the exclusion or sacrifice of the animal, which would in turn potentialize Aristotle's bios or political life as the origins of the state: "one might imagine that the animal, the animal-other, the other as animal, occupies the place of the third person and thus of the first appeal to justice, in between humans and the faces of those who look upon each other as brothers or neighbors."[87] However, Levinas elides entirely the question of the political status of the animal, thereby placing into question its exclusion altogether. Indeed, anyone who has ever lived with animals is familiar with their ability to act as thirds in a human-human encounter, interrupting the face-to-face and demanding a response.

The animal's position with respect to the law of hospitality, its very potential as the third and therefore the basis for both sociality and justice, can only be excluded by sovereign decree—that is, by naming them as animot and therefore an excluded class, categorically denied standing despite any affectivity they may inspire. Indeed, that primordial species exclusion as the basis for polity both precedes and makes possible the conceptualization of the citizen as brother, that is, of an entire chain of exclusions that are most often justified through animalization, which is to say dehumanization. Derrida leaves the question in a deconstructed state, although the implications are clear: if the animal can draw the human subject into a state of responsivity and is also capable of pretense (and therefore orientation toward the other), the animal necessarily can function as a third, placing the foundational demand for justice that constitutes the basis for both politics and the state. It is also in this sense that animals underpin the political order in Euro-American thought, as the foundational exclusion by which the law of hospitality and infinite justice transform into human/property rights enshrined in constitutional law (remembering that the foundational human right is the ownership of one's own body). The exclusionary political logic of brotherhood that Derrida deconstructs in *The Politics of Friendship* first relies on the exclusion of the animal, thus its reliance on animalizing tropes to justify gender, racial, and sexual exclusions (the equivalence drawn by some conservative politicians between homosexuality and bestiality immediately comes to mind).

The Forest as "Democracy-to-Come"

The transition from politics to a more-than-human cosmopolitics is beyond the purview of Derrida's essay, although his concept of the "democracy-to-come" necessarily implies that movement, particularly when read in tandem with *The Animal that Therefore I Am*. Nonetheless, cosmopolitics are not a mere hypothesis, a thought-experiment, an imagining of nonhuman rights akin to Cristopher Stone's famous essay "Should Trees Have Standing?" (1972) or Bruno Latour's "parliament of things." As I have shown in this chapter, the Yanomami and all other cultures that do not ascribe to the animot, to the human/nature divide, which is likely the numerical if not demographic majority of cultures throughout human history, have practiced for centuries or even millennia precisely this kind of cosmopolitics. Indeed, Derrida's thought tying together the first ethics of the face-to-face encounter with the emergence of justice and therefore the state through the third makes it clear that cosmopolitics always both precede and underpin the conceptualization of governance as such. This cosmopolitical basis is only overwritten through the induction into the political economy of humanism and its paradoxical reliance on demographic categorization as the basis for political representation, whereby the ethical orientation toward the other is displaced by biopolitical institutions that police these demographic categories through a carnophallogic of sacrifice and substitution.

Furthermore, Derrida's conceptualization of the "democracy-to-come" implies that the expansion of liberal rights to rightless humans and nonhumans did not in fact evolve organically as a logical extension of human dignity contra tyrannical forms of exclusion, but rather precisely from the aporia that emerges in the conflation of brotherhood with friendship, which is to say, through the attempt to impose legal strictures over the law of hospitality, to codify who, in fact, can be considered a third. Thus emancipation, women's rights, and animal rights do not emerge because of a re-categorization of enslaved people or women as fellow humans (brothers) or of animals as deficient humans, but rather because the aporia between the law of hospitality and the exclusionary figure of fraternity becomes overtly visible (usually due to systematic violence, as in the rise of the industrial slaughterhouse and vivisection laboratories in Europe in the nineteenth century) and therefore untenable at specific historical junctures. These junctures emerge from breaking points in political representation, in which it becomes clear that political representatives do not, in fact, serve the interests of the demographic categories they claim to represent (whether democratically or through sovereign power), but rather those of their own class (social, racial, gender, sexual, species) and those of the state itself as a hegemonic political formation.

It is at this moment in which constitutional law (enacted in political discourse) becomes perjurious in a secondary sense (following the initial perjury within the face-to-face relation that gives rise to the concept of justice or equality) and justice itself enters into contradiction, demanding redress, that is, legal reform. Nonetheless, no written law can ever fulfill the demand for absolute equality, that is "infinite hospitality" or "incalculable justice"; justice thus always haunts the law from within, exceeding it and demanding re-form. As Derrida concludes in *The Politics of Friendship*:

> For democracy remains to come; this is its essence in so far as it remains: not only will it remain indefinitely perfectible, hence always insufficient and future, but, belonging to the time of the promise, it will always remain, in each of its future times, to come: even when there is democracy, it never exists, it is never present, it remains the theme of a non-presentable concept. Is it possible to open up to the 'come' of a certain democracy which is no longer an insult to the friendship we have striven to think beyond the homo-fraternal and phallogocentric schema? When will we be ready for an experience of freedom and equality that is capable of respectfully experiencing that friendship, which would at last be just, just beyond the law, and measured up against its measurelessness? O my democratic friends . . .[88]

The Yanomami cosmopolitics of friendship, in its imperative to "acquire the traces of other" as the condition for engaging in political discourse, eschews entirely the logic of fraternity and its limits over hospitality, which is to say, who may act as a third and demand justice. Rather than the biopolitical institutions that Foucault accurately diagnosed at the heart of modern systems of governance (hospitals, mental institutions, prisons, and schools, as well as more orthodox political institutions such as congress and the courts), from which institutions designed to sequester the animal (pet stores, slaughterhouses, zoos, etc.) and "nature" itself (national parks, conservation reserves, etc.) cannot be excluded, the Yanomami recognize only two institutions: hospitality (not only that of the home as a spatial institution, but also that of the body as housing the traces of the other) and diplomacy. As I have argued, these are institutions that are designed to maintain fidelity not to the sovereign state and its constitutional order, but to justice itself, to the traces of the other. Furthermore, in viewing representation not as an act of over-writing but rather as the housing and enactment of the traces of the other, it becomes not only an act of intra-active diplomacy, but also of hospitality.

From this relational ontology, governance is reconceived as what I have referred to as "a state of plants," which is to say, a multispecies polis united in friendship relations (the face-to-face, but also always open to the de facto or potential third) and oriented toward the collective work of world build-ing, that is, the social production of what the Yanomami call the *Urihi-a*, the world-forest. The system of values that underpins this form of cosmopolit-ical governance is not commodification, with its reliance on the juridical persona-res distinction, but rather *në rope*, the value of growth, which is to say productive potential in intra-active relation. When the goal of the state is not producing docile, governable, and productive (in a capitalistic sense) citizens, but instead relations of reciprocal responsibility, the nature of insti-tutions—defined in a general sense as a political structures that maintain a particular form of governance—necessarily change. Rather than function-ing as what Foucault refers to as the panopticon, that is, coercive structures designed to produce self-discipline through the internalization of the sov-ereign gaze, the structures of governance in the state of plants emerge from within the encounter itself, as the reenactment of openness and ongoing fidelity to the traces of the other. Clearly, this is an other kind of state, but it is nevertheless a state in that it consists in a political structure that maintains itself from generation to generation through the enactment of law (the law of hospitality or incalculable justice) upheld by specific institutions (hospitality and diplomacy), and it constitutes citizenship through a system of reciprocal rights and obligations as well as communal territoriality (the ecosystem as what is proper, but not property, to the polis).

Indigenous Posthumanisms

Rethinking Modernity for Cosmopolitical Practice

As I discussed in the first two chapters of this book, the crucial problem that emerges in the implementation of rights of nature legislation is its fundamental incompatibility with Euro-American systems of representation, which extrapolate value (and therefore meaning and truth) through the abstraction of "essential" properties and their distribution in discrete, hierarchical categories that elide the messy materiality, multiplicity, and open-endedness of actual relations. This mode of conceiving of the relations between form and meaning generates polar oppositions between subjects and objects, humans and nature, and, in legal discourse, persona and res (property). In the Euro-American juridical framework, persona is not defined as either ontological singularity or nexus of relational multiplicities, but rather in seemingly pragmatic terms of autonomy in relation to property rights, as one who owns their own body and therefore retains the rights over it, which in turn affords them ownership rights over other forms of property. Clearly, this system of representation forecloses the possibility of any ethical orientation toward the "objects" that fall in the res category beyond a certain degree of flexibility in extending some degree of rights to entities that are seen as exhibiting proximity to rights holders through analogy, by demonstrating similar capacities for suffering and/or rational thought, usually through the metric of speech. This is why the vast majority of animal rights and nature conservation discourses rely on the utilitarian expansion of property rights. In the case of some, mainly domestic animals, evolutionary or affective proximity to the human body affords them a degree of self-ownership as long as they don't infringe on human rights such as access to food, freedom from real or imputed harm, and ownership for the purposes of companionship or work. Plants, insects, wild animals, and other organisms—especially those whose bodies are not easily equated to human bodies—are usually only granted a secondary degree of legal protection through human land ownership (as in public or private conservation easements) and/or in relation to preserving human freedom from harm or access to aesthetic pleasure. They are never considered to possess ownership over their own bodies.[1] Nonetheless, as Levinas argued regarding the "first" ethics of the face-to-face encounter and I discussed extensively in Chapters 3 through 5, the affectivity of intra-active relations always exceeds and problematizes categorical distinctions, thereby placing into question not only the bracketing of excluded classes from ethical and, ultimately, political standing, but also the legitimacy of abstract representation as a mode of approaching or approximating the other. It is precisely this ethical conundrum—the open-ended demand for justice—that modern social and political institutions are designed to supersede, reinforcing the validity of demographic categorization through what Foucault terms "subjectivation," or the construction of governable subjectivities that internalize state authority, which he figures through the metonym of the panopticon. Within this process, ethical responsibility is largely displaced from the individual to the state and its institutions, thereby eliding at least partially the sense of guilt that arises in committing the "perjury" that Derrida diagnosed in the displacement of the ethical demand for response placed on the subject by the other in face-to-face encounter. This is why Derrida contends that in order to create a truly democratic society, the carnophallogic underpinning political discourse—which relies on exclusionary figures of species, genealogical, and gender affinity—must be abandoned in favor of a politics of friendship, that is, an orientation toward the other, rather than the brother. The logic of friendship arising through "infinite hospitality" precludes the possibility of categorical exclusions, including animals, but also, as I argued in the last chapter regarding the Yanomami conceptualization of cosmopolitics, all entities capable of affecting others (leaving a trace), that is, all living beings and even the land itself.

It is undoubtedly challenging to imagine how this cosmopolitics of friendship might be put into practice in modern political systems, since it would appear to be largely incompatible with the modern state's biopolitical institutions, which are designed precisely to implement these demographic divisions and displace ethics from the purview of individual encounters to the realm of jurisprudence. Nonetheless, I will argue in this final chapter that such an engagement is indeed possible not only in theory, but also in practice. On the one hand, in what Crutzen and Stoermer refer to as the Anthropocene and Jason W. Moore reframes as the Capitalocene, that is, the global, anthropogenic modification/homogenization of environments at every scale since at least the Industrial Revolution, the human/nature conceptual divide has become untenable, and with it, the discourse of human exceptionalism that is underpinned by the persona/res distinction.[2] As these authors argue, environments never exist in isolation from human influence nor can humans ever live beyond environments; rather, they are coproduced through multi-scalar intra-actions between ecological and techno-cultural systems.

The invalidation of one of the foundational tenets of modern humanism—the human/nature divide—has in turn lead a number of Euro-American thinkers to redefine the grounds for the political to account for nonhuman agency. Broadly grouped under the umbrella of posthumanism, authors such as Karen Barad, Donna Haraway, Bruno Latour, and Isabelle Stengers have proposed a reappraisal of the hegemonic way of understanding the relations between humans and nonhumans through the persona/res distinction, usually through engaging scientific empiricism's mandate of objectivity, that is, the principle that knowledge about objects of study must come from the objects themselves. Indeed, one might argue that scientific knowledge engages to a degree in the representational practice of desistance or "detachment" in Latour's terminology, privileging the traces of the other within its representational framework.[3] Nonetheless, as Latour argues, this scientific knowledge is fully imbricated within the cult to the scientific "discoverer" as sovereign subject, who is seen as "making objects talk."[4] Within the scientific framework, the sense of objectivity is thus not produced through deferral to the object's own semiotic agency—that is, its ability to communicate information about itself—but rather through debate, experimental verification, and consensus within the scientific community, which effectively returns the powers of meaning and agency to human subjects and, in the process, reifies the phenomena in question as objects of human instrumentalization.

In the first part of this chapter, I discuss the nexus between objectivity, representational practices, ethical relations, and nonhuman political agency in the posthumanist theories of Haraway, Latour, and Stengers. I contend that while these theories represent ground-breaking attempts to rethink the relations between humans and nonhumans on the basis of intra-activity, their reliance on modern scientific methodologies effectively circumscribes any possibility for nonhuman political agency, since scientific knowledge always presupposes human mediation of ostensibly objective or unintentioned "data." In framing the signs displayed by nonhuman bodies as behavioral data or material properties, nonhuman bodies are depoliticized, rendered socially and politically inert, even when their ability to affect or influence human decision-makers is recognized. In short, this form of posthumanism tends to maintain the distinction between speech and affective agency that Barad, Derrida, and Hoffmeyer looked to deconstruct. In that sense, they provide no viable framework by which nonhumans can be said to represent themselves. And, as Tanasescu notes, there can be no political agency without representation, and no ethical or political standing without inclusion in a polity.[5]

It is for this reason that any serious attempt to put cosmopolitics in practice must take into account systems of representation in which nonhuman agency is not fully circumscribed by the symbolic order of language. Rather than the objectivity of scientific or political consensus, what Jason W. Moore called an "authentically multispecies politics of emancipation" would require a different form of objective representation, one that, as Derrida argued regarding animals, "would not be a matter of 'giving speech back' to animals but perhaps acceding to a thinking however fabulous and chimerical it might be, that thinks the absence of the name and of the word otherwise, and as something other than a privation."[6] Objectivity in this context would consist in the principle of maintaining open impartiality—what Lispector calls "objective" or "neutral life" and Derrida refers to as the "law of infinite hospitality"—toward the other in encounter, which in turn requires forms of representation that, rather than aiming to overwrite the other's singularity through demographic categorization and circumscribing the encounter through narrative emplotment, strive to maintain fidelity to it, deferring to their traces through the practice of desistance. As I discussed in Chapter 4 regarding Lispector's theorization of desistance (which she also calls objectivity), this form of representation neither erases/substitutes for the other's singularity through nominalization nor does it imply remaining in silence regarding the other. Instead, it approaches the other tentatively, as a nexus of potential relations of which the writing subject may form a part not only in the instant of encounter, but also through deferral to the other's traces within the reenactment of writing. In this sense, representation becomes an act of establishing and reenacting relations rather than an abstraction of either singularities or the social in the way that the latter is usually conceived, as an inferred totality or system of demographic categories such as gender, race, and economic class. This is why much of Lispector's work is nearly plotless; it is not about narrating the event of encounter, but re-enacting it as ongoing relation. And, as I argued in the last chapter, this way of viewing representation lies at the heart of cosmopolitical practice, as it implies that all others, human or not, function as thirds in the face-to-face relation, interpellating the subject from beyond the instant of encounter and demanding equal standing, that is, incalculable justice.

In short, cosmopolitical representation cannot be conceived of as the abstract capture and reiteration of either the extrapolated identitary essence or social interests of a human or nonhuman demographic, but instead must emerge through what Derrida called passive decision, that is, the deferral to the traces of the other and the enactment of relational potentials in the co-production of common differences. The Euro-American conceptualization of representation as essentially mimetic would have to be inverted to resemble Kopenawa's description of the relations between the *utupë* vital image and the body, wherein representation is not conceived of in terms of abstraction, but rather as the actualization of relational potentials within intra-action. Within this framework, virtual potentials—"vital images"—are nevertheless fully material in that they exist as properties or unactualized intra-active potentials within bodies, whereby bodies become "representatives" of actualized relations. As I argued in the last chapter, conceiving of representation in this way entails a fundamental shift away from the assignment of value based on abstract categorization and/or commodification (which, as Marx insisted, is essentially the abstraction of labor relations) toward one akin to the Yanomami concept of *në*, that is, potential productivity within multispecies labor relations. Cosmopolitical representation, then, cannot be oriented toward the values of economic growth or even human rights as such, but must instead focus on the common goal of *në rope* (the value of abundance), that is, of sustaining and reproducing life systems for all species, including humans, in their differences.

As theoretical as this proposition may appear, in the second part of this chapter I discuss how this mode of representation has been put into practice within modern political systems, usually as an intercultural, counterhegemonic strategy working to undermine the commodification of both nature and human labor within existing economic frameworks and juridical practice. Indeed, this is essentially the underlying principle of the Kichwa concept of *sumak kawsay* / buen vivir that anchors the 2008 Ecuadoran Constitution's rights of nature and social well-being provisions. While there are numerous other historical and current examples of Indigenous cosmopolitics engaging with modern political systems in transformational ways, I focus on two specific examples that exemplify cosmopolitical practice: the multi-ethnic Sin Maíz No Hay País (Without Maize, There is No Nation) food sovereignty movement in Mexico and the Ecuadoran Sarayaku Runa's proposal for a new international territorial designation called Kawsak Sacha (Living Forest), which was initially presented at the COP21 Climate Change Summit in Paris.

The Sin Maíz No Hay País movement weaves together the Indigenous view of intra-active becoming and world-making through multispecies work with the politics of national identity and economic sovereignty, arguing for a revalorization of the politics of corn production on the basis of entwined multispecies genealogies and reciprocal care. Similarly, Kawsak Sacha proposes an alternative to the Euro-American model of conservation, which emerged primarily in reaction to the unfettered expansion of commodities frontiers, whereby nature is protected through the exclusion of humans. Like the Yanomami, the Sarayaku Runa view the forest as a multispecies society bound together through biosemiotic communication and intra-active world-building, in which Indigenous communities play indispensable roles in maintaining the forest's health.[7] While engaging existing multicultural frameworks of Indigenous cultural preservation and property rights (within broader claims regarding territorial sovereignty) such as the 2007 United Nations Declaration on the Rights of Indigenous Peoples, the Kawsak Sacha proposal forces a reconsideration of the culture/territory, human/nature divide at the level of international law and governance. Both projects engage in a politics of interculturality, bringing Indigenous cosmopolitical frameworks into the terrain of modern legal practice, effectively demanding a renegotiation of the terms of modernity and humanism itself.

While posthumanist perspectives are usually associated with the deconstruction of the discourse of human exceptionalism from within Euro-American epistemological frameworks such as ecology, environmental history, ethology, neurobiology, and plant gnosophysiology, the key concern of cosmopolitics, or how nonhuman political agencies intra-act within social and political systems, necessarily emerges as a "common difference" or "partial connection" in what Viveiros de Castro would call "equivocal" (but not erroneous) relation with Indigenous ontologies. Indeed, many Euro-American proponents of posthumanist approaches acknowledge the potential for ostensibly "extramodern" relational ontologies to contribute to the project of reconceptualizing the grounds for subjectivity, the social, and the political in terms of complex networks of intra-activity, even when they recognize that they lack the conceptual tools for engaging Indigenous systems of thought in a rigorous and non-appropriative manner. However, many of the anthropologists I have cited throughout this book, among them Marisol de la Cadena, Philippe Descola, Eduardo Kohn, Marilyn Strathern, and Eduardo Viveiros de Castro, have touched upon the nexus between Euro-American posthumanist thought and Indigenous ontologies, at least tangentially, as in Kohn's deployment of Peircean biosemiotics to explain the Sarayaku Runa's apprehension of the forest as multispecies socius or Viveiros de Castro's engagement with Deleuze and Guattari's nomadology in his discussion of Amerindian perspectivism. Nonetheless, their disciplinary focus on ethnography tends to discourage an openly comparative, speculative approach toward intercultural political practice beyond the Indigenous communities they study.

In this chapter, I look to expand this work by undertaking a comparative analysis of the common differences that emerge between Indigenous cosmopolitical practice in what I have called the "state of plants" and Euro-American formulations of posthuman ethics and nonhuman political agency as they relate to the historical context of the Capitalocene. I engage the term "Indigenous posthumanisms" to underscore the ways in which Indigenous systems of thought have emerged following colonialization as contestatory, intercultural discourses from within modernity itself. Indeed, for posthumanist philosophy to have any transformational power, that is, for cosmopolitics to have practical implications, it cannot rely solely on the critique of its own humanistic premises or the recognition that nonhumans affect political systems, but must necessarily engage frameworks in which cosmopolitics function in practice, not only in theory. It is on this basis that I argue that the Sin Maíz No Hay País and Kawsak Sacha movements represent forms of Indigenous posthumanist activism that seek not to return to some idealized, precolonial past, but rather to transform in the present the terms of modern biogenetics and industrialized agriculture, in the first case, and the extractivism/nature conservation dialectic in the other.

Posthumanism: Thinking Past the Euro-American Human/Nature Dialectic

In his overview of posthumanist thought, Cary Wolfe notes that the deconstruction of the metaphysics of humanism—that is, the discursive construction of the human symbol—responded to two key movements in Euro-American philosophy, one related to the critical re-examination of the categorical distinctions between the human and the animal, often with an eye to drawing out the institutions that remove animals from ethical consideration and just treatment, and the other, frequently called transhumanism, emerging from the increasingly blurred lines between technologies and the "human" body.[8] In the first case, the Cartesian human/animal divide came into question with the rise of evolutionary biology in the nineteenth century, particularly following the massive cultural impact of Darwin's *The Origin of the Species* (1859). As would be expected, tracing humans' genetic origins to animals impelled a large volume of hyperhumanistic discourse seeking to reinforce species boundaries through tropes such as consciousness, speech, technology, and morality, to name only a few salient examples, which in turn have become the objects of analysis in ethological studies of animal and insect memory, sociality, and altruism; the exploration of the material basis of "consciousness" in the cognitive sciences; and the deconstruction of the discourse human exceptionalism and the sovereign subject in philosophy.

On the other hand, the hyperbolic growth since the 1950s of computer memory, processing speed, and algorithmic complexity, together with the rise of the internet (often framed by proponents of transhumanism not only as an informational network, but also a form of distributed cognition), have lead to a reconsideration of the meanings of intelligence and consciousness itself. At the same time, radical advances in medicine and human biology such as increasingly sophisticated limb, organ, and even neural prostheses; the use of in-vitro fertilization to produce human embryos; and gene editing and therapy technologies have placed into question just how "natural" the human body really is. In this context, transhumanist thought envisions a utilitarian future in which human and nonhuman bodies are fully managed for human well-being, that is, to minimize suffering, illness, disability, and "natural" limits on human capacities, up to and including death itself. Clearly, this would encompass not only individual human bodies, but also the technological modification for human benefit of other species and, ultimately, all environments at the planetary and even exoplanetary scales (for example, transhumanists like Elon Musk frequently dream of terraforming Mars).

In this context, Crutzen and Stoermer's proposal for the denomination of the Anthropocene as a new geological era could be seen as a posthumanist formulation from both the deconstructivist and transhumanist perspectives, since it indicates human technological agency over all environments at the planetary level, although proponents of the term do not usually share transhumanism's celebratory, often manic faith in human progress. Indeed, as Wolfe argues throughout his book, posthumanism and transhumanism are in a certain sense fundamentally oppositional even though they share the premise that the human/nature conceptual divide cannot be sustained. While deconstructive posthumanism looks to dismantle the discourse of human exceptionalism with the tacit or explicit goal of multispecies conviviality, transhumanism implies its full realization and generally only addresses ethics in terms of individual human well-being. As a wide range of critiques have made clear, transhumanism categorically downplays any ethical orientation not only toward nonhuman species, but also usually fails to address its ableist devaluation of non-normative human bodies, as well as the fundamental problem of equal access to the expensive technological "solutions" it promotes. In transhumanism, the human body is fully objectified as biological machine and consciousness is treated as informational (rather than transcendental), as bytes that may eventually be transferred to an external memory bank, a concept whose implications become truly dystopian when viewed in context, from within the hegemonic system of capitalistic extractivism and commodification.[9]

Donna Haraway: From Cyborgs to Depoliticized Companion Species

Feminist thinker Donna Haraway has been one of the most influential proponents of posthumanism in both its deconstructive and transhumanist aspects. Her 1985 "Cyborg Manifesto" prefigured Judith Butler's ground-shifting work in *Gender Trouble* and *Bodies that Matter*, arguing that human bodies are technocultural constructions embedded within what she calls an "infomatics of domination" that configures and naturalizes bodies in exploitative gender, class, and racial categories.[10] Despite itself being embedded within capitalist technoculture, Haraway envisions the cyborg as a deconstructive, emancipatory figure in its disavowal of the distinctions between nature and culture that have been used systematically to dehumanize women and nonwhite people as objects of domination. The cyborg's "illegitimate fusion of animal and machine" makes possible new, transgressive modes of kinship and polity that are not predicated on genealogical, gendered relational structures, but rather on horizontal association in encounter and partial connections (more along the lines of Deleuze and Guattari's "desiring machines" than Strathern's conceptualization of partial connections as an anthropological tool):

> The cyborg is resolutely committed to partiality, irony, intimacy, and perversity. It is oppositional, utopian, and completely without innocence. No longer

structured by the polarity of public and private, the cyborg defines a techno-logical polis based partly on a revolution of social relations in the *oikos*, the household. Nature and culture are reworked; the one can no longer be the re-source for appropriation or incorporation by the other.[11]

For Haraway, then, the cyborg is not simply the integration of machinery into the "natural" human body; it is a counterhegemonic mode of producing bodies in relational becoming, on the basis of what she calls in later works "sympoetic" intra-actions between bodies of all kinds, whether human, ani-mal, or machine.

Haraway deploys the term "sympoesis" to draw into productive tension Maturana and Varela's theorization of "autopoesis" as co-production within self-organizing systems and Lynn Margulis's conceptualization of "symbio-genesis," which looks to reframe the relative staticity of the biological concept of organismic symbiosis (in that symbionts are typically viewed as discrete entities) in terms of mutual evolution and becoming.[12] In *Staying with the Trouble*, she further relates it to Beth Dempster's early usage of the term to critique Maturana and Varela's conceptualization of autopoesis as occurring within self-enclosed systems; for Dempster, "collectively producing systems . . . do not have self-defined spatial or temporal boundaries. Information and control are distributed among components. The systems are evolution-ary and have the potential for surprising change."[13] However, Haraway is less interested in systematicity than emancipatory couplings; from her some-what anarchical perspective, sympoesis represents the possibility for dis-rupting or disempowering hegemonic systems at a relational level, through intra-activity between elements that are made artificially discrete through the infomatics of domination. Nevertheless, she does not view intra-activity as either prior to or existing beyond systems: "*sympoesis* is a word proper to complex, dynamic, responsive, situated historical systems. It is a word for worlding-with, in company. Sympoesis enfolds autopoeisis and generatively unfurls and extends it."[14] In that sense, what she looks to disrupt is the con-ceptualization of systems as self-contained and self-generating totalities comprised of discrete, interchangeable parts or components rather than concrete, intra-active relations between singularities. As in Barad's thought, the system emerges recursively through these intra-actions, rather than cir-cumscribing them fully.

While the "Cyborg Manifesto" clearly trends toward what would later be called transhumanism in its somewhat uncritical (in that it does not acknowl-edge the ethical and political implications of the necessarily unequal power relations involved in supposedly horizontal cyborg couplings) celebration of technological emancipation, it nevertheless also dismantles the nature/culture divide through integrating the animal third into the technoculture dyad. Animal rights thus come into play as cyborg technologies, as disruptors of the naturalization of the carnophallogic of domination: "movements for animal rights are not irrational denials of human uniqueness; they are a clear-sighted recognition of connection across the discredited breach of nature and culture."[15] However, the limitations of Haraway's thought for broaching cosmopolitical practice begin to emerge in this quote. While her focus increasingly shifted away from the figure of the cyborg toward multispecies relations in her work in the early 2000s, these relations always emerge from within capitalistic "nature-cultures" through the figure of domestication.

In *The Companion Species Manifesto* (2003), for instance, Haraway problematizes the family pet dog paradigm, arguing against the personification of dogs as "furry children" in favor of a mutual becoming-in-relation, whereby species differences are maintained and respected as "significant otherness."[16] This relation develops primarily through mutual work, through training practices or "technologies of behavioral management."[17] Despite opening her book with the query, "Whom and what do I touch when I touch my dog?," for Haraway, the dog is singular only as a companion, in relation with a human trainer. There is no problematization of the dog's demand for a response akin to Derrida's discussion of his cat's gaze. The animal's ethical standing emerges in practical working relation oriented toward mutual satisfaction and relative well-being, rather than operating at the level of subjectivity or intersubjectivity itself (a term she generally avoids, which in turn weakens her discussion of biosemiotic communications). Within this framework, the ethical orientation toward animals in sympoetic relations with humans essentially serves as a palliative for neoliberal transhumanism's excesses in relation to domesticated animals, that is, as a plea for the ethical relevance of animals on the basis of what they contribute to human lives as symbionts.

Nonetheless, Haraway's posthumanist approach to "companion species" would appear at face value to coincide in a general sense with many of the precepts of the Yanomami cosmopolitics of friendship that I examined in the last two chapters: the conceptualization of individuality as a multiplicity, as becoming-in-relation; the practice of interspecies exchange through embodied, biosemiotic communications; the goal of collaborative, multispecies work; and the idea that worlds or what she calls "worldings" are constructed relationally. However, Haraway's proposal eschews entirely any concept of political practice other than the deconstruction of the human/nature divide and the implementation of policies limiting animal abuse. As her usage of "worldings" over "worlds" implies, Haraway focuses on how humans conceive of their position in relation to an expansive network of relations from within the hegemonic technocultural system that ultimately institutes the human-nature divide, rather than the multispecies making of environments in the sense in which Indigenous thinkers conceive of worlds. It is for this reason that, despite her powerful critique of the colonial "god trick" whereby the sovereign Euro-American subject abstracts himself from the planet, transforming it into an object of analysis and planning from above, she repeatedly makes statements such as this one: "I was a kind of godhuman to Willem, a Great Pyrenees livestock guardian dog who worked on land in California that my family owns with a friend."[18] For Haraway, humans, animals, and machines co-create the world relationally, but only humans have the capacity to coordinate those relations in the production of social space.

In this scenario, nonhumans have no political agency other than the capacity to interpellate their human owners in an ambiguous way (usually through exhibiting suffering or pleasure), who then may or may not respond to their demand for nonabusive or rewarding, but not just or equitative treatment when it aligns with their own interests and/or empathetic capacities. In that sense, Haraway's theorization of companion species is a weak ethical formulation in comparison to that of Clarice Lispector, for example, for whom it is precisely the inhumanity of the animal other that constitutes the divine within the human, that is, absolute objectivity or openness (along the lines of Levinas's absolute other and Derrida's formulation of the law of infinite hospitality), which is similar to how the Yanomami view their relations with nonhumans. In both formulations, the "divine" stands in for political subjectivity, that is, the ability to decide and/or act for oneself and others. In contrast to the passive decision paradigm (the absolutely other deciding within and for me) and the institution of diplomacy in the state of plants, however, Haraway proposes a kind of humanistic monotheism, in which power is derived from the ability to create institutional frameworks from which one can manipulate and provide for those whom one chooses as companion species, that is, as significant others.

While she examines the roles of animals in a broader variety of institutions (the home, the farm/ranch, the laboratory, the industrialized chicken farm) in *When Species Meet*, the encounter with and the agency of the animal is always fully circumscribed by the institution in question. Unlike the Indigenous conceptualization of environment as a socius co-produced in working relation by all the species living within it, but who nevertheless work toward their own teloi, Haraway's working environments are fully human, techno-cultural spaces in the most limited sense, and they are oriented toward the capitalistic production of goods and services (including the social production of pleasure and a sense of achievement in the case of the dog competitions she references repeatedly).[19] Wild and stray domestic animals, who only make very brief appearances in Haraway's work, are devalued in a Hobbesian sense: they are animals that live "palpably fragile lives," in which they cannot reach their "full species potential" as defined by human trainers.[20] In that sense, her "contact zones" of human-animal encounter are not in fact open spaces of encounter, but rather institutions that circumscribe how intra-actions can play out within parameters delimited entirely by humans. It is in this sense in which she theorizes "encounter value": "trans-species encounter value is about relationships among a motley array of lively beings, in which commerce and consciousness, evolution and bioengineering, and ethics and utilities are all in play."[21]

In this formulation, the differences that emerge in relational encounter (Kopenawa's *õno* or Derrida's traces) are fully circumscribed by their institutional valorization, subordinated to the production of the institution itself: "working dogs produce and they reproduce, and in neither process are they their own 'self-directed' creatures in relation to lively capital, even though enlisting their active cooperation (self-direction) is essential to their productive and reproductive jobs. But they are not human slaves or wage laborers, and it would be a serious mistake to theorize their labor within those frameworks. They are paws, not hands."[22] All valorization is clearly derived from the production of economic and/or emotional capital (pleasure services), and ethical treatment is oriented toward maintaining the productive capacity of the work relations in question.[23] By extension, all animals who do not participate in narrowly defined symbiotic productive relations within specific anthropocentric institutions are devalued or valueless, that is, without representation. In that sense, when Haraway speaks of worldings, it is always within the bounds of what Jason W. Moore called the capitalist world-ecology, that is, the global production of business environments in the broadest sense, encompassing all phases of commercial activity up to and including natural resource extraction.[24]

During the early 2000s, when Francis Fukuyama's triumphalist prediction of the end of history under the peaceful hegemony of neoliberal consensus seemed more plausible than today, Haraway's companion species proposal based its claim for relevance on the pragmatic mitigation from within of the animal "killing machines" at work in capitalistic technocultures. However, as the consequences of anthropogenic climate change and global environmental devastation due to neoliberal extractive practices became increasingly impossible to downplay (among them war over dwindling resources and the horizon of a sixth great extinction event), she abandoned her apology of capitalistic technocultures to propose a more biocentric approach. This shift is marked by a change in slogans; whereas throughout her work she had proclaimed that "we were never individuals," in *Staying with the Trouble: Making Kin in the Chthulucene*, the catchphrase shifts from "we are all cyborgs" to "we are all lichens" or "corals."[25] Arguing against the apocalyptic end of history embedded within the terms "Anthropocene" and "Capitalocene," she proposes an alternative geocultural period/praxis called the "Chthulucene," which would be characterized by de-commodified forms of "monstrous" sympoetic relations oriented toward multispecies "kin-making" and the art of ethical "living on a damaged planet":

> Speaking resurgence to despair, the Chthulucene is the timespace of the sym-chthonic ones, the symbiogenetic and sympoetic earthly ones, those now submerged and squashed in the tunnels, caves, remnants, edges, and crevices of damaged waters, airs, and lands. The chthonic ones are those indigenous to the earth in myriad languages and stories, and decolonial Indigenous peoples and projects are central to my stories of alliance.[26]

Presented as a science fiction of a present that is already becoming postapocalyptic, the Chthulucene thus envisions a shift away from figures of resistance within domestic technocultures toward the wild and the Indigenous, which, as I discussed in the last two chapters, is a highly problematic conflation.[27]

In terms of political praxis, which is only alluded to nebulously, the Chthulucene would imply a return to Clastres's neo-Romantic formulation of Indigenous cultures as "societies against the state," in which kinship alliances are viewed as forms of grassroots resistance. Paradoxically, community emerges contra polity through a rigorous form of social engineering, in which "the decision to bring a new human infant into being is *strongly structured* to be a collective one for the emerging communities."[28] What this decision-making structure would look like or how it would be implemented is never discussed in depth, although a wide range of mainly Indigenous American samplings are invoked in passing, without any detailed discussion of ontologies, social structures, or political practice beyond acts of resistance.

Rather than technocultural work, human-animal relations would now be structured by ambiguous kinship ties, in which select animals become part of the family/community through human decision:

This freedom's most treasured power is the right and obligation of the human person, of whatever gender, who is carrying a pregnancy to choose an animal symbiont for the new child. All new human-members of the group who are born in the context of community decision-making come into being as symbionts with critters of actively-threatened species, and therefore with the whole patterned fabric of living and dying of those particular beings and all their associates, for whom the possibility of a future is very fragile.[29]

As these passages reveal, Haraway's proposal largely consists in an appropriation and decontextualization of actual Indigenous systems of thought, social structures, and cosmopolitical practices for the construction of a universal, ultimately humanistic theoretical framework, even when she cites certain Indigenous beliefs and cases of political activism as supporting evidence. And it is precisely this decontextualization, this failure to defer to multiple others' perspectives, that is, to imagine representation as something other than overwriting the other's traces, that weakens Haraway's proposal in terms of both ethical responsibility and viable cosmopolitical practice.

As a case in point, unlike the native Amazonian conceptualization of the forest as a multispecies socius, which requires ongoing diplomacy with non-human others, always before the specter of predation, Haraway's proposal subsumes difference almost entirely to the kinship relation. This is clearly evident in the just-quoted passage, which appropriates the recurrent Indigenous concept of the nahual or animal double, transforming it from a marker of becoming in multiplicity, in difference to the self, into a form of wardship.[30] For Haraway, political agency—decision-making for collectivities—is always the purview of the human; symbiotic animals are chosen by human parents and there is no face-to-face encounter with the animal as person, as singular other or *utupë* capable of affecting the human and coproducing the ecosocial order. The animal double is merely a protected class. Hospitality is thus not a passive decision, but a form of ecosocial engineering, of conservation. In turn, there is no need for diplomatic rapprochement, for addressing the other in their difference, among kin. As in the *Companion Species Manifesto*, all those who remain outside of the domestic relation are considered externalities, excluded from ethical or political standing.

In fact, kin-making becomes a eugenic exercise in *Staying with the Trouble*, a form of biopolitics that substitutes for the state (whether the modern state or what I called the state of plants). Following the long-standing North American conservationist tradition of framing the "Great Acceleration" in terms of human population growth (usually laying the blame on the "Third World") rather than capitalistic hyperproduction and overconsumption,

Haraway reimagines "decolonial feminist reproductive freedom" in terms of "making kin not babies": "kin-making as a means of reducing human numbers and demands on the earth, while simultaneously increasing human and other critters' flourishing, engaged intense energies and passions in the dispersed emerging worlds."[31] While her framing of this slogan initially appears relatively altruistic in terms of multispecies well-being and habitat conservation, it takes on more sinister overtones when read in conjunction with her apology of canine reproductive control on the basis of quality of life in *The Companion Species Manifesto*.[32] What emerges is a biopolitics of multispecies eugenics that could clearly only be implemented through some form of coercive institutionality. And biopolitics are always fundamentally opposed to cosmopolitics, since they consist in the full, bodily overwriting of the other's traces in the institutional production of standardized, governable bodies.

In the end, *Staying with the Trouble* offers a degree of solace in imaging an unalienated present-future among the ruins left by capitalistic modernity, but it fails to link ethics with justice and therefore the possibility for any new form of political praxis. Ethics are delimited by the kinship relation and the bounds of community, expanded only through the figure of migration and what Haraway refers to as "tentacular thinking" (a figure for appropriation?), while politics exist only in resistance, as societies against the state. There are no laws or institutions to generate equality (whether those of the liberal tradition or the incalculable justice of the state of plants), only a utopian conviviality suspiciously free of conflict. In short, the extraction of Indigenous tropes and concepts from concrete ontological frameworks and cosmopolitical practices has the effect of depoliticizing them, rendering them abstract, and transforming Haraway's ethos of sympoesis into a kind of mystical materialism that has no viable route to implementation other than apocalypse. The decomposition of all cultural, political, and social structures is required to allow the "Children of Compost" to emerge as the predominant social order or praxis (since it is fundamentally an anarchistic concept).

Latour's Parliament of Things

In contrast, French philosopher and sociologist Bruno Latour's form of posthumanism—or what he calls "redistributed humanism"—looks to transform current disciplinary and juridical practices through granting objects political standing in what he calls the "parliament of things." In *We Have Never Been Modern* (1993), he argues that the seventeenth century debate between natural philosopher Robert Boyle and political theorist Thomas Hobbes regarding the relations between scientific empiricism and political forms set the stage for the consolidation of the two as discrete fields, whereby the sciences were conceived as the realm of nature/objects and politics were limited to the sociology of human relations. From that point on, claims Latour, modern thought "had to see double . . . and not establish direct relations between the representation of nonhumans and the representation of humans, between the artificiality of facts and the artificiality of the Body Politic. The word 'representation' is the same, but the controversy between Hobbes and Boyle renders any likeness between the two senses of the word unthinkable."[33] Through the twin conceptual technologies of purification (the production of discrete essences) and translation (of the properties of objects and social collectivities), modern thought constituted the subject/object, human/nature division in terms of "the subject of law" and the "object of science": "the political spokespersons come to represent the quarrelsome and calculating multitude of citizens; the scientific spokespersons come to represent the mute and material multitude of objects. The former translate their principals, who cannot all speak at once; the latter translate their constituents, who are mute from birth."[34] In this way, disciplinary representational forms became technologies for slicing through the complex multiplicities of what he calls the "Gordian knot" of reality, in which nature and society are phenomenologically inseparable, at the same time freeing up the loose strands for disentanglement into new, ever more specialized disciplines that, in turn, allowed for the mass mobilization of both spheres (nature and society) in the ever-expanding production of new scientific, economic, and political technologies.[35]

However, these mobilizations necessarily affect both spheres, that of materiality and that of social relations, creating what Latour calls "quasi-objects" that elude or exceed the capacities of the technologies of purification and disciplinary translation. This happens because "the apparently reasonable division between material and social becomes just what is obfuscating any enquiry on how a collective action is possible," leading to postulations of chains of causality that are always partial (limited to the object of study rather than its relations in the broad sense) and therefore abstract, the product of disciplinary inference.[36] These quasi-objects exist simultaneously in the realms of nature and culture and thereby draw into question the validity of the disciplinary divisions between science and the social: "But quasi-objects continue to proliferate: those monsters of the first, second and third industrial revolutions, those socialized facts and these humans turned into elements of the natural world. No sooner are totalities closed in on themselves than they start cracking all over. The end of history is followed by history no matter what."[37] In a way akin to Michael Marder's discussion of plant heterotemporality, these quasi-objects possess their own temporal trajectories, moving simultaneously, yet asynchronously in human and natural history, thereby disrupting the conceptualization of history itself as the narrative of human progress, that is, modernity as a continual break with and "annihilation" of past forms.[38] In other words, these socially and naturally co-produced quasi-objects would disrupt both the modern logic of detached, disciplinary epistemologies and the conceptualization of progress as discontinuity with the past, which is why he claims that "we have never been modern."

According to Latour, modern thought attempts to mitigate these quasi-objects' threats to its foundational premises through the consolidation of what he refers to as a "Constitution," in both the senses of a foundational archive of inviolable juridical principles and of a template for constituting or mass-producing objects and social relations. He delineates "two constitutional guarantees of the moderns," "the universal laws of things and the inalienable rights of subjects," which are upheld through the sorting of quasi-objects' properties into four representational "repertoires" designed to parse them into discrete, controllable quantities: nature or external reality (the realm of science), society (the realm of social sciences and politics), meaning and narrative (semiotics and art), and being (philosophy and its "crossing out" of God).[39] Nonetheless, the practical application of these disciplinary repertoires endlessly generates new quasi-objects that always exist simultaneously in the materiality of nature and in social relations, thereby continually placing the modern Constitution and its disciplinary divisions into question: "the machine for creating differences is triggered by the refusal to conceptualize quasi-objects, because this very refusal leads to the uncontrollable proliferation of a certain type of being: the object, constructor of the social, expelled from the social world, attributed to a transcendent world that is, however, not divine—a world that produces, in contrast, a floating subject, bearer of law and morality."[40] In this way, the subject and object are revealed as co-constituting and ultimately inseparable even in the midst of the process of disciplinary representation.

This is why Latour advocates for a reformulation or amendment of this modern Constitution that would breach the gap between the "two branches of government," science as the government of things and politics as human government, in a "non-modern Constitution" upheld by a parliament of things. This would be accomplished through the institutional recognition that quasi-objects are never simply objects, but rather "actants" that run transversal to all four disciplinary repertoires, possessing "action, will, meaning, and even speech."[41] While the term "actant" is not rigorously defined in *We Have Never Been Modern*, in *Reassembling the Social* he clarifies that agency is never an inherent property, but rather is mobilized within intra-actions:

> If action is limited a priori to what "intentional," "meaningful" humans do, it is hard to see how a hammer, a basket, a door closer, a cat, a rug, a mug, a list, or a tag could act. They might exist in the domain of "material," "causal" relations, but not in the "reflexive," "symbolic" domain of social relations. By contrast, if we stick to our decision to start from the controversies about actors and agencies, then any thing that does modify a state of affairs by making a difference is an actor—or, if it has no figuration yet, an actant. Thus, the questions to ask about any agent are simply the following: Does it make a difference in the course of some other agent's action or not? Is there some trial that allows someone to detect this difference?[42]

Upon conceiving of material objects as agential in this sense, representation would be freed from the mandates of purification and translation into disciplinary categories, which transform "mediators" such as scientists and politicians into mere intermediaries between the segregated natural and social realms.

In the parliament of things, all quasi-objects become mediators who "delegate" information about themselves to other actants within the relational network. In that sense, they "transcend" their materiality through relating to the intra-active network, rather than by passing through disciplinary translation from the material to the abstraction of the episteme or the social:

> I call this transcendence that lacks a contrary "delegation." The utterance, or the delegation, or the sending of a message or a messenger, makes it possible to remain in presence—that is, to exist. When we abandon the modern world, we do not fall upon someone or something, we do not land on an essence, but on a process, on a movement, a passage—literally a pass, in the sense of this term as used in ball games. We start from a continuous and hazardous existence—continuous because it is hazardous—and not from an essence; we start from a presenting, and not from permanence. We start from the vinculum itself, from passages and relations, not accepting as a starting point any being that does not emerge from this relation that is at once collective, real, and discursive. We do not start from human beings, those latecomers, nor from language, a more recent arrival still. The world of meaning and the world of being are one

and the same world, that of translation, substitution, delegation, passing. We shall say that any other definition of essence is "devoid of meaning"; in fact, it is devoid of the means to remain in presence, to last. All durability, all solidity, all permanence will have to be paid for by its mediators.[43]

This amendment of re-presentation thus implies reconfiguring academic disciplines and political institutions to account simultaneously for the empirical and the relational, a process that requires the practice of analytical "symmetry"—that is, one in which the researcher positions themselves "at the median point where he can follow the attribution of both human and nonhuman properties."[44] In other words, researchers must apply the same analytical principles and methodologies used to describe objects—now actants—to those who were formerly conceived of as subjects.

The practice of empiricism would thus make possible a more objective analysis of relations through deferral to self-representation, in the sense in which science views objects as "speaking for themselves" with the scientist acting as mediator. In mediating the representations "delegated" by other actants, the human researcher becomes a "weaver of morphisms," capable of translating them to the human without anthropomorphizing them, that is, equating them to human subjectivity or intentionality.[45] The scientist still engages in translation, but the act of translation has changed fundamentally, becoming "a relation that does not transport causality but induces two mediators into coexisting."[46] In this scientific form of what Lispector called "desistance" and Viveiros de Castro denominates "controlled equivocation," the human is constituted not in opposition to nature, but as a conspicuous delegator: "it is true that by redistributing the action among all these mediators, we lose the reduced form of humanity, but we gain another form, which has to be called irreducible. The human is in the delegation itself, in the pass, in the sending, in the continuous exchange of forms. . . . Human nature is the set of its delegates and its representatives, its figures and its messengers."[47] In that sense, Latour proposes a reconceptualization of humanity not as transcendental category, but as a particular set of representational strategies fully embedded within material relations.

This way of conceiving of representation, designed to apprehend the objectivity of relations, would form the basis for political decision-making in that quasi-objects would act politically, as objective judges regarding claims made by human mediators regarding their own representations and therefore of decisions made on that basis. Nonetheless, despite Latour's nebulous claim that quasi-objects have "will," a question that he never fully problematizes (although Karen Barad's theory of intra-activity would provide some support), his proposal for a "Non-Modern Constitution" continues to associate objectivity with "Nature" and freedom with "Society."[48] From this perspective, nonhumans ostensibly act "willfully" not as singular individuals possessing the power of decision-making, but by affecting or structuring to a degree the social-material network around them, mobilizing other actants. Of course, from a fully materialist perspective such as that of Barad, one could certainly argue that this definition would apply to humans as well. Nonetheless, nonhumans would have only very limited access to freedom as Latour defines it: "third guarantee: freedom is redefined as the capacity to sort the combinations of hybrids that no longer depend on a homogeneous temporal flow."[49] One would infer that "sorting" would refer to categorization by kind, which necessarily requires a "purifying" technology that elevates a single or class of qualities as essential, while downplaying myriad differences. This kind of technology would be necessary for the object(ive) of politics as such: "fourth guarantee: the production of hybrids, by becoming explicit and collective, becomes the object of an enlarged democracy that regulates or slows down its cadence."[50] In this way, an object-oriented democracy would emerge possessing a greater degree of oversight over the collective production of all the quasi-objects that compose reality, which is, in the end, a veiled reference to economic regulation.

In an inversion of Haraway's formulation of an ethical society against the state rooted in kinship, Latour formulates an objective form of governance without ethics. Despite the shift from "matters of fact" to "matters of concern," whereby one might assume that quasi-objects have some form of ethical standing, Latour never really addresses the problem of justice, which is, in the end, the foundational telos of representation in the construction of the social, at least according to Levinas and Derrida.[51] Instead, these matters of concern emerge as such in relation to the decision-making body, which is composed of human practitioners still defined by disciplinary practices (science, politics, economics, moralism), but which are now oriented toward skill sets rather than governing principles.[52] These practitioners of "political ecology" would be divided among two congressional chambers or "houses" that would blend and replace what he sees as the current governing structure segregated into the "House of Scientific Inquiry" and the "House of Politics." The "Upper House" in this new political structure would be tasked with:

> detect[ing] the candidates for existence, translat[ing] their propositions into its own language, f[inding] for each the jury that can answer for its quality in

sponsoring it. In the terms of our historical fiction, this amounts to saying that each group of foreigners makes its solemn entrance into the city, behind a more or less vast group of members of the collective with whom they have established bonds of friendship or who have been designated as their judges, sponsors, constituents, or guarantors.[53]

In terms of "matters of concern," the human and nonhuman constituents of the parliament of things would thus be decided by this panel of experts on the basis of their relations to the collective, the degree to which they affect it and therefore require integration into governance or regulation. However, this Upper House would be concerned only with the "problem of taking into account ('How many are we?)" on the basis of difference; it would not itself make any "propositions" (which Latour substitutes for "laws" due to their contextual contingency on conditions at any given moment) regarding collective governance.[54] This task would fall to the "Lower House," which would evaluate the "question of compatibility, of the articulation of the propositions among those already recognized."[55] In turn, these contingent propositions regarding policy, always subject to re-evaluation, would take the place of rights (those of the subject, denied to the object) in the modern Constitution. While experts of the four disciplines outlined here would be responsible for analyzing specific aspects of these propositions, all would utilize his Actor-Network Theory as their guiding methodology, replacing the concept of the social with that of human-nonhuman collectivities.

Throughout *Politics of Nature*, Latour downplays ethics, equating them with ideological presuppositions that are rooted in universalizing systems of moral valuation that claim precedence over empirical practice.[56] Nonetheless, he continues to find a role for "moralists" (by which one assumes he refers to anyone concerned with justice, that is, philosophers of ethics, human and/or animal rights proponents, feminists, postcolonialists, environmentalists, theologians, etc.) within his scheme in that they continually reject disciplinary exclusions regarding the political (and therefore moral) standing of entities. Moralists would essentially be tasked with maintaining the collective's openness, permitting re-circulation between the two houses, so that no entity is forever excluded from political standing.[57] In that sense, Latour looks to remove ethical valuation from the purview of absolutist ideological frameworks and subject every ethical proposition to debate within the parliament of things. Paradoxically, there are in fact at least three unsupported ethical principles/injunctions that underpin Latour's formulation of political ecology: one, that diversity/multiplicity is good and reductivism is bad;

two, "the requirement to treat no entity simply as a means"; and three, that there is, in fact, a greater good (a "good world"), even if provisional and subject to revision.[58] Clearly, a consensus regarding those three principles would be absolutely necessary for the parliament of things to be put into practice.

Without a route from the individual encounter with the other to ethical relation to collective justice, the parliament of things can only remain a thought experiment, with little possibility for making any real political impact. This route is closed a priori due to the foundational precepts of science itself; even when scientific experimentalism may be capable of recognizing objects' affective or material agency, its imperative of impartial observation immediately overwrites any sense of responsibility that may emerge from within the "face-to-face" encounter with its objects of study. All that is left is a hollow network, an inference of forces that relate actants, and a passionate or dispassionate debate among a panel of experts regarding whether those forces' effects on its human and nonhuman constituents are positive or negative. This is why, unlike Derrida's democracy-to-come, which continually actualizes itself in the present whenever any form of democratic governance is practiced, the parliament of things, the "liberated State, a State freed from all forms of naturalization," is projected far into the future: "Gaia is not Mother Earth, a divine ancestor from whom our collective supposedly descends, but at best our remote great-grand-niece, whom only a civilized collective will be able to generate according to due process."[59] Nonetheless, Latour's methodology of Actor-Network Theory has had a notable impact in the social sciences, particularly in the sociology of commodities and the shift toward object-oriented ontologies in anthropology. In that sense, it clearly has the potential for transforming political practice, but, I argue, it must necessarily engage interculturally existing political forms such as the Indigenous cosmopolitical projects I analyze further on in this chapter.

Isabelle Stengers: Cosmopolitics and the Ecology of Practices

While not as explicitly posthumanist as Latour's thought, Isabelle Stengers's proposal for an "ecology of practices" rooted in cosmopolitics shares much with his critique of the science/social disciplinary divide, if from a somewhat distinct angle. In her multi-volume work *Cosmopolitics*, she undertakes an extensive analysis of the historical conceptualization of "natural laws" in physics, in which she demonstrates how these "laws" emerged not through the unproblematic, mathematical description of external and eternal "natural" forces, but rather from within the historical development of the nexus between experimental practices, debate within the scientific community, and broader social institutions. On the one hand, physics, as the "hardest" of the hard sciences, came to demand the rigorous separation of empiricism from both ideology and the social sphere despite its heavy reliance on mathematical abstraction and iterative scientific consensus. The demand for the correlation between theory and practice, oriented toward a unified theory explaining the totality of "natural" forces in the universe, resulted in a paradigm of "reciprocal capture," whereby the requirements and constraints placed by specific experimental methodologies produced "vectors of obligation" to which physicists and the questions they could legitimately ask were made to respond.[60] In this way, practitioners and scientific knowledge were bound together in "mutually referring identities" mobilized by and organized around what Stengers, following Latour, calls "factishes," that is, interpretations of data that are socially imbued with a sense of absolute truth.[61] As she summarizes, "factishes are a way of affirming the truthfulness of the relative, that is, a way of relating the power of truth to a *practical event* and not to a world to which practices would merely provide access."[62] This problem of "reciprocal capture" thus produced a system of thought and constellation of practices oriented toward divining/constructing a fundamental state of equilibrium, while disallowing any approach outside its own methodologies and disavowing the tumultuous debates and socially muddled process by which these facts came to be viewed as such, that is, as incontrovertible truths.

Nonetheless, the conceptualization of natural forces existing in a state of permanent stasis or equilibrium is continually put to the test by the emergence of "enigmatic factishes"—that is, facts that are unexplainable or "illegitimate" according to existing paradigms but that are nevertheless assumed to be true due to experimental evidence and/or mathematical proofs.[63] Citing the example of quantum physics and its description of the neutrino, these enigmatic factishes "weaken the intuitive power of the concept of a state" and draw attention to the limits of what may be known or intelligible to scientists.[64] In physics, this lead to a shift from mechanistic formulas to probabilities, which effectively "reflects the physicists' freedom not to take 'observable phenomena' into account but to discount them."[65] With the rise of quantum physics came a questioning of both the fundamental nature of the universe and of the fidelity or truthfulness (in an absolute sense) of our representations of it: "enigmatically but incontestably, the intelligibility of the world must make itself known, and the sign that it has done so is the wound it inflicts on our evidence."[66] This is why Stengers counters the conceptualization of the universe as a bounded space defined by invariable natural laws with that of the "cosmos," which alludes to the "unknown," what lies "outside" mechanical rationality and must therefore remain a matter of speculation and debate regarding the limits of empiricism and epistemologies.

The conceptualization of the cosmos is always political in that it destabilizes the staticity of the physical "state" as such, that is, as a permanent and invariable equilibrium that recovers any perturbations to its order. Furthermore, it extends beyond the debate in physics regarding the nature of the universe to other, competing cosmologies that modern science dismisses as non-factual or fetishistic and against which it engages in ontological "warfare" (thus her frequent references to "Science Wars"). As she summarizes in "The Cosmopolitical Proposal,"

> the cosmos must therefore be distinguished here from any particular cosmos, or world, as a particular tradition may conceive of it. It does not refer to a project designed to encompass them all, for it is always a bad idea to designate something to encompass those that refuse to be encompassed by something else. In the term cosmopolitical, cosmos refers to the unknown constituted by these multiple, divergent worlds and to the articulations of which they could eventually be capable. This is opposed to the temptation of a peace intended to be final, ecumenical: a transcendent peace with the power to ask anything that diverges to recognize itself as a purely individual expression of what constitutes the point of convergence of all. There is no representative of the cosmos as such; it demands nothing, allows no "and so . . .". And its question is therefore intended primarily for those who are masters of the "and so . . .," we who with our heavy doses of "and so . . ." may well, in all good will, identify ourselves with the representatives of problems that concern everyone, whether we like it or not.[67]

For this reason, she diverges from Latour's proposal for a parliament of things despite coinciding with many of his arguments. For Stengers, it is precisely the expert who must learn to live with a passing sense of "fright" that "scares self-assurance, however justified."[68] Therefore, no panel of experts (Latour's Houses) will ever be sufficiently broad to judge the truth value of any competing worldview or "proposition" relating to it. While not discarding the role of experts in presenting propositions derived from their specific worldviews, Stengers insists that cosmopolitics must always rely on acts of diplomacy between competing ontologies.

In that sense, she opposes the sense in which Kant deployed the term "cosmopolitics" in the service of transcendental idealism. In a non-transcendental cosmopolitics or "ecology of practices":

> Experts are the ones whose practice is not threatened by the issue under discussion since what they know is accepted as relevant. Their role will require them to present themselves and to present what they know, in a mode that does not foresee the way in which that knowledge will be taken into account. By contrast, diplomats are there to provide a voice for those whose practice, whose mode of existence and whose identity are threatened by a decision. "If you decide that, you'll destroy us." Diplomats' role is therefore above all to remove the anesthesia produced by the reference to progress or the general interest, to give a voice to those who define themselves as threatened, in a way likely to cause the experts to have second thoughts and to force them to think about the possibility that their favorite course of action may be an act of war.[69]

Stengers thus envisions cosmopolitical practice as acts of diplomacy between human mediators. Nonetheless, she opens a space for nonhumans through the mandate of consultation in decision-making, which would coincide with Latour's usage of the term as the reverse side of the "delegation" of the object's speech: "I chose the term consultation because it can apply both in the political domain and in places where 'invisibles' need to be convoked and consulted; these invisibles are insensitive to compromises and do not share human reasons but signify that humans are not the holders of what makes their identity."[70] In the case of those who are threatened by decisions but whose participation in the decision-making process cannot be "enforced," she suggests that a witness may stand in for them, making them present and "conveying what it may feel like to be threatened by an issue that one has nothing to contribute to."[71] In turn, this mode of presence complicates decision-making by invalidating the concept of externalities, that is, "any shortcut or simplification, any differentiation a priori between that which counts and that which does not."[72] It is in that sense in which she refers to the cosmos as "an operator of 'putting into equality,' in opposition to any notion of equivalence."[73]

The practice of diplomacy implies negotiation between multiple political forms, which is why she does not propose a single political structure akin to Haraway's anarchistic Children of Compost or Latour's more structured parliament of things. Since the ontologies that enter into diplomacy are always "divergent" in that, rather than common interests or a shared worldview, they come together through the dispute itself, in "connecting events" that define the contours of the common but contested grounds they inhabit.[74] In that sense, their form of relationality is fundamentally symbiotic, in that they "positively relate heterogeneous terms even as the terms diverge."[75] As she summarizes, "symbiotically related beings go on diverging, go on defining in their own manner what matters for them. Symbiosis means that these beings are related by common interests, but common does not mean having the same interest in common, only that diverging interests now need each other. Symbiotic events are a matter of opportunity, of partial connection, not of harmony."[76] In this context, diplomacy does not denote the possibility of arriving at consensus through the translation of opposing interests into a neutral (i.e. scientific, political, or economical) language, but rather agreeing to accept rapport, to engage in negotiation as an alternative to warfare.[77]

Furthermore, unlike experts, diplomats cannot make decisions on their own; they must always enter into agreement following consultation and ratification by the political bodies they represent.[78] All decision-making processes would thus necessarily arise through twin processes of diplomacy and consultation between multiple ontologies: "if politics is ontological, ontological clashes would have to be anticipated everywhere as no issue can any longer be considered a matter of free deliberation, putting into brackets the worlds it implies and the way it matters in these worlds. It would be diplomacy all the way down."[79] Within this framework, ethics would become a pragmatic matter, a question not of deferring to "the power of some greater reason," but of attention and discernment within each particular case or symbiotic event.[80] In this sense, Stenger's thought runs close to Badiou's and Lispector's formulations of ethics as maintaining fidelity to the truth of the event, that is, the encounter with the other. "Consultation" would thus emerge as the politicized aspect of Lispector's "desistance," that is, the form of representation most appropriate for evoking the traces of the other within the reenactment of the event of encounter during the decision-making process.

Posthumanism and Indigenous Ontologies

It is notable that, despite their deep reliance on the sciences for their critique of humanistic objectification/reification, all three of the "posthumanist" theorists I have discussed here return to Indigenous ontologies as foils and/or alternatives to the modern human/nature divide. While Haraway envisions a kind of decontextualized, de-racialized, neo-Indigenous sci-fi future, Latour evokes the deconstructive potential of what modern practitioners disavow as "premodern" ontologies in discerning the hybrid nature of quasi-objects.[81] However, shamans and other non-modern practitioners do not figure as experts in Latour's formulation of the parliament of things; they simply mark difference, that is, the possibility of alternatives to the modern human/nature divide. Stengers, on the other hand, does not engage Indigenous ontologies directly, but she opens the grounds for diplomatic exchange by locating the political practice of her formulation of an "ecology of practices" squarely within the purview of ontological diplomacy. Furthermore, she argues that modernity's first commandment, "thou shalt not regress," reveals a fundamental "fright" with respect to non-modern ontologies such as what has traditionally been described as "animism" in anthropology.[82]

For Stengers, animism and "magic" are practices that privilege what David Abrams calls the "art of immanent attention," that is, a form of sensorial being-in-the-world that allows one to conceive of agency not as the purview of the sovereign human subject, but as something that is proper to assemblages: "I do not exist and then enter into assemblages. The manner of my existence is my very participation in assemblages. I am not gifted with agency, the possessor of intentions or initiative. Animation, agency, intentionality, or what Deleuze and Guattari called 'desire,' belong to the assemblage as such."[83] Nonetheless, neither Stengers nor these other authors engage in direct diplomatic rapprochement with Indigenous ontologies in a rigorous manner, perhaps due to fears of cultural misappropriation. Haraway does cite several Indigenous beliefs and political acts, but she deploys them as examples or case studies subordinated to her overarching theoretical framework, while Latour's and Stengers's statements regarding Indigenous ontologies, rather than addressing culturally specific Indigenous thought directly, remain entirely in the negative, as what opposes the modern human/nature divide and therefore promises the possibility of cosmopolitical practice.

Nonetheless, in reframing science not as absolute, immutable truth, but rather as a set of social practices that vies for legitimacy within diverse social and political networks, these authors set the stage for its inclusion in what I called in the last chapter the "cosmopolitics of friendship." As Stengers's somewhat veiled critique of Latour's proposal for a parliament of things made clear, science alone cannot serve as the basis for a truly democratic system of governance capable of addressing divergent interests, including those of nonhumans. Furthermore, scientific practices are unlikely to solve through technocratic solutions the vast, systematic socio-ecological problems that they themselves have catalyzed, if not produced directly. As Stengers states pithily, "a world-destroying machine cannot fit with other worlds."[84] At the same time, few Euro-Americans are likely to accept a full disavowal of science and liberal constitutionalism in favor of Indigenous ontologies and cosmopolitical practices such as the Yanomami state of plants. It is only through ongoing diplomatic negotiations that a common, more inclusive cosmos or pluriverse may be forged in which competing ontologies are not erased or subordinated through relativistic discourse, but rather co-exist in and engage in the intercultural co-production of "a world in which many worlds fit," to cite the felicitous phrasing of the Ejército Zapatista de Liberación Nacional's "Fourth Declaration of the Selva Lacandona" (1996). Indeed, I would argue that it is only through this cosmopolitical conceptual framework that the 2008 Ecuadoran Constitution, with its emphasis on interculturality, pluralism, and the equal validity of incommensurate ontologies, becomes not only legible, but viable in practice. In that sense, one might view it as the first working example of Latour's "non-modern" constitution, wherein science, human rights, Indigenous ontologies, and the rights of nature act as an intricate set of checks and balances over political power, assuring that no one interest may dominate or be peremptorily excluded from the decision-making process.

Furthermore, when politics are reconceived of as cosmopolitics in the sense in which Stengers uses the term, the state of plants can be viewed not as a political system that either precedes or may replace liberal constitutionalism, but rather as one that competes with it as an other political ontology within an ecology of practices. It surfaces in the Ecuadoran Constitution not as the formal codification of Indigenous cosmopolitical practices or through the discourse of multicultural tolerance, but rather in the mandate for consultation, consultation that is not limited to Indigenous communities but also extends to nonhumans themselves in the rights of nature provisions in Articles 71 and 72 regarding freedom from harm and the right to restoration. In similar fashion, the two posthumanist Indigenous cosmopolitical projects that I examine at the end of this chapter engage in intercultural diplomacy and a broad ecology of practices with the goal of bringing the state of plants into modern political and economic practices relating to transgenic organisms, food production, and the conservation/extractivism dialectic.

As Latour's analysis of the Boyle-Hobbes debate and my discussion of Hobbes's state of nature in Chapter 5 show, the conceptual divide between science as the government of things and politics as human governance had the effect of framing Indigenous cosmopolitical systems that did not recognize the human/nature divide as premodern and therefore prehistorical. In this context, humanism became a weapon in the war against competing ontologies, as the famous sixteenth-century debate between Bartolomé de las Casas and Juan Ginés de Sepúlveda regarding what Sepúlveda called "justus belli causus" (just cause for war) against American Indigenous peoples made clear. While Las Casas argued that Pope Alexander VI had tacitly recognized that Amerindian peoples had human souls when, in his 1493 "Inter Caetera" papal bull, he authorized the conquest of the Americas on the condition that the conquered Indigenous peoples be converted to Catholicism and treated as royal subjects, Sepúlveda famously equated them to monkeys and argued that they were incapable of self-governance.

Similar tropes of animalization were frequently deployed by social Darwinists in nineteenth century post-independence debates regarding Indigenous peoples' capacities for participating in the newly founded Latin American democracies. In both cases, Indigenous people's resistance to full acculturation into Euro-American political ontologies—an acculturation that was in any case made purposefully impossible by colonial and postcolonial racial hierarchies supporting exploitative labor regimes—was used to dehumanize them, representing them as defective or, in Alcides Arguedas's words, "sickly" humans.[85] From within this paradigm (which was not fully hegemonic, as the biopolitical status of Indigenous peoples was a matter of continual debate within governing elites), all Indigenous political discourse and activism during the colonial and postcolonial periods would effectively be posthumanist and cosmopolitical in the sense in which Stengers defines the term, seeking to alter the terms of modern humanism through diplomatic engagement or, at times, insurrection.

Indeed, after more than five hundred years of living under colonial and postcolonial regimes and furnishing not only much of the labor and raw materials for modern production, but also being placed at the center of modern biopolitical regimes (usually as objects of control) and cultural discourse (as both constitutive others and precursors in nationalistic identitary narratives), it is clearly a gross mischaracterization to portray Indigenous peoples in the Americas as being somehow premodern or living outside modernity, even in the few cases in which Indigenous communities maintained relative isolation from national political and economic infrastructures. The "underdevelopment" paradigm through which Euro-Americans and local elites most often view Indigenous communities frames the persistence of ancestral cultural practices and sustainable technologies in highly reductive terms, as outmoded ("prehistoric") ways of life and/or as the product of economic marginalization and exploitation, when in many, if not most cases,

Indigenous communities have consciously decided to conserve particular ancestral forms of knowledge, political structures, and life technologies in the midst of diverse modernizing initiatives.

This is certainly not to say that Indigenous peoples have no interest in modern technologies, but rather that they wish to retain the right to decide which of these technologies to implement in their communities and how to use them in accordance with their own ontological frameworks. When one approaches the question of "development" in Indigenous communities, then, one must necessarily distinguish between and problematize in context-specific and non-binary terms the issues of access to (economic exclusion) and ontological appropriateness of modern forms. Furthermore, this process always hinges on diplomatic negotiations within modern political and economical structures, whether those of colonial governments, the nation state, or international governance. Clearly, these are most often not democratic negotiations, since coercion is often employed to force Indigenous peoples to acculturate into modern systems. Nonetheless, it is a major methodological error to assume that Indigenous communities have had no agency in this process and therefore no impact on modern economic, social, and political forms.

Even in the colonial period, Indigenous peoples were often able to negotiate at least limited concessions from colonial powers with respect to territorial rights, cultural practices, and political representation.[86] As a case in point, the Repúblicas de Indios in the Spanish colonies were not only sources of forced labor and conversion to Catholicism (purportedly isolated from the heresies of the Protestant Reformation); they also maintained intact to some degree the communal land tenure, political and social structures, and linguistic and cultural practices of the Indigenous communities, as long as they were not viewed by Franciscan or Jesuit overseers as relating to "idolatry," that is, Indigenous religious practices at their most visible and transgressive.[87] Despite the systematic destruction of sacred idols, architecture, and texts, Indigenous ontologies persisted not only through syncretism with Catholicism, but also in everyday relations with the environment.[88] This was the case with sacred topographies, which could not readily be destroyed by Spanish colonizers, but also in rituals and other cultural practices relating to hunting, gathering, and agriculture. Following independence, many colonial forms of oppression persisted in Latin American nations, including military, economic, and cultural violence and discrimination, but Indigenous peoples acquired a greater degree of negotiating power through reclassification as citizens of the nation state, in name if not always in practice.[89] Once again, territorial rights—which in Indigenous thought are never viewed as mere property ownership, but rather as political ontologies—took center stage.

The Cosmopolitics of Indigenous Territorial Rights

In one form or another, territorial rights have been the prime political concern for most Indigenous peoples from the independence period through the present. For instance, many Mexican Indigenous groups counter-intuitively supported the 1861–1867 French intervention and Second Mexican Empire that temporarily overthrew the liberal government of Mexico's first and only Indigenous president, Benito Juárez. This seeming irony has often been explained away as being due to local Catholic priests' sway over Indigenous communities (combatting Juárez's attempts to secularize Mexican governance and minimize the influence of the Church) or in racist terms as a supposed Indigenous predilection for autocracy, but it has much more to do with the liberal regime's 1856 Lerdo Law, which privatized the Catholic Church's and Indigenous communal lands, the latter being postcolonial remnants of the Repúblicas de Indios.[90] Many Indigenous communities initially supported Austro-Hungarian emperor Maximilian because he had promised to restore the colonial land concessions to Indigenous communities, which also included a degree of political and ontological autonomy.[91]

At the same time, the liberal proposal to privatize and therefore tax Indigenous communal lands was viewed by the Indigenous communities as an attempt to reinstate the colonial tribute levied on Indigenous peoples. In addition to the liberal theory that linked responsible democratic citizenship with property ownership (through having a stake in the economic development of the nation), the main impulse for this project was the need to raise funds to pay off the national debt, whose default served as the justification for repeated French interventions in nineteenth-century Mexico, as well as to finance modern infrastructure projects.[92] Privatization was thus essentially a revocation of the tax-exempt status of Indigenous communities and the Catholic Church, but it was also envisioned by its liberal proponents as the basis for a societal revolution that would lead to the implementation of capitalism in rural areas. In that sense, Indigenous peoples' concerns about economic exploitation were inseparable from cosmopolitics, since enforcement of the Lerdo Law would necessarily imply the radical transformation of Indigenous communities' relations with their environments.

Following Juárez's triumph over the Franco-Austrian occupiers and the consolidation of liberal hegemony, Indigenous and mixed-race campesinos who had received land titles very frequently suffered expropriation, due both to the inability to pay property taxes (most of them were subsistence farmers with little access to capital) and because the government declared lands that were not being developed for agriculture or ranching to be "baldíos" (empty or unused land) that could be confiscated by the state and granted to developers. These expropriations thus occurred because agrarian communities typically engaged in low-impact, sustainable agricultural practices for subsistence purposes, leaving large swathes of forest or savannah untouched (as common hunting/gathering areas, as well as space for rotational swidden agriculture), rather than large-scale deforestation to implement extractive monoculture and intensive ranching practices.[93] Clearly, this reticence was not due to a lack of "initiative" or any of the other pejorative qualities that nineteenth-century social Darwinists associated with the Indigenous or mixed-race "character," but rather to an ethical and, ultimately, ontological conflict: the largely Indigenous campesinos viewed the environment as a living socius of which they formed part and its wholesale destruction was akin to an act of genocide.

At the same time, this cosmopolitical view of the environment was not limited solely to Indigenous peoples as we usually conceive of this demographic term from the United States and Europe. Following the abolition of the colonial caste system, Indigenous tributes, and forced labor in the mita and repartimiento systems, ethnic divisions became increasingly blurred in rural areas. Even during the colonial period, a large number of interethnic agrarian communities had arisen, whether on hacienda lands or in unincorporated areas, that were not differentiated from Indigenous communities through skin color, language, or cultural practices, but rather by the system of privileges and obligations imposed within the caste system. Syncretic Catholicism was practiced within both the "pueblos de indios" and these interethnic communities, but so were many of the ancestral Indigenous cosmopolitical rituals involved in everyday interactions with the local environment, now reframed as agricultural and hunting techniques.

In part, these practices were engrained linguistically, within the lexicon of specialized work, since Indigenous languages continued to predominate in everyday social interactions, with Spanish being used primarily in political, juridical, and (sometimes) religious discourse. Indeed, this kind of rural, intercultural hegemony was transparently the norm rather than the exception in nearly every region in which Indigenous peoples formed the bulk of the population, which is why one still commonly finds mixed-race Quechua or Aymara speakers in the Andes, Náhuatl speakers in Central Mexico, and Guaraní speakers in Paraguay, to name only a few of the most salient examples. Similarly, in colonial Brasil, the Tupi-Nheengatu language, called by the Portuguese colonizers "Língua Geral" (the Common Language), was considerably more widely used than Portuguese other than in the most heavily colonized regions. In general terms, Spanish and Portuguese only became demographically hegemonic languages in the twentieth century, following the widespread implementation of public education in rural areas, which also generally accompanied the uneven construction of modern infrastructure and induction into the capitalist economy.

Nonetheless, even in rural areas in which Spanish and Portuguese are now the hegemonic languages, Indigenous terms or conceptual translations linked to cosmopolitical practices often persist. To cite one example, the folk stories in Juan Carlos Galeano's *Folktales of the Amazon* and Candace Slater's *Entangled Edens*, gathered from multiethnic communities in Spanish and Portuguese rather than Indigenous languages, detail the widespread persistence of the conceptualization of the Amazonian rainforest as a multispecies socius inhabited by powerful beings akin to the *xapiri* in Kopenawa's *The Falling Sky*.[94] As these stories make clear, cosmopolitical conceptualizations of the environment are capable not only of persisting in the midst of modernization, but actually adapt to it, as when Yakumama, the anaconda mother, is described as having eyes like boat lights; a road to nowhere in the middle of the jungle is attributed to a giant anaconda with a bulldozer blade under his neck; or when Kopenawa described invading gold prospectors as children of the white-lipped peccary (renowned for uprooting trees).[95] Rather than ascribing to the persona/res distinction, even machines are viewed as agential, due to the apprehension of agency through the production of material effects in relation rather than abstract intentionality. Throughout rural Amazonia, anything capable of producing effects on other bodies is judged as having personhood and therefore must be addressed through cosmopolitical negotiations.

These shared, intercultural identities cannot be extracted from the ontologies and cosmopolitical practices that form their way of life and worldview. As Hutchins and Wilson point out, "the constant exchanges between these different Amazonian inhabitants has led to the emergence of shared intellectual traditions and social spaces and the formation of kin ties between groups that are often incorrectly treated separately (as Indigenous and mestizo)."[96] Furthermore, the Amazonian multiethnic, multispecies cosmopolitical framework is not the product of isolation from modernizing movements; on the contrary, the region's long history of natural resource extraction, fraught with violence, contributed to the rise of a non-Western cosmopolitanism that bridges ethnic and species boundaries. As Uzendoski argues, Amazonian concepts of relations "do not oppose locality and globality; they show that people are defined simultaneously by the local and the global, part and whole, the one and the many."[97] It is in this sense that I contended in "Amazonian Flows" that, "Indigenous thought regarding the relations between bodies and natural flows became generalized to explain how globalized flows of capital, commodities, and labor function at the local level. Rather than forcing a disjunction with prior Amazonian notions of identity, then, capital flows were assimilated into the pre-existing cultural framework, which also adjusted to accommodate it. In this way, Amazonian thought minimalized the Western human/nature binomial that underpins globalized capitalism, transforming capitalism instead into one among many flows through which material subjectivities arise."[98] At the same time, however, these multiethnic communities and alliances often collaborate to resist threats to their territories and way of life posed by extractive, export-oriented activities, as was the case with Chico Mendes's rubber tapper union in the Brazilian state of Acre, multiethnic protests against oil pollution throughout Amazonia, and the Sarayaku Runa's proposal for an new international territorial designation called Kawsak Sacha (living forest).

As I hope this cursory summary has shown, Indigenous peoples and their affiliates have actively negotiated political and ontological agency within distinct modernizing paradigms since colonization. While religious beliefs were generally downplayed through cultural subordination as the mytho-historical roots of national identity, Indigenous political engagement has nearly always been related to territorial sovereignty and the political autonomy necessary to make decisions regarding land use practices more so than equal human rights within the liberal tradition. This is not to say by any means that Indigenous claimants have had no interest in obtaining justice for human rights violations, only that those rights were always viewed as inseparable from the key issues of territorial control and self-governance at the local level. This occurs due to the historical relations between the liberal state and the implementation of capitalism in Latin America, whereby the expansion of the frontiers of capitalistic land management and extractivism produced human rights violations as the norm, not the exception. And, as the Wixáritari people stated eloquently in the passage I quoted in Chapter 5, but which bears repeating here:

> Territory, from an Indigenous perspective, constitutes the natural space of life, conceived of as a fundamental ecological unity, in which life develops in its multiple expressions and forms; this natural space is the source of knowledge

and wisdom, culture, identity, tradition, and rights. In this sense, a territory integrates all of life's elements in its natural and spiritual diversity: the land with its diversity of soils, ecosystems, and forests, the diversity of plants and animals, the rivers, lakes, and marshes. Natural ecosystems are considered by Indigenous peoples to be the habitat of gods that protect this diversity of life and who maintain the integrity and balance of the forest, rivers, and the lakes, as well as the soil's fertility, which allows the plants and animals to live and reproduce.[99]

Clearly, property ownership is not the only or even primary concern of Indigenous peoples in territorial claims. For Indigenous peoples, territory is a cosmopolitical system, a form of "government" in Kopenawa's words; the claim for territorial rights is inseparable from the claim for political and ontological autonomy.

The Sarayaku Runa's "Living Forest" Project as Posthumanist Intervention

Indigenous posthumanisms thus operate from within the humanistic system of Euro-American governance, but take it in another direction, working to make it compatible with Indigenous cosmopolitics. The degrees of success these political projects have are clearly constrained by the parameters of the systems in place; nevertheless, they cannot be viewed simply in terms of acculturation, that is, of the abandonment of Indigenous ontologies and acceptance of the principles underpinning Euro-American humanism. In that sense, Indigenous thought and political activism is continually pushing the boundaries of the human in ways that are not always so different from the work carried out by Euro-American posthumanists such as Haraway, Latour, and Stengers or non-Indigenous Latin American writers like Cortázar and Lispector. In short, I am arguing for a reading of works such as the Zapatista manifestos, Rigoberta Menchú's *Me llamo Rigoberta Menchú y así me nació la conciencia*, José Gualinga's "Kawsak Sacha Declaration," and Davi Kopenawa's *The Falling Sky* as posthumanist manifestos that are not limited to opening a multicultural space of tolerance and equal rights, but rather look to transform modern practices to create a "world in which many worlds fit," including the worlds of nonhumans.

This kind of posthumanist cosmopolitical activism is clearly the goal of the Sarayaku Runa's proposal for a new international territorial designation called "Kawsak Sacha," the Living Forest. This initiative was formally adopted by the General Assembly of the Pueblo Originario Kichwa de Sarayaku (Kichwa Indigenous Community of Sarayaku) in 2012 with revisions in 2018, and it was presented at the COP21 Paris Climate Summit in 2015 and the IUCN World Conservation Congress in Hawaii in 2016. However, the roots of the proposal can be traced back to the 1992 Indigenous movements, in which members of the Sarayaku community marched to Quito to demand the legal title to their ancestral territories.[100] Despite official recognition of those property rights in the same year, the Ecuadoran government included the Sarayaku territories in an oil concession granted to the Argentinean consortium CGC (Compañía General de Combustibles) in 1996. To create a façade of Indigenous consent, CGC engaged in a propaganda campaign in nearby communities dominated by the rival Asociación Indígena Evangélica de Pastaza (Indigenous Evangelical Christian Association of Pastaza), which signed an agreement with the consulting firm Daimiservices allowing oil prospection on Sarayaku lands despite the majority of the Indigenous residents' opposition.[101] The Sarayaku Runa took their case to the Inter-American Commission on Human Rights, which decided in their favor in 2003 and 2004 on the basis of international human and Indigenous rights laws.

Nevertheless, the Ecuadoran government did not respect this decision, even following Rafael Correa's election as president in 2007 and the approval of the 2008 constitution that ostensibly protected both Indigenous communities' rights to prior consultation regarding extractive projects and the rights of nature. In 2009, Correa's administration pushed through a new mining law revalidating prior oil concessions that was stridently opposed as unconstitutional by the Confederación de Nacionalidades Indígenas del Ecuador (CONAIE; Confederation of Indigenous Nations of Ecuador), and in 2012 the oil concessions in Sarayaku territories were re-approved. A delegation of Sarayaku travelled anew to the Inter-American Court, which judged in their favor on the grounds that the Ecuadoran government had violated its own constitution as well as international law in multiple ways, including delegating the right to prior consultation to the corporation, the use of a fraudulent consultation process that removed the decision from the hands of the legally constituted local government, the threat and use of violence against individuals, failing to respect collective rights over territory and natural resources, and neglecting constitutional rights regarding the preservation of cultural identities, traditions, customs, and way of life.[102] Clearly, even the 2008 Ecuadoran Constitution, with its Indigenous rights and rights of nature provisions, has not been able to consolidate itself fully in practice; it is only through ongoing cosmopolitical diplomacy and litigation at the local, national, and international scales that the constitution can be actualized in each specific case or conflict.

As this summary has made clear, the Sarayaku proposal originated as a territorial claim within national law regarding Indigenous collective property rights; however, it rapidly evolved at both the ontological and political scales, becoming an explicitly (rather than veiled) cosmopolitical proposal that extended beyond the Pastaza region to the entire planet. The Sarayaku Runa engage in a variety of sophisticated diplomatic modes tailored to different audiences, ranging from ecotours of their lands, national and international media reporting, performances in national and international public spaces, meetings with politicians, testimony before the Ecuadoran congress and international governance organizations, and a strong presence in the internet and social media. In each of these forums, the underlying message is the same, but the language and emphasis shifts according to the context and the audience in question. For instance, the Kawsak Sacha website (kawsaksacha.org), buttressed by documentary clips featuring community members interacting with forest species, focuses on the ties between the Sarayaku Runa's cultural practices and the health of the local environment, avoiding contextual abstraction and appealing for support for the project. The website's text presents a reduced version of the 2018 Declaration, appropriate for web surfers with limited engagement, that emphasizes the aspects of the declaration related to ancestral knowledges, religious beliefs, and the genealogical relation to the land. In this sense, it caters to a non-specialist, international audience that conflates Indigenous cultures with an "enchanted" way of life that is unalienated from nature, as well as the discourse of multicultural tolerance. It thus supports the Sarayaku Runa's territorial claims primarily on the basis of cultural and environmental conservation at the local level.

Somewhat in contrast (but not opposition), the version of the Declaration presented by José Gualinga, aimed at academics and policy makers, focuses to a much greater degree on extending the Kawsak Sacha model to the planetary scale through tying it into broader anthropological, ecological, and political discourses. The opening paragraph, which is clearly inflected by Eduardo Kohn's reading of the Sarayaku Runa's relational ontology in *How Forests Think*, frames the proposal specifically in cosmopolitical terms, whereby the forest is presented as a multispecies society relying on biosemiotic communications:

Kawsak Sacha (The Living Forest) is a proposal for living together with the natural world that grows out of the millennial knowledge of the Indigenous Peoples who inhabit the Amazonian rainforest, and it is one that is also buttressed by recent scientific studies. Whereas the Western world treats nature as an undemanding source of raw materials destined exclusively for human use, Kawsak Sacha recognizes that the forest is made up entirely of living selves and the communicative relations they have with each other. These selves, from the smallest plants to the supreme beings who protect the forest, are persons (runa) who inhabit the waterfalls, lagoons, swamps, mountains, and rivers, and who, in turn, compose the Living Forest as a whole. These persons live together in community (llakta) and carry out their lives in a manner that is similar to human beings. To summarize, in the Living Forest the economic system is an ecological web; the natural world is also a social world.[103]

Following this introduction, the Declaration immediately links this project to the Ecuadoran Constitution's well-being provisions through the trope of sumak kawsay/buen vivir (and thereby placing the Ecuadoran government's hypocrisy at the forefront): "Kawsak Sacha, understood as sacred territory, is the primordial font of Sumak Kawsay (Buen Vivir, "Good Living"). Not only does it provide a home for all of its inhabitants, it also emotionally, psychologically, physically, and spiritually revitalizes them. In this way it regenerates the Indigenous Peoples who live in community with these sylvan selves. That is, the Living Forest nourishes and augments life."[104] Tacitly countering the Ecuadoran government's insistence that funds garnered through oil extraction are necessary for social well-being, the Sarayaku Runa contend that the forest itself is what provides social well-being for all of its species.

Furthermore, they subtly argue against the "national park" paradigm of nature conservation, underscoring the common Indigenous contention that Indigenous peoples play integral roles in ecosystemic health: "In essence, the forest is neither simply a landscape for aesthetic appreciation nor a resource for exploitation. It is, rather, the most exalted expression of life itself. It is for this reason that continued coexistence with the Living Forest can lead to Sumak Kawsay."[105] Finally, they present the Kawsak Sacha proposal as a new model for global initiatives oriented not at environmental conservation through the exclusion of humans, but rather at a form of multispecies worldbuilding that produces well-being for all species: "this encourages us to propose that maintaining this lively space, based on a continuous relation with its beings, can provide a global ethical orientation as we search for better ways to face the worldwide ecological crisis in which we live today. In this manner Sumak Kawsay can become a planetary reality."[106]

This introduction leads up to three proposals for action. The first is the national and international recognition of Kawsak Sacha as "a new legal category of protected area" that would be considered "Sacred Territory and Biological and Cultural Patrimony of the Kichwa People of Ecuador" and which would be off-limits to intensive extractive practices of any kind. The second point promotes Kawsak Sacha as a "viable economic model," in which wealth would be reframed as well-being and development would consist in maintaining the forest's fertility, living in community, and preserving knowledge and practices linked to the forest. The third is aimed simultaneously at engaging in cosmopolitical diplomacy with outsiders and demarcating the territorial limits of the Kawsak Sacha. The authors state that the Sarayaku Runa territory:

> is now demarcated by a border of flowering and fruiting trees visible form the air. We call this vital cordon a Frontier of Life or Trail of Flowers (*Jatun Kawsak Sisa Ñampi*). By means of the flower's ephemeral beauty, the Frontier of Life conveys the fragility of life and the fertility of the Living Forest that it both surrounds and protects. In keeping with the central pillar of Kawsak Sacha—that the forest is composed entirely of communicative relations among the various selves that make it up—this Frontier of Life aims to communicate to outsiders the delimitation and existence of the area categorized as Kawsak Sacha. Any outsider can thus appreciate the beauty of the Living Forest and the living presence of Mother Earth (Pachamama) thanks to a multi-colored cloak of flowers. At the same time it creates the possibility of beginning to dialogue with the beings that make up the Living Forest.[107]

This border of flowering and fruiting trees thus serves the pragmatic function of notifying outsiders that they are now on Sarayaku land (and thus cannot proceed with extractive activities such as illegal lumber harvesting) as well as an ontological fence of sorts, whereby the extractivist mentality will ostensibly be left behind as the outsider enters the paradigm of fertility and multispecies well-being as wealth, and as a frontier or contact zone of cosmopolitical diplomacy. As the Declaration summarizes, "the Frontier of Life is a symbol of life that manifests Kawsak Sacha's principles at the same time that it serves as a tool for its protection. The message it delivers is aimed at the entire world with the goal of reaching the hearts and minds of human beings everywhere, encouraging us all to reflect on the close relation between Human Rights and the Rights of Nature."[108] Finally, the Declaration addresses the incompatibility of the subject/object, human/nature dichotomy with the rights of nature paradigm: "in order to extend rights to Nature, one must first recognize its entities as persons (and not mere objects). As persons, the beings of the forest relate to one another as well as to the Indigenous People that share their land. So, based on our continuous life together with the beings of the forest, Kawsak Sacha emerges as an authentic way of guaranteeing the Rights of Nature in those spaces that have not yet been decimated."[109]

In this way, Kawsak Sacha is presented as a concrete proposal for remediating the Ecuadoran government's failure to implement fully both the rights of nature and the sumak kawsay/buen vivir provisions of the 2008 constitution. At the same time, it rejects the predominant, international ' national park" model of environmental conservation, proposing viewing environments as multispecies societies whose relations are continually enacted and maintained and portraying Indigenous peoples worldwide as their custodians. Finally, it tacitly rejects capitalistic greenwashing both in the reinscription of value and therefore wealth not in terms of either economic production or sustainability, but of multispecies well-being, and in terms of modern planning and economic modelling. The Kawsak Sacha as a model for world-making clearly looks to replace what Haraway called the colonial "god-trick" of the modern, global cartographic imagination, but also other, more ethical modes of apprehending the planet such as Jennifer Wenzel's "planetary imagination from below" as a "better kind of borderlessness."[110] Playing ironically on the 1970s techno-environmentalist trope of "spaceship Earth" and the humanist expression "we are all in the same boat" (in which one envisions a group of humans navigating across an empty ocean), the Sarayaku Runa took an 800lb hand-carved canoe with them to the COP21 Paris Summit and paraded it through the streets. Rather than collective isolation in empty (outer) space, "we are all in the same canoe" implies navigating the river of life in the midst of the species-rich forest. Clearly, preserving the canoe alone will not preserve life, there can be no life without the forest or the river, that is, the cosmos. In that sense, the Sarayaku Runa's "Kawsak Sacha Declaration" downplays both the globe and the planet as valid ways of "worlding"; "a world in which many worlds fit" must be constructed through an ecology of practices at the local level, through multispecies relations that nevertheless are never bounded by cartographic or demographic divisions, but always open to diplomatic rapprochement.

Interestingly, following the 2008 Ecuadoran Constitution's adoption of the *sumak kawsay* / buen vivir equivalence, which was initially proposed by

Sarayaku Runa scholar and activist Carlos Gualinga Viteri, it has acquired international valence as an intercultural, decolonial political model designed to revalidate traditional Indigenous cultural and environmental management practices and draw them into dialogue with modern liberal constitutionalism, with its emancipatory push for gender, racial, and social equality, as well as the precepts of modern ecology and environmental stewardship. As Kauffman and Martin note, "Buen vivir is not a specific policy outcome, but a concept that refers to humans' constantly changing relationship with nature and a set of norms regarding the need for dialog within and among communities to determine the best way to live within their natural environment in a balanced way. Because buen vivir refers to a process, advocates say it can, and should, be applied globally."[111] Similarly, Jorge Marcone observes that "the thinkers and practitioners of BV do not recognize it as a static concept, but as a project that is continually being created. Therefore, BV should not be understood as a restorative nostalgia for a distant precolonial time, but as a reflective unearthing of Indigenous cosmologies. It encourages Indigenous and non-Indigenous communities to reflect on Indigenous beliefs and values as alternatives."[112]

Due to its cosmopolitical mandate for diplomacy and its processual, intercultural orientation, the buen vivir model is able to adapt to drastic cultural and environmental differences, making it attractive for Indigenous movements worldwide. It rapidly spread throughout the Andean region into other South American nations, with the 2009 Bolivian Constitution and 2010 rights of nature laws incorporating the Aymara concept of *suma qamaña*, and Indigenous political movements in Chile, Paraguay, and Peru deploying similar political platforms.[113] Indeed, Indigenous activists and organizations throughout the Americas have begun elaborating similar cosmopolitical initiatives designed not only to strengthen traditional local cultural practices, but also to transform political frameworks. In Guatemala, the Confluencia Nuevo B'aqtun group, formed of a variety of Mayan organizations, created a proposal entitled *El UtzlläJ K'aslemal· El Raxnaqull K'aslemal: "El Buen Vivir" de los Pueblos de Guatemala*, while similar formulations have emerged among the Nna'ncue (*tsjomnancue*), P'urhepecha (*sesi irekani*), O'dam (*jix bhai' chu kioka'*), and Tseltal (*lekil kuxlejal*) in Mexico, to cite only a few examples.[114] Clearly, these Indigenous movements are decentralized and yet mutually influencing, engaging each other and local, national, and international organizations and bodies of governance in diplomacy to implement policy changes. It is precisely in this sense in which the "internationalization" or "scaling-up" of buen vivir must be viewed; not as the globalization of a single model for policy-making, but as the viral expansion of an effective model for diplomatic political engagement between Indigenous communities and external policy makers and practitioners.

Intercultural Cosmopolitical Practice: The Sin Maíz No Hay País Food Sovereignty Movement

With the exception of Ecuador's and Bolivia's national constitutions, the buen vivir movement continues to be circumscribed by external observers in most cases as a form of ethnic politics, which subverts its intercultural goals and subjects it to neoliberalism's multicultural machinery. This is why I would like to address in closing another popular movement that demonstrates how Indigenous cosmopolitics can converge with other civic movements into the "mainstream" of national and international politics. The Sin Maíz No Hay País and Red en Defensa del Maíz Nativo food sovereignty movements emerged in Mexico in response to the 2007 "tortillazo," in which the price of masa, or corn flour, and tortillas nearly doubled due to speculation on the global grain market. These price increases were devastating for the Mexican working class, for whom corn is a main staple, and it became all the more intimidating given the fact that, according to the terms of NAFTA (the North American Free Trade Agreement), Mexico's protectionist tariffs on corn and bean imports from the US were slated to be removed the following year. Mexican producers, both large and small, feared that the national market would be inundated with subsidized US GMO corn, forcing prices down and driving them out of business. Furthermore, the debate over the legalization of GMOs in Mexico, especially Monsanto's Round-Up Ready Corn, came into play with respect to the potential health effects of GMOs, concern over cross-pollination with native species of corn, and because Monsanto had patented their seed corn genome, whereby farmers would no longer be allowed to retain seed from one year to the next.[15] Many independent campesinos and small farm cooperatives viewed this as a move by the Mexican government to eliminate them from the countryside, making their land available for industrialized agriculture and forcing them to migrate to Mexican cities or the US to find work.

The Sin Maíz No Hay País movement, whose formal name is "Campaña en Defense de la Soberanía Alimentaria y la Revitalización del Campo Mexicano" (Campaign to Defend Food Sovereignty and Revitalize Mexican Rural Areas), was inaugurated at the Museo Nacional in Mexico City on June 25,

2007 with the initial goal of collecting one million signatures on a petition to cancel NAFTA's mandate to open the Mexican market to corn and bean imports from the US.[116] More than three hundred campesino and popular organizations at the local, state, and national levels joined the movement, as well as several Indigenous organizations and a slate of celebrity actors and musicians. As the movement's "Convocatoria" (Call to Action) makes clear, the movement arose specifically in opposition to the post-1982 neoliberal turn in Mexico, which was consolidated with the implementation of NAFTA in 1994, and its effects on agricultural production in Mexico, leading not only to the loss of small farmer's livelihoods, but also food dependence and insecurity, hunger, and malnutrition due to the proliferation of processed foods and US fast-food chains.[117]

While various demands were presented in different forums, often tailored to specific audiences, the *Revista ANEC*, which served as the main forum for distributing information about the movement, summarizes them in the following way:

1. Remove corn and beans from NAFTA. Have Congress implement a permanent regulatory procedure for corn and beans (and their related products).
2. Prohibit planting GMO corn in Mexico. Protection and improvement of the genetic legacy of Mexican corn varieties, incentivize the production of native and organic corns.
3. Have the Constitutional Right of Access to Food approved by Congress and the Agricultural Foods and Nutritional Sovereignty and Security Planning Law approved by the Senate.
4. Fight against monopolies in the agricultural food production sector. Prevent market manipulation and speculation, as well as deceptive advertising for "junk" foods.
5. Advocate for Mexican corn and related cultural expressions to be included as soon as possible in the UNESCO list of Oral and Intangible Cultural Heritages of Humanity.[118]

Participants in the movement engaged in a broad range of activities to draw attention to its demands, including a nationwide campaign to plant corn in public spaces in which celebrities featured prominently, mass marches, a hunger strike, occupying public spaces such as Mexico City's central Zócalo and plazas in state capitals, concerts and artistic charity events, publicity campaigns oriented toward the implementation of a national fair trade designation (Comercio Justo México; Fair Trade Mexico), and a tractor caravan from Zacatecas, among other forms of activism.

On the surface, the Sin Maíz No Hay País movement appears primarily as a popular, nationalistic anti-globalization movement, seemingly having little to do with Indigenous cosmopolitics other than the fact that a sizeable proportion of Mexican campesinos identify as members of Indigenous communities. Likewise, there seems to be little direct connection to environmental ethics other than the rejection of GMOs and, indirectly, the ecological problems caused by globalization in the neoliberal model. Nonetheless, both Indigenous ontologies and environmental concerns creep in to the movement's discourse at various junctures, such as the incentive to produce native Mexican corn species organically in the second demand or the petition to list Mexican corn species and "the cultural expressions it is involved with" as a protected class under UNESCO's Intangible Cultural Heritage category in the fifth. Indeed, the nexus between Indigenous ways of life and food sovereignty emerges explicitly throughout the movement's documents in statements such as the following:

> The neoliberal dream of a campo [rural zone] without campesinos or Indigenous peoples is nothing more than a nightmare and a vain illusion. Either there is a Mexico with campesinos and Indigenous peoples or there is no Mexico. Because without corn there is no nation [sin maíz no hay país]. Campesino and Indigenous organizations as well as environmentalist, human rights, consumer protection, non-governmental, researcher, scientist, artist, intellectual, and grass roots organizations we all raise our voices to call for civil society to defend our right to food, of the right of Indigenous peoples and campesinos to exist with their own cultures and ways of life; to establish agricultural policies that promote the national production of the enormous variety of Mexican corns.[119]

Rather than an appropriation of indigeneity for ulterior ends (as occurred with the nationalistic discourse of mestizaje), the coterminousness of campesinos/Indigenous peoples emerges here as an intercultural strategy akin to the covalence of nature/Pachamama in the Ecuadoran constitution. Neither term erases or subordinates the other; instead, their co-valence indicates the presence of irreducible common differences, that is, of divergent interests that share the common grounds of resistance against globalized industrial agriculture, which affects both parties negatively, but in somewhat different ways.

While Indigenous ontologies are not readily visible in most of the movement's documents, the cosmopolitical aspect nevertheless emerges through contextual referentiality and the refusal to separate its anti-globalization posture and its demands for food sovereignty and sustainable agricultural practices from Indigenous and campesino territorial and cultural rights. In Mexico, one cannot speak of Indigenous peoples and corn in the same space without evoking Indigenous cosmologies and iconographies, particularly following the 1910–1920 Mexican Revolution. The post-Revolution government's civic education programs forged a unifying concept of Mexican nationality in which pre-Columbian Indigenous cultures were portrayed as the roots of the nation (despite often marginalizing Indigenous peoples in the present), a concept that was often represented in nationalistic art through the figure of corn. As is well known, people are viewed as descendants of corn in many Meso-American Indigenous cosmologies, and the "native" corn species alluded to in the documents cited above were themselves developed by Indigenous peoples over thousands of years by selectively breeding the Teosintle or Teocinte (*Zea perennis*) grass. This is why Mexican anthropologist Guillermo Bonfil Batalla eloquently affirms in *El maíz: Fundamento de la cultura popular mexicana* (Corn: The Foundation of Mexican Popular Culture; 1982) that "corn is a human plant" and that "in cultivating corn, Man cultivated himself."[120] In this way, Bonfil captures how corn and humans "became" together sympoetically, through mutual affectivity and nurture. Furthermore, corn has also traditionally been associated with symbiotic polycultures in the *milpa* form of agricultural production, whereby the human-corn face-to-face is interrupted by the third presences of beans, squash, and chile.

This sacred sense of mutual becoming in relation through agricultural practice, which is not limited to Indigenous cultures but has also become a key trope in Mexican nationalism through the centrality of the campesino figure, thus serves to counter corn's iconicity in the "Green Revolution" of industrialized agriculture, where it has become emblematic of monocultures and the technological manipulation of plants using agrochemicals and genetic engineering. In this way, the Sin Maíz No Hay País movement's references to Indigenous and campesino corn cultures serve to disrupt big agro's euphoric transhumanism, which claims that technological innovations will magically produce an end to hunger and, implicitly, that the dispossession of small farmers and environmental degradation are the prices that must be paid. In contrast, for Indigenous Mexicans, corn and humans must cultivate one another with respect, since corn forms the conceptual basis for both personhood and the multispecies socius centered around the *milpa* or polyculture plot. As Rodríguez Wallenius and Concheiro Bórquez emphasize, this is precisely the relational structure that ties together the diverse actors and divergent interests that have coalesced in the Sin Maíz No Hay País movement: "these collective actions express a perspective of food sovereignty constructed from below, based on the rural campesino economy and sustaining itself through the corn-milpa-social land ownership [referring to the ejido system in Mexico] triad for the development of sustainable agriculture, in which the multifunctional character [in terms of economic, cultural, social, and environmental sustainability] of campesino agriculture is recognized."[121]

At the same time, one cannot speak of anti-globalization movements in Mexico without evoking the 1994 Zapatista Indigenous uprising in Chiapas, which began on January 1, the day NAFTA entered into effect. In this sense, the Sin Maíz No Hay País movement necessarily refers back not only to the Ejército Zapatista de Liberación Nacional's acts of resistance, but also its cosmopolitical proposal to build a "world in which many worlds fit," as well as its sociopolitical organization into "Caracoles" or "Juntas," structures of decentralized, communal governance that put into practice an ecology of practices rooted in the Mayan cosmology. Indeed, the collective decision-making process in the Sin Maíz No Hay País movement mirrors several key Zapatista principles regarding governance, among them that of "mandar obedeciendo" (governing by obeying [the popular will]) and "representar, no suplantar" (represent, not supplant):

> Our Assembly was developed within the framework of plurality, inclusion, deliberation, enthusiasm, and resistance from a great diversity of campesino, Indigenous, and women's rights organizations, from environmentalist, human rights, social welfare, and fair trade organizations, from community radio and nutrition, agronomy, and agro-ecology professional associations, as well as students, academics, researchers, intellectuals, artists, homemakers, radio listeners, and citizens.[122]

In this sense, both Zapatismo and the Sin Maíz No Hay País movement put into practice cosmopolitics as Stengers envisions them, that is, through diplomatic negotiations and collective policy-making that does not require the hegemonic subordination of differences to common interests. Here, the partially diverging and partially converging, sometimes contradictory and never fully coincident interests of Indigenous peoples (particularly regarding political and territorial autonomy), campesinos (who want to keep their lands and lifestyles, as well as making a living), women's organizations (gender equality and food security), environmentalists (conservation and the preservation of biodiversity), social activists (empowering the people), nutritionists and proponents of organic foods, and even celebrities (showing solidarity, but also reinforcing their celebrity image) come together in a single, decentralized movement pushing not only policy change, but also social and even political transformation.

Finally, I would argue that corn itself forms a key part of this cosmopolitical assemblage not only as a thematic axis, but even more so as itself, that is, as a plant that has co-evolved with humans through mutual nurture. Clearly, transhumanist GM corn is alienated in multiple senses, not the least of which being that is it engineered to be sterile and to be bathed in toxic glyphosate, which kills most other plants and has been shown to cause cancer in humans and other animals. From this perspective, non-GMO corn would clearly makes its "interests" or teloi known; its release of pollen is aimed at open propagation and its wilting and dying when exposed to glyphosate clearly communicate a failure to thrive and even suffering, if the capacity to suffer is removed from human exceptionalism. Indigenous peoples and campesinos know and feel this (the term "sentipensar" [to know and feel] has become common in Indigenous and popular activist discourse) because they are open to seeing it, while the transhumanist simple views corn as an object that can be manipulated with no ethical or juridical repercussions.

As the Sarayaku Runa's Kawsak Sacha proposal for both transforming modern conservation practices and reorienting them toward Indigenous ontologies and the Sin Maíz No Hay País's milpa-zation of public space (which necessarily implies reconceiving of lived environments in terms of Indigenous relational ontologies) show, the most viable route to putting Haraway's, Latour's, and Stengers posthumanist thought into practice runs through intercultural diplomacy with Indigenous ontologies and political activism, a fact that all three recognized explicitly in their work. Furthermore, these movements also dismantle the long-standing Euro-American colonial perspective that Indigenous thought is pre-historical, outmoded, and at odds with modernity. Since modernity is conceived of as the future of all humanity, any ontology labelled pre-modern would necessarily have no place in this future, a neocolonialist position vigorously resisted by Indigenous peoples globally. In contrast, Indigenous thought emerges in its present as a contestatory discourse that not only offers a critique of modern discourse and practices, but also ethical and political alternatives that can function from within and transform modernity itself. Once the human/nature divide as the conceptual machine that has produced what Moore calls the Capitalist world-ecology is invalidated as the basis for modern thought, a cosmopolitical world-ecology rooted in Indigenous principles of reciprocity, sustainability, and respect can emerge. It is in this sense that I speak of "Indigenous posthumanisms."

As emerging events make clear, social and political change is inevitable when confronted with intensifying worldwide ecological, political, and social crises as capitalism exhausts its conditions of production of wealth. The question then becomes: what kind of world(s) can we build going forward? Will the future look how Brazilian writer Ignácio Loyola de Brandão envisioned it in his satirical but all too prescient *Não verás país nenhum* (*And Still the Earth*; 1982), in which capitalism has been divested from democratic politics, doubling down on its iron-clad grip over all facets of life in a fascistic dystopia where consumption is mandated by the state, plant life has died out and the Amazonian rainforest is now the world's largest desert, "factitious" food is produced in laboratories and drugged with sedatives to keep the populace in a state of complacency, and history is no longer taught and therefore no alternatives can be imagined?[123] Or will it be a posthumanist future in which cosmopolitics become the predominant political practice in the multispecies construction of environments that are livable for all species? Clearly, only one of these offers a viable future for humanity, as the ending of Brandão's novel suggests. As global warming and the depletion of the ozone layer turns sunlight deadly, the surviving inhabitants of Brazil are squashed together in the shade created by the fascist regime's final public works project: a series of huge concrete canopies whose shapes, viewed from space, spell out BRAZIL. As the case may be, the human/nature distinction can no longer be upheld: either nature and consequently humans will be eradicated as in Brandão's novel or we will have to accept that we are part of a multispecies society to whom we owe ethical and political standing.

NOTES

INTRODUCTION

1. Juan Alberto Lecaros Urzúa. "La ética medioambiental: Principios y valores para una ciudadanía responsable en la sociedad global," *Acta Bioethica* 19, no. 2 (2013): 178–79.

2. Donna Haraway defines "sympoesis" as a making/becoming with other species in *When Species Meet* (Minneapolis: University of Minnesota Press, 2008), 31–33, and in chapter 3 of *Staying with the Trouble* (Durham, NC: Duke University Press, 2016).

3. Jacques Derrida, *The Gift of Death and Literature in Secret*, trans. David Wills (Chicago: University of Chicago Press, 1999), 131.

4. Luis Costa Lima, "Social Representation and Mimesis," *New Literary History* 16, no. 3 (1985): 448.

5. As I discuss at length in Chapter 2 of this book, Derrida argues this point most explicitly in *Speech and Phenomena, and Other Essays on Husserl's Theory of Signs*, trans. David Allison (Evanston, IL: Northwestern University Press, 1973).

6. Costa Lima, "Social Representation," 461.

7. Andrés Bello, "Silva a la agricultura de la zona tórrida," Biblioteca Cervantes Virtual, https://www.cervantesvirtual.com/obra-visor/poesias--35/html/ff5cfcdc-82b1-11df-acc7-0021852e6064_20.html, line 231.

8. Gary Snyder, "Language Goes Two Ways," in *The Green Studies Reader: From Romanticism to Ecocriticism*, ed. Laurence Coupe (London: Routledge, 2000), 127–28.

9. Marília Librandi Rocha, "Becoming Natives of Fiction: Towards an Ontology of the Mimetic Game (Lévi Strauss, Costa Lima, Viveiros de Castro, and the Nambikwara Art Lesson)," *Culture, Theory, and Critique* 54, no. 2 (2013): 173.

10. On this point, see Julie Stone Peters, "'Literature,' the 'Rights of Man,' and Narratives of Atrocity: Historical Backgrounds to the Culture of Testimony," in *Theoretical Perspectives on Human Rights and Literature*, ed. Elizabeth Swanson Goldberg and Alexandra Schultheis Moore (New York: Routledge, 2013), 19–40.

11. Esteban Echeverría, *El matadero; La cautiva*, ed. Leonor Flemming (Madrid: Cátedra, 1986).

12. Mark Anderson, "Violent Transactions and the Politics of Dying in Neoliberal Mexico," *Revista de Estudios Hispánicos* 53, no. 1 (2019): 211–34.

13. Michael Niblett, "World Economy, World-Ecology, World Literature," *Green Letters* 16, no. 1 (2012): 20.

14. For a summary of common Indigenous principles on relations with environments, see Laurie Ann Whitt et al., "Indigenous Perspectives," in *A Companion to Environmental Philosophy*, ed. Dale Jamieson, 3–20 (Malden, MA: Blackwell, 2001).

15. Darren Ranco and Jamie Haverkamp, "Storying Indigenous Life(Worlds): An Introduction," *Genealogy* 6, no. 25 (2022): 2.

16. Whitt et al., "Indigenous Perspectives," 16.

17. Lesley Wylie, *The Poetics of Plants in Spanish American Literature* (Pittsburgh, PA: University of Pittsburgh Press, 2020), 20.

18. Leyla Perrone-Moises, "Literary Nationalism in Latin America," in *Literary Cultures of Latin America: A Comparative History*, vol. 1, ed. Mario J. Valdés and Djelal Kadir (Oxford: Oxford University Press, 2004), 195–96.

19. Jennifer L. French, *Nature, Neo-Colonialism, and the Spanish American Regional Writers* (Hanover, NH: Dartmouth College Press, 2005), 13.

20. This novel was originally penned in 1887, but it was lost in a shipwreck and rewritten shortly before Asunción Silva's suicide in 1896. It would only be published thirty years later, in 1925.

21. See the introduction to Ericka Beckman's *Capital Fictions: The Literature of Latin America's Export Age* (Minneapolis: University of Minneapolis Press, 2013).

22. Beckman, *Capital Fictions*, xxvii.

23. Victoria Saramago, *Fictional Environments: Mimesis, Deforestation, and Development in Latin America* (Evanston, IL: Northwestern University Press, 2021), 6–7.

24. Saramago, *Fictional Environments*, 13.

25. John McNeill and Peter Engelke, *The Great Acceleration: An Environmental History of the Anthropocene since 1945* (Harvard: Harvard University Press, 2016); Jens Andermann, *Tierras en trance: Arte y naturaleza después del paisaje* (Santiago de Chile: Metales Pesados, 2018), 425.

26. Pablo Neruda, "Oda a la erosión en la Provincia de Malleco," in *Nuevas odas elementales* (Buenos Aires: Losada, 1964).

27. See Andermann, *Tierras en trance*; Laura Barbas-Rhoden, *Ecological Imaginations in Latin American Fiction* (Gainesville: University Press of Florida,

2011); Beckman, *Capital Fictions*; Scott Devries, *A History of Ecology and Environmentalism in Spanish American Literature* (Lanham, MD: Bucknell University Press, 2013); Jennifer L. French, *Nature*; Gisela Heffes, *Políticas de la destrucción; poéticas de la preservación: Apuntes para una lectura (eco)crítica del medioambiente en América Latina* (Buenos Aires: Beatriz Viterbo, 2013); Adrian Kane, ed., *The Natural World in Latin American Literatures: Ecocritical Essays on Twentieth-Century Writings* (Jefferson, NC: McFarland, 2010); Jorge Marcone, "De retorno a lo natural: *La serpiente de oro*, 'la novela de la selva' y la crítica ecológica," *Hispania* 81, no. 2 (1998): 299–308; Malcolm McNee, *The Environmental Imaginary in Brazilian Poetry and Art* (New York: Palgrave Macmillan, 2014); Kerstin Oloff, "Greening the Zombie: Caribbean Gothic, World-Ecology, and Socio-Ecological Degradation," *Green Letters* 16, no. 1 (2012): 31–45; Lizabeth Paravisini-Gebert, "Endangered Species: Caribbean Ecology and the Discourse of the Nation," in *Displacements and Transformations in Caribbean Cultures*, ed. Lizabeth Paravisini-Gebert and Ivette Romero-Cesareo (Gainesville: University of Florida Press, 2008), 8–23; Saramago, *Fictional Environments*; Steven F. White, *Arando el aire: La ecología en la poesía y la música de Nicaragua* (León, Nicaragua: 400 Elefantes; Alcaldía Municipal de León, 2011); and Wylie, *Poetics of Plants*.

28. Scott Devries, *Creature Discomfort: Fauna-Criticism, Ethics, and the Representation of Animals in Spanish American Fiction and Poetry* (Leiden: Brill, 2016); Gabriel Giorgi, *Formas comunes: Animalidad, cultura, biopolítica* (Buenos Aires: Eterna Cadencia, 2014); Maria Esther Maciel, *Literatura e animalidade* (Rio de Janeiro: Civilização Brasileira, 2016); Patrícia Vieira, "Interspecies Literature: Clarice Lispector's Zoophytographia," *Journal of Lusophone Studies* 2, no. 2 (2017): 70–85, and "Phytofables: Tales of the Amazon," *Journal of Lusophone Studies* 1, no. 2 (2016): 116–34; Carolyn Fornoff, *Subjunctive Aesthetics: Mexican Cultural Production in the Era of Climate Change* (Nashville, TN: Vanderbilt University Press, 2024); Vera Coleman, "Beyond the Anthropocene: Multispecies Encounters in Contemporary Latin American Literature, Art, and Film," PhD diss., Arizona State University, 2017.

29. Lucia Sá, *Rainforest Literatures: Amazonian Texts and Latin American Culture* (Minneapolis: University of Minnesota Press, 2004); Carolyn Fornoff, "The Nature of Revolution in Rafael F. Muñoz's *Se llevaron el cañon para Bachimba*," in *Mexican Literature in Theory*, ed. Ignacio Sánchez Prado (New York: Bloomsbury, 2018), 93–110.

30. Héctor Hoyos, *Things with a History: Transcultural Materialism and the Literatures of Extraction in Contemporary Latin America* (New York: Columbia University Press, 2019).

31. Jacques Derrida, *Adieu to Emmanuel Levinas*, trans. Pascale-Anne Brault and Michael Naas (Stanford: Stanford University Press, 1999), 11.

CHAPTER 1

Epigraph. Mihnea Tanasescu, *Environment, Political Representation, and the Challenge of Rights: Speaking for Nature* (New York: Palgrave Macmillan, 2016), 80.

1. Constitutional Assembly, *Constitution of Ecuador, Political Database of the Americas*, January 31, 2011, https://pdba.georgetown.edu/Constitutions/Ecuador/english08.html.

2. Alberto Acosta, president of the Constitutional Assembly tasked with rewriting the constitution, declares the following in the abstract to his essay on "El Buen Vivir como alternativa del desarrollo": "we propose a transition toward a sustainable economy rooted in solidarity, which will include the degrowth of extractivism and a recentering toward local, participative politics. The Buenos Convivires [Good Coexistence], as a way of life than a concept, open the door for us to construct a world in which all worlds fit, in which all human beings can live with dignity." "El Buen Vivir como alternativa al desarrollo. Algunas reflexiones económicas y no tan económicas," *Política y Sociedad* 52, no. 2 (2015): 299. This and all translations in this book were done by the author unless otherwise noted. Acosta is an Ecuadorian economics professor who worked closely with the Pachakutik Indigenous movement and was briefly Minister of Energy and Mining in Ecuador in 2007 under Rafael Correa's administration before becoming president of the Constitutional Assembly.

3. See chapters 2 and 3 of Rodrick Nash's *The Rights of Nature: A History of Environmental Ethics* (Madison, WI: University of Wisconsin Press, 1989) regarding early debates on animal rights and the rights of nature in Europe and the United States. Clearly, legislation such as the 1966 US Endangered Species Preservation Act and the 1973 US Endangered Species Act were key moments in the trajectory toward affording non-human beings legal protections, as was the 1973 approval of the CITES (Convention on the International Trade in Endangered Species of Wild Fauna and Flora) resolution regulating the traffic in endangered species, the Rio Declaration on Environment and Development and Agenda 21 approved at the 1992 Rio Earth Summit (officially known as the United Nations Conference on Environment and Development), the follow-up 2012 UN Conference on Sustainable Development (also held in Rio de Janeiro), and the 2015 UN Framework Convention on Climate Change's Paris Agreement. The majority of Latin American nations' legislation pertaining to the environment was passed during the 1980s and 1990s, including statutes

and policies regarding protected and endangered species, land use, water and forest conservation, biodiversity, and so on. On this point, see the first chapter of Eduardo Gudynas's *El mandato ecológico: Derechos de la Naturaleza y políticas ambientales en la nueva Constitución* (Quito: Abya Yala; Universidad Politécnica Salesiana, 2009); chapter 6 of David R. Boyd's *The Environmental Rights Revolution: A Global Study of Constitutions, Human Rights, and the Environment* (Vancouver: University of British Columbia, 2012); Felipe Paez's "Environmental Framework Laws in Latin America," *Pace Environmental Law Review* 13 (1996): 625–84; and Lila Katz de Barrera-Hernández and Alistair R. Lucas's development-oriented appraisal in "Environmental Law in Latin America and the Caribbean: Overview and Assessment," *Georgetown International Environmental Law Review* 12 (1999): 207–45. María Akchurin provides a concise summary of the history of environmental legislation in Ecuador building up to the 2008 constitution in "Constructing the Rights of Nature: Constitutional Reform, Mobilization, and Environmental Protection in Ecuador," *Law and Social Inquiry* 40, no. 4 (2015): 937–68.

4. See, for instance, Kelly Kay, "Breaking the Bundle of Rights: Conservation Easements and the Legal Geographies of Individuating Nature," *Environment and Planning A* 48, no. 3 (2018): 504–22, and Jerilyn Church, Chinyere O. Ekechi, Aila Hoss, and Anika Jade Larson's "Tribal Water Rights: Exploring Dam Construction in Indian Country," *Journal of Law, Medicine, and Ethics* 43, no. 1 (2015): 60–63. On the other hand, Lídia Cano Pecharroman notes that, beyond the liberal framework, rivers have been granted legal personhood in Ecuador (Vilcabamba River), India (Ganges and Yamuna Rivers), New Zealand (Whanganui River), and Colombia (Atrato River); "Rights of Nature: Rivers that Can Stand in Court," *Resources* 7, no. 13 (2018): 1–14.

5. See chapter 5 of Tanasescu's *Environment.* Regarding Latin American judicial activism, Idelber Avelar notes that the Brazilian prosecutor involved in one of twenty-two lawsuits brought to halt the construction of the Belo Monte dam on the Xingu River argued that the rights of nature were being infringed upon; "Amerindian Perspectivism and Non-Human Rights," *Alter/nativas* 1 (2013): 17. As Tanasescu discusses, an important precursor to the Ecuadorian constitution was the 2006 Tamaqua Borough, Pennsylvania municipal ordinance 612, which states that: "Borough residents, natural communities, and ecosystems shall be considered to be 'persons' for purposes of the enforcement of the civil rights of those residents, natural communities, and ecosystems;" Tanasescu, *Environment,* 108. The NGO with which the local government consulted in developing the ordinance, the Community Environmental Legal Defense Fund (CELDF), was also instrumental, together with the Ecuadorian NGO

Fundación Pacha Mama, in promoting the inclusion of rights of nature provisions in the Ecuadorian constitution, and it continues to promote similar legislation worldwide. In Latin America, Chilean lawyer Godofredo Stutzin was an early proponent of the rights of nature, beginning with work dating back to the 1950s, the founding of the Chilean National Committee for the Defense of Fauna and Flora in 1968, and influential articles on the rights of nature published in 1976 and 1984. This project was taken up prominently in the 1990s and 2000s by Ecuadorian economist Alberto Acosta and Uruguayan socio-ecologist Eduardo Gudynas, among others.

6. Tanasescu frames this new legislation as the result of "moral progressivism," that is the expansion of the Euro-American traditions of the "rights of man" and "human rights" to encompass the non-human (*Environment*, 102). However, her book largely discounts the decolonial paradigm, viewing both Indigenous perspectives and Indigenous activism as largely ancillary or even decorative to the Euro-American liberal rights paradigm and influence of Euro-American animal rights and environmentalist discourse. In what follows, I problematize this perspective.

7. The preamble opens with the following wording:

> We women and men, the sovereign people of Ecuador,
> RECOGNIZING our age-old roots, wrought by women and men from various peoples,
> CELEBRATING nature, the Pacha Mama, of which we are a part and which is vital to our existence,
> INVOKING the name of God and recognizing our diverse forms of religion and spirituality,
> CALLING UPON the wisdom of all the cultures that enrich us as a society,
> AS HEIRS to social liberation struggles against all forms of domination and colonialism
> AND with a profound commitment to the present and to the future,
> Hereby decide to build
> A new form of public coexistence, in diversity and in harmony with nature, to achieve the good way of living, the sumak kawsay;
> A society that respects, in all its dimensions, the dignity of individuals and community groups;
> A democratic country, committed to Latin American integration—the dream of Simón Bolívar and Eloy Alfaro—, peace and solidarity with all peoples of the Eart

Constitutional Assembly, *Constitution of Ecuado8*.

8. According to the Ecuadorian page of the *World Directory of Minority and Indigenous Peoples* compiled by the Minority Rights Group International and housed by the United Nations High Commissioner for Refugees, "minority

and Indigenous groups include fourteen distinct Indigenous peoples—including Tsáchila, Chachi, Epera, Awa, Quichua, Shuar, Achuar, Shiwiar, Cofán, Siona, Secoya, Zápara, Ancoa y Waorani, and Afro-Ecuadorians (7.2 percent). According to the most recent census in 2010, 6.8 percent of the population of Ecuador self-identify as Indigenous, compared to 6.1 per cent counted in the 2001 census. Yet many other estimates of the Indigenous population are considerably higher: for instance, the Confederation of Indigenous Nationalities of Ecuador (Confederación de Nacionalidades Indígenas del Ecuador, CONAIE) believes that Indigenous peoples comprise somewhere between 25 and 30 percent of the total population. Similarly, there is a large gap between the official figures for Afro-Ecuadorians (5 percent) and NGO estimates (10 percent). These differences have to do with questions of classification of Afro-descendants and Indigenous peoples, including the self-identification of those who have intermarried with non-black or non-Indigenous people, and those who live in urban areas"; Minority Rights Group International, "Ecuador," *World Directory of Minorities and Indigenous Peoples*, May 2018, https://minorityrights.org/country/ecuador/. Marc Becker's ¡*Pachakutik! Indigenous Movements and Electoral Politics in Ecuador* (Lanham, MD: Rowman & Littlefield, 2011) provides a concise history of these ethnic popular movements and their relation to the writing of the new constitution. Regarding the shift away from economic nationalism, see Christopher Brogan's *The Retreat from Oil Nationalism in Ecuador: 1976–1983* (Working Papers. University of London: Institute of Latin American Studies, 1984), Allen Gerlach's *Indians, Oil, and Politics: A Recent History of Ecuador* (Wilmington, DE: Scholarly Resources, 2003), and Suzana Sawyer's *Crude Chronicles: Indigenous Politics, Multinational Oil, and Neoliberalism in Ecuador* (Durham, NC: Duke University Press, 2004). See Michael Cepek's *Life in Oil: Cofán Survival in the Petroleum Fields of Amazonia* (Austin: University of Texas Press, 2018) for a more recent discussion of the effects of oil extraction on Indigenous communities in Oriente, as well as the relationships between the oil spills and Indigenous political activism.

9. Cumbre Continental de Pueblos y Organizaciones Indígenas, *Declaración de Quito, Ecuador*, Continental Summit of Indigenous Peoples and Nationalities Abya Yala, http://www.cumbrecontinentalindigena.org/quito_es.php)

10. As Jorge Marcone notes regarding Indigenous environmental activism in Latin America, "we must understand the complexity of popular environmentalisms' local, national, and transnational political scenarios; the alliances and exchanges that are demanded by such complexity; the balance between restoration of traditional knowledge and technological and social innovation; the fluidity of their identities as their struggles are carried out; the self-imposed

respect for the diversity within and among the movements; and the prominence of unexpected links that are revealed by the study of such complexity"; "The Stone Guests: Buen Vivir and Popular Environmentalisms in the Andes and Amazonia," in *The Routledge Companion to the Environmental Humanities*, ed. Ursula K. Heise, Jon Christensen, and Michelle Niemann (London: Routledge, 2017), 227.

11. The toponym "America" was proposed by German mapmaker Martin Waldseemüller in 1507 in honor of Italian explorer Amerigo Vespucci, who was the first European to suggest that Columbus had "discovered" a new continent.

12. Daniel Bonilla Maldonado, "El constitucionalismo radical ambiental y la diversidad cultural en América Latina: Los derechos de la naturaleza y el buen vivir en Ecuador y Bolivia," *Revista Derecho del Estado* 42 (2019): 8. Regarding the antecedents, deliberations, and negotiations between different stakeholders in the formulation of the new constitution, see Akchurin's "Constructing the Rights of Nature" and chapter 3 of Gudynas's *El Mandato ecológico*.

13. As Tanasescu points out, this is a common denominator in rights of nature movements, nearly all of which arise in response to federal and state governments' inaction regarding specific environmental catastrophes affecting local communities; *Environment*, 111.

14. Cletus Gregor Barié, "Nuevas narrativas constitucionales en Bolivia y Ecuador: El buen vivir y los derechos de la naturaleza," *Latinoamérica* 59 (2014): 24. On the other hand, Paola Villavicencio Calzadilla and Louis J. Kotzé argue that, "even though the Bolivian Constitution does not constitutionalize the rights of Mother Earth, it recognizes at the highest constitutional level the importance of ecological integrity, which enables people to create a new future for themselves through a new constitutional framework: without the integrity of nature, a new constitutional democracy will be impossible. It might even be said that the Constitution recognizes ecological integrity as the basis of the Bolivian constitutional state"; "Living in Harmony with Nature? A Critical Appraisal of the Rights of Mother Earth in Bolivia," *Transnational Environmental Law* 7, no. 3 (2018): 403.

15. Constitutional Assembly, *Constitution of Ecuador*.

16. Constitutional Assembly, *Constitution of Ecuador*. Regarding the use of toxic agrochemicals in the Drug War, see Rachel Massey, "The 'Drug War' in Colombia: Echoes of Vietnam," *Journal of Public Health Policy* 22, no. 3 (2001): 280–85.

17. Constitutional Assembly, *Constitution of Ecuador*.

18. This language is specific to the particularities of the Texaco-Chevron oil spill case; in 2011, three years after the promulgation of the new constitution, Chevron was ordered by an Ecuadorian court to pay $US 19 billion in damages to

more than 30,000 plaintiffs as well as carry out full remediation of the polluted environment, a decision that Chevron fought to have overthrown in the US court system, accusing the plaintiffs' Ecuadorian and US lawyers of racketeering. This countersuit relied primarily on the argument that Chevron complied in full with the environmental remediation plan stipulated by the Ecuadorian government in 1995, a claim whose patent misrepresentation is placed on display in Joe Berlinger's documentary *Crude* (Entrendre Films, 2009). For a more academic recounting of this case, see former Ecuadorian Ambassador to the US Nathalie Cely's "Balancing Profit and Environmental Sustainability in Ecuador: Lessons Learned from the Chevron Case," *Duke Environmental Law and Policy Forum* 24, no. 353 (2014): 353–73.

19. Erin Fitz-Henry, "The Natural Contract: From Lévi-Strauss to the Ecuadoran Constitutional Court," *Oceania* 82 (2012): 264. As she expands, "too often the limited extension of cultural rights to Indigenous communities in Latin America . . . has gone hand in hand with an unwavering commitment to neoliberal economic restructuring. The result has been a kind of tokenistic 'multiculturalism' that officially celebrates 'pluri-nationality' or 'pluri-culturalism' but does not allow for the most important practices of *actual* Indigenous autonomy—for example, in economic decision-making that threatens valuable state resources or questions macro-economic decisions"; Fitz-Henry, "The Natural Contract," 265. Regarding this form of "new extractivism' associated with leftist "Pink Tide" governments, see Eduardo Gudynas, "Estado compensador y nuevos extractivismos: Las ambivalencias del progreso sudamericano," *Nueva Sociedad* 237 (2012): 128–46.

20. See the International Center for Not-For-Profit Law's website "Civic Freedom Monitor: Ecuador" (February 3, 2023, https://www.icnl.org/resources/civic-freedom-monitor/ecuador) and the Fundación Pacha Mama's website. The ITT-Yasuní initiative was a proposal by which Correa's government would protect the Yasuní rainforest from oil development if it received $US 3.2 billion from international donors; only $200 million were pledged by 2012.

21. See Marcone, "Stone Guests," 232. I refer here to the environmental degradation and social conflicts arising from Chavismo's reliance on oil extraction and monocultures in Venezuela; see Emiliano Terán-Mantovani, "Inside and Beyond the Petro-State Frontiers: Geography of Environmental Conflicts in Venezuela's Bolivarian Revolution," *Sustainability Science* 13 (2018): 677–91, as well as that of Kirchnerismo in Argentina; see Lucas Savino, "Landscapes of Contrast: The Neo-Extractivist State and Indigenous Peoples in 'Post-Neoliberal' Argentina," *The Extractive Industries and Society* 3 (2016): 404–15; and Lulismo in Brazil, see Fábio de Castro, "Environmental Policies in the

Lula Era: Accomplishments and Contradictions," in *Brazil Under the Worker's Party: Continuity and Change from Lula to Dilma*, ed. Fábio de Castro, Kees Koonings, and Marianne Wiesebron (Houndmills: Palgrave Macmillan UK, 2014), 229–55), both of which relied heavily on GMO soy and other forms of export monoculture, which are associated with intensive deforestation as well as the massive use of agrochemicals.

22. Dan Collyns, "Bolivia Approves Highway Through Amazon Diversity Hotspot," *Guardian*, August 15, 2017, https://www.theguardian.com/environment/2017/aug/15/bolivia-approves-highway-in-amazon-biodiversity-hotspot-as-big-as-jamaica.

23. Villavicencio Calzadilla and Kotzé, "Living in Harmony," 405.

24. Bolivia, Asamblea Legislativa Plurinacional, 2010, *Ley de Derechos de la Madre Tierra*, No. 071, 21 December.

25. Bolivia, Asamblea Legislativa Plurinacional, 2012, *Ley Marco de la Madre Tierra y Desarrollo Integral para Vivir Bien*, No. 300, 16 October.

26. Villavicencio Calzadilla and Kotzé, "Living in Harmony," 413–15. Organizations such as the Defensores de la Madre Tierra and the Mensajeros de la Madre Tierra continue to pressure the government to comply with this provision, leading to the 2021 proposed legislation. Nonetheless, the law was tabled due to opposition from entrenched economic interests and ongoing political instability arising from conservative politician Jeanine Añez Chávez's coup ousting Evo Morales in 2019.

27. Quoted in Villavicencio Calzadilla and Kotzé, "Living in Harmony," 418.

28. Villavicencio Calzadilla and Kotzé, "Living in Harmony," 419.

29. Eduardo Gudynas, "Development Alternatives in Bolivia: The Impulse, the Resistance, and the Restoration." *NACLA Report on the Americas* 46, no. 1 (2013): 25.

30. Global Alliance for the Rights of Nature, "Commission of the International Rights of Nature Tribunal Examines Controversial Road Project in the Heart of TIPNIS," *Movement Rights Blog*, September 4, 2018, https://www.movementrights.org/commission-of-international-rights-of-nature-tribunal-examines-the-controversial-road-project-in-the-heart-of-tipnis/.

31. See the summaries of this court case in Cano Pecharroman's "Rights of Nature," 7; Erin Daly's "The Ecuadorian Exemplar: The First Ever Vindications of Constitutional Rights of Nature," *Review of European Community and International Environmental Law* 21, no. 1 (2012): 63–66; and Tanasescu, *Environment*, chapter 6. Nevertheless, little was done to comply with this ruling; Daly, "Ecuadorian Exemplar," 63–64; David R. Boyd, *The Rights of Nature: A Legal Revolution that Could Save the World* (Toronto: ECW, 2017), 163–64.

32. Cely, "Balancing Profit," 360.

33. Daly notes that although the provincial government did not comply in full with the ruling in the Vilcabamba River case, in the second rights of nature case to come before Ecuadorian courts, the court ordered an immediate cessation to illegal gold mining operations in the San Lorenzo and Eloy Alfaro districts, as well as the mobilization of the national police and military to enforce the ruling; "Ecuadorian Exemplar," 65. Nevertheless, the state was criticized for taking this hardline approach to local artisanal miners while largely ignoring the damage caused by transnational mineral corporations and its own state-owned extractive industries.

34. Bonilla Maldonado, "Constitucionalismo radical ambiental," 19–20.

35. Javier Cuestas-Caza, "Sumak Kawsay is not Buen Vivir," *Alternautas* 5, no. 1 (2018): 50. Regarding the European degrowth movement, see Giacomo D'Alisa, Federico Demaria, and Giorgos Kallis's edited volume *Degrowth: A Vocabulary for a New Era* (New York: Routledge, 2015) and Luis I. Prádanos's *Postgrowth Imaginaries: New Ecologies and Counterhegemonic Culture in Post-2008 Spain* (Liverpool: University of Liverpool Press, 2018). For a comparative discussion, see Koldo Unceta Satrustegui, "Decrecimiento y buen vivir: ¿paradigmas convergentes? Debates sobre el postdesarrollo en Europa y América Latina," *Revista de Economía Mundial* 35 (2013): 21–45.

36. Cuestas-Caza, "Sumak Kawsay is not Buen Vivir," 56.

37. Norman E. Whitten, Jr. and Dorothea Scott Whitten, "Clashing Concepts of the 'Good Life': Beauty, Knowledge, and Vision versus National Wealth in Amazonian Ecuador," in *Images of Public Wealth or the Anatomy of Well-Being in Indigenous Amazonia*, ed. Fernando Santos-Granero (Tucson: University of Arizona Press, 2015), 193.

38. Whitten and Scott Whitten, "Clashing Concepts," 193.

39. Cuestas Caza makes this argument explicit in this passage: "'the classic' Buen-Vivir (Oviedo, 2014) and the 'current' Buen-Vivir (neodevelopmentalist or post-developmentalist) share the Western DNA. In this way, when academics and politicians allude to Kichwa words 'as a discursive construction critical to conventional developmentalism but firmly based on the Western episteme' (Bretón-Solo, 2013, p. 80) what they are really doing is ignoring the ontology of the terms Buen-Vivir and Sumak Kawsay"; "Sumak Kawsay Is Not Buen Vivir," 56.

40. Macarena Gómez Barris, *The Extractive Zone: Social Ecologies and Decolonial Perspectives* (Durham, NC: Duke University Press, 2017), 5.

41. In addition to the Native American material and linguistic commerce with European cultures in what environmental historian Alfred Crosby baptized as the "Columbian Exchange," it is impossible to speak of capitalism itself

without taking into account its roots in the Spanish colonization of Indigenous and African labor, which Wallerstein views as the foundational moment in the capitalist "world system." Indeed, Enrique Dussel has argued that modernity, rather than some kind of Euro-American teleological essence, has always been a transmodernity, an intercultural if unequal formation arising from the relations between European colonizers and colonial subjects. See Dussel, "Transmodernity and Interculturality: An Interpretation from the Philosophy of Liberation," *Transmodernity* 1, no. 3 (2012): 28–59. Returning to the more specific context of this discussion, the political weight in Ecuadorian politics of the Indigenous Pachakutik movement and the Confederación de Nacionalidades y Pueblos Indígenas del Ecuador is undeniable.

42. Joe Quick and James T. Spartz, "On the Pursuit of Good Living in Highland Ecuador: Critical Indigenous Discourses of Sumak Kawsay," *Latin American Research Review* 53, no. 4 (2018): 766.

43. See Carlos Viteri Gualinga, "Biografía," Wordpress, https://carlosviterigualinga.wordpress.com/biografia/ and "Visión indígena del desarrollo en Amazonía," *Polis* 3 (2002): 1–6, http://journals.openedition.org/polis/7678. Asier Martínez de Bringas backs up this claim, noting that the term "Sumak Kawsay" first appeared in a Spanish text in the mimeographed 1992 Amazanga Plan formulated by the Organización de Pueblos Indígenas de Pastaza, now known as the Coordinadora Kichwa de Pastaza, in which Alfredo Viteri and Carlos Viteri Gualinga had leadership roles; "Selva Viviente: El corazón de la autonomía Kichwa en Sarayaku," *Revista d'Estudis Autonòmics i Federals* 34 (2021): 104, note 32.

44. Quick and Spartz, "On the Pursuit," 764.

45. For an overview of these arguments, see Quick and Spartz, "On the Pursuit," 758. Indeed, the Sarayaku Runa suggest as much in their *El libro de la vida de Sarayaku para defender nuestro futuro*: "We, ancestral peoples, have been forced to define, label, and give a name to many things that are part of our lives, like nature itself, with the goal of defending what belongs to us, our inheritance"; In *Sumak kawsay yuyay: Antología del pensamiento indigenista ecuatoriano sobre el sumak kawsay*, ed. Hidalgo Capitán, Antonio Luis and Alejandro Guillén García, Nancy Deleg Guazha (Huelva: CIM; FIUCUHU; Pyudlos, 2014), 85.

46. Quick and Spartz, "On the Pursuit," 759.

47. Tanasescu, *Environment*, 133.

48. As María Akchurin notes regarding the constitutional assembly's deliberations on the rights of nature, "the case represents an instance in which Indigenous politics influenced non-Indigenous systems of state authority. Though

Indigenous movements did not actively pursue the constitutional rights of nature, their political presence and the recognition of the cosmologies of Indigenous groups provided a conceptual opening, permitting assembly participants to think differently about environment-society relations and to consider the creation of a new set of rights. Consequently, an idea placing the intrinsic worth of nature and its elements alongside that of human beings, and muting the separation between nature and society by emphasizing the interconnectedness between natural ecosystems and social worlds, became part of a bureaucratic rational-legal system. Ecocentric ideas had been present in other contexts, such as in the United States in the 1970s, but they were never transformed into radical legal reforms"; "Constructing the Rights of Nature," 939. Quick and Spartz cite the Sarayaku community's Kawsak Sacha (Living Forest) project as another example of this form of interethnic political outreach, one that is not limited to the mediation of the Ecuadorian state: "more recently, Sarayaku has invited nonIndigenous people to join its efforts. In a proposal submitted to the 2015 Paris Climate Conference it urged the world community to strive for a fundamental metamorphosis: 'We need to shift from a modernizing model of development—a model that treats nature as material resource—to the alternative of Kawsak Sacha, which recognizes that forming community with many kinds of selves with whom we share our world is a better way to orient our economic and political activities'"; "On the Pursuit," 763.

49. Whitten and Scott Whitten, "Clashing Concepts," 207.
50. Regarding this concept, see Deleuze and Guattari's *Kafka: Toward a Minor Literature*, trans. Dana Polan (Minneapolis: University of Minnesota Press, 1986). On the biopolitical construction of racialized demographic and labor categories based on "the colonial difference," see Aníbal Quijano's "Colonialidad del poder, cultura y conocimiento en América Latina," *Dispositio* 24, no. 51 (1999): 137–48 and Walter Mignolo's *The Darker Side of Western Modernity: Global Futures, Decolonial Options* (Durham, NC: Duke University Press, 2011).
51. Constitutional Assembly, *Constitution of Ecuador*.
52. As Catherine Walsh argues, "While multiculturalism maintains the production and administration of difference within the national order, rendering it operative within the expansion of neoliberalism, interculturality, understood from its significance for Indigenous movements, points toward radical changes to this order. Its intent is not simply the recognition, tolerance, or incorporation of difference within the existing structure and matrix. On the contrary, it is a challenge, proposal, process, and project that uses difference to provoke an implosion within the colonial structures of power; it

forces a reconceptualization and refounding of structures that foreground and create equitable relations between logics, practices, and diverse cultural modes of thinking, acting, and living. In that sense, it suggests an active and permanent process of negotiation and interrelation in which cultural specificity does not lose its difference, but rather has the opportunity and capacity to contribute from its difference to the creation of new understandings, collaborations, and forms of solidarity and collective life. For this reason, interculturality is not a fixed social fact, but rather something in a permanent process of insurgency, construction, and becoming." "Interculturalidad, plurinacionalidad y decolonialidad: Las políticas político-epistémicas de refundar el Estado," *Tabula Rasa* 9 (2008): 141.

53. Constitutional Assembly, *Constitution of Ecuador*.

54. For a concise summary of this debate, see David Sobrevilla, "Transculturación y heterogeneidad: Avatares de dos categorías literarias en América Latina," *Revista de Crítica Literaria Latinoamericana* 54 (2001): 21–33.

55. Antonio Cornejo Polar, *Escribir en el aire: Ensayo sobre la heterogeneidad sociocultural en las literaturas andinas* (Lima: Centro de Estudios Literarios "Antonio Cornejo Polar"; Latinoamericana, 2003), 11.

56. Whitten and Scott Whitten, "Clashing Concepts," 202.

57. I use Marisol de la Cadena's translation of the Andean term *tirakuna* as "earth beings" here in full recognition that such a term is only an abstract and therefore homogenizing approximation to the specific conceptualizations of inspirited natural phenomena in Afro-Ecuadorian and Amazonian cultures. There are large bodies of ethnographic work on the cosmologies and religious practices of Afro-Ecuadorian and Amazonian ethnic groups; Marta Escobar Konanz's *La frontera imprecisa: lo natural y lo sagrado en la cultura negra del norte de Esmeraldas* (Quito: Centro Cultural Afro-Ecuatoriano; Abya Yala, 1990) provides a good, ethnographic introduction to Afro-Ecuadorian religious practices, while Eduardo Kohn's *How Forests Think: Toward an Anthropology Beyond the Human* (Berkeley: University of California Press, 2013) and Michael Cepek's *Life in Oil* provide fascinating accounts of the interfaces between Amazonian shamanistic practices, colonial Catholicism, and the negotiation of modern Euro-American beliefs and cultural practices in the ethnic Runa community of Ávila and the Cofán of Dureno, respectively. If not exemplary of all Amazonian cultures and cosmologies, Kohn's and Cepek's books nevertheless provide insight into the complex, mutually constitutive, intercultural interactions among belief systems in Ecuadorian Amazonia. Clearly, none of these cosmologies can be subsumed to the Andean belief

system of which Pacha Mama has become emblematic, even when they sometimes refer to her (another product of intercultural heterogeneity).

58. Constitutional Assembly, *Constitution of Ecuador*.

59. Atuq Eusebio Manga Qespi, "Pacha: Un concepto andino de espacio y tiempo," *Revista Española de Antropología Americana* 24 (1994): 155.

60. Asamblea Legislativa Plurinacional, *Ley de Derechos de la Madre Tierra*.

61. Asamblea Legislativa Plurinacional, *Ley de Derechos de la Madre Tierra*. I use italics here to underscore the relativistic language in this passage.

62. Asamblea Legislativa Plurinacional, *Ley de Derechos de la Madre Tierra*, Article 4. The language regarding ethnicity in the Bolivian constitution is some-what convoluted and is not directly translatable due to the fact that Latin American concepts of indigeneity are quite different from the definitions of "Native American" used in the United States, for example. When the Bolivian laws speak of "naciones y pueblos indígena originario campesinos", the three adjectives (Indigenous, native/aboriginal, and agrarian/peasant) speak to the complexity of ethnic identification in many Latin American nations in which race is not the sole determining factor in indigeneity. People who are mixed-race and may not consider themselves Indigenous or live in communities that identify as Indigenous may nevertheless share many cultural practices and religious beliefs with Indigenous peoples. In that sense, someone who is "originario" may or may not consider themselves Indigenous. On the other hand, the "campesino" component indicates a particular form of agricultural labor oriented toward a subsistence economy that is closely tied to care for the land; the reverse would seem to claim somewhat problematically that migrants to urban areas, whether ethnically Indigenous or mixed race, would necessarily lose that connection to the land and become fully accultured within the modern Euro-American worldview.

63. Eduardo Gudynas, *Ecología, economía y ética del desarrollo sostenible* (Quito: ILDIS-FES; Abya Yala, 2003), 155–56.

64. Eduardo Gudynas, *Mandato*, 32. Ramachandra Guha calls out the "ideology of scientific conservation" in the third chapter of *Environmentalism: A Global History* (New York: Longman, 2000). See also Enrique Leff, *Racionalidad ambiental: La reapropriación social de la naturaleza* (Mexico City: Siglo XXI, 2004).

65. Interestingly, neither Thomas Berry nor Latin American "liberation ecologists" such as Ernesto Cardenal and Leonardo Boff are generally cited by these authors, perhaps because of their Catholic theological orientation, which could be seen as blunting the decolonial thrust of rights of nature legislation in Latin America.

66. It is well known that Aldo Leopold was deeply influenced by his interactions with Diné and Apache communities when he worked as a forest ranger in Arizona; see Dan Shilling, "Aldo Leopold Listens to the Southwest," *Journal of the Southwest* 51, no. 3 (2009): 317–50, while deep ecology draws so heavily on Indigenous environmental perspectives that some critics have derided it as a form of cultural appropriation or even genocidal erasure. See the discussion of this issue in Guha's "Radical American Environmentalism and Wilderness Preservation: A Third World Critique," *Environmental Ethics* 11, no. 1 (1989): 71–83, and Bron Taylor's "Earthen Spirituality or Cultural Genocide? Radical Environmentalism's Appropriation of Native American Spirituality," *Religion* 27 (1997): 183–215.

67. Marcone, "Stone Guests," 234. Whitten and Scott Whitten make a similar assessment: "if we in the West take what appears to be a cultural contrast and turn it into an analytical contrast, then we miss the significance of the clashing concepts that we have identified in the first part of this presentation; Whitten 2011, 329–31. We miss the processes involved in interculturality, the very processes written into the 2008 Constitution of the Republic of Ecuador and recently enacted by Amazonian Runa on both sides of the semantic divide"; "Clashing Concepts," 205.

68. Sarayaku Runa, *Libro de la vida*, 99.

69. See, for instance, Andrew Brei, "Rights & Nature: Approaching Environmental Issues by Way of Human Rights," *Journal of Agricultural and Environmental Ethics* 26 (2013): 393–408; Carlos Martín Beristaín, *El derecho a la reparación en los conflictos socioambientales: Experiencias, aprendizajes y desafíos prácticos* (Bilbao: Universidad del País Vasco; Hegoa, 2010); Cano Pecharroman, "The Rights of Nature"; Joel Colón Ríos, "Comment: The Rights of Nature and the New Latin American Constitutionalism," *Nasaraw Journal of Public and International Law* 13 (2015): 107–13; Fitz-Henry, "The Natural Contract"; Katz and Lucas, "Environmental Law in Latin America and the Caribbean: Overview and Assessment"; Kay, "Breaking the Bundle of Rights"; Paez, "Environmental Framework Laws in Latin America"; and Tanasescu, *Environment*.

70. I use the term "posthegemonic" here in the sense in which early users of the term such as George Yúdice, "Civil Society, Consumption, and Governmentality in an Age of Global Restructuring: An Introduction," *Social Text* 45 (1995): 1–25 engaged it, as the transnational decentering (but not equalizing) of economic power and the consequent dissipation of the power of the nation-state under neoliberal capitalism (which, as I have argued, is the grounds for the Ecuadorian constitution), as well as in the sense in which Jon Beasley-Murray discusses it as the affective relationality through which

"multitudes" and the state constitute and reconstitute themselves mutually in *Posthegemony: Political Theory and Latin America* (Minneapolis: University of Minnesota Press, 2010). This in contrast to the more traditionally Gramscian view of hegemony, in which the individual citizen enters into a political pact with the state that is made possible and reinforced through the cultural hegemony of nationalism, that is, a discursive framework largely controlled by a state-oligarchy alliance.

71. For a summary of proposed legislation, see the Community Environmental Legal Defense Fund's "Rights of Nature: Timeline," CELDF, https://celdf.org/rights-of-nature/timeline/.

72. Brent Patterson et al., eds. *The Rights of Nature: The Case for a Universal Declaration of the Rights of Mother Earth* (San Francisco, CA: Council of Canadians; Fundación Pachamama; Global Exchange, 2011), 9.

73. Department of Economic and Social Affairs, United Nations, "General Assembly Convenes Dialogue on Harmony with Nature," April 17, 2014, https://www.un.org/en/development/desa/news/sustainable/harmony-with-nature.html

74. See, for example, Eduardo Viveiros de Castro's push in *Cannibal Metaphysics* for anthropology, rather than classifying Indigenous cultural practices and beliefs according to preformulated classificatory schema, to recognize Indigenous beliefs as rational philosophical systems, a procedure that "consists in treating Indigenous ideas as concepts and then following the consequences of this decision: defining the preconceptual ground or plane of immanence the concepts presuppose, the conceptual persona they conjure into existence, and the matter of the real that they suppose. Treating these ideas as concepts does not involve objectively determining them as something other than what they are, such as another kind of actual object." *Cannibal Metaphysics: For a Post-Structural Anthropology*, trans. Peter Skafish (Minneapolis: University of Minnesota Press, 2017), 187.

75. Librandi Rocha, 'Becoming Natives," 173.

76. Coleman, "Beyond the Anthropocene," 55.

77. Bolsonaro was widely accused by politicians and environmental activists of tacitly permitting or even orchestrating massive forest fires to burn out of control in the Brazilian Amazon, since he has actively promoted the expansion of the beef and soy industries in the area due to increased demand from China during the US-China trade war.

CHAPTER 2

Epigraph. Alain Pottage, "Introduction: The Fabrication of Persons and Things," in *Law, Anthropology, and the Constitution of the Social: Making Persons and Things*, ed. Alain Pottage and Martha Mundy (Cambridge: Cambridge University Press, 2004), 38.

1. Consolidating prior legal practice, Roman jurist Gaius formalized the distinction between *personae*, *res*, and *actiones* (legal actions) in his *Institutes* (c. 160 CE).

2. Tellingly, the *res/persona* division was anchored in a body/mind opposition derived from the more general Aristotelian nature/culture one. As the late classical Roman jurist Paul wrote in *Commentary on the Praetor's Edict*, "things that are corporeal can be possessed" and "we acquire possession *corpore et animo* (with body and intent)," quoted in Herbert Hausmaninger and Richard Gamauf, *Casebook on Roman Property Law*, trans. George Sheets (New York: Oxford University Press, 2012), 2. Self-possession is thus the condition for legal personhood and property rights: "we acquire possession through ourselves. A lunatic or ward acting without the authority of his guardian cannot commence to possess"; Paul, quoted in Hausmaninger and Gamauf, *Casebook*, 2.

3. Classical notions of rights or legal privileges were generally centered on ownership. Agamben notes that in ancient Greek philosophy, the person/thing distinction in relation to animate bodies was linked to oppositional conceptualizations of life: natural life, or *zoe*, and *bios*, or life within the polis. For Agamben, non-citizens who nevertheless lived within society fell between these two categories, living a rightless "bare life" permanently exposed to the possibility of death without recourse or retribution at the hands of sovereign power; see Giorgio Agamben, *Homo sacer: Sovereign Power and Bare Life*, trans. Daniel Heller-Roazen (Stanford, CA: Stanford University Press, 1998). Although he doesn't develop this point fully, natural life would thus be closely linked to coerced production (the labor of animals or humans), and while no human would be considered to exist fully within *zoe* due to the hierarchy of being in natural law (in which culture constitutes the basis of human superiority over other species), those humans who are excluded from polity could be utilized as if they were things, their potential *bios* legally nullified. For this reason, Pottage argues that law was the original biotechnology: "it produced human life by techniques of personification and reification which were just as radically creative as the techniques of commercial biotechnology"; Pottage, "Introduction," 39. In this same vein, Gabriel Giorgi argues that "the person functions as a regime of biopolitical domination, which distributes positions and struggles around the exercise of powers, resistances, and dispossessions on a mobile cartography of relations with the living, which are always relations of control and property"; *Formas comunes: Animalidad, cultura, biopolítica* (Buenos Aires: Eterna Cadencia, 2014), 24.

4. This is the thesis Michel Foucault developed in his lectures on *Security, Territory, Population: Lectures at the Collège de France, 1977–1978,* ed. Michel Senellart, trans. Graham Burchell (London: Palgrave Macmillan, 2007).

5. Pottage, "Introduction," 1.

6. Pottage, "Introduction," 4–5.

7. Pottage, "Introduction," 5.

8. Tanasescu, *Environment,* 16. She draws here on Judith Butler's thesis in *Gender Trouble,* which Butler states in the following manner: "Foucault points out that juridical systems of power produce the subjects they subsequently come to represent. Juridical notions of power appear to regulate political life in purely negative terms . . . But the subjects regulated by such structures are, by virtue of being subjected to them, formed, defined, and reproduced in accordance with the requirements of those structures. If this analysis is right, then the juridical formation of language and politics that represents women as 'the subject' of feminism is itself a discursive formation and effect of a given version of representationalist politics. And the feminist subject turns out to be discursively constituted by the very political system that is supposed to facilitate its emancipation." *Gender Trouble: Feminism and the Subversion of Identity* (New York: Routledge, 1990), 2.

9. Pottage, "Introduction," 11.

10. Tanasescu, *Environment,* 163.

11. Tanasescu, *Environment,* 60.

12. Tanasescu, *Environment,* 60.

13. Tanasescu, *Environment,* 59.

14. Early animal rights proponents such as Jeremy Bentham argued that animals, like humans, have the capacity to suffer and therefore have moral standing; later thinkers such as Peter Singer and Tom Regan drew closer parallels to human rights discourse by tracing genotypal, cognitive, and behavioral equivalencies between humans and other animals.

15. Respectively in *Dissensus: On Politics and Aesthetics* (London: Continuum, 1999) and *Being and Event* (London: Continuum, 2006), Jacques Rancière and Alain Badiou argue that political action consists in the disruption of the demographic accounting of liberal democratic political representation, particularly within the institutionalized classification and control of majority and minority voting blocks and political speech. Giorgi takes this conceptualization of politics as his point of departure in affirming that in post-1960s Latin American literature, "the animal, who had functioned as the sign of a heterogeneous alterity, the mark of an inassimilable outside to social order—and onto which hierarchies and racial, class, sexual, and gendered exclusiones

were projected—this animal becomes internal, proximate, contiguous, the instantiation of a closeness for which there is no precise 'place' and which dislocates the mechanisms that ordered bodies and meanings"; *Formas comunes*, 13.

16. If nature was primary a category of irrationality constructed in opposition to human thought in Euro-American philosophy, in the natural sciences it is postulated as the summa of all that is observable and bears witness to immutable physical laws. Even in this latter perspective, however, the unity of nature remains elusive, as the sciences have yet to decipher a "unified theory" explaining the existence of all observable phenomena.

17. Tanasescu, *Environment*, 118–19 and 142–45.

18. Tanasescu, *Environment*, 93 and 133.

19. Tanasescu, *Environment*, 162.

20. Isabelle Stengers repurposed the term "cosmopolitics" to overcome the limitations on political negotiation of those who cannot or refuse to negotiate, thereby disrupting the normal functioning of politics: "the prefix 'cosmo-' aims at making the disruption matter. It proposes to characterize the disruptive event as the entering on the scene of human deliberation of 'causes' that do not accept dependence on a regime of deliberation and transaction. The cosmos is not an argument and nobody can purport to be its spokesperson, but it signals that together with issues, worlds are in the balance." Isabelle Stengers, "The Challenge of Ontological Politics," in *A World of Many Worlds*, ed. Marisol de la Cadena and Mario Blaser (Durham, NC: Duke University Press, 2018), 94. She then cites her book *Cosmopolitics II* in underscoring that "it makes present, helps resonate the unknown affecting our questions, an unknown that our political tradition is at significant risk of disqualifying." Stengers, *Cosmopolitics II* (Minneapolis: University of Minnesota Press, 2011), 355.

21. Tanasescu, *Environment*, 164.

22. Tanasescu, *Environment*, 145.

23. Tanasescu, *Environment*, 166.

24. In *Politics of Nature*, Latour borrows the semiotic term "actant" to describe "acting agents, interveners" within a political assemblage: "Let us suppose now that someone comes to find you with an association of humans and nonhumans, an association whose exact composition is not yet known to anyone, but about which a series of trials makes it possible to say that its members act, that is, quite simply, that they modify other actors through a series of trials that can be listed thanks to some experimental protocol. This is the minimal, secular, nonpolemical definition of an actor." *Politics of Nature: How to Bring the Sciences into Democracy* (Cambridge, MA: Harvard University Press, 2004), 75.

25. One might argue that the metaphysical is a specific form or configuration of materiality, that of the symbol. Indeed, as I discuss below, Karen Barad makes a convincing argument to this effect in "Posthumanist Performativity: Toward an Understanding of How Matter Comes to Matter," *Signs* 28, no. 3 (2003): 801–31.

26. As Jacques Derrida notes, "Saussure was also careful to distinguish between the real word and its image. He also saw the expressive value of a 'signifier' only in the form of the 'sound-image.'" *Speech and Phenomena, and Other Essays on Husserl's Theory of Signs* (Evanston, IL: Northwestern University Press, 1973), 46.

27. Jacques Lacan, "The Function and Field of Speech and Language in Psychoanalysis," in *Ecrits* (New York: Norton, 1996), 248.

28. Writing in the late nineteenth century, Pierce anticipated the psychoanalytical turn in semiotics in his distinction between "immediate objects" as linguistic representations and "dynamic objects" as the unmediated physical object-in-itself. Tellingly, he referred to the relationship between the indexical sign and its object as a contiguous "real" or "factual" relation that depends on position rather than interpretation (regarding this point, see Albert Atkin, "Pierce on the Index and Indexical Reference," *Transactions of the Charles S. Pierce Society* 41, no. 1 [2005]: 163). In this formulation, the immediate object of an indexical sign would be factually indistinguishable from the dynamic object, a question that Derrida problematizes (through Husserl rather than Pierce) in *Speech and Phenomena.*

29. Jesper Hoffmeyer, *Biosemiotics: An Examination into the Signs of Life and the Life of Signs* (Scranton, PA: University of Scranton, 2009); Kalevi Kull's "Ecosystems are Made of Semiosic Bonds: Consortia, Umwelten, Biophony, and Ecological Codes," *Biosemiotics* 3 (2010): 347–57; Eduardo Kohn's *How Forests Think: Toward an Anthropology Beyond the Human* (Berkeley: University of California Press, 2013), and Thomas Sebeok's *Perspectives in Zoosemiotics* (The Hague: Mouton, 1972).

30. For some interesting discussions of these phenomena, see the essays in Connor and Obler's edited volume *Neurobehavior of Language and Cognition: Studies of Normal Aging and Brain Damage. Honoring Martin L. Albert* (Boston: Kluwer, 2000), and Marie-Loup Eustache et al., "Sense of Identity in Advanced Alzheimer's Dementia: A Cognitive Dissociation between Sameness and Selfhood?" *Consciousness and Cognition* 22, no. 4 (2013): 1,456–67.

31. Jacques Derrida, *Of Grammatology*, trans. Gayatri Chakravorty Spivak (Baltimore, MD: Johns Hopkins University Press, 1997), 158.

32. Derrida, *Speech and Phenomena*, 86. Elaborating on this point, he writes that "but this pure difference [between the inference of the past and that of being

in the present], which constitutes the self-presence of the living present, introduces into self-presence from the beginning all the impurity putatively excluded from it. The living present springs forth out of its nonidentity with itself and from the possibility of a retentional trace. It is always already a trace. This trace cannot be thought out on the basis of a simple present whose life would be within itself; the self of the living present is primordially a trace. The trace is not an attribute; we cannot say that the self of the living present 'primordially is' it. Being-primordial must be thought on the basis of the trace, and not the reverse. This protowriting is at work at the origin of sense. Sense, being temporal in nature, as Husserl recognized, is never simply present; it is always already engaged in the 'movement' of the trace, that is, in the order of 'signification.'" *Speech and Phenomena*, 85.

33. On this point, Derrida writes: "Considered from a purely phenomenological point of view, within the reduction, the process of speech has the originality of presenting itself already as pure phenomenon, as having already suspended the natural attitude and the existential thesis of the world. The operation of 'hearing oneself speak' is an auto-affection of a unique kind. On the one hand, it operates within the medium of universality; what appears as signified therein must be idealities that are *idealiter* indefinitely repeatable or transmissible as the same. On the other hand, the subject can hear or speak to himself and be affected by the signifier he produces, without passing through an external detour, the world, the sphere of what is not 'his own.' Every other form of auto-affection must either pass through what is outside the sphere of 'ownness' or forego any claim to universality. When I see myself, either because I gaze upon a limited region of my body or because it is reflected in a mirror, what is outside the sphere of 'my own' has already entered the field of this auto-affection, with the result that it is no longer pure. In the experience of touching and being touched, the same thing happens. In both cases, the surface of my body, as something external, must begin by being exposed in the world." *Speech and Phenomena*, 78–79.

34. Derrida, *Speech and Phenomena*, 38.

35. Derrida provides the following summary of Husserl's distinction: "The indicative sign falls outside the content of absolutely ideal objectivity, that is, outside truth. Here again, the very possibility of this exteriority, or rather this extrinsic character of the indicative sign, is inseparable from the possibility of all the forthcoming reductions, be they eidetic or transcendental. Having its 'origin' in the phenomena of association, and always connecting empirical existents in the world, indicative signification in language will cover

everything that falls subject to the 'reductions': factuality, worldly existence, essential nonnecessity, nonevidence, etc. Would we not be already justified in saying that the whole future problem of the reduction and all the conceptual differences in which it is articulated (fact/essence, worldliness/transcendentality, and all the oppositions systematically involved with it) are opened up in a divergence between two kinds of signs?" *Speech and Phenomena*, 30. He glosses Husserl's concept of expression in the following terms: "The meaning (bedeuten) intends an outside which is that of an ideal ob-ject. This outside is then ex-pressed and goes forth beyond itself into another outside, which is always 'in' consciousness"; *Speech and Phenomena*, 32. Of course, he then proceeds to deconstruct this binary opposition.

36. Derrida, *Speech and Phenomena*, 34.

37. Clearly, I am not arguing that non-sentient matter can experience events subjectively (that is, incorporate its encounters with other bodies into a chronological, symbolic narrative); however, I concur with Karen Barad that all matter bears witness to its history, when history is taken not as a chronology of human life, but rather as one of the causality of intra-active material encounters that produce the world phenomenally.

38. Anna Tsing, "Unruly Edges: Mushrooms as Companion Species," *Environmental Humanities* 1 (2012): 141.

39. See Karen Barad's discussion of Butler's *Bodies that Matter* in *Meeting the Universe Halfway: Quantum Physics and the Entanglement of Matter and Knowing* (Durham, NC: Duke University Press, 2007), 150–53.

40. Barad traces the monadic conceptualization of being back to Democritus and atomism, which she views as the beginnings of anthropocentric representationalism, that is "the idea that the world is composed of individuals with separately attributable properties"; "Posthumanist Performativity," 813. In contrast, she argues that "phenomena are constitutive of reality. Reality is not composed of things-in-themselves or things behind-phenomena but 'things'-in-phenomena" (817). As she summarizes in *Meeting the Universe Halfway*, her formulation of posthumanism "eschews both humanist and structuralist accounts of the subject that position the human as either pure cause or pure effect, and the body as the natural and fixed dividing line between interiority and exteriority" (136).

41. Barad, "Posthumanist Performativity," 815.

42. Barad, "Posthumanist Performativity," 818.

43. Barad, "Posthumanist Performativity," 814.

44. Barad, "Posthumanist Performativity," 819.

45. Barad, "Posthumanist Performativity," 821.

46. As she notes, citing Bohr, "the measurement can be said to express particular facts about that which is measured; that is, the measurement is a causal intra-action and not 'any old playing around.'" Barad, *Meeting the Universe Halfway*, 140.

47. Donna Haraway, *The Companion Species Manifesto: Dogs, People, and Significant Otherness* (Chicago: Prickly Paradigm, 2003), 5.

48. Barad, "Posthumanist Performativity," 817.

49. Gilles Deleuze, *The Fold: Leibniz and the Baroque*, trans. Tom Conley (Minneapolis: University of Minnesota Press, 1992). Indeed, Donna Haraway's theorization of "sympoesis," or "making with," developed in dialogue with Lynn Margulis's and other organismic biologists' work with holobionts, suggests just such a process of involutive, symbiotic co-creation; see chapter 3 of *Staying with the Trouble: Making Kin in the Chthulucene* (Durham, NC: Duke University Press, 2016).

50. Throughout *Biosemiotics,* Hoffmeyer provides a vast array of evidence from organismic biology to support this thesis, mostly in relation to intra- and intercellular communication in multicellular organisms.

51. Derrida, *Speech and Phenomena*, 39.

52. Barad, "Posthumanist Performativity," 818.

53. Jacques Derrida, *The Animal that Therefore I Am*, ed. Marie-Louise Mallet, trans. D. Wills (New York: Fordham University Press, 2008), 133.

54. Derrida, *Animal*, 135.

55. Derrida, *Animal*, 135.

56. In *The Open: Man and Animal*, Giorgio Agamben proposes that humanism and the concept of the human have historically functioned as an "anthropological machine": "*Homo sapiens*, then, is neither a clearly defined species nor a substance; it is, rather, a machine or device for producing the recognition of the human"; *The Open: Man and Animal* (Palo Alto, CA: Stanford University Press, 2004), 26.

57. In her essay on Latin American bio-art, Azucena Castro provides some provocative insights into the possible forms such co-representation might take: "in [Luciana Paoletti's] *Portraits* the microorganisms are taken from the hair, skin or breath of those posing for the picture, but then these miniscule entities are cultivated artificially in dishes and sometimes modified by biotechniques to make them grow. In these artworks, the image created, be it in the photographs or in Jeff's inscription artwork, is related to *cultivation* rather than *imitation* or reproduction. This insight means then that the becoming of the self depends on how life forms are cultivated, how they enter the web of life, and in what spaces—rather than on the repetition or duplication of a model.

The new agencies and assemblages deconstruct the dominant imaginary of artistic creation based on Kantian mimesis that colonized the conception of aesthetic experience"; "At the Biocultural Borderland: The Unfolding of Multispecies Encounters in Latin American Bioart," *452° Fahrenheit* 21 (2019): 31. Castro ties this notion into Haraway's "sympoesis," which draws on biologist Lynn Margulis's reframing of symbiosis as "the intimacy of strangers" to posit representation as a "making-with" and "unfolding together" akin to Barad's notion of intra-activity; see Haraway, *Staying with the Trouble*, 58–60. Many poets and writers within Latin America and beyond have developed strategies designed to bring out this collaborative aspect of literary creation, as I will discuss in the chapters that follow. Malcolm McNee has studied some of these strategies in *Environmental Imaginary*, coining terms such as "riomorphism" to describe how Astrid Cabral narrates from the river.

58. This is the case even in Donna Haraway's notion of "staying with the trouble" and the politics of care proposed by María Puig de la Bellacasa in *Matters of Care: Speculative Ethics in More Than Human Worlds* (Minneapolis: University of Minnesota Press, 2017).

59. Stengers goes as far as to state that "the global West is not a 'world' and recognizes no world. Referring to Deleuze and Guattari, I would rather characterize it as a 'machine,' destroying both politics and ontologies. No peace is possible with this hegemonic machine, because it knows only, as Bruno Latour emphasized (using another of its names: the advancing front of modernization), 'pacification,' or police operations. Those who oppose modernization are just 'backward' or 'misled.'" "Challenge," 86. As she summarizes, "a world-destroying machine cannot fit in with other worlds" (86). Nonetheless, she proposes that "modern practitioners" may break with the "agents of modernization" to establish diplomatic relations with members of other worlds.

60. Bruno Latour, "Scientific Objects and Legal Objectivity," in *Law, Anthropology, and the Constitution of the Social: Making Persons and Things*, ed. Alain Pottage and Martha Mundy (Cambridge: Cambridge University Press, 2004), 82.

61. Latour, "Scientific Objects," 88–89.

62. Barad, *Meeting the Universe Halfway*, 140.

63. See the introduction to Marisol de la Cadena's *Earth Beings: Ecologies of Practice across Andean Worlds* (Durham, NC: Duke University Press, 2015).

64. On this notion of the "bundling" of effects and the openness of bodies, see Webb Keane, "Signs Are Not the Garb of Meaning: On the Social Analysis of Material Things," in *Materiality*, ed. Daniel Miller (Durham, NC: Duke University Press, 2005), 182–205.

65. De la Cadena, *Earth Beings*, 26.

66. De la Cadena, *Earth Beings*, 27.
67. Marilyn Strathern, "Opening Up Relations," in *A World of Many Worlds*, ed. Marisol de la Cadena and Mario Blaser, (Durham, NC: Duke University Press, 2018), 25.
68. Ejército Zapatista de Liberación Nacional, "Cuarta declaración de la selva lacandona," January 1, 1996, *Enlace Zapatista*, https://enlacezapatista.ezln.org.mx/1996/01/01/cuarta-declaracion-de-la-selva-lacandona/. Isabelle Stengers notes that the term "pluriverse," was first employed by William James: "Unsatisfied with the choice on offer in metaphysics between, on the one hand, a universe, with its ready-made oneness, justifying efforts at overcoming discordance, and, on the other hand, a multiverse, made of disconnected parts indifferent to each other, James proposed that the world is a pluriverse in the making. Connections are in the making, breaking indifference but bringing no encompassing unity. Plurality means divergences that communicate, but partially, always partially"; "Comparison as a Matter of Concern," *Common Knowledge* 17, no. 1 (2011): 60–61.
69. On this point, see Elizabeth A. Povinelli's discussion of "geontologies" in the introduction to her book of the same name: *Geontologies: A Requiem to Late Liberalism* (Durham, NC: Duke University Press, 2016).
70. Mario Blaser and Marisol de la Cadena, "Introduction: Pluriverse, a Proposal for a World of Many Worlds," in *A World of Many Worlds*, ed. Marisol de la Cadena and Mario Blaser (Durham, NC: Duke University Press, 2018), 2.
71. Val Plumwood, *Feminism and the Mastery of Nature* (London: Routledge, 1993).
72. See Stengers, "Comparison," 60 and "Introductory Notes on an Ecology of Practices," *Cultural Studies Review* 11, no. 1 (2005): 193; Blaser and De la Cadena, "Introduction," 4–10; and note 16 of this chapter regarding Badiou's and Rancière's theories of politics.
73. Blaser and de la Cadena, "Introduction," 4.
74. Stengers, "Introductory Notes," 193.
75. As Strathern notes, with reference to the Hagen culture of Papua New Guinea, "there is no culture, in the sense of the cumulative works of man, and no nature to be tamed and made productive"; "No Nature, No Culture: The Hagen Case," in *Nature, Culture, and Gender*, ed. Carol MacCormack and Marilyn Strathern (Cambridge: Cambridge University Press, 1980), 219. In turn, Rarámuri anthropologist Enrique Salmón notes that Indigenous terms referring to the natural world typically coalesce around notions of mutually "nurturing life" rather than exteriority; "Kincentric Ecology: Indigenous Perceptions of the Human-Nature Relationship," *Ecological Applications* 10, no. 5 (2000): 1331.

76. Viveiros de Castro writes that "the Amerindian words which are usually translated as 'human being' and which figure in those supposedly ethno-centric self-designations do not denote humanity as a natural species. They refer rather to the social condition of personhood, and they function (pragmatically when not syntactically) less as nouns than as pronouns. They indicate the position of the subject; they are enunciative markers, not names." "Cosmological Deixis and Amerindian Perspectivism," *The Journal of the Royal Anthropological Institute* 4, no. 3 (1998): 476.

77. Viveiros de Castro, *Cannibal Metaphysics: For a Post-Structural Anthropology*, trans. Peter Skafish (Minneapolis: University of Minnesota Press, 2017), 156–57. In "Cosmological Deixis and Amerindian Perspectivism," Viveiros de Castro summarizes perspectivism in the following way: "Typically, in normal conditions, humans see humans as humans, animals as animals and spirits (if they see them) as spirits; however, animals (predators) and spirits see humans as animals (as prey) to the same extent that animals (as prey) see humans as spirits or as animals (predators). By the same token, animals and spirits see themselves as humans: they perceive themselves as (or become) anthropomorphic beings when they are in their own houses or villages and they experience their own habits and characteristics in the form of culture—they see their food as human food. Jaguars see blood as manioc beer, vultures see the maggots in rotting meat as grilled fish, etc.), they see their bodily attributes (fur, feathers, claws, beaks etc.) as body decorations or cultural instruments, they see their social system as organized in the same way as human institutions are (with chiefs, shamans, ceremonies, exogamous moieties, etc.). This 'to see as' refers literally to percepts and not analogically to concepts, although in some cases the emphasis is placed more on the categorical rather than on the sensory aspect of the phenomenon. In sum, animals are people, or see themselves as persons" (470).

78. Stengers, "Challenge," 85.

79. In his use of the cannibal trope, Viveiros de Castro draws both on the long history of anthropological studies on cannibalism and "savagery" as well as the playful Brazilian modernist "Anthropophagist" movement, which proposed Tupí cannibalism as a methodology for reconciling the postcolonial conundrum of achieving cultural autonomy when national culture was dominated by the "imitation" of European models. In his famous "Anthropophagist Manifesto," Oswald de Andrade argued for the indiscriminate consumption of both European and Indigenous Brazilian cultural tropes in the creation of a new national cultural corpus. While some critics consider this proposal a superficial cultural appropriation of Indigenous tropes into a Eurocentric

modernist discourse (akin to European avant-garde primitivism), Viveiros de Castro rejects oedipal approaches to this problem, reframing it through his ethnographic fieldwork with Arawaté communities and Deleuze and Guattari's theorization of becoming and filiation.

80. Eduardo Viveiros de Castro, *The Relative Native: Essays on Indigenous Conceptual Worlds* (Chicago: Hau, 2015), 180–81.

81. Viveiros de Castro, *Cannibal Metaphysics*, 144.

82. Viveiros de Castro, *Cannibal Metaphysics*, 151–52.

83. Viveiros de Castro, *Cannibal Metaphysics*, 151.

84. Viveiros de Castro, *Cannibal Metaphysics*, 142–43.

85. On this point, Viveiros cites a shaman from Igulik quoted by Bodenhorn: "*Life's greatest danger lies in the fact that man's food consists entirely of souls,*" cited in Viveiros de Castro, *Relative Native*, 175; the italics are his.

86. Viveiros de Castro, *Cannibal Metaphysics*, 152.

87. As Samantha Frost notes, Thomas Hobbes famously viewed fear as the prime motivator in politics, compelling humans to accept sovereign power in exchange for security; "Fear and the Illusion of Autonomy," in *New Materialisms: Ontology, Agency, Politics*, ed. Diana Coole and Samantha Frost (Durham, NC: Duke University Press, 2010), 158. Somewhat against the grain, she argues that Hobbes's account implies that fear plays a key role in the autonomy of the subject; it is the willful displacement of fear onto sovereign power that foregrounds the subject's agency; Frost, "Fear," 172. While this perspective seems plausible within the history of Euro-American political thought, I argue that Amazonian ontologies proffer an alternative relation between fear and political subjectivities, in which subjectivity emerges not through displacement, but rather ingestion.

88. Adorno argues that "identity, the condition of freedom, is immediately and simultaneously the principle of determinism." *Negative Dialectics* (New York: Continuum, 1973), 216–17. As he further elaborates, "men are unfree because they are beholden to externality, and this externality in turn consists also of men themselves" (219) and "it is the nature-controlling sovereignty and its social form, dominion over people, that suggest the opposite to our consciousness: the idea of freedom" (220). In this formulation, the tyranny of nature would have been seen as an extension of the tyranny of God and the Church.

89. Viveiros de Castro, *Relative Native*, 176.

90. Viveiros generalizes this situation in the following terms: "This is the 'war of the worlds' that forms the backdrop to Amerindian cosmopraxis. The typical confrontation takes place in the encounter outside the village between a person who is alone (a hunter, a woman collecting firewood, etc.) and a

being that at first sight looks like an animal or a person—sometimes a relative (living or dead) of the subject. The entity then interpellates the human: the animal, for example, speaks to the hunter, protesting against his treatment of itself as prey; or it looks strangely at him, while the hunter's arrows fail to injure it; the pseudo-relative invites the subject to follow it, or to eat something it is carrying. The reaction to the entity's initiative is decisive. If the human accepts the dialogue or the invitation, if he or she responds to the interpellation, the person is lost: he/she will inevitably be overpowered by the non-human subjectivity, passing over to its side, transforming him/herself into a being of the same species as the speaker. Anyone responding to a 'you' spoken by a non-human accepts the condition of being its 'second person' and when assuming it, in turn, the position of 'I' does so already as a non-human. The canonical form of these encounters, then, consists in suddenly finding out that the other is 'human' or, rather, that *it is the other that is human*, which automatically dehumanizes and alienates the interlocutor." *Relative Native*, 181–82.

91. Viveiros de Castro, *Cannibal Metaphysics*, 124.
92. Viveiros de Castro, *The Relative Native*, 171. Regarding Roberto Esposito's theory of biopolitics, see *Immunitas: The Protection and Negation of Life* (Cambridge: Polity, 2011).
93. Stengers theorizes the role of fright in an "ecology of practices" in several of her later works, particularly in "Challenge" and "Comparison."
94. Daniel Shargel and Jesse Prinz, "An Enactivist Theory of Emotional Content," in *The Ontology of Emotions*, ed. Hichem Naar and Fabrice Teroni (Cambridge: Cambridge University Press, 2017), 110.
95. Jean Paul Sartre, *Sketch for a Theory of the Emotions* (London: Routledge, 2004), 58.
96. Anthony Hatzimoysis, "Emotions in Heidegger and Sartre," in *The Oxford Handbook of Philosophy of Emotion*, ed. Peter Goldie (Oxford: Oxford University Press, 2009), 231.
97. Quoted in Hatzimoysis, "Emotions," 223.
98. Sartre, *Sketch*, 43.
99. Viveiros de Castro, *Relative Native*, 172.
100. Emmanuel Levinas, *Totality and Infinity: An Essay on Exteriority* (Pittsburgh, PA: Duquesne University Press, 1969), 116 and 112, respectively.
101. See Badiou's discussion of Levinas's first ethics in the second chapter of *Ethics: An Essay on the Understanding of Evil*, trans. Peter Hallward (London: Verso, 2001).
102. Levinas, *Totality and Infinity*, 102.

103. Derrida comes very close to making this affirmation in "Eating Well": "For everything that happens at the edge of the orifices (of orality, but also of the ear, the eye-and all the 'senses' in general) the metonymy of 'eating well' (bien manger) would always be the rule. The question is no longer one of knowing if it is 'good' to eat the other or if the other is 'good' to eat, nor of knowing which other. One eats him regardless and lets oneself be eaten by him. The so-called nonanthropophagic cultures practice symbolic anthropophagy and even construct their most elevated socius, indeed the sublimity of their morality, their politics, and their right, on this anthropophagy." "'Eating Well' or the Calculation of the Subject: An Interview with Jacques Derrida," in *Who Comes After the Subject?* ed. Eduardo Cadava, Peter Connor, and Jean-Luc Nancy (New York: Routledge, 1991), 114. Or perhaps even more to the point: "One must eat well-here is a maxim whose modalities and contents need only be varied, ad infinitum. This evokes a law of need or desire (I have never believed in the radicality of this occasionally useful distinction), orexis, hunger, and thirst ('one must ,' 'one must [eat] well'), respect for the other at the very moment when, in experience (I am speaking here of metonymical 'eating' as well as the very concept of experience), one must begin to identify with the other, who is to be assimilated, interiorized, understood ideally (something one can never do absolutely without addressing oneself to the other and without absolutely limiting understanding itself, the identifying appropriation), speak to him in words that also pass through the mouth, the ear, and sight, and respect the law that is at once a voice and a court (it hears itself, it is in us who are before it)." Derrida, "Eating Well," 115.

104. Derrida, *Speech and Phenomena*, 38.

105. Derrida, *Speech and Phenomena*, 67.

106. Viveiros de Castro is careful to underscore that this form of subjectivity is not synthetic, but rather heterogeneous: "Every point of view is 'total,' and no point of view knows its like or equivalent. . . . The relation between points of view (the relation that is a point of view qua multiplicity) is of the order of a disjunctive synthesis or immanent exclusion, and not of a transcendent inclusion. In sum, the perspectivist system is in perpetual disequilibrium, to once again invoke Lévi-Strauss's characterization of Amerindian cosmologies." *Cannibal Metaphysics*, 157.

107. Derrida, *Speech and Phenomena*, 54.

CHAPTER 3

First epigraph. Clarice Lispector, *Água viva* (Rio de Janeiro: Rocco, 1998), 49; Second epigraph. Lispector, *Água viva*, 54. In these epigraphs and in several passages throughout this chapter and the subsequent two (all marked), I have used my own translations of the Portuguese original as the published English translations often lose some key subtleties, especially in the case of Lispector's writing. In this particular case, the word "being" was removed from the English translation, transforming "dexei de existir sendo" into "I've stopped existing." Clarice Lispector, *The Stream of Life*, trans. Elizabeth Loew and Earl Fitz (Minneapolis: University of Minnesota Press, 1989), 43.

1. Julio Cortázar, "Axolotl," in *End of the Game and Other Stories*, trans. Paul Blackburn (New York: Pantheon, 1967), 4.

2. As Irus Braverman notes, "at the zoo, direct physical contact between zoo animals and zoogoers is not only discouraged but also physically prevented. Fences, moats, cages, and separate air and water systems ensure that animals and humans cannot touch one another, and to a lesser extent, that they cannot smell one another. Sight— the strongest, safest, and most sanitary of human senses— emerges as the only possible contact between the two populations. Of all the senses, the zoo's preference toward sight is not incidental, nor is it unproblematic." *Zooland: The Institution of Captivity* (Palo Alto, CA: Stanford University Press, 2012), 71.

3. Cortázar, "Axolotl," 9.

4. Tellingly, R. Lane Kauffman reads the story in an allegorical mode as an ultimately failed exploration of the possibilities for a non-ethnocentric ethnography of the other, but he never suggests that it may be a non-anthropocentric one (failed or otherwise). On the contrary, he views the axolotls as "avatars of the Aztecs" ("Julio Cortázar y la apropiación del otro: 'Axololt' como una fábula etnográfica," *Revista Mexicana de Sociología* 63, no. 4 [2001]: 227–28).

5. Graciela Capacci de Giovani, "'Axolotl' de Julio Cortázar. Un reclamo desde el silencio: Intertextualidad social en la literatura del exilio," in *Literatura como intertextualidad: IX Simposio de Internacional de Literatura*, ed. Juana Alcira Arancibia, 193–204 (Buenos Aires: Vinciguerra, 1993); Laura García Moreno, "Cuerpos interrogantes: La mirada en 'El búfalo' de Clarice Lispector y 'Axolotl' de Julio Cortázar," *La Torre* 6, nos. 20–21 (2001): 309–30; and Brett Levinson, "The Other Origin: Cortázar and Identity Politics," *Latin American Literary Review* 22, no. 44 (1994): 5–19; among others, approach the story through Lacanian psychoanalysis; however, their analyses of the construction of subjectivity through desire for the other sidesteps entirely the problem of the axolotls' animality. Sara Castro-Klarén, "Ontological Fabulation: Toward Cortázar's Theory of Literature," in *The Final Island: The Fiction of Julio Cortázar*, ed. Jaime Alazraki and Ivar Ivask, 140–50 (Norman: University of Oklahoma Press, 1978) analyzes Cortázar's surrealist postulation of fantasy as a methodology for

accessing other subjectivities, an approach that Joana Videira Álvarez, "Esquizoánalisis del deseo y literatura fantástica," *Brumal* 3, no. 2 (2015): 155–75, and Malva Vásquez Córdoba, "Devenir-otro: Capitalismo y esquizofrenia en relatos de Cortázar," *Chasqui* 41, no. 2 (2012): 124–36, amplify through Deleuze and Guattari's procedure of schizoanalysis. In a similar vein, Torbjörn Gustafsson Chorell reads the story as an allegory for the role of "fascination" in the creative process, in which the "author becomes trapped in the artwork, buried alive as it were." "Fascination in Julio Cortázar's 'Axolotl,'" *Partial Answers* 17, no. 1 (2019): 53. However, Gabriel Giorgi offers a powerful counter-reading of the roles of the animal in fantastic fiction that hinges on its political potential: "if we think of texts by Cortázar, Silvina Ocampo, Rodolfo Wilcock, or Borges and Margarita Guerrero's *Manual de la zoología fantástica* [*Book of Imaginary Beings*], the operation surrounding the animal has a principle framing: that of responding to the disappearance of wild animals as a consequence of modernization—to its political and economic ordering of bodies—and relocating it as a power of fiction, as an incontrollable force that overflows and puts into a state of crisis the perceptual frameworks of the real; the animal in fantasy comes with an other time, which is that of ghostly nature, trace of a universe prior to modernity and a disruption of the evidences of the present. We are dealing with a virtual animal: which is to say, [the animal] as a threshold or line of passage between the real and the imaginary, between the given and the potential"; *Formas comunes*, 66. As he summarizes, these texts "aim to make of the fantastic a space that channels the challenge to the real that comes from these indomitable bodies, this energy that cannot be reduced to commerce and taming, but that no longer deploys itself as 'wild' or savage nature, but which is instead transcribed within the domain and powers of imagination"; *Formas comunes*, 67. Nevertheless, I will argue that what are usually taken as fantastical elements in this particular story do not in fact correspond strictly to fantastical aesthetics, since these animals actually exist, but rather to the materiality of intersubjective encounter. What seems fantastical to the humanist is the potential subjectivity of the axolotl—a potentiality that nevertheless approximates it to the disruptive powers of the fantastical that Giorgi describes.

6. Critics as varied as Capacci, "Axolotl," 193–204; Francis Fontmarty, "Xolotl, Mexolotl, Axolotl: Una metamorfosis recreativa," in *Lo lúdico y lo fantástico en la obra de Cortázar: Coloquio Internacional*, vol. 2, 79–88 (Madrid: Editorial Fundamentos, 1998); Kauffmann, "Julio Cortázar," 223–32; Jacques Leenhardt, "La americanidad de Julio Cortázar: El otro y su mirada." *Inti* 22–23 (1985–1986): 307–15; Levinson, "The Other Origin," 5–19; and Bertín Ortega, "Cortázar:

'Axolotl' y la cinta de Moebius," *Nuevo Texto Crítico* 2, no. 3 (1989): 135–40, have approached this story as a postcolonial allegory dealing with the repression of Indigenous cultural histories in the construction of Latin American identities. These readings contest those of Maurice Bennet, "Dialogue of Gazes: Metamorphosis and Epiphany in Julio Cortázar's 'Axolotl,'" *Studies in Short Fiction* 23, no. 1 (1986): 57–62; E. C. Graf, "'Axolotl' de Julio Cortázar: Dialéctica entre las mitologías azteca y dantesca," *Bulletin of Spanish Studies* 79, no. 5 (2002): 615–36; and Roberto González Echeverría, "Los reyes: Cortázar's Mythology of Writing," in *The Final Island: The Fiction of Julio Cortázar*, ed. Jaime Alazraki and Ivar Ivask, 63–72 (Norman: University of Oklahoma Press, 1978), which focus on integrating Cortázar's writing into the Western cultural canon, usually following a Jungian myth criticism approach in which Cortázar's axolotls would appear as reinscriptions of Western classical myths such as those in Dante's Inferno (Graf) or Greek mythology (Bennet and González Echeverría, who, although he does not address this specific story, relates Cortázar's writing process in general to bricolage in myth-making).

7. Jacob von Uexküll. *A Foray Into the Worlds of Animals and Humans, with A Theory of Meaning*, trans. Joseph D. O'Neil (Minneapolis: Minnesota University Press, 2010).

8. As the 2012 *Cambridge Declaration on Consciousness*, originally authored by Philip Low and amended and approved by the Francis Crick Memorial Conference attendees, states, "the absence of a neocortex does not appear to preclude an organism from experiencing affective states. Convergent evidence indicates that non-human animals have the neuroanatomical, neurochemical, and neurophysiological substrates of conscious states along with the capacity to exhibit intentional behaviors. Consequently, the weight of evidence indicates that humans are not unique in possessing the neurological substrates that generate consciousness. Nonhuman animals, including all mammals and birds, and many other creatures, including octopuses, also possess these neurological substrates." Philip Low et al., "Cambridge Declaration on Consciousness," July 7, 2012, *Francis Crick Memorial Conference*, https://fcmconference.org/img/CambridgeDeclarationOnConsciousness.pdf. In this context, thinking or mind would not be limited to symbolic representation or language, which may or may not be a possibility for many animal species, but rather in terms of iconic representation, of images or what Uexküll called "magical shadows" in his discussion of how chickens remembered the presence of a predator in their enclosure long after it had disappeared. Uexküll, *Foray*, 124. In citing Uexküll, I feel it imperative to state that I completely disavow his racist portrayal of the young African man in his discussion

of the perception of a ladder (94). It is clear to me that this particular example indicates a problem of cultural equivocation, not biological difference—by which I mean to say that what was probably not clear to the young man was the cultural logic behind Von Uexküll's request—his expectations; see Uexküll, *Foray*, 94. Nevertheless, this episode also brings to the surface the problem of equivocation in his representations of animal perception as well, an issue that I address below in my discussion of multispecies diplomacy.

9. Cortázar, "Axolotl," 7.

10. Spiritists did typically believe that animals had immortal souls, but they were not self-conscious or capable of transmigration; according to the founder of spiritism, Allan Kardec (the pen name of Hippolyte Léon Denizard Rivail), animal souls or vital energies were immediately reassigned to other animal bodies by higher spirits upon their death without any memory of their prior lives; see *The Spirits' Book*, trans. E. G. Dutra (Sheridan, WY: Luchnos, 2021), fragments 592–606.

11. On this point, see John Berger's chapter "Why Look at Animals?" in *About Looking* (New York: Pantheon, 1980).

12. Cortázar, "Axolotl," 9. One might argue that this reference to the image from the axolotl's perspective constitutes a projection of the human narrator, who apprehends the axolotl bodies within a representational rather than indexical mode. However, it is important to remember that in cosmological perspectivism, the human who becomes other always retains traces of the human's perspective on their own othered self. In that sense, this awareness of the human narrator's perception of the axolotl as entrapped within an immobile image does not necessarily contradict the logic of shamanistic transformation or transmigration (both phenomena exist within Indigenous ontologies).

13. Cortázar, "Axolotl" (Spanish), 163. This quote is my literal translation from the Spanish version, since Blackburn's English translation changed both the wording and the grammar of this passage, losing a substantial portion of the meaning.

14. Viveiros de Castro, *Relative Native*, 175–82. He underscores that, "what defines these perspectival multiplicities is their incompatibility. A human and jaguar cannot be people at the same time; it is impossible to experience blood as beer without having-already-become a jaguar. Perspectivism states that each species sees itself as people. However, it also states that two species cannot see each other simultaneously as people" (*Relative Native*, 178).

15. Cortázar, "Axolotl," 6. Unfortunately, this passage cannot be translated adequately due to the English language's lack of a null subject position, although one can come close by taking "That" as an ambiguous subject. In the Spanish

original, the subject of the first two sentences is entirely ambiguous—it could be the narrator or it could be the axolotl, which reinforces the melding of the two subject perspectives throughout the story. Also "reclamar" is a bit different than "claim," since it can also be translated as "complain" or "protest," that is, petition for the recognition of equal standing and remediation of an injustice.

16. Cortázar, "Axolotl," 8.

17. See the first chapter of Derrida's *The Animal that Therefore I Am.* He argues that this singularity consists in "an existence that refuses to be conceptualized" (9).

18. John Berger, *About Looking,* 28.

19. In *Homo Sacer,* Agamben approached this problem through a perceived distinction in classical Greek thought between *bios* (as political and productive life), *zoe* (as natural social life), and "bare life" (life exposed to death) in the constitution of sovereign power, that is the ability of the sovereign to exempt itself from law and exercise the "unconditional power of death" over bare life, or life that "may be killed, but not sacrificed" (since the sacred would ostensibly embody the conjunction of bios and zoe in ancient Greek politics). According to Agamben, it is precisely this exception that allows for the sacred and therefore politics to be instituted. While many scholars of classical thought have problematized Agamben's selective extrapolation of these terms from Aristotle's philosophy, in which they are often ambivalent, Fabián Ludueña Romandini makes the convincing case in *La comunidad de los espectros* (Buenos Aires: Miño y Dávila, 2010) that, since its beginnings in classical Greek thought, Euro-American political philosophy has primarily been concerned with the administration of human animality, what he denominates zoopolitics. In his study of the treatment of "illegitimate" newborns and those born with deformities, the decision over life and death was not based strictly on the "bare life" of animality as Agamben argued, but rather on induction into the bios. The future citizenship of the infant was simultaneously a sovereign decision of the citizen father and an institutional power adjudicated by the state. This institutional power was rooted in a eugenic logic that was applied to both humans and animals based on what was seen as a natural order of able bodies.

20. Viveiros de Castro, *Cannibal Metaphysics,* 142–43.

21. In "Derrida y el pensamiento amazónico," Juan Duchesne Winter postulates that this difference is exemplified by the fundamental distinction in the conceptualization of governance between the centrality of the sovereign/wolf metaphor that Derrida diagnoses at the heart of Western theorizations of sovereign power and the common (although not exclusive) Amazonian associatiof

shamans with jaguars. As Duchesne Winter writes, "the shaman's power and knowledge do not conform to the Western concept of sovereignty, in the sense that they do not configure a sole and indivisible subject of power, nor are they based on a unilateral relation with a world-object, besides not presupposing total control over any partiality"; "Derrida y el pensamiento amazónico (La bestia y el soberano/el jaguar y el chamán," *Cuadernos de Literatura* 21, no. 41 (2017): 173. While Derrida notes that the association of sovereign with wolf locates sovereign power in a position of exteriority with respect to the law, thereby revealing its co-constitutive relationship to it, the shaman's relationship with the jaguar is diplomatic; it is a form of negotiation with a colleague. In that sense, the primary political form in Amazonian thought is cosmopolitical diplomacy rather than the sovereign power to create institutions.

22. In that sense, Ralph Acampora's comparison of zoological exhibition to pornography in "Zoos and Eyes" does not seem particularly far fetched. He argues that "zoos are pornographic in that they make the nature of their subjects disappear precisely by overexposing them." "Zoos and Eyes: Contesting Captivity and Seeking Successor Practices," *Society and Animals* 13, no. 1 (2005): 69.

23. Regarding how amphibians distinguish prey and predators, see chapter 4 of Jörg-Peter Ewert's *Neuroethology: An Introduction to the Neurophysiological Fundamentals of Behavior* (Berlin: Springer-Verlag, 1980).

24. Cortázar, "Axolotl," 7.

25. Cortázar, "Axolotl," 6.

26. On this point, see also Akira Mizuta Lippit's discussion of the sublimity of the "animal cry" in Burke and Hegel in the introduction to *Electric Animals: Toward a Rhetoric of Wildlife* (Minneapolis: University of Minnesota Press, 2000). Furthermore, Mizuta Lippit notes that Lyotard finds a form of sublimity in the animal as its cry, ostensibly a form of expression without subjectivity, "opens up a channel of unconscious communication that carries with it the possibility of an unconscious world, the world of the unconscious. It is thus toward the unconscious that modern philosophy inevitably edges. The figure of the animal leads, in many ways, that progression: dispossessed of language and mortality, and excluded from the philosophical community of beings, the animal recedes into what Lyotard terms a 'time before *logos*': a time, that is, before the human subject" (50). Of course, entrapped within the sound-damping walls of glass and water, the axolotls in Cortázar's stories are effectively muted. There is only the gaze.

27. See Heidegger, *Fundamental Concepts*, 177.

28. Emmanuel Levinas, *Totality and Infinity*, 198–200.

29. Cortázar, "Axolotl," 7.
30. Derrida, *Animal*, 47–48.
31. Playing on Derrida's usage of the term dissemination, Cixous writes that, "at first sight, a text is not readable. It cannot be summarized. It is free. It diffuses and spreads"; *Reading with Clarice Lispector*, ed. and trans. by Verena Andermatt Conley (Minneapolis: Minnesota University Press, 1990). 99.
32. Cortázar, "Axolotl," 168. Again, this is my literal translation from the Spanish version, since Blackburn's rewording of this passage changes the meaning.
33. I follow here Badiou's theorization of the event as the disruption of sameness by a multiplicity, and of ethics as fidelity to the "truth" of that disruptive event; *Being and Event*, chapter 3.
34. See the first chapter of Deleuze and Guattari, *Kafka*.
35. Samuel Alberti, ed., *The Afterlives of Animals: A Museum Menagerie* (Charlottesville: University of Virginia Press, 2011).
36. Geoffrey Swinney, "An Afterword on Afterlife," in *The Afterlives of Animals: A Museum Menagerie*, ed. Samuel Alberti (Charlottesville: University of Virginia Press, 2011), 221. Swinney's arguments on this point parallel Berger's more general theorization of the virtualization of animals in modern technosociety: "even in their premortem existence, these animals were appropriated and reconstructed in our image. They were anthropomorphized and fashioned to embody human emotions and values; constructed as creatures with which we were able to empathize. Death allows such roles to be consolidated, and the postmortem reconstruction of an animal is both material and epistemological. Preservation and reconstruction divest the animal of those aspects of its animality—its beastliness—which serve to remind we humans of our own biology and of the beast within." "Afterword," 221. In an interesting counterpoint to this perspective, however, Garry Marvin argues that hunters' trophies serve a quite different function, preserving the hunter-prey relationship beyond the death of the prey through memorialization; "Enlivened Through Memory: Hunters and Hunting Trophies," in *The Afterlives of Animals: A Museum Menagerie*, ed. Samuel Alberti (Charlottesville: University of Virginia Press, 2011), 202–17.
37. Berger, *About Looking*, 21.
38. I refer not only to the presence-value of these zoo animals, which visually counteracts the extinction narrative at a visceral if not quantitative level, but also the captive-breeding programs that are often associated with zoos; see chapter 3 of Irus Braverman's *Wild Life: The Institution of Nature* (Palo Alto, CA: Stanford University Press, 2015).

39. On this point, see Braverman's penetrating study of wildlife conservation and management in *Wild Life*, in which she argues that the long-standing conceptual division between *in-situ* (natural) and *ex-situ* (institutional) conservation has become untenable. For Braverman, wildlife management consists in a form of institutional biopolitics: "conservation's contemporary biopolitical characteristics include both its foundational goal of affirmatively saving life and its operations on the macro-scale of the species" (227).

40. Braverman argues that the concept of animal wildness has itself become dissociated from "wilderness" in conservation practice, if not always discourse: "this realignment of conservation around wildness has enabled a more dynamic and relational modus vivendi: it is no longer necessary to understand conservation in extreme terms; a species can be 'wilder' and a site can be 'semi-wild' or 'as wild as possible,' with neither being 'wilderness' per se. In other words, the wild has come to be perceived as a multidimensional matrix of possibilities"; *Wild Life*, 227.

41. Cary Wolfe, *Before the Law: Humans and Other Animals in a Biopolitical Frame* (Chicago: University of Chicago Press, 2012), 10.

42. See for instance, Gabriel Giorgi's discussion in *Formas comunes* of the spatial regime of the house in *The Passion According to G. H.* (92).

43. Clarice Lispector, "The Buffalo," in *Family Ties*, trans. Giovanni Ponteiro (Austin: University of Texas Press, 1972), 147.

44. Lispector, "Buffalo," 152.

45. Lispector, "O búfalo," in *Laços de família: Contos* (Rio de Janeiro: Rocco, 2009), 128; my translation.

46. While Freud theorized the death drive as a destructive biological instinct to self-harm and harm others rooted in a return to the inorganic, Lacan reframed it successively as the drive to return to the pre-symbolic imaginary order and as the foundational movement of the symbolic itself, in the subject's impossible drive to satiate and therefore exhaust its own desires in *jouissance*, thereby producing the repetitive displacement of affective objects and the transference or exchange of signs between them. On this point, see Bruno Vincent's "Jouissance and Death Drive in Lacan's Teaching," *Ágora* 23, no. 1 (2020): 49–56. Lispector's representation of the "will to kill" in *The Passion* places her closer to Lacan. She describes killing the cockroach in terms of extreme pleasure: "And I shivered with great delight, as though I were finally in touch with the grandeur of an instict that was horrible, totally and completely sweet—as though I were finally experiencing, and within myself, a grandeur greater than myself. I was for the first time drunk with a hatred as clean as water from a spring, I was becoming drunk with the desire, justified or not,

to kill"; *The Passion According to G. H.*, trans. Ronald W. Sousa (Minneapolis: University of Minneapolis Press, 1988), 45. The series of similes (como) suggests a recursive movement regarding this "desire" to kill as something that aporetically constitutes and transcends subjectivity through jouissance. In that sense, what is presented as instinctual is closer to Lacan's conceptualization of the drive. Nevertheless, the cockroach does not die, and its affective demand for a response—its gaze—problematizes its position as object of desire; between life and death, it is an ambivalent presence that forces the character to abdicate her sovereignty and, eventually, incorporate its perspective on her into her own: "Alive and looking at me. I turned my eyes aside in a quick, violent reaction"; Lispector, *Passion*, 47; "But it was then that I saw the cockroach's face"; Lispector, *Passion*, 47; "An instant earlier, I probably would still have been unable to see the cockroach's face on its visage" (ter visto na cara da barata o seu rosto). Lispector, *A paixão segundo G. H.* (Rio de Janeiro: Rocco, 2009), 54; my translation.

47. Lispector, "Buffalo," 149.

48. On this point, see Derrida's discussion of Lacan's thinking regarding the animal in chapter 3 of *The Animal That Therefore I Am*. Lacan's distinction relies on the what he diagnoses as the animal's inability to "pretend to pretend," that is, to make the sovereign decision to misrepresent its (indexical) representation of itself or "erase its tracks"; Derrida dismantles this argument through his theorization of the trace (including animal tracks) as always already the trace of a trace. *Animal*, 133–36.

49. In *The Passion According to G. H.*, she describes neutral life as "the vital element linking things," which manifests itself in the subject precisely as what is "unexpressive of/in me," thereby anticipating Derrida's theorization of the trace (92). Neutrality would thus indicate a desire to maintain fidelity to these traces, as the very grounds for an excessive objectivity that is fundamentally ontological or perspectival rather than epistemological in a scientific sense: "The great, neutral reality of what I was experiencing outstripped me in its extreme objectivity. I felt unable to be as real as the reality that was reaching me" (Lispector, *Passion*, 92). Similarly, in *Água viva*, she describes oblique life as "the mystery of the impersonal that is the 'it': I have the impersonal within me and it's not rotten and corruptible by the personal that sometimes drenches me: but I dry myself in the sun and I'm impersonal, made of a dry, germinating seed" (Lispector, *Stream of Life*, 22). A few pages on, she writes that "I don't think but I feel the *it*. With eyes closed, I search blindly for the breast: I want thick milk. Nobody taught me to want [querer, also love]. But now I want [love]" (*Stream of Life*, 27–28). As Giorgi notes, "this life is never

'individual,' it is not conjugated around a formal principle, but is always a knotting of forces, spaces, and relations" (*Formas comunes*, 36).

50. Thales Augusto Barreto de Castro notes that the narrator also plays a role establishing this parallel, since both the female protagonist and the animals share the condition of being "unnamed." "Perspectivas híbridas, concepções descentradas: estéticas do porvir em *Laços de família*," *Mundo Amazónico* 9, no. 1 (2018): 58.

51. Lispector, "The Buffalo," 156.

52. Lispector, "The Buffalo," 155.

53. In *The Passion*, she distinguishes between the apprehension of the futurity of death as the horizon of subjectivity and the non-being of the subject in the instant: "Of my own death, yes, I was indeed aware, for death was the future and is imaginable, and I always had time to imagine. But the instant, the very instant—the right now—*that* is unimaginable, between the right now/and the I there is no space: it is just now, inside me" (70). In Derridean terms, the subject is always a projection toward the future; subjectivity can never manifest itself in the instant except as the flicker of an absence. For this reason, Lispector states that, "the moment of living is so hellishly inexpressive that it is nothingness" (*Passion*, 71). Nevertheless, her proposal for an aesthetics of neutral life requires a prolongation of the immediate as a flow, rather than the truncation that the term "instant" implies: "the future will be precisely a now again" (*Passion*, 73).

54. Lispector, "Buffalo," 156.

55. Lispector, "Buffalo," 156.

56. As Evando Nascimento notes, "the exchange [of perspectives in Lispector's writing] deterritorializes ontological identities, opening historical or existential immanence to irreducible difference"; "Rastros do animal humano: a ficção de Clarice Lispector," in *Pensar/escrever o animal: Ensaios de zoopoética y biopolítica*, ed. Maria Esther Maciel (Florianópolis: Editora da Universidade Federal de Santa Catarina, 2011), 135.

57. Viveiros de Castro, *Relative Native*, 59.

58. Viveiros de Castro, *Relative Native*, 65.

59. Lispector, *Stream of Life*, 57.

60. Lispector, "Buffalo," 156.

61. Jacques Derrida, *The Politics of Friendship*, trans. George Collins (London: Verso, 1994), 68–69.

62. Derrida, *Politics of Friendship*, 69. Lispector describes this responsivity in very similar terms in *The Passion* when the narrator discusses her response to the cockroach upon having crushed it with a cabinet door, exposing its insides:

"even in secret, freedom does not absolve guilt" (79). However, the morality of guilt is suspended in the affectivity of the instant, transformed into pure responsivity without interpretation: "there had to be a goodness [bondade, kindness] so other that it wouldn't resemble goodness [kindness]" (80). This form of kindness consists not in helping the cockroach in some way (whether healing it or killing it to end its suffering), but rather in opening herself to it: "And now I began to let it touch me" (80). Tellingly, this sequence leads to her ingesting the cockroach in an act that can only be described as cannibalistic (given her explicit will to self-animalize) in the sense in which Viveiros de Castro uses the term, that is, as an eating of relations: "then, through the door of condemnation, I ate life and was eaten by life. I understood that my kingdom is of this world" (112).

63. This trend is transparently the case in critical essays such as A. M. Wheeler's "Animal Imagery as Reflection of Gender Roles in Clarice Lispector's *Family Ties*," *Critique* 28, no. 3 (1987): 125–34; Martin Mauro's "Tanta vida mutua (mujeres y precaridad animal)," *Alea* 20, no. 2 (2018): 17–35; Ingrid Muller's "The Problematics of the Body in Clarice Lispector's *Family Ties*," *Chasqui* 20, no. 1 (1991): 34–42; and Maria Peixoto's "Family Ties: Female Development in Clarice Lispector," in *The Voyage In: Fictions of Female Development*, ed. Elizabeth Abel, Marianne Hirsch, and Elizabeth Langland, 287–303 (Dartmouth, NH: University Press of New England for Dartmouth College, 1983), and *Passionate Fictions: Gender, Narrative, and Violence in Clarice Lispector* (Minneapolis: University of Minnesota Press, 1997).

64. This reinstatement is clear in passages such as this one: "Clarice works on language itself and on its relationship to the body, on the paradox that makes it so that things without body and reality are found and said more easily because they are nothing but words, for example, the law. She works on differences between humans and animals. She regrets not having been born an animal. In other words, she has to find the animal in herself. At stake for her is not the realm of science but that of life and death, of love. This agrees with what Freud had described as the formidable narcissism of animals, of the singular power of animals that goes with the fact that they have no intellect nor unconscious. They have another relation to life that can teach us a lot. This is what the law wants to avoid at all cost. It does not want us to feel regret, or desire, for a mode of life that would take as an example not God and the saints, but animals. This mode would not repress the animal part in us: 'An animal never substitutes one thing for another,' says Clarice. It could be said that an animal does not speak, therefore it cannot substitute one thing for another"; Cixous, *Reading*, 12. Nevertheless, this is the very point that

Derrida deconstructs in his discussion of Lacan in *The Animal that Therefore I Am*; I would suggest that Clarice performs a similar deconstruction in her representation of the buffalo. Furthermore, many ethological studies on altruism and animal sociality (for instance, those of Frans de Waal and Marc Beckhoff) place into question Freud's postulation of narcissism as a primary animal characteristic.

65. In that sense, Lispector's political project with respect to gender and sexuality hinges on the deconstructive gesture, as Maider Tornos Urzainki notes: "in this way, through uncertain contact with irreducible otherness, the becoming-animal construes a multiple and de-hierarchicalized sexuality, on the margins of the duplicative logic of the arborescent system, which, as a consequence of the inclusive disjunction of a heterogeneous grouping of sexual markings, disarticulates the conventions of the body and the text. It has to do with constructing a politics of rhythm and movement to think sexual difference beyond opposites, without succumbing to the categorical reduction of two sexes, with the goal of recovering the multiple, productive potential of difference, against the phallogocentric system of the Western world"; "El devenir-animal en *La pasión según G. H.* de Clarice Lispector (en lengua extranjera)," *Arte y Políticas de Identidad* 16 (2017): 159.

66. Earl Fitz laid the groundwork for this kind of poststructuralist reading of Lispector, arguing that, "returning to the ancient epistemological fount of philosophy and poetry, Lispector's generically hybrid texts can, collectively, be taken as a grand and endlessly self-reflective discourse on language and being, with the problem of meaning (and therefore of identity, both individual and cultural) functioning as their thematic and structural ground"; *Sexuality and Being in the Poststructuralist Universe of Clarice Lispector: The Difference of Desire* (Austin: University of Texas Press, 2001), 16.

67. Jutta Ittner, "Becoming Animal? Zoo Encounters in Rilke, Lispector, and Kronauer," *KulturPoetik* 3, no. 1 (2003): 37.

68. Rodolfo Piskorski, "The Light That Therefore I Give (to): Paleonymy and Animal Supplementarity in Clarice Lispector's *The Apple in the Dark*," in *What is Zoopoetics? Texts, Bodies, Entanglement*, ed. Kári Driscoll and Eva Hoffman (Cham: Palgrave Macmillan, 2018), 105.

69. Piskorski, "Light," 104.

70. Irving Goh, "*Le Toucher, le cafard*, or, On Touching—the Cockroach in Clarice Lispector's *Passion according to G. H*," *MLN* 131 (2016): 465.

71. Lispector, *Stream of Life*, 16.

72. Lispector, *Stream of Life*, 19.

73. Lispector, *Stream of Life*, 16.

74. Lispector, *Passion,* 131.
75. Gilles Deleuze, *Difference and Repetition* (New York: Columbia University Press, 1994), 10. As he writes, "the theatre of repetition is opposed to the theatre of representation, just as movement is opposed to the concept and to representation which refers it back to the concept. In the theatre of repetition, we experience pure forces, dynamic lines in space which act without intermediary upon the spirit, and link it directly with nature and history, with a language which speaks before words, with gestures which develop before organised bodies, with masks before faces, with spectres and phantoms before characters—the whole apparatus of repetition as a 'terrible power'" (10). "Theatre" here implies not mimetic representation, but rather presentation itself, as enactment; in this perspective, presentation may be framed by discourse as mimetic (representational theater), but it is essentially singular and immanent to the instant.
76. Nascimento, "Rastros," 133.
77. Tornos Urzainki, "Devenir," 152.
78. Lispector, *Passion,* 117.
79. Lispector describes this passivity in the following terms: "What still frightened me was that even that very unpunishable horror would be benignly reassorbed into the abyss of endless time, into the abyss of endless heights, into the profound abyss of God: absorbed into the core of an indifference"; *Passion,* 114.
80. Lispector, *Passion,* 114.
81. As Peter Hallward notes, Deleuze's monadism implies that, "far from disrupting the specified self, for Deleuze the Other is its very organizing principle. His Other is neither object nor subject per se, but 'a structure of the perceptual field,' an enabling condition of the subject (LS, 307). The Other distinguishes figure from ground (LS, 312, 305). The Other mediates. The Other opens the gap between subject and object. 'The fundamental effect [of the Other] is the distinction of my consciousness and its object' (306; cf. 31 0)"; "Deleuze and the 'World Without Others,'" *Philosophy Today* 41, no. 1 (1997): 536. Deleuze views thought as arising in material encounter precisely in the absence of this mediating function of the Other: "in the absence of the Other, 'the whole of our [Given] perceived world collapses in the interest of something else' (LS, 310)—namely, the immediate Real. 'In the Other's absence, consciousness and its object are one. There is no longer any possibility of error. . . . Consciousness ceases to be a light cast upon objects in order to become a pure phosphorescence of things in themselves' (LS, 311)." Hallward, "Deleuze," 536.

82. As Hallward notes, "[Deleuze's] work shares with global capitalism a certain faith in limitless expansion along an infinitely extendible 'frontier,' on the all too familiar American model"; "Deleuze," 537.

83. Nevertheless, Hallward diagnoses several parallels with absolutist political philosophy, although he is careful to point out that it is an "absolutism by other means" (539). Furthermore, he notes that "between fascism and Deleuze's anti-fascism, there is little formal or substantial difference. There is only the difference of affect, 'good' against 'bad'" (540). Given Deleuze's explicit anti-moralism, I can only infer that 'good' here would refer to openness to attachment, and 'bad' to the static, stratified, and detached.

CHAPTER 4

Epigraph. Lispector, *Água viva*, 66.

1. Lispector, *Passion*, 157.
2. Lispector, *Passion*, 163.
3. See chapter 4 of Alain Badiou, *Ethics*.
4. Clarice Lispector, *A paixão segundo G. H.* (Rio de Janeiro: Rocco, 2009), 163; my translation.
5. Lispector, *Água viva*, 13 and 29.
6. Lispector, *Água viva*, 90.
7. Lispector, *Passion*, 158.
8. Lispector, *Passion,* 157.
9. Lispector, *Passion*, 158.
10. Lispector, *Passion*, 158.
11. Jacques Derrida, *The Gift of Death and Literature in Secret*, trans. David Wills (Chicago: University of Chicago Press, 1999).
12. Lispector, *Passion*, 159–60.
13. Lispector, *Stream*, 9.
14. Julia Kristeva, *Powers of Horror: An Essay on Abjection*, trans. Leon Roudiez (New York: Columbia University Press, 1982).
15. Lispector, *Passion* 170.
16. Lispector, *Passion*, 171.
17. Deleuze, "A Philosophical Concept," 94.
18. Lispector, *Passion*, 58.
19. Derrida, *Gift*, 126.
20. Derrida, *Gift*, 137.
21. Regarding this secret, which Derrida argues lies at the heart of literature, he writes, "for the secret of secrecy about which we shall speak does not consist in hiding *something*, in not revealing the truth, but in respecting the absolute

singularity, the infinite separation of what binds me or exposes me to the unique, to the one as to the other, to the *One as to the Other*.' *Gift*, 122–23. He clarifies its relation to literature on pages 156–57.

22. Derrida, *Gift*, 138.
23. Lispector, *Passion*, 170.
24. Derrida, *Speech and Phenomena*, 104.
25. Lispector, *Stream*, 71.
26. Dialoguing with Heidegger and the question of Dasein as a "throwing/being-thrown" into consciousness, Derrida insists that, rather than an appropriation of the trace or a reappropriation of the self, the becoming-subject consists in an ex-appropriation: "And ex-appropriation does not form a boundary, if one understands by this word a closure or a negativity. It implies the irreducibility of the relation to the other. The other resists all subjectivation, even to the point of the interiorization-idealization of what one calls the work of mourning." Derrida, "Eating Well," 107.
27. Lispector, *Passion*, 171.
28. Lispector, *Passion*, 162.
29. Lispector, *Passion*, 163.
30. Lispector, *Passion*, 162.
31. Deleuze, "A Philosophical Concept," 95.
32. As Tornos Urzainki writes, citing Deleuze and Guattari: "it is a minorization of the major language that escapes the control of the dominant system, with an eye to creating this minor community that is always in-becoming through a violent contortion of syntax, which motivates the creation of a language within language. . . . The deterritorialization of the dominant language in the revolutionary process that guarantees the becoming-other of writing, allows one to deconstruct the self-satisfying autarky of the phallogocentric system by introducing in the hegemonic discourse a discomforting estrangement (*unheimlich*), which de-authorizes the arrogance exhibited by the symbolic order of language." "El Devenir-animal," 157.
33. Lispector, *Passion*, 169.
34. Giorgi, *Formas comunes*, 81–82.
35. Giorgi, *Formas comunes*, 34.
36. While I coincide with Simone de Ribeiro da Costa Curi's assessment in *A escritura nómade em Clarice Lispector* (Chapecó: Argos, 2001) of the relations between micropolitics and minor language, I think it is perhaps a disservice to Lispector's thought to read her writing as a straightforward example of literary nomadism in the sense in which Deleuze and Guattari use the word, as I discuss in what follows.

37. Clarice Lispector, "The Egg and the Chicken," in *The Complete Stories*, ed. Benjamin Moser, trans. Katrina Dodson (New York: New Directions, 2015), 277.

38. Lispector, "Egg," 277.

39. Lispector, *Água viva*, 45.

40. Clarice Lispector, "Family Ties," in *The Complete Stories*, ed. Benjamin Moser, trans. Katrina Dodson (New York: New Directions, 2015), 191.

41. Lispector, "Family Ties," 193.

42. Lispector, "Family Ties," 194.

43. Lispector, "Family Ties," 195–96.

44. Lispector, "Family Ties," 197.

45. Lispector, "Family Ties," 197.

46. Viveiros de Castro, *Relative Native*, 72.

47. Viveiros de Castro, *Relative Native*, 72.

48. Clarice Lispector, "The Crime of the Mathematics Teacher," in *The Complete Stories*, ed. Benjamin Moser, trans. Katrina Dodson (New York: New Directions, 2015), 218.

49. Lispector, "Crime," 219.

50. Lispector, "Crime," 217–18.

51. Lispector, "Crime," 218.

52. Lispector, "Crime," 219.

53. Lispector, "Crime," 218.

54. Lispector, "Crime," 218.

55. The math teacher laments that neither judicial law nor the law of the church can administer justice in this case (Lispector, "Crime," 220).

56. Lispector, "Crime," 219.

57. Clarice Lispector, "A Chicken," in *The Complete Stories*, ed. Benjamin Moser, trans. Katrina Dodson (New York: New Directions, 2015), 127.

58. Lispector, "Chicken," 127.

59. Lispector, "Chicken," 128. I should point out that in Spanish and Portuguese, "raza/raça" can refer to "people" or "species," not only skin color or ethnicity.

60. Lispector, "Chicken," 128.

61. Lispector, "Chicken," 128.

62. Lispector, "Chicken," 129.

63. Lispector, "Chicken," 129.

64. Lispector, "Chicken," 129.

65. Lispector, "Chicken," 129.

66. Lispector, "Chicken," 129.

67. Lispector, "Chicken," 129–30.

68. Lispector, "Chicken," 130.

69. See, for instance, T. R. Forbes's "The Crowing Hen: Early Observations on Spontaneous Sex Reversal in Chickens," *The Yale Journal of Biology and Medicine* 19, no. 6 (1947): 955–70.

70. Clarice Lispector, *A Breath of Life (Pulsations)*, ed. Benjamin Moser, trans. Johnny Lorenz (New York: New Directions, 2012), 51.

71. Henry Schwarz argues that, "the chicken is free because it defies the order of its world, which is to serve as food. And after it is captured again, the chicken of the short story suddenly lays an egg, another act of defiance, an act of regeneration of chicken life and existence." "Cartesian Literature: The Narrative Mathematics of Being in Clarice Lispector," *Canadian Journal of Latin American and Caribbean Studies* 39, no. 1 (2014): 63.

72. Lispector, "Chicken," 130.

73. As Evando Nascimento points out, "The hen distinguishes itself as the emblem of a certain form of femininity that is historically determined, but whose emergence constantly becomes irrepressible. Remember that, in colloquial Brazilian Portuguese, 'hen' is used to allude to a vulgar and promiscuous woman according to the masculine gaze (and the same goes for 'piranha'). In contrast, 'rooster' has positive meanings due to its propensity of sleeping with many females." "Rastros," 141.

74. Lispector problematizes this in a very interesting, cross-species way in "The Egg and the Chicken": "The chicken must not know that she has an egg. Or else she would save herself as a chicken, which is no guarantee either, but she would lose the egg. So she doesn't know. The chicken exists so that the egg can use the chicken. She was only meant to be fulfilled, but she liked it. The chicken's undoing comes from this: liking wasn't part of being born. To like being alive hurts" (280).

75. Derrida, "Eating Well," 113.

76. Derrida, "Eating Well," 113.

77. Derrida, "Eating Well," 114.

78. Derrida, "Eating Well," 114.

79. Derrida, "Eating Well," 115.

80. Derrida, "Eating Well," 115.

81. As Giorgi argues, critical zoographies produce an other biopolitics, a concept of "what is alive less as human property and root of human autonomy, but as a range of diverse forms of agentization, always already in relation with other bodies, always already collective, the threshold of multiplicity: as virtuality and experimental judgment. What is alive, the *bios*, then, less as

object of appropriation, of privatization derived from the individual, than as the threshold for the creation of modes of commonality between bodies and between species." *Formas comunes*, 41–42.

82. Gilles Deleuze and Felix Guattari, *A Thousand Plateaus: Capitalism and Schizophrenia*, trans. Brian Massumi (Minneapolis: University of Minnesota Press, 1987), 358.

CHAPTER 5

Epigraph. Davi Kopenawa and Bruce Albert, *The Falling Sky: Words of a Yanomami Shaman*, trans. Nicholas Elliot and Alison Dundy (Cambridge, MA: Harvard University Press, 2013), 323–24.

1. As Derrida explores throughout *Politics of Friendship*, democratic political equality in the liberal tradition of "liberté, egalité, fraternité" is premised on the aporetic identification with the other as "brother," a conceptualization of democratic polity that necessarily relies on the exclusion of differences. Historically, these exclusions have included gender, social class, and ethnicity; how much more so in the case of other species, particularly when human exclusions are often predicated on the basis of animalization.

2. Barad, *Meeting the Universe*, 148–49.

3. Barad defines an "agential cut" in the following way: "the apparatus [which may or may not be 'technological' in the sense in which we usually conceive of the term] enacts an agential cut—a resolution of the ontological indeterminacy—*within* the phenomenon, and *agential separability—the agentially enacted material condition of exteriority-within-phenomena—provides the condition for the possibility of objectivity*. This agential cut also enacts a local causal structure in the marking of the measuring instrument (effect) by the measured object (cause), where local means within the phenomenon." *Meeting the Universe*, 175; the italics are Barad's. In this particular case, the apparatus that enacts the human/animal agential cut would effectively be humanism itself, which works within phenomenal intra-actions to inscribe humans as subjects and nonhumans as objects. The question of objectivity would arise here within the ostensibly empirical evidence (language, culture, etc.) supporting the premise of human exceptionalism.

4. See Derrida, *Politics of Friendship*, 306, and Jason W. Moore, "The Capitalocene, Part 1: On the Nature and Origins of Our Ecological Crisis," *Journal of Peasant Studies* 44, no. 3 (2017): 599, https://www.tandfonline.com/doi/full/10.1080/03066150.2016.1235036. Bruno Latour in *Politics of Nature* and Isabelle Stengers in *Cosmopolitics* and other texts have made similar proposals for "a parliament of things" and "cosmopolitics" respectively; however, while their

approaches advocate for incorporating nonhuman entities' knowledge about themselves into political practice, they continue to rely fully on human "parliamentary" representation of nonhumans' "interests." While this argument may be inevitable with respect to the possibilities of nonhuman political agency within political structures dominated by humans, I feel that neither author problematizes sufficiently the discursive structure of representation itself, particularly regarding nonhuman political agency.

5. Michael Marder, *Plant Thinking: A Philosophy of Vegetal Life* (New York: Columbia University Press, 2013).

6. Marder, *Plant Thinking*, 96–101. By "bare life," I do not refer explicitly to Agamben's oft-criticized reading of Aristotle's distinction between zoe and bios, although there are certainly points of connection, but rather to Marder's observation that, "after we strip life of all its recognizable features, vegetal beings go on living; plant-soul is the remains of the psyche reduced to its non-human and non-animal modality. It is life in its an-archic bareness, inferred from the fact that it persists in the absence of the signature features of animal vivacity, and it is a source of meaning, which is similarly bare, non-anthropocentric, and yet ontologically vibrant. In a word, life as survival." *Plant Thinking*, 22.

7. Marder, *Plant Thinking*, 98–99.

8. See the introduction to Wylie, *Poetics*.

9. Wylie, *Poetics*, 16 and Juan Duchesne Winter, *Plant Theory in Amazonian Literature* (New York: Palgrave Macmillan, 2019).

10. In this chapter, I primarily quote the Spanish original (José Eustasio Rivera, *La vorágine* [Bogotá: Biblioteca Popular de Cultura Colombiana, 1946]) due to changes in wording that affect key passages in John Chasteen's translation (*The Vortex*, trans. John Charles Chasteen [Durham, NC: Duke University Press, 2018]).

11. Jorge Marcone, "De retorno a lo natural: *La serpiente de oro*, 'la novela de la selva' y la crítica ecológica," *Hispania* 81, no. 2 (1998): 299.

12. Marcone, "Retorno," 307.

13. See chapter 1 of Margarita Serje's *El revés de la nación: Territorios salvajes, fronteras y tierras de nadie* (Bogotá: Universidad de los Andes, 2005). Regarding Hobbes, I refer to the famous quote in *Leviathan* in which he describes the "life of man" in the "state of nature" as "solitary, poor, nasty, brutish, and short." *Leviathan or the Matter, Forme, & Power of a Commonwealth, Ecclesiastic and Civil*, Part 1, Chapter 13, Project Gutenberg, https://www.gutenberg.org/files/3207/3207-h/3207-h.htm.

14. The crane rookery and feather harvesting appears in Rivera, *La vorágine*, 132–35.

15. See Sylvia Molloy, "Contagio narrativo y gesticulación retórica en *La vorágine*," in *La vorágine: Textos críticos*, ed. Montserrat Ordóñez (Bogotá: Alianza Editorial Colombiana, 1987), 494. Regarding the illness hypothesis, see for example Luis Eyzaguirre's "Patología en *La vorágine* de José Eustasio Rivera," *Hispania* 56, no. 1 (1973): 81–90, and chapter 3 of Charlotte Rogers's *Jungle Fever: Exploring Madness and Medicine in Twentieth-Century Tropical Narratives* (Nashville, TN: Vanderbilt University Press, 2012).

16. See, for example, Molloy, "Contagio," 746–51; David Viñas, "*La vorágine*: Crisis, populismo y mirada," *Hispamérica* 3, no. 8 (1974): 6–7; and Lesley Wylie, *Colonial Tropes, Postcolonial Tricks: Rewriting the Tropics in the Novela de la Selva* (Liverpool: Liverpool University Press, 2009), 23–26. Regarding the continuity of the Regenerationist project of national integration and economic modernization beyond the administrations of Rafael Núñez and Miguel Antonio Caro and the position of the Colombian Amazonia within this project, consult Felipe Martínez Pinzón's "Héroes de la civilización: La Amazonía como cosmópolis agroexportadora en la obra del General Rafael Reyes," *Anuario Colombiano de Historia Social y de la Cultura* 40, no. 2 (2013): 145–77.

17. Rivera, *La vorágine*, 228; my translation. Chasteen's version changes substantially the wording and meaning of this passage and several others that I cite in the following pages. Since I am engaging in a close reading of the Spanish original here, my translations will tend toward the literal.

18. In "Ecology, Capital, and the Nature of Our Times: Accumulation & Crisis in the Capitalist World-Ecology" (*Journal of World Systems Research* 17, no. 1 [2011]: 107–46), Jason W. Moore referred to "Nature's free gifts" as one of the "3 Cheaps" (the other two being energy and human labor) or inputs required for the accumulation of capital; he later rephrased this term as "Nature's unpaid work" to draw out how capitalism relies on the devaluation of the work of animals, enslaved peoples, women, and environments to produce profit; see Moore, "The Capitalocene, Part 1."

19. Mark Anderson, "The Natural Baroque: Opacity, Impenetrability, and Folding in Writing on Amazonia," *Amazonian Literatures*, ed. Lesley Wylie, *Hispanic Issues On-Line* 16 (2014): 57–83.

20. Rivera, *Vortex*, 81.

21. Camilo Jaramillo, "Green Hells: Monstrous Vegetations in Twentieth-Century Representations of Amazonia," in *Plant Horror: Approaches to the Monstrous Vegetal in Fiction and Film*, ed. Dawn Keetley and Angela Tengla (London: Palgrave Macmillan, 2016), 91. Simon Estok defines ecophobia as "an irrational and groundless hatred of the natural world, as present and subtle in our daily lives and literature as homophobia and racism and sexism." "Theorizing

in a Space of Ambivalent Openness: Ecocriticism and Ecophobia," *ISLE* 16, no. 2 (2009): 208.

22. Anderson, "The Natural Baroque," 74–75.

23. Rivera, *La vorágine*, 122; my translation.

24. Rivera, *La vorágine*, 121–22.

25. Ursula Biemann, "The Cosmo-Political Forest: A Theoretical and Aesthetic Discussion of the Video *Forest Law*," *GeoHumanities* 1, no. 1 (2015): 157–70.

26. This theory forms the basis of much of Foucault's work; see, for example, the lectures in *Security, Territory, Population*.

27. This conceptualization of the triadic relation between the subject, the other, and the arche of language surfaces throughout Derrida's writing; it is developed throughout his earliest work; see *Of Grammatology*; *Speech and Phenomena, and Other Essays on Husserl's Theory of Signs;* and *Writing and Difference*.

28. See chapter 7 of Charles S Pierce, *Philosophical Writings of Pierce*, ed. Justus Buchler (New York: Dover, 1955), which unites several sections on semiotics drawn from Pierce's *Collected Papers*.

29. Hoffmeyer, *Biosemiotics*, 19.

30. Hoffmeyer, *Biosemiotics*, 15.

31. Hoffmeyer defines "analog" and "digital" in the following terms: "I will use *analog coding* as a common designation for codings based on some kind of similarity *in the spatial-temporal continuity*, or on internal relations such as part-to-whole, or cause-and-effect. *Digital coding*, in contrast, will be used to designate sign systems where the relations of sign to signified are due to a demarcation of purely *conventional* or *habitual* origin." *Biosemiotics,* 89. For Hoffmeyer, digital codes are "abstract" in that "possible as well as impossible messages may be expressed in digital codes," they do not depend on actualization in the present (they are "time-independent" and thus are able to conserve past events as memory), and they are external to both the sender and the receiver and mediate their relation. *Biosemiotics,* 86–87.

32. Hoffmeyer, *Biosemiotics,* 5 and 15.

33. Hoffmeyer, *Biosemiotics*, 65.

34. Regarding matter as a becoming within phenomenon, Barad writes that "*matter is substance in its intra-active becoming—not a thing, but a doing, a congealing of agency. Matter is a stabilizing and destabilizing process of iterative interactivity.* Phenomena—the smallest material units (relational 'atoms')—come to matter through this process of ongoing intra-activity. 'Matter' does not refer to an inherent, fixed property of abstract, independently existing objects; rather, 'matter' refers to phenomena in their ongoing materialization." *Meeting the Universe*, 151; italics in the original.

35. Barad, *Meeting the Universe*, 140; the italics are Barad's.
36. Quoted in Hoffmeyer, *Biosemiotics*, 22.
37. Hoffmeyer, *Biosemiotics,* 285; the italics are Hoffmeyer's.
38. Barad, *Meeting the Universe*, 149.
39. Barad, *Meeting the Universe,* 178; italics in the original.
40. Barad, *Meeting the Universe*, 146–47.
41. Barad rarely uses the term "body" due to its connotations of static self-containment; for Barad, body would indicate an "agential cut" within an intra-action, a specific way of materializing the relation within the bounds of a subject/object divide. For this reason, she prefers "matter" in the double connotation made famous by Judith Butler in *Bodies that Matter*, as materiality that means (in fact, from both Butler and Barad's perspectives, there can be no meaningless matter). When the word "body" appears in Barad's texts, it is usually in order to engage other theorists who use the term. I follow in her footsteps in using the term "body" as shorthand for an ongoing locus of intra-actions.
42. Barad, *Meeting the Universe*, 149.
43. As I mentioned in Chapter 2, Derrida refers to this logic of domination as "carnophallogocentrism," drawing out not only its privileging of rationality as the basis for subjectivity, but also its roots in the sacrifice or exclusion of both women and animals in the construction of "Man" as sovereign subject (see, for instance, Derrida's interview in "Eating Well," 113).
44. Rivera, *La vorágine*, 121–22; my translation.
45. I refer here to the nineteenth-century Positivist doctrine of species progress as exemplified in the writings of Herbert Spencer, among many others, which was transparently designed to justify European colonialism and global white supremacy.
46. Jacques Lacan, "The Subversion of the Subject and the Dialectic of Desire," in *Ecrits*, trans. Bruce Fink (New York: Norton, 1996), 683. As I discuss at length in the next chapter, Derrida deconstructs this affirmation in chapter 3 of *The Animal that Therefore I Am*.
47. Derrida, *Animal*, 135.
48. Derrida, *Animal*, 135.
49. There may be exceptions to this categorical affirmation, as some animals have revealed themselves able to use symbols in experiments, while there may be some isolated cases in nature. However, Hoffmeyer coincides with Terrence Deacon's affirmation in *The Symbolic Species* that, while human language usage emerges from and maintains continuity with animal semiosis,

animals are generally "pre maladapted" for symbolic communication: "That chimpanzees are *pre-maladapted* for symbolic reference means no more (and no less) than that they, in their natural state, are not very apt to master this particular kind of reference—just as humans, in their natural state, are not very good at sleeping in an erect position, or in distinguishing friend from foe by smell alone. Thus, the expression *pre-maladapted* implies that the difference between humans and apes is not necessarily based on some sort of general intelligence (much less a specific 'gene for' explanation)—but rather on a much more specific *talent* that humans have developed and chimpanzees haven't" (Hoffmeyer, *Biosemiotics,* 283). This would almost certainly never be the case with plants, however, as their nervous system is not centralized in a brain organ, which most neuroscientists view as the basis for abstraction in the primal function of image storage in memory. On the other hand, it has been proven in a variety of experiments that at least some plants do have memory (that is not genetically encoded species memory). On this point, see Monica Gagliano et al., "Experience Teaches Plants to Learn Faster and Forget Slower in Environments Where It Matters," *Oecologia* 175 (2014): 63–72.

50. This is why, in *Totality and Infinity*, Levinas associates the face not only with the singular other, with whom one necessarily finds some degree of commonality across difference in the face-to-face encounter, but also with the "absolute" other, the one who always remains distant, who can never become the same. As Derrida discusses at length in *Adieu to Emmanuel Levinas* (Palo Alto, CA: Stanford University Press, 1999), this absoluteness or infinite difference is what makes possible the law in the sense of equal and objective justice across differences. I refer to Agamben's discussion of *Homo sacer* as the foundational exclusion that makes it possible to conceive of the polis as such, a thesis that holds true despite Agamben's oft-critiqued oversimplification of Aristotle's distinction between zoe (domestic life) and bios (political life).

51. Rivera, *La vorágine,* 136; my translation.

52. Hobbes famously defined the "state of nature" in the following terms: "whatsoever therefore is consequent to a time of Warre, where every man is Enemy to every man; the same is consequent to the time, wherein men live without other security, than what their own strength, and their own invention shall furnish them withall. In such condition, there is no place for Industry; because the fruit thereof is uncertain; and consequently no Culture of the Earth; no Navigation, nor use of the commodities that may be imported by Sea; no commodious Building; no Instruments of moving, and removing such things as require much force; no Knowledge of the face of the Earth; no account of

Time; no Arts; no Letters; no Society; and which is worst of all, continuall feare, and danger of violent death; And the life of man, solitary, poore, nasty, brutish, and short" (*Leviathan*, Chapter 13).

53. For a summary of these arguments, see Pat Moroney, "Hobbes, Savagery, and International Anarchy," *American Political Science Review* 105, no. 1 (2011): 189–204. As Moroney notes, Hobbes did not address colonialism explicitly, since he was more focused on the origins of governance (189); however, his intellectual successor John Locke used his theory of the state of nature to justify explicitly European colonialism.

54. Francisco de Vittoria, *De Indis et de Ivre Belli Reflectiones*, ed. Ernest Nys, trans. John Pawley Bate (Washington, DC: Carnegie Institute, 1917), 160–61.

55. As Moroney points out, Hobbes viewed violent competition over resources as rational, since it responded to the logic of individual self-preservation: "living by plunder was a rational course of action in the state of nature given that subsistence was uncertain and private property rights had yet to be established" ("Hobbes," 198).

56. Rivera, *La vorágine*, 136.

57. Rivera, *La vorágine*, 136.

58. Gabriela Nouzeilles, "The Transcultural Mirror of Science: Race and Self-Representation in Latin America," in *Literary Cultures of Latin America: A Comparative History*, Vol. 3, ed. Mario J. Valdés and Djelal Kadir (Oxford: Oxford University Press, 2004), 284–99.

59. In that sense, "Indigenous silence" emerges in *La* vorágine through the conflation of the narrator's own derogatory silencing of his Indigenous informants through the invalidation of their way of life and worldview and what Doris Sommer refers to as "secrecy," that is the withholding of ontologically privileged information that must be garnered through a long process of cultural initiation or embedding within the culture itself; see Doris Sommer, "Rigoberta's Secrets," *Latin American Perspectives* 18, no. 3 (1991): 32–50.

60. Jean Jacques Rousseau, *The Social Contract & Discourses* (London and Toronto: Dent; New York: Dutton, 1920) and Charles de Secondat, Baron de Montesquieu, *The Spirit of Laws*, trans. Thomas Nugent (Kitchener: Batoche, 2001).

61. Anthropologist Marilyn Strathern's 1980 essay "No Nature, No Culture: The Hagen Case," set the tone for this break with structuralist anthropology, which has been expanded by Strathern in later work as well as a large number of other anthropologists including Marisol de la Cadena, Philippe Descola, Pedro Favarón, Bruno Latour, Aparecida Vilaça, and Eduardo Viveiros de Castro, to mention only a few. The deconstruction of the nature/culture opposition in relation to the metaphysics of the sovereign subject is also the

subject of much of Derrida's work, beginning with his analysis in *Writing and Difference* of Lévi-Strauss's *The Raw and the Cooked* and *The Savage Mind*, and it is also a central argument in ecofeminist thought such as that of Val Plumwood in *Feminism and the Mastery of Nature.*

62. It must be noted that the categories of the "Indigenous" and "native" are clearly colonial demographic constructions that erase all linguistic, political, cultural, and religious differences between vastly heterogenous societies, subordinating them in geopolitical relation to European colonizers and Europeanized postcolonial states. In that sense, both terms closely mirror the European colonial conceptual models deconstructed by Edward Said in his analysis of orientalism. When I use these terms, then, it is specifically with reference to their status as colonized others within the modern geopolitical order.

63. Pierre Clastre, *Society Against the State: Essays in Political Anthropology,* trans. Robert Huxley and Abe Stein (Cambridge: Cambridge, MA: Zone, 1987).

64. See, for example, Oscar Fernando Gamba-Barrón, Daniel Esteban Unigarro-Caguasango, and Nohora Inés Carvajal-Sánchez, "Indigenous Territoriality: External Discourses and Native Perspectives on the Space Inhabited by Tegria's U'wa Community," *Revista U.D.C.A Actualidad & Divulgación Científica* 24, no. 1 (2021): 1–10; Paul Liffman, "Indigenous Territorialities in Mexico and Colombia," Regional Worlds at the University of Chicago, University of Chicago, Center for International Studies. http://regionalworlds.uchicago.edu/indigenousterritorialities.pdf; and Heike Schroeder and Nidia González, "Bridging Knowledge Divides: The Case of Indigenous Ontologies of Territoriality and REDD+," *Forest Policy and Economics* 100 (2019): 198–206. Clearly, cartography is also an ongoing, practical enactment of space, but it displaces its legitimacy from its own culturally determined practice onto its archival status, thereby reifying the lived environment as immutable, bounded space, that is, as *res* (abstract property).

65. On this point, see Whitt et al, "Indigenous Perspectives."

66. Quoted in Abigail Pérez Aguilera, "Mining and Indigenous Cosmopolitics: The Wirikuta Case," in *Ecological Crisis and Cultural Representation in Latin America: Ecocritical Perspectives on Art, Film, and Literature,* ed. Mark Anderson and Zélia Bora (Lanham, MD: Lexington, 2016), 187.

67. Kopenawa and Albert, *Falling Sky,* 295.

68. In *The Falling Sky,* Yanomami shaman and Indigenous activist Davi Kopenawa describes this process in the following way, contrasting it with modern land management practices: "unlike the white people, we take care of [the land/forest], like our elders before us, because without it we could not live. This

is why the spirit of hunger always remained far away from it. We want our children and our grandchildren to keep on feeding themselves from the forest when they grow up. We do not cut many of its trees, only enough to open our gardens. We plant manioc, banana plants, yams, taros, sweet potatoes, sugarcane, papaya trees, and *rasa si* peach palms. Then after some time we abandon our old gardens and let the tangled vegetation overrun them and the trees grow back little by little. If you always replant in the same plot, the plants no longer yield. They become too hot, like bare land that has lost its forest smell. They become stunted and dried up. Then nothing comes anymore. This is why our elders moved around the forest, from one garden to another, when their plantations declined and game became scarce around their houses" (Kopenawa and Albert, *Falling Sky*, 383).

69. See chapter 7 of Viveiros de Castro's *Cannibal Metaphysics*.

70. Viveiros de Castro summarizes Deleuze's conceptualization of multiplicity and disjunctive synthesis in the following way: "multiplicity is a system defined by a modality of relational synthesis different from a connection or conjunction of terms. Deleuze calls it *disjunctive synthesis* or *inclusive disjunction*, a relational mode that does not have similarity or identity as its (formal or final) cause, but divergence or distance; another name for this relational mode is 'becoming.'" *Cannibal Metaphysics*, 112.

71. Viveiros de Castro, "Perspectival Anthropology and the Methodology of Controlled Equivocation," *Tipiti* 2, no. 1 (2004): 18.

72. Viveiros de Castro, "Perspectival Anthropology," 20.

73. As de la Cadena writes, "uncommons does not work through sameness or its twin, difference; it does not emerge from constitutive commonality. Rather, participant entities may come into commonality without becoming the same. The conceptual condition underpinning uncommons is what Isabelle Stengers (2001) calls divergence: rather than a relation (of similarity or difference) between entities, divergence constitutes practices in their heterogeneity as they become together, even through each other, while remaining distinct. Like orchid and wasp, through an interest in common that is not the same interest, practices self-make with others as they diverge in their own positivity" ("Uncommons," Editor's Forum: Theorizing the Contemporary, Society for Cultural Anthropology, https://culanth.org/fieldsights/uncommons).

74. John Locke, *Two Treatises of Government*, ed. Peter Lasslet (New York: Cambridge University Press, 1988), 122.

75. Kopenawa and Albert, *Falling Sky*, 299–300.

76. Kopenawa states that if a younger man whose knowledge has not been validated by the community attempts to speak in *hereamuu*, he is mocked and

effectively laughed off the stage: "I had to learn to discourse in front of out-siders when I was very young. It is true! I was already addressing the white people harshly before I even dared to speak like my elders in my own house. My mouth was ashamed because if I had tried to exhort my own people at the time, they would have shut me up with their mockery" (*Falling Sky*, 300).

77. Kopenawa and Albert, *Falling Sky,* 366–68.

78. Kopenawa and Albert, *Falling Sky*, 300.

79. Kopenawa and Albert, *Falling Sky*, 545, note 3.

80. The mechanism for this genealogical transmission of shamanic powers is quite interesting. The Yanomami believe that procreation is an ongoing, ac-cretive process by which the father's sperm becomes the fetus's flesh; in the case of shamans. the father's *xapiri* (primordial being) allies sometimes con-tribute their own nonhuman sperm to the growth of the fetus, whereby the fetus is more likely to be able to perceive and interact with the *xapiri*, and, in turn, be recognized as one of their own. Kopenawa and Albert, *Falling Sky*, 45–46; see also 493 note 24

81. Kopenawa and Albert, *Falling Sky,* 329.

82. Kopenawa and Albert, *Falling Sky*, 333–34. I call these pacts of nonaggression because Kopenawa emphasizes that the Yanomami do not engage in inter-tribal warfare in the way that Euro-American observers such as Napoleon Chagnon in *Yanomamo: The Fierce People* (1968) usually frame it. According to Kopenawa, all attacks on other communities are carried out to enact ret-ribution for the real or perceived killing of family members through physical violence or shamanic attacks. These revenge attacks are carried out by small groups of family members and generally target only the guilty party and those who defend him: "it is true that our long-ago elders engaged in raids, just like the white people had their own wars. But theirs proved far more dangerous and fierce than ours. We never killed each other without restraint, the way they did. We do not have bombs that burn houses and all their inhabitants. When in old times our warriors wanted to arrow their enemies, it was a truly different thing. Above all, they tried to strike men who had already killed and whom we therefore call * õrokaerima tʰë pë*. Seized with the anger of mourning for their dead kin, they carried out raids until they were able to avenge them." Kopenawa and Albert, *Falling Sky,* 357. For this reason, there is no need for pacts of mutual defense or war alliances with other communities; instead, Yanomami alliances are primarily trade and marriage alliances with the un-derstanding that the allied communities will not engage in raids or shamanic attacks on each other. Furthermore, Kopenawa also notes that these raids have become almost non-existent since contact with outsiders beginning in

the 1950s, due primarily to the precipitous decline of the Yanomami population from epidemics.

83. Kopenawa and Albert, *Falling Sky,* 302.

84. Kopenawa, *Falling Sky,* 262.

85. Kopenawa and Albert, *Falling Sky,* 301.

86. The Yanomami believe that animals are the descendants of primordial humans called *yarori* who transformed into animals following the titular cataclysmic event—the collapse of the ancient sky, *Hutukara*, which became the current land surface. Kopenawa and Albert, *Falling Sky*, 55. This is why Kopenawa frequently makes affirmations such as the following: "the spider monkeys that we call *paxo* are humans like us. They are spider monkey humans, *yanomae t^hë pë paxo pë*, but we arrow them and smoke them when we gather game for our *reahu* feasts. Despite this, in their eyes, we are still their fellow creatures. Though we are humans, they give us the same name they give themselves. This is why I think our inner part is identical to that of the game and that we only attribute to ourselves the name of human beings by pretending to do so. Animals consider us their fellow creatures who live in houses while they are people of the forest. This is why they say 'humans are the game that live in houses'" (387). As Viveiros de Castro notes, this view of animals as being fundamentally human and sharing human culture (but seeing the same things in different ways, from a different perspective) is common among native American cultures and is commensurate with conceiving of environment as a multispecies socius (see chapters 2 and 3 of *Cannibal Metaphysics*).

87. Ellen Basso, *A Musical View of the Universe: Kalapalo Myth and Ritual Performances* (Philadelphia: University of Pennsylvania Press, 1985), 70.

88. Basso, *Musical View*, 9.

89. Kopenawa and Albert, *Falling Sky,* 304.

90. Kopenawa and Albert, *Falling Sky,* 93–95.

91. See Kopenawa and Albert, *Falling Sky,* 501, note 19 and 495, note 19.

92. Kopenawa and Albert, *Falling Sky,* 59; Albert uses bold type to indicate words that Kopenawa used in Portuguese rather than Yanomami during their interviews.

93. Kopenawa and Albert, *Falling Sky,* 142–44 and 510, note 25.

CHAPTER 6

Epigraph. Kopenawa and Albert, *The Falling Sky*, 313.

1. Kopenawa and Albert, *The Falling Sky*, 207.

2. Kopenawa and Albert, *The Falling Sky*, 13.

3. See, for example, Kopenawa and Albert, *The Falling Sky*, 24, 232, and 327.

4. Barad, *Meeting the Universe*, 140. Italics in the original.

5. See, once again, Derrida's *Politics of Friendship*, 336 and Jason W. Moore, "Capitalocene, Part 1," 6.

6. Marder, *Plant Thinking*, 51.

7. Marder, *Plant Thinking*, 103–4.

8. See, for instance, Hoffmeyer's discussion of embryonics and endosemiotics as self-organizing communicative systems in part 2 of *Biosemiotics*. It is important to underscore that Marder uses the concepts "soul" and "psyche" not as synonyms of the abstract concepts of "spirit" and "mind," but with reference to Aristotle's definition of the *arché ton zoon* in *De Anima* as the "principle of animal life": "it is the *arkhe* of animal life in the sense of acting as its *first* manifestation and as an *authority* that organizes and commands its further development, guiding it, in the words of Plotinus, 'without effort or noise' toward its ownmost flourishing." Marder, *Plant Thinking*, 21.

9. Marder, *Plant Thinking*, 135–38.

10. On this point, see the essays in Frans de Waal and Peter Tyack's edited volume on *Animal Social Complexity: Intelligence, Culture, and Individualized Societies* (Cambridge, MA: Harvard University Press, 2005). Unconvincingly, evolutionary biologists most often frame altruistic behavior across species as exceptional cases of "misidentification."

11. See chapter 4 of Marder's *Plant Thinking*, entitled "The Freedom of Plants," regarding the complementarity of plant and human ontological freedoms with respect to the alienation of labor. Although he doesn't address it in depth, I would argue that the freedoms afforded by plant excessive vitality have their parallel in forms of human labor that are not fully commodifiable, including the production of pleasure in sex (especially sex in which reproduction is not the telos, as per Bataille in *Visions of Excess*).

12. See note 19 of the last chapter.

13. While this may be most evident in the case of seemingly immobile entities such as plants and minerals, one might note that domestication consists in a process of rendering animals passive or open to humans; in this relation, animal lives are taken, but they are also given.

14. Marder, *Plant Thinking*, 122.

15. This seemingly philosophical affirmation has been upheld by recent advances in plant sciences. See, for instance, Suzanne Simard's discussion of tree communicativity and sociality through mycelia networks in *Finding the Mother Tree: Discovering the Wisdom of the Forest* (New York: Knopf, 2021). In fact, one might argue somewhat contra Marder that fungal mycelia exemplify this function to an even greater degree, given their symbiotic relations with plant roots.

Indeed, recent studies of electrical impulses in mycelia networks show that fungi communicate using packets of information that resemble uncannily how words appear in the human brain; see Andrew Adamatzky, "Language of Fungi Derived from Their Electrical Spiking Activity," *Royal Society Open Science* 9, no. 4 (2022): 1–15. However, so little was known or thought of fungi in the humanistic tradition that it would not have given Marder much material for critique from within the history of philosophy.

16. Marder, *Plant Thinking*, 127.
17. As Hoffmeyer notes, "in the biological world, signs incite the generation of interpretants in the form of actions which are future-oriented, inasmuch as living beings always seek signs for survival and for reproduction. That organisms react to signs necessarily implies that these signs are meaningful, and that they are directed toward latent activities, whether now or later." *Biosemiotics*, 65.
18. Hoffmeyer, *Biosemiotics*, 309–10.
19. Hoffmeyer, *Biosemiotics*, 19.
20. Hoffmeyer, *Biosemiotics*, 32–35.
21. Derrida arrives at similar conclusions in his deconstruction of "carnophallogocentrism" in "Eating Well," whereby the morality of eating can no longer defer to the humanist institution, that is, the categorical sacrifice of the animal to institute the human subject, but must view predation as a fundamentally ethical act, an act oriented toward the eaten other, toward their traces: "One eats him regardless and lets oneself be eaten by him" (114). Eating effectively becomes an act of desistance. This in turn, implies the deconstruction of the sovereign subject, which, in the absence of the logic of sacrifice, becomes multiple, other to itself: "I don't know, at this point, who is "who," no more than I know what "sacrifice" means; to determine what this last word means, I would retain this clue: need, desire, authorization, the justification of putting to death, putting to death as denegation of murder. The putting to death of the animal, says this denegation, is not a murder. I would link this de-negation to the violent institution of the "who" as subject" (115). Indeed, for Derrida, symbolic representation is itself always a cannibalistic act, one that generates a double bind in which the sacrifice of the singular other in the act of naming (the erasure of their singularity) is also always the integration of their irreducible difference in trace form: "the so-called nonanthropophagic cultures practice symbolic anthropophagy and even construct their most elevated socius, indeed the sublimity of their morality, their politics, and their right, on this anthropophagy" (114).

22. Kopenawa and Albert, *Falling Sky,* 333. As Albert notes, "most Yanomami 'exchanges' are made in this relatively blurry deferred mode. More than bartering, the essential here is to show that one is prepared to give up the requested goods without too much concern for compensation. The verbal roots designating this operation refer essentially to the idea of giving away (*hipɨ-*, "give"; *topɨ*, "offer"; *weyë-*, 'distribute"). On the other hand, acquiring a coveted good through defined compensation is known as *rurai* (a term that now also describes a commercial purchase), and direct exchange is described by the verb *nomihiai*, which denotes immediate reciprocation." *Falling Sky,* 549–50, note 12.

23. Kopenawa and Albert, *Falling Sky,* 334.

24. Kopenawa and Albert, *Falling Sky,* 55; as noted in the last chapter, Albert employs bold type to indicate words that Kopenawa used in Portuguese rather than Yanomami.

25. *Utupë* cannot accurately be translated as "soul," despite its proximity to some key conceptualizations of the soul in Euro-American thought. Unlike Plato and later Christian theologians, the Yanomami do not view the *utupë* as the immaterial and immortal essence of a person; in fact, human *utupë* may be devoured by evil beings (although he does state that *xapiri* are immortal). Furthermore, Plato and most Christian theologians do not ascribe any clear relation between the soul and the body; the body is merely inhabited by the soul temporarily (and for Plato, it could reincarnate as any living body, including nonhumans). Aristotle's perspective runs much closer to the Yanomami concept, since he viewed the *pneuma* (soul, breath of life) as fundamentally material, as "the first actuality of a body that has life potentially." Aristotle, *De anima*, ed. Ronald Polanksy (Cambridge: Cambridge University Press, 2009), II, 412a, 27. Aristotle's theorization of the soul as coordinating principle or totality that gives common purpose to all the body's parts is similar to the Yanomami one in viewing it as a relation between form and matter, but it diverges in that it is essentialist, limited to the body itself as monad in contrast to the Yanomami conceptualization of the body as multiplicity. In that sense, Aristotle's conceptualization of the relation between matter and form runs quite close, but inverse to that of the Yanomami: "the body cannot be soul; the body is the subject or matter, not what is attributed to it. Hence the soul must be a substance in the sense of the form of a natural body having life potentially within it. But substance is actuality, and thus soul is the actuality of a body as above characterized" (Aristotle, *De Anima,* II, 412a, 17–21). For Aristotle, then, the soul transcends the body as the governing principle that

emerges from the intra-actions between its parts, while for the Yanomami the body is the actualization of the utupë in serial, mutable relation with others. In other words, Aristotle views form as the emergent, self-organizing meaning of matter, while the Yanomami view matter as the actualization of the form in relational meaning. Nonetheless, both perspectives attribute singularity itself to this principle of interrelation that is simultaneously material and potential.

26. As Istvan Praet argues regarding South American Indigenous ontologies, "while 'humans' and 'spirits' are distinct, this distinction is never qualitative; both positions are entirely equivalent. The Amerindian expressions that are translated as such do not denote specific categories or classes but what I will call shapes." Praet, "Shamanism and Ritual in South America: An Inquiry into Amerindian Shape-Shifting," *Journal of the Royal Anthropological Institute* 15 (2009): 738.

27. As Barad frames it: "matter does not refer to a fixed substance; rather, *matter is substance in its intra-active becoming—not a thing, but a doing, a congealing of agency. Matter is a stabilizing and destabilizing process of iterative intra-activity.* Phenomena—the smallest material units (relational 'atoms')—come to matter through this process of ongoing intra-activity. 'Matter' does not refer to an inherent, fixed property of abstract, independently existing objects; rather, *'matter' refers to phenomena in their ongoing materialization.*" *Meeting the Universe,* 151, italics are Barad's. While Barad does not refer specifically to "form" in this discussion, since she gives precedence to the lexicon of physics, it seems clear to me that "form" would correspond to a specific patterning of "phenomena" or relational matrix of matter that emerges intra-actively at any given point in space-time.

28. Kopenawa and Albert, *Falling Sky,* 328. As Albert notes, body paintings are not considered simple decoration. They are viewed as the traces of primordial beings that effectively activate an other body/skin: "human body paintings are considered 'marks of the human/animal ancestors' (*yarori pë õno pë*)." Kopenawa and Albert, *Falling Sky,* 560, note 12. Likewise, Viveiros de Castro notes that, "the manifest form of each species is a mere envelope (a 'clothing') which conceals an internal human form, usually only visible to the eyes of the particular species or to certain trans-specific beings such as shamans. This internal form is the 'soul' or 'spirit' of the animal: an intentionality or subjectivity formally identical to human consciousness, materializable, let us say, in a human bodily schema concealed behind an animal mask. At first sight then, we would have a distinction between an anthropomorphic essence of a spiritual type, common to animate beings, and a variable bodily

appearance, characteristic of each individual species but which rather than being a fixed attribute is instead a changeable and removable clothing. This notion of 'clothing' is one of the privileged expressions of metamorphosis—spirits, the dead and shamans who assume animal form, beasts that turn into other beasts, humans that are inadvertently turned into animals—an omnipresent process in the 'highly transformational world' (Riviere 1994: 256) proposed by Amazonian ontologies" ("Cosmological Deixis," 470–71). Nonetheless, I would argue that Viveiros's language here is somewhat misleading, since it gives the impression that what the Yanomami refer to as the *utupë* is envisioned as a homunculus, a "little human" inside each sentient body-skin or clothing, when it seems clear to me that it refers to personhood prior to or even opposed to representation, in the sense of the latency of agential intra-activity within relations. As I discussed in note 12, the *utupë* does not denote an immutable essence (the abstract image of the self) akin to the "soul" in Euro-American thought, but rather a matrix of relational potentials capable of producing specific bodily effects in intra-action with other *utupë*. In that sense, the *utupë* would not be a person who changes clothes, but rather the range of persons that may come into being upon putting on a certain type of clothing in a given setting, again when personhood is conceived of as an intra-active assemblage, not an essence. Indeed, this is why Viveiros writes further on that, "what I call 'body' is not a synonym for distinctive substance or fixed shape; it is an assemblage of affects or ways of being that constitute a *habitus*." "Cosmological Deixis," 478. In other words, Indigenous peoples see clothes (at least in the context of mythology) as an enactment, not a garment or re-presentation.

29. See Viveiros de Castro, "Cosmological Deixis," 477.
30. Kopenawa and Albert, *Falling Sky*, 540, note 39.
31. Kopenawa and Albert, *Falling Sky*, 495, note 19.
32. Kopenawa and Albert, *Falling Sky*, 11 and 160.
33. Kopenawa applies this same language to himself when speaking in Portuguese: "these new words about protecting the forest came to me gradually, during my trips in the forest and among the white people. They settled inside me and increased little by little, linking up to each other, until they formed a long path in my mind. I used them to start speaking in the cities, even if in Portuguese my tongue still seemed as tangled as a ghost's!" (*Falling Sky*, 262).
34. Kopenawa and Albert, *Falling Sky*, 501, note 19.
35. Kopenawa and Albert, *Falling Sky*, 83–95.
36. Kopenawa and Albert, *Falling Sky*, 295.
37. See chapter 2, "Repetition for Itself," of Deleuze's *Difference and Repetition*.

38. Deleuze, *Difference*, 269–70.
39. Kopenawa and Albert, *Falling Sky,* 60–61.
40. Kopenawa and Albert, *Falling Sky,* 61.
41. Kopenawa and Albert, *Falling Sky,* 493, note 24.
42. Kopenawa and Albert, *Falling Sky,* 45–46.
43. Kopenawa frequently describes sexual coupling in terms of "eating a [woman]'s vulva" (Kopenawa and Albert, *Falling Sky,* 46) and, as Albert notes, "the Yanomami consider any type of lethal aggression, whether human (war, sorcery) or nonhuman (evil beings, enemy shamanic spirits), visible or invisible, as a form of cannibalism" (Kopenawa and Albert, *Falling Sky,* 496, note 24).
44. Kopenawa and Albert, *Falling Sky,* 146.
45. Kopenawa and Albert, *Falling Sky,* 505, note 14.
46. Stengers, "Comparison," 59–62.
47. Kopenawa address directly this fundamental incommensurability between the Yanomami the conceptualization of value as multispecies productive potential and capitalistic exchange value: "I do not know how to make **accounts** like they do. I only know that our land is more solid than our life and that it does not die. I also know that it is the forest that makes us eat and live. It is not gold or merchandise that makes the plants grow or feeds and fattens the game we hunt! This is why I say that its value is very high and very heavy. All the white people's merchandise will never be enough to exchange for its trees, fruits, animals, and fish. The paper skins of their money will never be numerous enough to compensate for the value of its burned trees, its desiccated ground, and its dirty waters. Nothing of this could return the value of the dead caimans and the vanished peccaries. The rivers are too **expensive**, and nothing can pay the value of game. Everything that grows and moves in the forest or under the waters, as well as the *xapiri* and human beings, has a value far too **important** for the white people's merchandise and money. Nothing is solid enough to restore the sick forest's value. No merchandise can **buy** all the human beings devoured by the epidemic fumes. No money will be able to return to the spirits their dead fathers' value!" *Falling Sky*, 280–81. Tellingly, most of the bolded (Portuguese) words are related to capitalistic economics, thereby drawing attention to their incommensurability with the Yanomami worldview.
48. Kopenawa and Albert, *Falling Sky,* 328.
49. Kopenawa and Albert, *Falling Sky,* 328.
50. Kopenawa and Albert, *Falling Sky,* 293.
51. Regarding the grammar of the *në* proclitic, see Helder Peri Ferreira, *Yanomama Clause Structure* (Utrecht: LOT, 2017), 251.

52. Kopenawa and Albert, *Falling Sky,* 496, note 24.

53. For example, Albert notes that, "human body paintings are considered 'marks of the human/animal ancestors' (*yarori pë õno pë*)." Kopenawa and Albert, *Falling Sky,* 560, note 12. The same logic applies to symptoms of illness: "these 'marks' (*õno*) are left on sick people's 'images' (*utupë*) by the pathogenic weapons/objects/substances of evil entities and human aggressors who are held responsible for disease and death." Kopenawa and Albert, *Falling Sky,* 503, note 51.

54. Derrida, *Politics of Friendship,* 68–69.

55. Kopenawa and Albert, *Falling Sky,* 496, note 23.

56. See the first chapter of Derrida's *Politics of Friendship.*

57. Derrida, *Politics of Friendship,* 87.

58. Derrida, *Politics of Friendship,* 91.

59. Derrida, *Politics of Friendship,* 238–39 and "Eating Well," 113–14.

60. Derrida, *Politics of Friendship,* 93.

61. Derrida, *Politics of Friendship,* 261.

62. Viveiros de Castro, "Perspectival Anthropology," 18.

63. Derrida, *Adieu,* 22–23.

64. This is why Derrida apprises Levinas in referring to an "ethics before and beyond ontology, the State, or politics, but also ethics beyond ethics" (the latter referring to ethical discourse, that is, the rational code of conduct regulating one's relations with the other; *Adieu,* 4).

65. Derrida, *Adieu,* 31.

66. Derrida, *Adieu,* 32.

67. Derrida, *Adieu,* 41–42.

68. Derrida, *Adieu,* 42. Derrida cites here Franz Rosenzweig, *The Star of Redemption,* translated by William W. Hallo, Notre Dame: Notre Dame University Press, 1985, 300.

69. David L. Clark, "On Being the 'Last Kantian in Nazi Germany': Dwelling with Animals after Levinas," in *Animal Acts: Configuring the Human in Western History,* ed. Jennifer Ham and Matthew Senior (New York: Routledge, 1997), 165–98. As Derrida points out regarding Descartes, Levinas, and all other ontological theorists that define the human in opposition to the animal, "their 'I am' is always 'I am after the animal even when I don't know it.' And this disavowal of foreclosure is just as powerful when they don't speak of it or when they speak of it in order to deny to the *animot* everything they attribute to the human" (*Animal,* 113).

70. Clark, "On Being," 44–45.

71. Emmanuel Levinas, "The Paradox of Morality: An Interview with Emmanuel Levinas," in *The Provocation of Levinas: Rethinking the Other,* ed. Robert

Bernasconi and David Wood, trans. Andrew Benjamin and Tamara Wright (London: Routledge, 1988), 169.

72. Heidegger, *Fundamental Concepts,* 177.
73. Clark, "On Being," 68.
74. Agamben, *Open,* 75.
75. Derrida, *Animal,* 135; italics are Derrida's.
76. Derrida, *Animal,* 104.
77. Derrida, *Animal,* 94.
78. Derrida, *Animal,* 95.
79. Derrida, *Animal,* 95.
80. Hoffmeyer bases this affirmation on Pierce's "law of mind," in which he argued that the "final causality" at work in the universe—that is, the telos of all semiosis—is modification; see Hoffmeyer, *Biosemiotics,* 62–68. From this point of view, "higher order" organisms would be more adept at interpreting signs and therefore capable of manipulating their environments to a greater degree, which Hoffmeyer refers to as "semiotic freedom." However, the teleological view of evolution as tending toward greater organismic complexity has been shown to be empirically questionable, as has any transcendental interpretation of evolution as leading toward anything other than contextual adaptation to ecological niches. Species complexify or simplify according to environmental cues. For instance, the water flea *Daphnea pulex* has approximately 31,000 genes, compared to Homo sapiens' 23,000, while the *Paris japonica* plant has 28,000 genes and the worlds largest genome at 152 billion nucleotides, roughly 50 times larger than the human genome; see National Science Foundation, "The Most Genes in an Animal? Tiny Crustacean Holds the Record," National Science Foundation News, February 3, 2011. On the other hand, scientists have shown that in plants at least, larger genomes actually make extinction more likely due to both highly specific adaptations to local environments (and thus greater susceptibility to habitat loss and extreme environmental conditions) and greater probability for lethal mutations caused by pollution; see Royal Botanic Gardens, Kew, "Rare Japanese Plant Has Largest Genome Known to Science," ScienceDaily, October 7, 2010. The notion that *Homo sapiens* is the culmination of evolutionary complexity is thus disproven; the human exception must therefore be viewed as something other than the pinnacle of evolution. Nonetheless, as Hoffmeyer points out, it is undeniable that humans have attained the greatest semiotic complexity, even when no clear set of "language genes" has been identified. In either case, one must approach Hoffmeyer's conceptualization of "semiotic freedom" with a certain skepticism, since, as Adorno noted in *Negative Dialectics*, freedom can only be conceived of as a negation, a "freedom from." What is it, then,

that symbolic language would free humans from? That question clearly leads back to what Derrida critiques in *The Animal that Therefore I Am*, that is, the idea that consciousness is fundamentally, essentially symbolic (and cannot be found in other forms of semiosis).

81. Derrida, *Animal*, 135.
82. Derrida, *Animal*, 133.
83. Derrida, *Animal*, 60.
84. See, for instance, Bruce E. Lyon and Robert Montgomerie, "Sexual Selection is a Form of Social Selection," *Philosophical Transactions of the Royal Society B* 367 (2012): 2,266–73.
85. Derrida, *Animal,* 61.
86. Derrida, *Animal*, 48.
87. Derrida, *Animal,* 112.
88. Derrida, *Politics*, 306.

CONCLUSION

1. The exception to this rule would be endangered species protections such as the 1973 US Endangered Species Act.
2. Paul Crutzen and Eugene Stoermer, "The 'Anthropocene,'" *Global Change Newsletter* 41 (2000): 17–18. In *Capitalism in the Web of Life* (London: Verso, 2015), Moore traces the roots of the current planetary socioecological crisis back ever further, to the Spanish conquest and colonization of the Americas in the sixteenth century, which provided the influx of precious metals that catalyzed European capitalism as well as the radical transformation of environments and labor regimes in the Americas to maximize their potential for export-oriented commodity production.
3. Latour, "Scientific Objects,' 83.
4. Latour, "Scientific Objects,' 81.
5. See chapter 7 of Tanasescu's *Environment.*
6. Derrida, *The Animal*, 48.
7. See Eduardo Kohn's *How Forests Think.*
8. See the introductory chapter of Wolfe's *What is Posthumanism?* (Minneapolis: University of Minnesota Press, 2009) regarding the emergence of the term itself and the threads of thought that converged in it.
9. Alex Rivera's dystopian sci-fi film *Sleep Dealer* (Likely Story, 2008, 1 hr., 30 min.) provides a penetrating look what such a transhumanist society would likely look like in practice.
10. Donna Haraway, "A Manifesto for Cyborgs: Science, Technology, and Socialist Feminism in the 1980s," in *The Haraway Reader* (New York: Routledge, 2004), 20.

11. Haraway, "Manifesto for Cyborgs," 9.

12. Donna Haraway, *When Species Meet* (Minneapolis: University of Minnesota Press, 2008), 31–33.

13. Quoted in Donna Haraway, *Staying with the Trouble: Making Kin in the Chthulucene* (Durham, NC: Duke University Press, 2016), 61.

14. Haraway, *Staying with the Trouble*, 58.

15. Haraway, "Manifesto for Cyborgs," 10.

16. Donna Haraway, *The Companion Species Manifesto: Dogs, People, and Significant Otherness.* (Chicago: Prickly Paradigm, 2003), 15–16.

17. Haraway, *Companion Species*, 44–45.

18. Haraway, *When Species Meet*, 39. Regarding the "colonial god trick" she diagnoses at the heart of globalized capitalism, see Donna Haraway, "Situated Knowledges: The Science Question in Feminism and the Privilege of Partial Perspective," *Feminist Studies* 14, no. 3 (1988): 575–99.

19. The title of the second chapter of *When Species Meet* is highly indicative of this tendency: "Value Added Dogs and Lively Capital."

20. Haraway, *When Species Meet*, 279.

21. Haraway, *When Species Meet*, 46.

22. Haraway, *When Species Meet*, 55–56.

23. In *When Species Meet*, her ethics are summed up in the following way: opposing "unidirectional relations of use" in favor of a usage of animals in which humans take on a "responsible sharing of suffering" (Haraway, *When Species Meet*, 71–72). She contends that, "taking animals seriously as workers without the comfort of humanist frameworks for people or animals is perhaps new and might help stem the killing machines" (Haraway, *When Species Meet*, 73).

24. For instance, Haraway frequently speaks of "dogland," which is clearly not any specific environment, but rather a transnational social sphere within the capitalist world-ecology.

25. Haraway, *Staying with the Trouble*, 72.

26. Haraway, *Staying with the Trouble*, 71.

27. As she describes it, "staying with the trouble does not require such a relationship to times called the future. In fact, staying with the trouble requires learning to be truly present, not as a vanishing pivot between awful or edenic pasts and apocalyptic or salvific futures, but as mortal critters entwined in myriad unfinished configurations of places, times, matters, and meanings." Haraway, *Staying with the Trouble*, 1.

28. Haraway, *Staying with the Trouble*, 139; my italics.

29. Haraway, *Staying with the Trouble*, 139–40.

30. In contrast, see Rigoberta Menchú's discussion of the significance of the na-hual in K'Iché Mayan culture in Menchú and Elizabeth Burgos Debray, *Me llamo Rigoberta Menchú y así me nació la conciencia* (Mexico City: Siglo XXI, 1985), 39–41.
31. Haraway, *Staying with the Trouble*, 138.
32. Haraway, *Companion Species*, 88–92.
33. Latour, *Modern*, 27.
34. Latour, *Modern*, 29.
35. Latour, *Modern*, 43.
36. Latour, *Reassembling*, 74.
37. Latour, *Modern*, 57.
38. Latour, *Modern*, 47–48.
39. Latour, *Modern*, 88.
40. Latour, *Modern*, 112.
41. Latour, *Modern*, 136.
42. Latour, *Reassembling*, 71.
43. Latour, *Modern*, 129.
44. Latour, *Modern*, 96.
45. Latour, *Modern*, 137.
46. Latour, *Reassembling*, 108.
47. Latour, *Modern*, 138.
48. Latour, *Modern*, 141.
49. Latour, *Modern*, 141.
50. Latour, *Modern*, 141.
51. In the end, Latour's primary goal is dismantling the nature/culture divide in the social sciences, rather than granting objects a pathway to ethical or polit-ical standing: "a natural world made up of matters of fact does not look quite the same as a world consisting of matters of concern and thus cannot be used so easily as a foil for the 'symbolic-human intentional' social order. This is why what could be referred to as the second empiricism doesn't look at all like the first: its science, its politics, its esthetics, its morality are all differ-ent from the past. It is still real and objective, but it is livelier, more talkative, active, pluralistic, and more mediated than the other." *Reassembling*, 114–15.
52. Bruno Latour, *Politics of Nature: How to Bring the Sciences into Democracy* (Cam-bridge, MA: Harvard University Press, 2004), 115.
53. Latour, *Politics*, 172.
54. Latour, *Politics*, 172–73.
55. Latour, *Politics*, 172.
56. Latour, *Politics*, 98.

57. Latour, *Politics,* 159.
58. Latour, *Politics,* 156 and 187–88.
59. Latour, *Politics,* 206, 199.
60. Stengers, *Cosmopolitics I,* 90–91 and 223.
61. Stengers, *Cosmopolitics I,* 222.
62. Stengers, *Cosmopolitics I,* 24; italics are Stengers's.
63. Stengers, *Cosmopolitics I,* 222.
64. Stengers, *Cosmopolitics I,* 168.
65. Stengers, *Cosmopolitics I,* 260.
66. Stengers, *Cosmopolitics I,* 260.
67. Stengers, "Cosmopolitical Proposal," 995.
68. Stengers, "Cosmopolitical Proposal," 996.
69. Stengers, "Cosmopolitical Proposal," 1,002–3.
70. Stengers, "Cosmopolitical Proposal," 1,003.
71. Stengers, "Cosmopolitical Proposal," 1,003.
72. Stengers, "Cosmopolitical Proposal," 1,003.
73. Stengers, "Cosmopolitical Proposal," 1,003.
74. Stengers, "Comparison," 60.
75. Stengers, "Comparison," 60.
76. Stengers, "Comparison," 60.
77. Stengers, "Comparison," 55. In the *Politics of Nature*, Latour coincides with this neutrality of the diplomat: "at no moment does the diplomat use the notion of a common world of reference, since it is to construct that common world that he confronts all the dangers; at no moment, either, does he regard 'simple formulations' with respectful contempt, since any one of them, however impalpable, may hold the key to the agreement that nothing has guaranteed in advance. He consents only, quite rightly, to 'parley,' in the fine diplomatic expression, and to 'make representations.' He never speaks of what may be rational or irrational. In other words, the distribution of essences and habits depends on the talks. Never (and here lies the greatness of his mission) does he resign himself, either, to the incommensurable—that is, at bottom, to war" (212–13). However, for Latour, the diplomat is only responsible for establishing relations; they do not figure among his panels of experts in the parliament of things.
78. Stengers, "Challenge," 83.
79. Stengers, "Challenge," 95.
80. Stengers, "Introductory Notes," 188.
81. He thus locates the "premodern" not as an empirical, historical, or even cultural distinction, but as an ontological weapon used by modern practitioners

to eliminate rival ontologies that do not distinguish categorically between nature and culture (and, one must add, to justify colonialism): "Moderns do differ from premoderns by this single trait: they refuse to conceptualize quasi-objects as such. In their eyes, hybrids present the horror that must be avoided at all costs by a ceaseless, even maniacal purification." *Modern,* 112.

82. Stengers, "Challenge," 99.

83. Stengers, "Challenge," 105.

84. Stengers, "Challenge," 86.

85. See Alcides Arguedas's *Pueblo enfermo* (Santiago de Chile: Ercilla, 1937). As Nouzeilles notes. this kind of dehumanizing discourse rooted in pseudo-scientific rhetoric was common in positivistic discourse in Latin America up through the mid twentieth century; "Transcultural Mirror," 284.

86. On this point, see Ana Díaz Serrano, "La República de Tlaxcala ante el rey de España en el siglo XVI," *Historia Mexicana* 61, no. 3 (2012): 1,049–107; Alcira Dueñas, "The Lima Indian Letrados: Remaking the Repúblicas de Indios in the Bourbon Andes," *The Americas* 72, no. 1 (2015): 55–75; Edgar Franco-Vivancos, "Justice as Checks and Balances: Indigenous Claims in the Courts of Mexico," *World Politics* 73, no. 4 (2021): 712–83; and Luis J. García Ruíz, "La territorialidad de la República de Indios de Orizaba. Entre la separación de los sujetos y la preponderancia española: 1,740–1,828," *Historia Mexicana* 4 (2015): 1,415–61, to cite just a few examples of the vast body of scholarship that has been carried out on this topic.

87. Indeed, many of the "traditional" political structures that we commonly associate with Indigenous communities throughout the former Spanish colonies were negotiated during this period. See, for instance, chapter 1 of Maurice Crandal's *These People Have Always Been A Republic: Indigenous Electorates in the US-Mexico Borderlands, 1598–1912* (Chapel Hill: University of North Carolina Press, 2019) for a fascinating account of this process during the Spanish colonization of "Puebloan" cultures in New Mexico. Tellingly, the term "Pueblo" in this context refers precisely to the colonial "Pueblo de Indios" ethnopolitical and territorial designation, which was, again, the product of negotiation within the parameters of the Spanish Empire's Leyes de Indias.

88. See, for example, Amara Solari's *Maya Ideologies of the Sacred: The Transfiguration of Space in Colonial Yucatán* (Austin: University of Texas Press, 2013).

89. See, for instance David Mejilla Velilla's "Leyes republicanas de indios: Aportación de la Independencia a la Legislación Civil en pro de los indígenas. Antecedentes y período de 1821–1843," *Díkaion* 4 (1995): 41–53, whose surprisingly retrograde text also reproduces nitidly the ontological conflict between Indigenous conceptualizations of territoriality and postcolonial liberals' views

regarding the nexus between citizen rights and property ownership. As Daniel Marino points out, Indigenous petitioners and their allies were adept at engaging the juridical language in force at any given moment, particularly in terms of the relation between citizenship and property rights, while at the same time pushing for collective rights that were often not explicitly recognized in law. "'Ahora que Dios nos ha dado padre': El Segundo Imperio y la cultura jurídica-política campesina en el Centro de México," *Historia Mexicana* 55, no. 4 (2006): 1,401–2.

90. This law's full title was "Ley de Desamortización de Fincas Rústicas y Urbanas Propiedad de Corporaciones Civiles y Eclesiásticas" (Law Regarding the Confiscation of Rural and Urban Plots Owned by Civil and Ecclesiastic Corporate Bodies).

91. As Jean Meyer notes, Maximilian's Second Empire passed laws in 1865 that explicitly recognized Indigenous communities as collective juridical personas and recognized their rights to communal land ownership, as well as promising to grant lands to Indigenous communities lacking them. Meyer, "La Junta Protectora de las Clases Menesterosas: Indigenismo y agrarismo en el Segundo Imperio," in *Indio, nación y comunidad en el México del siglo XIX*, ed. Antonio Escobar Ohmstede y Patricia Lagos Preisser (México: Centro de Estudios Mexicanos y Centroamericanos; Centro de Investigaciones y Estudios Superiores en Antropología Social, 1993), 329. However, Maximilian in general saw himself as a liberal modernizer, and he did not reverse the Lerdo law, since he also viewed property ownership as a means to developing responsible citizenship (330).

92. For an in-depth study of the political and economic ramifications of the Lerdo Law for Indigenous and mixed race campesinos, see Carlos Alberto Murgueitio Manrique, "Proceso de desamortización de las tierras indígenas durante las repúblicas liberales de México y Colombia, 1853–1876," *Anuario de la Historia Regional y de las Fronteras* 20, no. 1 (2015): 73–95 and Jennie Purnell, "With All Due Respect: Popular Resistance to the Privatization of Communal Lands in Nineteenth-Century Michoacán," *Latin American Research Review* 34, no. 1 (1999): 85–121.

93. See, for instance, nineteenth-century Colombian author Medardo Rivas's *Los trabajadores de tierra caliente* (The Lowland Developers, Bogotá: Universidad Nacional, 1946), which provides a nitid summary of this shift in land management practices from local agrarian economies of subsistence toward capitalistic natural resource extraction and intensive cattle ranching destined for exportation. As Marcela Reales and I discussed in "Extracting Nature: Toward an Ecology of Colombian Narrative," in *A History of Colombian Literature*, ed.

Raymond Leslie Williams, 353–405 (New York: Cambridge University Press, 2016), this process was not only an economic one, but also carried with it a radical ontological shift in which the concept of abstract, tropical "nature" emerged in opposition to the lived experience of environments as societies.

94. Juan Carlos Galeano, *Folktales of the Amazon*, trans. R. Morgan and K. Watson (Westport, CT: Libraries Unlimited, 2009) and Candace Slater, *Entangled Edens: Visions of the Amazon* (Berkeley: University of California Press, 2002).

95. See Galeano, *Cuentos*, 12–13, and chapter 15 of Kopenawa and Albert's *The Falling Sky*.

96. Frank Hutchins and Patrick C. Wilson, ed., "Introduction," in *Editing Eden: A Reconsideration of Identity, Politics, and Place in Amazonia* (Lincoln: University of Nebraska, 2011), xxiv.

97. Michael Uzendoski, "Fractal Subjectivities: An Amazonian Inspired Critique of Globalization Theory," in *Editing Eden: A Reconsideration of Identity, Politics, and Place in Amazonia*, ed. Frank Hutchins and Patrick C. Wilson (Lincoln: University of Nebraska, 2011), 39.

98. Mark Anderson, "Amazonian Flows, Ecological Cosmopolitanism, and the Question of Material Subjectivities," in *Transatlantic Landscapes. Environmental Awareness, Literature, and the Arts,* ed. José Manuel Marrero Henríquez (Alcalá de Henares: Instituto Franklin, 2016), 130.

99. Quoted in Pérez Aguilera, "Mining," 187.

100. Martínez de Bringas, "Selva viviente," 91.

101. Martínez de Bringas, "Selva viviente," 92.

102. Martínez de Bringas, "Selva viviente," 93.

103. José Gualinga and the Sarayaku Runa, "Kawsak Sacha—Living Forest," Amazonwatch.org. https://amazonwatch.org/assets/files/2016-kawsak-sacha-proposal-english.pdf.

104. Gualinga and Sarayaku Runa, "Kawsak Sacha."

105. Gualinga and Sarayaku Runa, "Kawsak Sacha."

106. Gualinga and Sarayaku Runa, "Kawsak Sacha."

107. Gualinga and Sarayaku Runa, "Kawsak Sacha."

108. Gualinga and Sarayaku Runa, "Kawsak Sacha."

109. Gualinga and Sarayaku Runa, "Kawsak Sacha."

110. See Haraway's "Situated Knowledges" and Wenzel's "Planet vs. Globe," *English Language Notes* 52, no. 1 (2014): 19–30.

111. Craig M Kauffman and Pamela L. Martin, "Scaling up Buen Vivir: Globalizing Local Environmental Governance from Ecuador," *Global Environmental Politics* 14, no. 1 (2014): 56.

112. Marcone, "Stone Guest," 230.

113. As Roger Merino notes in "An Alternative to 'Alternative Development'? Buen Vivir and Human Development in Andean Countries," equivalents to sumak kawsay have been used by the Ashuar in Ecuador (*Shiir waras*), the Awajun and the Ashaninka in the Peruvian Amazon (*Tajimat Pujut* and *Kametsa Asaike*, respectively) the Guaraní in Paraguay (*Ñandereko*), and the Mapuche in Chile (*Küme Mongen*).

114. See Omar Cruz, "Producción y reproducción de la vida desde la visión de los Nna'ncue: Xochistlahuaca, Guerero," *La Jornada del Campo*. 15 Oct. 2016; Alicia Lemus Jiménez, "Una reflexión sobre los conceptos de honor y prestigio y kaxumbekua/honorabilidad," *La Jornada del Campo*, October 15, 2016,; Honorio Mendía Soto, "La justicia oral y comunal O'dam," *La Jornada del Campo*, October 15, 2016; and Dionisio Toledo Hernández, "Cosmovisión Tseltal en la búsqueda del lekil kuxlejal (la vida buena)," *La Jornada del Campo*, October 15, 2016.

115. The debate over GMOs in Mexico began shortly after Sinalopasta (a subsidiary of Campbell's), was granted permission to grow GMO corn in Mexico in 1988. Popular outcry lead to a moratorium on commercial GMO crops from 1999 through 2005, when Vicente Fox's administration passed the "Ley de Bioseguridad de Organismos Modificados" (GMO Biosecurity Law), which was popularly known as the "Ley Monsanto," since it allowed GMO crops to be farmed upon approval by a commission of experts, several of whose members had ties to Monsanto.

116. The shorter name by which the movement is popularly known comes from its slogan: "Sin Maíz No Hay País y Sin Frijol Tampoco: Pon a México en tu Boca" (Without Corn and Beans There Can Be No Nation: Put Mexico in Your Mouth).

117. Asociación Nacional de Empresas Comercializadoras de Productores del Campo, *Revista ANEC* 3, nos. 22/23 (2008): 6–12.

118. Asociación Nacional de Empresas Comercializadoras de Productores del Campo, *Revista ANEC* 3, nos. 17/18 (2007): 22.

119. Asociación Nacional de Empresas Comercializadoras de Productores del Campo, *Revista ANEC* 3, nos. 17/18 (2007): 5

120. Guillermo Bonfil Batalla, *El maíz: Fundamento de la cultura popular mexicana* (Mexico City: Museo Nacional de Culturas Populares, 1982), 5.

121. Carlos Rodríguez Wallenius and Luciano Concheiro Bórquez, "Sin Maíz No Hay País: Luchas indígenas por la soberanía alimentaria y un proyecto de nación en México," *Revista NERA* 19, no. 32 (2016): 214.

122. Asociación Nacional de Empresas Comercializadoras de Productores del Campo, *Revista ANEC* 3, nos. 22/23 (2008): 24.

123. Ignácio de Loyola Brandão *Não verás pais nenhum: Memorial descritivo* (Rio de Janeiro: Codecri, 1981).

BIBLIOGRAPHY

Acampora, Ralph. "Zoos and Eyes: Contesting Captivity and Seeking Successor Practices." *Society and Animals* 13, no. 1 (2005): 69–88.

Acosta, Alberto. "El Buen Vivir como alternativa al desarrollo. Algunas reflexiones económicas y no tan económicas." *Política y Sociedad* 52, no. 2 (2015): 299–330.

Acosta, Alberto, and Esperanza Martínez, ed. *La naturaleza con derechos: De la filosofía a la política.* Quito: Universidad Politécnica Salesiana; Abya Yala, 2011.

Adamatzky, Andrew. "Language of Fungi Derived From Their Electrical Spiking Activity." *Royal Society Open Science* 9, no. 4 (2022): 1–15.

Adorno, Theodor. *Negative Dialectics.* New York: Continuum, 1973.

Agamben, Giorgio. *Homo sacer: Sovereign Power and Bare Life.* Translated by Daniel Heller-Roazen. Palo Alto, CA: Stanford University Press, 1998.

———. *The Open: Man and Animal.* Translated by Kevin Attell. Palo Alto, CA: Stanford University Press, 2004.

Akchurin, María. "Constructing the Rights of Nature: Constitutional Reform, Mobilization, and Environmental Protection in Ecuador." *Law and Social Inquiry* 40, no. 4 (2015): 937–68.

Alberti, Samuel, ed. *The Afterlives of Animals: A Museum Menagerie.* Charlottesville: University of Virginia Press, 2011.

Andermann, Jens. *Tierras en trance: Arte y naturaleza después del paisaje.* Santiago de Chile: Metales Pesados, 2018.

Anderson, Mark. "Amazonian Flows, Ecological Cosmopolitanism, and the Question of Material Subjectivities." In *Transatlantic Landscapes. Environmental Awareness, Literature, and the Arts.* Edited by José Manuel Marrero Henríquez, 125–45. Alcalá de Henares: Instituto Franklin, 2016.

———. "The Natural Baroque: Opacity, Impenetrability, and Folding in Writing on Amazonia." *Amazonian Literatures*. Edited by Lesley Wylie. *Hispanic Issues On-Line* 16 (2014): 57–83.

———. "Violent Transactions and the Politics of Dying in Neoliberal Mexico." *Revista de Estudios Hispánicos* 53, no. 1 (2019): 211–34.

Anderson, Mark, and Marcela Reales. "Extracting Nature: Toward an Ecology of Colombian Narrative." In *A History of Colombian Literature*. Edited by Raymond Leslie Williams, 363–405. New York: Cambridge University Press, 2016.

Arguedas, Alcides. *Pueblo enfermo.* Santiago de Chile: Ercilla, 1937.

Aristotle. *De anima.* Edited by Ronald Polanksy. Cambridge: Cambridge University Press, 2009.

Asociación Nacional de Empresas Comercializadoras de Productores del Campo. *Revista ANEC* 17/18 (2007): 1–108.

———. *Revista ANEC* 22/23 (2008): 1–36.

Atkin, Albert. "Pierce on the Index and Indexical Reference." *Transactions of the Charles S. Pierce Society* 41, no. 1 (2005): 161–188.

Avelar, Idelber. "Amerindian Perspectivism and Non-Human Rights." *Alter/nativas* 1 (2013): 1–21.

Badiou, Alain. *Being and Event.* Translated by Oliver Feltham. London: Continuum, 2006.

———. *Ethics: An Essay on the Understanding of Evil.* Translated by Peter Hallward. London: Verso, 2001.

Barad, Karen. *Meeting the Universe Halfway: Quantum Physics and the Entanglement of Matter and Knowing.* Durham, NC: Duke University Press, 2007.

———. "Posthumanist Performativity: Toward an Understanding of How Matter Comes to Matter." *Signs* 28, no. 3 (2003): 801–831.

Barbas-Rhoden, Laura. *Ecological Imaginations in Latin American Fiction.* Gainesville: University Press of Florida, 2011.

Barié, Cletus Gregor. "Nuevas narrativas constitucionales en Bolivia y Ecuador: El buen vivir y los derechos de la naturaleza." *Latinoamérica* 59 (2014): 9–40.

Barreto de Castro, Thales Augusto. "Perspectivas híbridas, concepções descentradas: estéticas do porvir em *Laços de família*." *Mundo Amazónico* 9, no. 1 (2018): 50–71.

Basso, Ellen. *A Musical View of the Universe: Kalapalo Myth and Ritual Performances.* Philadelphia: University of Pennsylvania Press, 1985.

Beasley-Murray, Jon. *Posthegemony: Political Theory and Latin America.* Minneapolis: University of Minnesota Press, 2010.

Becker, Marc. *Pachakutik: Indigenous Movements and Electoral Politics in Ecuador.* Lanham, MD: Rowman & Littlefield, 2011.

Beckman, Ericka. *Capital Fictions: The Literature of Latin America's Export Age.* Minneapolis: University of Minneapolis Press, 2013.

Bello, Andrés. "Silva a la agricultura de la zona tórrida." Biblioteca Cervantes Virtual. https://www.cervantesvirtual.com/obra-visor/poesias--35/html/ ff5cfcdc-82b1-11df-acc7-002185ce6064_20.html.

Bennet, Maurice. "Dialogue of Gazes: Metamorphosis and Epiphany in Julio Cortázar's 'Axolotl.'" *Studies in Short Fiction* 23, no. 1 (1986): 57–62.

Berger, John. *About Looking.* New York: Pantheon, 1980.

Beristaín, Carlos Martín. *El derecho a la reparación en los conflictos socioambientales: Experiencias, aprendizajes y desafíos prácticos.* Bilbao: Universidad del País Vasco; Hegoa, 2010.

Berlinger, Joe, director. *Crude.* Entrendre Films, 2009. 1hr., 40 min.

Berros, Valeria. "Ética animal en diálogo con recientes reformas en la legislación de países latinoamericanos." *Revista de Bioética y Derecho* 33 (2015): 82–93.

Biemann, Ursula. "The Cosmo-Political Forest: A Theoretical and Aesthetic Discussion of the Video *Forest Law.*" *GeoHumanities* 1, no. 1 (2015): 157–70.

Blanco Wells, Gustavo and María Griselda Günther. "De crisis, ecologías y transiciones: Reflexiones sobre teoría social latinoamericana frente al cambio ambiental global." *Revista Colombiana de Sociología* 42, no. 1 (2019): 19–40.

Blaser, Mario, and Marisol de la Cadena. "Introduction: Pluriverse, a Proposal for a World of Many Worlds." In *A World of Many Worlds.* Edited by Marisol de la Cadena and Mario Blaser, 1–22. Durham, NC: Duke University Press, 2018.

Bonfil Batalla, Guillermo. *El maíz: Fundamento de la cultura popular mexicana.* Mexico City: Museo Nacional de Culturas Populares, 1982.

Bonilla Maldonado, Daniel. "El constitucionalismo radical ambiental y la diversidad cultural en América Latina: Los derechos de la naturaleza y el buen vivir en Ecuador y Bolivia." *Revista Derecho del Estado* 42 (2019): 3–23.

Boyd, David R. *The Environmental Rights Revolution: A Global Study of Constitutions, Human Rights, and the Environment.* Vancouver: University of British Columbia, 2012.

———. *The Rights of Nature: A Legal Revolution that Could Save the World.* Toronto: ECW, 2017.

Braverman, Irus. *Wild Life: The Institution of Nature.* Palo Alto: Stanford University Press, 2015.

———. *Zooland: The Institution of Captivity.* Palo Alto: Stanford University Press, 2012.

Brei, Andrew. "Rights & Nature: Approaching Environmental Issues by Way of Human Rights." *Journal of Agricultural and Environmental Ethics* 26 (2013): 393–408.

Brogan, Christopher. *The Retreat from Oil Nationalism in Ecuador: 1976–1983.* Working Papers. University of London, Institute of Latin American Studies, 1984.

Butler, Judith. *Bodies that Matter: On the Discursive Limits of Sex.* New York: Routledge, 1993.

———. *Gender Trouble: Feminism and the Subversion of Identity.* New York: Routledge, 1990.

Cadena, Marisol de la. *Earth Beings: Ecologies of Practice across Andean Worlds.* Durham, NC: Duke University Press, 2015.

———. "Uncommons." Editor's Forum: Theorizing the Contemporary. Society for Cultural Anthropology. https://culanth.org/fieldsights/uncommons.

Cadena, Marisol de la, and Mario Blaser, ed. *A World of Many Worlds.* Durham, NC: Duke University Press, 2018.

Cano Pecharroman, Lidia. "Rights of Nature: Rivers that Can Stand in Court." *Resources* 7, no. 13 (2018): 1–14.

Capacci de Giovani, Graciela. "'Axolotl' de Julio Cortázar. Un reclamo desde el silencio: Intertextualidad social en la literatura del exilio." In *Literatura como intertextualidad: IX Simposio de Internacional de Literatura.* Edited by Juana Alcira Arancibia, 193–204. Buenos Aires: Vinciguerra, 1993.

Carrillo Trueba, César. *El pluriverso: Un ensayo sobre el conocimiento indígena.* Mexico City: Universidad Nacional Autónoma de México, 2014.

Castro, Azucena. "At the Biocultural Borderland: The Unfolding of Multispecies Encounters in Latin American Bioart." *452° Fahrenheit* 21 (2019): 22–34.

Castro-Klarén, Sara. "Ontological Fabulation: Toward Cortázar's Theory of Literature." In *The Final Island: The Fiction of Julio Cortázar.* Edited by Jaime Alazraki and Ivar Ivask, 140–50. Norman, OK: University of Oklahoma Press, 1978.

Cely, Nathalie. "Balancing Profit and Environmental Sustainability in Ecuador: Lessons Learned from the Chevron Case." *Duke Environmental Law and Policy Forum* 24, no. 353 (2014): 353–73.

Cepek, Michael. *Life in Oil: Cofán Survival in the Petroleum Fields of Amazonia.* Austin: University of Texas Press, 2018.

Church, Jerilyn, and Chinyere O. Ekechi, Aila Hoss, Anika Jade Larson. "Tribal Water Rights: Exploring Dam Construction in Indian Country." *Journal of Law, Medicine, and Ethics* 43, no. 1 (2015): 60–63.

Cixous, Hélène. *Reading with Clarice Lispector.* Edited and translated by Verena Andermatt Conley. Minneapolis: Minnesota University Press, 1990.

Clark, David L. "On Being the 'Last Kantian in Nazi Germany': Dwelling with Animals After Levinas." In *Animal Acts: Configuring the Human in Western History*. Edited by Jennifer Ham and Matthew Senior, 165–98. New York: Routledge, 1997.

Clastre, Pierre. *Society Against the State: Essays in Political Anthropology*. Translated by Robert Huxley and Abe Stein. Cambridge: Cambridge, MA: Zone, 1987.

Coleman, Vera. "Beyond the Anthropocene: Multispecies Encounters in Contemporary Latin American Literature, Art, and Film." PhD diss., Arizona State University, 2017.

Collier, John. "Signs Without Minds." In *Pierce and Biosemiotics: A Guess at the Riddle of Life*. Edited by Vinicius Romanini and Eliseo Fernández, 183–97. Dordrecht: Springer, 2014.

Collyns, Dan. "Bolivia Approves Highway Through Amazon Diversity Hotspot." *The Guardian*, August 15, 2017. https://www.theguardian.com/environment/2017/aug/15/bolivia-approves-highway-in-amazon-biodiversity-hotspot-as-big-as-jamaica.

Colón Ríos, Joel. "Comment: The Rights of Nature and the New Latin American Constitutionalism." *Nasaraw Journal of Public and International Law* 13 (2015): 107–13.

Community Environmental Legal Defense Fund. "Rights of Nature: Timeline." CELDF. https://celdf.org/rights-of-nature/timeline/.

Confluencia Nuevo B'aqtun. *El Utzlläj K'aslemal· El Raxnaqull K'aslemal: "El Buen Vivir" de los Pueblos de Guatemala*. Guatemala City: N. pub., 2014. http://www.altaalegremia.com.ar/Archivos-Website/BUEN_VIVIR_Pueblos_Guatemala.pdf.

Connor, Lisa Tabor, and Loraine K. Obler, ed. *Neurobehavior of Language and Cognition: Studies of Normal Aging and Brain Damage. Honoring Martin L. Albert*. Boston: Kluwer, 2000.

Constitutional Assembly. *Constitution of Ecuador*. Political Database of the Americas. January 31, 2011. https://pdba.georgetown.edu/Constitutions/Ecuador/english08.html.

Coole, Diana, and Samantha Frost, ed. *New Materialisms: Ontology, Agency, Politics*. Durham, NC: Duke University Press, 2010.

Cornejo Polar, Antonio. *Escribir en el aire: Ensayo sobre la heterogeneidad sociocultural en las literaturas andinas*. Lima: Centro de Estudios Literarios "Antonio Cornejo Polar"; Latinoamericana, 2003.

Cortázar, Julio. "Axolotl." In *End of the Game and Other Stories*. Translated by Paul Blackburn, 3–10. New York: Pantheon, 1967.

———. "Axolotl." In *Final del juego*, 161–68. Buenos Aires: Sudamericana, 1968.

Costa Lima, Luis. "Social Representation and Mimesis." *New Literary History* 16, no. 3 (1985): 447–66.

Crandal, Maurice. *These People Have Always Been A Republic: Indigenous Electorates in the US-Mexico Borderlands, 1598–1912.* Chapel Hill: University of North Carolina Press, 2019.

Crosby, Alfred W., Jr. *The Columbian Exchange: Biological and Cultural Consequences of 1492.* Westport, CT: Praeger, 2003.

Crutzen, Paul, and Eugene Stoermer. "The 'Anthropocene.'" *Global Change Newsletter* 41 (2000): 17–18.

Cruz, Omar. "Producción y reproducción de la vida desde la visión de los Nna'ncue: Xochistlahuaca, Guerero." *La Jornada del Campo.* 15 Oct. 2016. https://www.jornada.com.mx/2016/10/15/cam-produccion.html.

Cruz Rodríguez, Edwin. "Del derecho ambiental a los derechos de la naturaleza: Sobre la necesidad del diálogo intercultural." *Jurídicas* 1, no. 11 (2014): 95–116.

Cumbre Continental de Pueblos y Organizaciones Indígenas. *Declaration of Quito, Ecuador.* Continental Summit of Indigenous Peoples and Nationalities Abya Yala. http://www.cumbrecontinentalindigena.org/quito_es.php.

Cuestas-Casa, Javier. "Sumak Kawsay is not Buen Vivir." *Alternautas* 5, no. 1 (2018): 49–63.

D'Alisa, Giacomo, and Federico Demaria, Giorgos Kallis, ed. *Degrowth: A Vocabulary for a New Era.* New York: Routledge, 2015.

Daly, Erin. "The Ecuadorian Exemplar: The First Ever Vindications of Constitutional Rights of Nature." *Review of European Community and International Environmental Law* 21, no. 1 (2012): 63–66.

Dawkins, Richard. *The Selfish Gene.* Oxford: Oxford University Press, 1973.

De Castro, Fábio. "Environmental Policies in the Lula Era: Accomplishments and Contradictions." In *Brazil Under the Worker's Party: Continuity and Change from Lula to Dilma,* edited by Fábio de Castro, Kees Koonings, and Marianne Wiesebron, 229–55. Houndmills: Palgrave Macmillan UK, 2014.

Devries, Scott. *Creature Discomfort: Fauna-Criticism, Ethics, and the Representation of Animals in Spanish American Fiction and Poetry.* Leiden: Brill, 2016.

———. *A History of Ecology and Environmentalism in Spanish American Literature.* Lanham: Bucknell University Press, 2013.

Deleuze, Gilles. *Difference and Repetition.* New York: Columbia University Press, 1994.

———. *The Fold: Leibniz and the Baroque.* Translated by Tom Conley. Minneapolis: University of Minnesota Press, 1992.

————. "A Philosophical Concept." In *Who Comes After the Subject?* Edited by Eduardo Cadava, Peter Connor, and Jean-Luc Nancy, 94–95. New York: Routledge, 1991.

Deleuze, Gilles, and Félix Guattari. *Kafka: Towards a Minor Literature.* Translated by Dana Polan. Minneapolis: University of Minnesota Press, 1986.

————. *A Thousand Plateaus: Capitalism and Schizophrenia.* Translated by Brian Massumi. Minneapolis: University of Minnesota Press, 1987.

DeLoughrey, Elizabeth, and George Handley, ed. *Postcolonial Ecologies: Literatures of the Environment.* Oxford: Oxford University Press, 2011.

Department of Economic and Social Affairs. United Nations. "General Assembly Convenes Dialogue on Harmony with Nature." April 17, 2014. https://www.un.org/en/development/desa/news/sustainable/harmony-with-nature.html.

Derrida, Jacques. *Adieu to Emmanuel Levinas.* Translated by Pascale-Anne Brault and Michael Naas. Stanford: Stanford University Press, 1999.

————. *The Animal that Therefore I Am.* Edited by Marie-Louise Mallet. Translated by D. Wills. New York: Fordham University Press, 2008.

————. "'Eating Well' or the Calculation of the Subject: An Interview with Jacques Derrida." In *Who Comes After the Subject?* Edited by Eduardo Cadava, Peter Connor, and Jean-Luc Nancy, 96–119. New York: Routledge, 1991.

————. *The Gift of Death and Literature in Secret.* Translated by David Wills. Chicago: University of Chicago Press, 1999.

————. *Of Grammatology.* Translated by Gayatri Chakravorty Spivak. Baltimore: Johns Hopkins University Press, 1997.

————. *The Politics of Friendship.* Translated by George Collins. London: Verso, 1994.

————. *Speech and Phenomena, and Other Essays on Husserl's Theory of Signs.* Translated by David Allison. Evanstone, IL: Northwestern University Press, 1973.

————. *Writing and Difference.* Translated by Alan Bass. Chicago: University of Chicago Press, 1978.

Descola, Philippe. *Beyond Nature and Culture.* Translated by Janet Lloyd. Chicago: University of Chicago Press, 2013.

Díaz Serrano, Ana. "La República de Tlaxcala ante el rey de España en el siglo XVI." *Historia Mexicana* 61, no. 3 (2012): 1049–1107.

Duchesne Winter, Juan. "Derrida y el pensamiento amazónico (*La bestia y el soberano* / El jaguar y el chamán." *Cuadernos de Literatura* 21, no. 41 (2017): 168–93.

————. *Plant Theory in Amazonian Literature.* New York: Palgrave Macmillan, 2019.

Dueñas, Alcira. "The Lima Indian Letrados: Remaking the Repúblicas de Indios in the Bourbon Andes." *The Americas* 72, no. 1 (2015): 55–75.

Dussel, Enrique. "Transmodernity and Interculturality: An Interpretation from the Philosophy of Liberation." *Transmodernity* 1, no. 3 (2012): 28–59.

Echeverría, Esteban. *El matadero; La cautiva*. Edited by Leonor Flemming. Madrid: Cátedra, 1986.

Ejército Zapatista de Liberación Nacional. "Cuarta declaración de la selva lacandona." 1 Jan. 1996. *Enlace Zapatista*. https://enlacezapatista.ezln.org.mx/1996/01/01/cuarta-declaracion-de-la-selva-lacandona/.

Escobar Konanz, Marta. *La frontera imprecisa: Lo natural y lo sagrado en la cultura negra del norte de Esmeraldas*. Quito: Centro Cultural Afro-Ecuatoriano; Abya Yala, 1990.

Esposito, Roberto. *Immunitas: The Protection and Negation of Life*. Cambridge: Polity, 2011.

Estok, Simon. "Theorizing in a Space of Ambivalent Openness: Ecocriticism and Ecophobia." *ISLE* 16, no. 2 (2009): 203–25.

Eustache, Marie-Loup, and Mickaël Laisney, Aurelija Juskenaite, Odile Letortu, Hervé Platel, Francis Eustache, Béatrice Desgranges. "Sense of Identity in Advanced Alzheimer's Dementia: A Cognitive Dissociation between Sameness and Selfhood?" *Consciousness and Cognition* 22, no. 4 (2013): 1456–67.

Ewert, Jörg-Peter. *Neuroethology: An Introduction to the Neurophysiological Fundamentals of Behavior*. Berlin: Springer-Verlag, 1980.

Eyzaguirre, Luis. "Patología en *La vorágine* de José Eustasio Rivera." *Hispania* 56, no. 1 (1973): 81–90.

Figueroa, Isabela. "La subjetivación de la naturaleza (y sus trampas jurídicas, éticas y epistémicas)." *Revista Catalana de Dret Ambiental* 2, no. 1 (2011): 1–19.

Fitz, Earl. *Sexuality and Being in the Poststructuralist Universe of Clarice Lispector: The Difference of Desire*. Austin: University of Texas Press, 2001.

Fitz-Henry, Erin. "The Natural Contract: From Lévi-Strauss to the Ecuadoran Constitutional Court." *Oceania* 82 (2012): 264–77.

Fontmarty, Francis. "Xolotl, Mexolotl, Axolotl: Una metamorfosis recreativa." In *Lo lúdico y lo fantástico en la obra de Cortázar: Coloquio Internacional*. Vol. 2, 79–88. Madrid: Editorial Fundamentos, 1998.

Forbes, T. R. "The Crowing Hen: Early Observations on Spontaneous Sex Reversal in Chickens." *The Yale Journal of Biology and Medicine* 19, no. 6 (1947): 955–70.

Fornoff, Carolyn. "The Nature of Revolution in Rafael F. Muñoz's *Se llevaron el cañon para Bachimba*." In *Mexican Literature in Theory*. Edited by Ignacio Sánchez Prado, 93–110. New York: Bloomsbury, 2018.

———. *Subjunctive Aesthetics: Mexican Cultural Production in the Era of Climate Change.* Nashville, TN: Vanderbilt University Press, 2024.

Forns-Broggi, Roberto. "Los retos del ecocine en nuestras Américas: Rastreos del buen vivir en *Tierra sublevada.*" *Revista de Crítica Literaria Latinoamericana* 40 no. 79 (2014): 315–32.

Foucault, Michel. *Security, Territory, Population: Lectures at the Collège de France, 1977–1978.* Edited by Michel Senellart. Translated by Graham Burchell. London: Palgrave Macmillan, 2007.

Franco-Vivancos, Edgar. "Justice as Checks and Balances: Indigenous Claims in the Courts of Mexico." *World Politics* 73, no. 4 (2021): 712–783.

French, Jennifer L. *Nature, Neo-Colonialism, and the Spanish American Regional Writers.* Hanover, NH: Dartmouth College Press, 2005.

Friis, Elisabeth. "In My Core I have the Strange Impression that I Don't Belong to the Human Species: Clarice Lispector's *Água viva* as Life Writing?" In *Narrating Life: Experiments with Human and Animal Bodies in Literature, Science and Art.* Edited by Stefan Herbrechter and Elisabeth Friis, 33–55. Leiden: Brill-Rodopi, 2016.

Frost, Samantha. "Fear and the Illusion of Autonomy." In *New Materialisms: Ontology, Agency, Politics.* Edited by Diana Coole and Samantha Frost, 158–77. Durham, NC: Duke University Press, 2010.

Gagliano, Mónica, and Michael Renton, Martial Depczynski, Stefan Mancuso. "Experience Teaches Plants to Learn Faster and Forget Slower in Environments Where It Matters." *Oecologia* 175 (2014): 63–72.

Galeano, Juan Carlos. *Folktales of the Amazon.* Translated by R. Morgan and K. Watson. Westport, CT: Libraries Unlimited, 2009.

Gamba-Barrón, Oscar Fernando, Daniel Esteban Unigarro-Caguasango, and Nohora Inés Carvajal-Sánchez. "Indigenous Territoriality: External Discourses and Native Perspectives on the Space Inhabited by Tegria's U'wa Community." *Revista U.D.C.A Actualidad & Divulgación Científica* 24, no. 1 (2021): 1–10.

García Moreno, Laura. "Cuerpos interrogantes: La mirada en 'El búfalo' de Clarice Lispector y 'Axolotl' de Julio Cortázar." *La Torre* 6, nos. 20–21 (2001): 309–30.

García Ruíz, Luis J. "La territorialidad de la República de Indios de Orizaba. Entre la separación de los sujetos y la preponderancia española: 1740–1828." *Historia Mexicana* 4 (2015): 1415–61.

Gerlach, Allen. *Indians, Oil, and Politics: A Recent History of Ecuador.* Wilmington, DE: Scholarly Resources, 2003.

Giorgi, Gabriel. *Formas comunes: Animalidad, cultura, biopolítica.* Buenos Aires: Eterna Cadencia, 2014.

Global Alliance for the Rights of Nature. "Commission of the International Rights of Nature Tribunal Examines Controversial Road Project in the Heart of TIPNIS." *Movement Rights Blog*. September 4, 2018. https://www.movementrights.org/commission-of-international-rights-of-nature-tribunal-examines-the-controversial-road-project-in-the-heart-of-tipnis/.

Goh, Irving. "*Le Toucher, le cafard,* or, On Touching—the Cockroach in Clarice Lispector's *Passion According to G. H.*" *MLN* 131 (2016): 461–80.

Gómez Barris, Macarena. *The Extractive Zone: Social Ecologies and Decolonial Perspectives*. Durham, NC: Duke University Press, 2017.

González Echeverría, Roberto. "*Los reyes:* Cortázar's Mythology of Writing." In *The Final Island: The Fiction of Julio Cortázar*. Edited by Jaime Alazraki and Ivar Ivask, 63–72. Norman, OK: University of Oklahoma Press, 1978.

Graf, E. C. "'Axolotl' de Julio Cortázar: Dialéctica entre las mitologías azteca y dantesca." *Bulletin of Spanish Studies* 79, no. 5 (2002): 615–36.

Gualinga, José, and the Sarayaku Runa. "Kawsak Sacha—Living Forest." Amazonwatch.org. https://amazonwatch.org/assets/files/2016-kawsak-sacha-proposal-english.pdf.

Gudynas, Eduardo. "Development Alternatives in Bolivia: The Impulse, the Resistance, and the Restoration." *NACLA Report on the Americas* 46, no. 1 (2013): 22–26.

———. *Ecología, economía y ética del desarrollo sostenible*. Quito: ILDIS-FES; Abya Yala, 2003.

———. "Environmental Ethics in Latin America: In Search of a Utopian Vision." *The Trumpeter* 6, no. 4 (1989): 151–55.

———. "Estado compensador y nuevos extractivismos: Las ambivalencias del progreso sudamericano." *Nueva Sociedad* 237 (2012): 128–46.

———. *El mandato ecológico: Derechos de la Naturaleza y políticas ambientales en la nueva Constitución*. Quito: Abya Yala; Universidad Politécnica Salesiana, 2009.

Guha, Ramachandra. *Environmentalism: A Global History*. New York: Longman, 2000.

———. "Radical American Environmentalism and Wilderness Preservation: A Third World Critique." *Environmental Ethics* 11, no. 1 (1989): 71–83.

Gustafsson Chorell, Torbjörn. "Fascination in Julio Cortázar's 'Axolotl.'" *Partial Answers* 17, no. 1 (2019): 49–63.

Hallward, Peter. "Deleuze and the 'World Without Others." *Philosophy Today* 41, no. 1 (1997): 530–44.

Haraway, Donna. *The Companion Species Manifesto: Dogs, People, and Significant Otherness*. Chicago: Prickly Paradigm, 2003.

————. "A Manifesto for Cyborgs: Science, Technology, and Socialist Feminism in the 1980s." In *The Haraway Reader*, 7–45. New York: Routledge, 2004.

————. "Situated Knowledges: The Science Question in Feminism and the Privilege of Partial Perspective." *Feminist Studies* 14, no. 3 (1988): 575–99.

————. *Staying with the Trouble: Making Kin in the Chthulucene*. Durham, NC: Duke University Press, 2016.

————. *When Species Meet*. Minneapolis: University of Minnesota Press, 2008.

Hatzimoysis, Anthony. "Emotions in Heidegger and Sartre." In *The Oxford Handbook of Philosophy of Emotion*. Edited by Peter Goldie, 215–35. Oxford: Oxford University Press, 2009.

Hausmaninger, Herbert, and Richard Gamauf. *Casebook on Roman Property Law*. Translated by George Sheets. New York: Oxford University Press, 2012.

Heffes, Gisela. *Políticas de la destrucción, poéticas de la preservación: Apuntes para una lectura (eco)crítica del medioambiente en América Latina*. Buenos Aires: Beatriz Viterbo, 2013.

Heidegger, Martin. *The Fundamental Concepts of Metaphysics: World, Finitude, Solitude*. Bloomington: Indiana University Press, 1995.

Hernández, Ernesto O. "Climate Change and Philosophy in Latin America." *Journal of Global Ethics* 7, no. 2 (2011): 161–72.

Heyd, Thomas. "Themes in Latin American Environmental Ethics: Community, Resistance, and *Environmental Values*Autonomy." 13, no. 2 (2004): 223–42.

Hidalgo Capitán, Antonio Luis, Alejandro Guillén García, and Nancy Deleg Guazha, eds. *Sumak kawsay yuyay: Antología del pensamiento indigenista ecuatoriano sobre el sumak kawsay*. Huelva: CIM; FIUCUHU; Pyudlos, 2014.

Hobbes, Thomas. *Leviathan, or the Matter, Forme, & Power of a Common-wealth, Ecclesiastic and Civil*. 1651. Project Gutenberg. https://www.gutenberg.org/files/3207/3207-h/3207-h.htm.

Hoffmeyer, Jesper. *Biosemiotics: An Examination into the Signs of Life and the Life of Signs*. Scranton, PA: University of Scranton, 2009.

Hoyos, Héctor. *Things with a History: Transcultural Materialism and the Literatures of Extraction in Contemporary Latin America*. New York: Columbia University Press, 2019.

Hutchins, Frank, and Patrick C. Wilson, eds. *Editing Eden: A Reconsideration of Identity, Politics, and Place in Amazonia*. Lincoln: University of Nebraska, 2011.

The International Center for Not-For-Profit Law. "Civic Freedom Monitor: Ecuador." February 3, 2023. https://www.icnl.org/resources/civic-freedom-monitor/ecuador.

Ittner, Jutta. "Becoming Animal? Zoo Encounters in Rilke, Lispector, and Kronauer." *KulturPoetik* 3, no. 1 (2003): 24–41.

Jaramillo, Camilo. "Green Hells: Monstrous Vegetations in Twentieth-Century Representations of Amazonia." In *Plant Horror: Approaches to the Monstruous Vegetal in Fiction and Film*. Edited by Dawn Keetley and Angela Tengla, 91–109. London: Palgrave Macmillan, 2016.

Kane, Adrian, ed. *The Natural World in Latin American Literatures: Ecocritical Essays on Twentieth-Century Writings*. Jefferson, NC: McFarland, 2010.

Kardec, Allan. *The Spirit's Book*. Translated by E. G. Dutra. Sheridan, WY: Luchnos, 2021.

Katz de Barrera-Hernández, Lila, and Alistair R. Lucas. "Environmental Law in Latin America and the Caribbean: Overview and Assessment." *Georgetown International Environmental Law Review* 12 (1999): 207–45.

Kauffman, Craig M., and Pamela L. Martin. "Scaling up Buen Vivir: Globalizing Local Environmental Governance from Ecuador." *Global Environmental Politics* 14, no. 1 (2014): 40–58.

Kauffmann, R. Lane. "Julio Cortázar y a la apropiación del otro: 'Axololt' como una fábula etnográfica." *Revista Mexicana de Sociología* 63, no. 4 (2001): 223–32.

Kawsak Sacha, Sarayaku, Living Forest. Oficina de Coordinación del Pueblo Originario Kichwa de Sarayaku. https://kawsaksacha.org.

Kay, Kelly. "Breaking the Bundle of Rights: Conservation Easements and the Legal Geographies of Individuating Nature." *Environment and Planning A* 48, no. 3 (2018): 504–22.

Keane, Webb. "Signs Are Not the Garb of Meaning: On the Social Analysis of Material Things." In *Materiality*. Edited by Daniel Miller, 182–205. Durham, NC: Duke University Press, 2005.

Kohn, Eduardo. *How Forests Think: Toward an Anthropology Beyond the Human*. Berkeley: University of California Press, 2013.

Kopenawa, Davi, and Bruce Albert. *The Falling Sky: Words of a Yanomami Shaman*. Translated by Nicholas Elliot and Alison Dundy. Cambridge, MA: Harvard University Press, 2013.

Kristeva, Julia. *Powers of Horror: An Essay on Abjection*. Translated by Leon Roudiez. New York: Columbia University Press, 1982.

Kull, Kalevi. "Ecosystems are Made of Semiosic Bonds: Consortia, Umwelten, Biophony and Ecological Codes." *Biosemiotics* 3 (2010): 347–57.

Lacan, Jacques. "The Subversion of the Subject and the Dialectic of Desire." In *Ecrits*. Translated by Bruce Fink, 671–702. New York: Norton, 1996.

———. "The Function and Field of Speech and Language in Psychoanalysis." In *Ecrits*. Translated by Bruce Fink, 237–68. New York: Norton, 1996.

Latour, Bruno. *Politics of Nature: How to Bring the Sciences into Democracy*. Cambridge, MA: Harvard University Press, 2004.

———. *Reassembling the Social: An Introduction to Actor Network Theory*. Oxford: Oxford University Press, 2005.

———. "Scientific Objects and Legal Objectivity." In *Law, Anthropology, and the Constitution of the Social: Making Persons and Things*. Edited by Alain Pottage and Martha Mundy, 73–114. Cambridge: Cambridge University Press, 2004.

———. *We have Never Been Modern*. Translated by Catherine Porter. Cambridge, MA: Harvard University Press, 1993.

Lecaros Urzúa, Juan Alberto. "La ética medioambiental: Principios y valores para una ciudadanía responsable en la sociedad global." *Acta Bioethica* 19, no. 2 (2013): 177–88.

Leenhardt, Jacques. "La americanidad de Julio Cortázar: El otro y su mirada." *Inti* 22–23 (1985–1986): 307–15.

Leff, Enrique. *La racionalidad ambiental: La reapropriación social de la naturaleza*. Mexico City: Siglo XXI, 2004.

Lemus Jiménez, Alicia. "Una reflexión sobre los conceptos de honor y prestigio y kaxumbekua/honorabilidad." *La Jornada del Campo*. October 15, 2016. https://www.jornada.com.mx/2016/10/15/cam-honor.html.

Levinas, Emmanuel. "The Name of a Dog, or Natural Rights." In *Difficult Freedom: Essays on Judaism*. Translated by Seán Hand, 151–53. London: Athlone, 1990.

———. "The Paradox of Morality: An Interview with Emmanuel Levinas." In *The Provocation of Levinas: Rethinking the Other*. Edited by Robert Bernasconi and David Wood. Translated by Andrew Benjamin and Tamara Wright, 168–80. London: Routledge, 1988.

———. *Totality and Infinity: an Essay on Exteriority*. Pittsburgh: Duquesne University Press, 1969.

Levinson, Brett. "The Other Origin: Cortázar and Identity Politics." *Latin American Literary Review* 22, no. 44 (1994): 5–19.

Librandi Rocha, Marília. "Becoming Natives of Fiction: Towards an Ontology of the Mimetic Game (Lévi Strauss, Costa Lima, Viveiros de Castro, and the Nambikwara Art Lesson)." *Culture, Theory, and Critique* 54, no. 2 (2013): 166–82.

Liffman, Paul. "Indigenous Territorialities in Mexico and Colombia." Regional Worlds at the University of Chicago. University of Chicago. Center for International Studies. http://regionalworlds.uchicago.edu/indigenousterritorialities.pdf.

Lispector, Clarice. *Água viva*. Rio de Janeiro: Rocco, 1998.

———. *A Breath of Life (Pulsations)*. Edited by Benjamin Moser. Translated by Johnny Lorenz. New York: New Directions, 2012.

———. "The Buffalo." In *Family Ties*. Translated by Giovanni Ponteiro, 147–56. Austin: University of Texas Press, 1972.

————. "O búfalo." In *Laços de família: Contos*, 126–35. Rio de Janeiro: Rocco, 2009.

————. "A Chicken." In *The Complete Stories*. Edited by Benjamin Moser. Translated by Katrina Dodson, 127–30. New York: New Directions, 2015.

————. "O crime do professor de matemática." In *Laços de família: Contos*, 118–25. Rio de Janeiro: Rocco, 2009.

————. "The Crime of the Mathematics Teacher." In *The Complete Stories*. Edited by Benjamin Moser. Translated by Katrina Dodson, 214–21. New York: New Directions, 2015.

————. "The Egg and the Chicken." In *The Complete Stories*. Edited by Benjamin Moser. Translated by Katrina Dodson, 276–86. New York: New Directions, 2015.

————. "Family Ties." In *The Complete Stories*. Edited by Benjamin Moser. Translated by Katrina Dodson, 190–99. New York: New Directions, 2015.

————. "Uma galinha." In *Laços de família: Contos*, 30–33. Rio de Janeiro: Rocco, 2009.

————. "Os laços de família." In *Laços de família: Contos*, 94–103. Rio de Janeiro: Rocco, 2009.

————. *A paixão segundo G. H.* Rio de Janeiro: Rocco, 2009.

————. *The Passion According to G. H.* Translated by Ronald W. Sousa. Minneapolis: University of Minneapolis Press, 1988.

————. *Um sopro de vida (pulsações)*. Rio de Janeiro: Rocco, 1999.

————. *The Stream of Life*. Translation of *Água Viva*. Translated by Elizabeth Loew and Earl Fitz. Minneapolis: University of Minnesota Press, 1989.

Locke, John. *Two Treatises of Government*. Edited by Peter Lasslet. New York: Cambridge University Press, 1988.

Low, Philip, Jaak Panksepp, Diana Reiss, David Edelman, Bruno Van Swinderen, and Christof Koch. "Cambridge Declaration on Consciousness." July 7, 2012. *Francis Crick Memorial Conference*. https://fcmconference.org/img/CambridgeDeclarationOnConsciousness.pdf.

Loyola Brandão, Ignácio de. *Não verás país nenhum: Memorial descritivo*. Rio de Janeiro: Codecri, 1981.

Ludueña Romandini, Fabían. *La comunidad de los espectros*. Buenos Aires: Miño y Dávila, 2010.

Lyon, Bruce E., and Robert Montgomerie. "Sexual Selection is a Form of Social Selection." *Philosophical Transactions of the Royal Society B* 367 (2012): 2266–2273.

Maciel, Maria Esther. *Literatura e animalidade*. Rio de Janeiro: Civilização Brasileira, 2016.

Manga Qespi, Atuq Eusebio. "Pacha: Un concepto andino de espacio y tiempo." *Revista Española de Antropología Americana* 24 (1994): 155–89.

Marcone, Jorge. "De retorno a lo natural: *La serpiente de oro*, 'la novela de la selva' y la crítica ecológica." *Hispania* 81, no. 2 (1998): 299–308.

———. "The Stone Guests: *Buen Vivir* and Popular Environmentalisms in the Andes and Amazonia." In *The Routledge Companion to the Environmental Humanities*. Edited by Ursula K. Heise, Jon Christensen, and Michelle Niemann, 227–35. London: Routledge, 2017.

Marder, Michael. *Plant Thinking: A Philosophy of Vegetal Life*. New York: Columbia University Press, 2013.

Marino, Daniel. "'Ahora que Dios nos ha dado padre': El Segundo Imperio y la cultura jurídica-política campesina en el Centro de México." *Historia Mexicana* 55, no. 4 (2006): 1353–1410.

Martínez de Bringas, Asier. "Selva Viviente: El corazón de la autonomía kichwa en Sarayaku." *Revista d'Estudis Autonòmics i Federals* 34 (2021): 85–111.

Martínez Pinzón, Felipe. "Héroes de la civilización: La Amazonía como cosmópolis agroexportadora en la obra del General Rafael Reyes." *Anuario Colombiano de Historia Social y de la Cultura* 40, no. 2 (2013): 145–77.

Marvin, Garry. "Enlivened Through Memory: Hunters and Hunting Trophies." In *The Afterlives of Animals: A Museum Menagerie*. Edited by Samuel Alberti, 202–17. Charlottesville: University of Virginia Press, 2011.

Massey, Rachel. "The 'Drug War' in Colombia: Echoes of Vietnam." *Journal of Public Health Policy* 22, no. 3 (2001): 280–85.

Mauro, Martin. "Tanta vida mutua (mujeres y precariedad animal)." *Alea* 20, no. 2 (2018): 17–35.

McNee, Malcolm. *The Environmental Imaginary in Brazilian Poetry and Art*. New York: Palgrave Macmillan, 2014.

McNeill, John, and Peter Engelke. *The Great Acceleration: An Environmental History of the Anthropocene since 1945*. Harvard: Harvard University Press, 2016.

Mejilla Velilla, David. "Leyes republicanas de indios: Aportación de la Independencia a la Legislación Civil en pro de los indígenas. Antecedentes y periodo de 1821–1843." *Díkaion* 4 (1995): 41–53.

Melo, Mario. *Sarayaku Before the Inter-American Human Rights System: Justice for the People of the Zenith and their Living Forest*. Bogotá: De Justicia, 2019.

Menchú, Rigoberta, and Elizabeth Burgos Debray. *Me llamo Rigoberta Menchú y así me nació la consciencia*. Mexico City: Siglo XXI, 1985.

Mendía Soto, Honorio. "La justicia oral y comunal O'dam." *La Jornada del Campo*. October 15, 2016. https://www.jornada.com.mx/2016/10/15/cam-justicia.html.

Merino, Roger. "An Alternative to 'Alternative Development"? Buen Vivir and Human Development in Andean Countries." *Oxford Development Studies* 44, no. 3 (2016): 271–86

Meyer, Jean. "La Junta Protectora de las Clases Menesterosas: Indigenismo y agrarismo en el Segundo Imperio." In *Indio, nación y comunidad en el México del siglo XIX*. Edited by Antonio Escobar Ohmstede y Patricia Lagos Preisser, 329–64. México: Centro de Estudios Mexicanos y Centroamericanos; Centro de Investigaciones y Estudios Superiores en Antropología Social, 1993.

Mignolo, Walter. *The Darker Side of Western Modernity: Global Futures, Decolonial Options*. Durham, NC: Duke University Press, 2011.

Minority Rights Group International. "Ecuador." World Directory of Minorities and Indigenous Peoples. May 2018. https://minorityrights.org/country/ecuador/.

Mizuta Lippit, Akira. *Electric Animal: Toward a Rhetoric of Wildlife*. Minneapolis: University of Minnesota Press, 2000.

Molloy, Sylvia. "Contagio narrativo y gesticulación retórica en *La vorágine*." In *La vorágine: textos críticos*. Edited by Montserrat Ordoñez, 489–513. Bogotá: Alianza Editorial Colombiana, 1987.

Montesquieu, Charles de Secondat, Baron de. *The Spirit of Laws*. Translated by Thomas Nugent. Kitchener: Batoche, 2001.

Moore, Jason W. *Capitalism in the Web of Life*. London: Verso, 2015.

———. "The Capitalocene, Part 1: On the Nature and Origins of Our Ecological Crisis." *Journal of Peasant Studies* 44, no. 3 (2017): 594–630. https://www.tandfonline.com/doi/full/10.1080/03066150.2016.1235036.

———. "Ecology, Capital, and the Nature of Our Times: Accumulation & Crisis in the Capitalist World-Ecology." *Journal of World Systems Research* 17, no. 1 (2011): 107–46.

Moroney, Pat. "Hobbes, Savagery, and International Anarchy." *American Political Science Review* 105, no. 1 (2011): 189–204.

Muller, Ingrid R. "The Problematics of the Body in Clarice Lispector's *Family Ties*." *Chasqui* 20, no. 1 (1991): 34–42.

Murgueitio Manrique, Carlos Alberto. "Proceso de desamortización de las tierras indígenas durante las repúblicas liberales de México y Colombia, 1853–1876." *Anuario de la Historia Regional y de las Fronteras* 20, no. 1 (2015): 73–95.

Nascimento, Evando. "Rastros do animal humano: A ficção de Clarice Lispector." In *Pensar/escrever o animal: Ensaios de zoopoética y biopolítica*. Edited by Maria Esther Maciel, 117–48. Florianópolis: Editora da Universidade Federal de Santa Catarina, 2011.

Nash, Rodrick Frazier. *The Rights of Nature: A History of Environmental Ethics*. Madison, WI: University of Wisconsin Press, 1989.

National Science Foundation. "The Most Genes in an Animal? Tiny Crustacean Holds the Record." National Science Foundation News, February 3, 2011. https://www.nsf.gov/news/news_summ.jsp?cntn_id=118530.

Neruda, Pablo. "Oda a la erosión en la Provincia de Malleco." In *Nuevas odas elementales*. Buenos Aires: Losada, 1964.

Niblett, Michael. "World Economy, World-Ecology, World Literature." *Green Letters* 16, no. 1 (2012): 15–30.

Nouzeilles, Gabriela. "The Transcultural Mirror of Science: Race and Self-Representation in Latin America." In *Literary Cultures of Latin America: A Comparative History*. Vol 3. Edited by Mario J. Valdés and Djelal Kadir, 284–99. Oxford: Oxford University Press, 2004.

Oloff, Kerstin. "Greening the Zombie: Caribbean Gothic, World-Ecology, and Socio-Ecological Degradation." *Green Letters* 16, no. 1 (2012): 31–45.

Ortega, Bertín. "Cortázar: 'Axolotl' y la cinta de Moebius." *Nuevo Texto Crítico* 2, no. 3 (1989): 135–40.

Paez, Felipe. "Environmental Framework Laws in Latin America." *Pace Environmental Law Review* 13 (1996): 625–84.

Paravisini-Gebert, Lizbeth. "Endangered Species: Caribbean Ecology and the Discourse of the Nation." In *Displacements and Transformations in Caribbean Cultures*, edited by Lizbeth Paravisini-Gebert and Ivette Romero-Cesareo, 8–23. Gainesville: University of Florida Press, 2008.

Patterson, Brent, Emma Lui, Melissa Dick, Jan Malek, Andrea Harden-Donahue, Brant Thompson, Dylan Penner, Matt Ramsden, Carleen Pickard, Shannon Biggs, and Julianne Stelmaszyk, eds. *The Rights of Nature: The Case for a Universal Declaration of the Rights of Mother Earth*. San Francisco, CA: Council of Canadians; Fundación Pachamama; Global Exchange, 2011.

Peixoto, Marta. "Family Ties: Female Development in Clarice Lispector." In *The Voyage In: Fictions of Female Development*. Edited by Elizabeth Abel, Marianne Hirsch, and Elizabeth Langland, 287–303. Dartmouth, NH: University Press of New England for Dartmouth College, 1983.

———. *Passionate Fictions: Gender, Narrative, and Violence in Clarice Lispector*. Minneapolis: University of Minnesota Press, 1997.

Pérez Aguilera, Abigaíl. "Mining and Indigenous Cosmopolitics: The Wirikuta Case." In *Ecological Crisis and Cultural Representation in Latin America: Ecocritical Perspectives on Art, Film, and Literature*. Edited by Mark Anderson and Zélia Bora, 179–98. Lanham, MD: Lexington, 2016.

Peri Ferreira, Helder. *Yanomama Clause Structure*. Utrecht: LOT, 2017.

Perrone-Moises, Leyla. "Literary Nationalism in Latin America." In *Literary Cultures of Latin America: A Comparative History*, vol. 1. Edited by Mario J. Valdés and Djelal Kadir, 193–99. Oxford: Oxford University Press, 2004.

Peters, Julie Stone. "'Literature,' the 'Rights of Man,' and Narratives of Atrocity: Historical Backgrounds to the Culture of Testimony." In *Theoretical Perspectives on Human Rights and Literature*. Edited by Elizabeth Swanson

Goldberg and Alexandra Schulteis Moore, 19–40. New York: Routledge, 2013.

Pierce, Charles S. *Philosophical Writings of Pierce.* Edited by Justus Buchler. New York: Dover, 1955.

Piskorski, Rodolfo. "The Light That Therefore I Give (to): Paleonymy and Animal Supplementarity in Clarice Lispector's *The Apple in the Dark.*" In *What is Zoopoetics? Texts, Bodies, Entanglement.* Edited by Kári Driscoll and Eva Hoffman, 103–28. Cham: Palgrave Macmillan, 2018.

Plumwood, Val. *Feminism and the Mastery of Nature.* London: Routledge, 1993.

Pottage, Alain. "Introduction: The Fabrication of Persons and Things." Pottage and Mundy, *Law*, 1–39.

Pottage, Alain, and Martha Mundy, eds. *Law, Anthropology, and the Constitution of the Social: Making Persons and Things.* Cambridge: Cambridge University Press, 2004.

Povinelli, Elizabeth A. *Geontologies: A Requiem to Late Liberalism.* Durham, NC: Duke University Press, 2016.

Prádanos, Luis I. *Postgrowth Imaginaries: New Ecologies and Counterhegemonic Culture in Post-2008 Spain.* Liverpool: University of Liverpool Press, 2018.

Praet, Istvan. "Shamanism and Ritual in South America: An Inquiry into Amerindian Shape-Shifting." *Journal of the Royal Anthropological Institute* 15 (2009): 737–54.

Puig de la Bellacasa, María. *Matters of Care: Speculative Ethics in More Than Human Worlds.* Minneapolis: University of Minnesota Press, 2017.

Purnell, Jennie. "With All Due Respect: Popular Resistance to the Privatization of Communal Lands in Nineteenth-Century Michoacán." *Latin American Research Review* 34, no. 1 (1999): 85–121.

Quick, Joe, and James T. Spartz. "On the Pursuit of Good Living in Highland Ecuador: Critical Indigenous Discourses of Sumak Kawsay." *Latin American Research Review* 53, no. 4 (2018): 757–69.

Quijano, Aníbal. "Colonialidad del poder, cultura y conocimiento en América Latina." *Dispositio* 24, no. 51 (1999): 137–48.

Rancière, Jacques. *Dissensus: On Politics and Aesthetics.* Translated by Steven Corcoran. London: Continuum, 1999.

Ranco, Darren, and Jamie Haverkamp. "Storying Indigenous Life(Worlds): An Introduction." *Genealogy* 6, no. 25 (2022): 1–9.

Ribeiro da Costa Curi, Simone. *A escritura nómade em Clarice Lispector.* Chapecó: Argos, 2001.

Rivas, Medardo. *Los trabajadores de tierra caliente.* Bogotá: Universidad Nacional, 1946.

Rivera, Alex, director. *Sleep Dealer*. Likely Story, 2008. 1 hr., 30 min.

Rivera, José Eustasio. *La vorágine*. Bogotá: Biblioteca Popular de Cultura Colombiana, 1946.

———. *The Vortex*. Translated by John Charles Chasteen. Durham, NC: Duke University Press, 2018.

Rodríguez Wallenius, Carlos, and Luciano Concheiro Bórquez. "Sin Maíz No Hay País: Luchas indígenas por la soberanía alimentaria y un proyecto de nación en México." *Revista NERA* 19, no. 32 (2016): 214–35.

Rogers, Charlotte. *Jungle Fever: Exploring Madness and Medicine in Twentieth-Century Tropical Narratives*. Nashville: Vanderbilt University Press, 2012.

Rousseau, Jean Jacques. *The Social Contract & Discourses*. London and Toronto: Dent; New York: Dutton, 1920. Project Gutenberg. https://www.gutenberg. org/ebooks/46333.

Royal Botanic Gardens, Kew. "Rare Japanese Plant Has Largest Genome Known to Science." ScienceDaily. October 7, 2010. https://www.sciencedaily.com/ releases/2010/10/101007120641.htm.

Sá, Lucia. *Rainforest Literatures: Amazonian Texts and Latin American Culture*. Minneapolis: University of Minnesota Press, 2004.

Salmón, Enrique. "Kincentric Ecology: Indigenous Perceptions of the Human-Nature Relationship." *Ecological Applications* 10, no. 5 (2000): 1327–1332.

Saramago, Victoria. *Fictional Environments: Mimesis, Deforestation, and Development in Latin America*. Evanston, IL: Northwestern University Press, 2021.

Sarayaku Runa. *El libro de la vida de Sarayaku para defender nuestro futuro*. In *Sumak kawsay yuyay: Antología del pensamiento indigenista ecuatoriano sobre el sumak kawsay*. Edited by Hidalgo Capitán, Antonio Luis and Alejandro Guillén García, Nancy Deleg Guazha, 77–102. Huelva: CIM; FIUCUHU; Pyudlos, 2014.

Sartre, Jean Paul. *Sketch for a Theory of the Emotions*. London: Routledge, 2004.

Savino, Lucas. "Landscapes of Contrast: The Neo-Extractivist State and Indigenous Peoples in 'Post-Neoliberal' Argentina." *The Extractive Industries and Society* 3 (2015): 404–15

Sawyer, Suzana. *Crude Chronicles: Indigenous Politics, Multinational Oil, and Neoliberalism in Ecuador*. Durham, NC: Duke University Press, 2004.

Schwarz, Henry. "Cartesian Literature: The Narrative Mathematics of Being in Clarice Lispector." *Canadian Journal of Latin American and Caribbean Studies* 39, no. 1 (2014): 56–71.

Schroeder, Heike, and Nidia González, "Bridging Knowledge Divides: The Case of Indigenous Ontologies of Territoriality and REDD+." *Forest Policy and Economics* 100 (2019): 198–206.

Sebeok, Thomas. *Perspectives in Zoosemiotics*. The Hague: Mouton, 1972.

Serje, Margarita. *El revés de la nación: Territorios salvajes, fronteras y tierras de nadie*. Bogotá: Universidad de los Andes, 2005.

Shargel, Daniel, and Jesse Prinz. "An Enactivist Theory of Emotional Content." In *The Ontology of Emotions*. Edited by Hichem Naar and Fabrice Teroni, 110–29. Cambridge: Cambridge University Press, 2017.

Shilling, Dan. "Aldo Leopold Listens to the Southwest." *Journal of the Southwest* 51, no. 3 (2009): 317–50.

Simard, Suzanne. *Finding the Mother Tree: Discovering the Wisdom of the Forest*. New York: Knopf, 2021.

Singer, Peter. *Animal Liberation: A New Ethics for Our Treatment of Animals*. New York: Harper Collins, 2004.

Slater, Candace. *Entangled Edens: Visions of the Amazon*. Berkeley: University of California Press, 2002.

Snyder, Gary. "Language Goes Two Ways." In *The Green Studies Reader: From Romanticism to Ecocriticism*. Edited by Laurence Coupe, 127–31. London: Routledge, 2000.

Sobrevilla, David. "Transculturación y heterogeneidad: Avatares de dos categorías literarias en América Latina." *Revista de Crítica Literaria Latinoamericana* 54 (2001): 21–33.

Solari, Amara. *Maya Ideologies of the Sacred: The Transfiguration of Space in Colonial Yucatán*. Austin: University of Texas Press, 2013.

Sommer, Doris. "Rigoberta's Secrets." *Latin American Perspectives* 18, no. 3 (1991): 32–50.

Stengers, Isabelle. "The Challenge of Ontological Politics." In *A World of Many Worlds*. Edited by Marisol de la Cadena and Mario Blaser, 83–111. Durham, NC: Duke University Press, 2018.

———. "Comparison as a Matter of Concern." *Common Knowledge* 17, no. 1 (2011): 48–63.

———. *Cosmopolitics I*. Translated by Robert Bononno Minneapolis: University of Minnesota Press, 2010.

———. *Cosmopolitics II*. Translated by Robert Bononno. Minneapolis: University of Minnesota Press, 2011.

———. "The Cosmopolitical Proposal." Translated by Liz Carey-Libbrecht. In *Making Things Public: Atmospheres of Democracy*. Edited by Bruno Latour and Peter Weibel, 994–1003. Karlsurhe: ZKM; Cambridge, MA: MIT Press, 2005.

———. "Introductory Notes on an Ecology of Practices." *Cultural Studies Review* 11, no. 1 (2005): 183–96.

Stone, Christopher. *Should Trees Have Standing? Law, Morality, and the Environment.* Oxford: Oxford University Press, 2010.

Strathern, Marilyn. "No Nature, No Culture: The Hagen Case." In *Nature, Culture, and Gender.* Edited by Carol MacCormack and Marilyn Strathern, 174–222. Cambridge: Cambridge University Press, 1980.

———. "Opening Up Relations." In *A World of Many Worlds.* Edited by Marisol de la Cadena and Mario Blaser, 23–52. Durham, NC: Duke University Press, 2018.

Stutzin, Godofredo. "Should We Recognize Nature's Claim to Legal Rights? An Essay." *Environmental Policy and Law* 2 (1976): 129.

Swinney, Geoffrey. "An Afterword on Afterlife." In *The Afterlives of Animals: A Museum Menagerie.* Edited by Samuel Alberti, 219–33. Charlottesville: University of Virginia Press, 2011.

Tanasescu, Mihnea. *Environment, Political Representation, and the Challenge of Rights: Speaking for Nature.* New York: Palgrave Macmillan, 2016.

Taylor, Bron. "Earthen Spirituality or Cultural Genocide? Radical Environmentalism's Appropriation of Native American Spirituality." *Religion* 27 (1997): 183–215.

Terán-Mantovani, Emiliano. "Inside and Beyond the Petro-State Frontiers: Geography of Environmental Conflicts in Venezuela's Bolivarian Revolution." *Sustainability Science* 13 (2018): 677–91.

Toledo Hernández, Dionisio. "Cosmovisión Tseltal en la búsqueda del lekil kuxlejal (la vida buena)." *La Jornada del Campo*, 15 Oct. 2016. https://www.jornada.com.mx/2016/10/15/cam-vida.html.

Tornos Urzainki, Maider. "El devenir-animal en *La pasión según G. H.* de Clarice Lispector (en lengua extranjera)." *Arte y Políticas de Identidad* 16 (2017): 145–60.

Tsing, Anna. "Unruly Edges: Mushrooms as Companion Species." *Environmental Humanities* 1 (2012): 141–54.

Uexküll, Jacob von. *A Foray Into the Worlds of Animals and Humans, with A Theory of Meaning.* Translated by Joseph D. O'Neil. Minneapolis: Minnesota University Press, 2010.

Unceta Satrustegui, Koldo. "Decrecimiento y buen vivir: ¿Paradigmas convergentes? Debates sobre el postdesarrollo en Europa y América Latina." *Revista de Economía Mundial* 35 (2013): 21–45.

Uzendoski, Michael. "Fractal Subjectivities: An Amazonian Inspired Critique of Globalization Theory." In *Editing Eden: A Reconsideration of Identity, Politics, and Place in Amazonia.* Edited by Frank Hutchins, and Patrick C. Wilson, 38–69. Lincoln: University of Nebraska, 2011.

Vilaça, Aparecida. "Chronically Unstable Bodies: Reflections on Amazonian Corporalities." *Journal of the Royal Anthropological Institute* 11 (2005): 445–64.

Villavicencio Calzadilla, Paola, and Louis J. Kotzé. "Living in Harmony with Nature? A Critical Appraisal of the Rights of Mother Earth in Bolivia." *Transnational Environmental Law* 7, no. 3 (2018): 397–424.

Vieira, Patrícia. "Interspecies Literature: Clarice Lispector's Zoophytographia." *Journal of Lusophone Studies* 2, no. 2 (2017): 70–85.

———. "Phytofables: Tales of the Amazon." *Journal of Lusophone Studies* 1, no. 2 (2016): 116–34.

Vincent, Bruno. "Jouissance and Death Drive in Lacan's Teaching." *Ágora* 23, no. 1 (2020): 49–56.

Viñas, David. "*La vorágine*: Crisis, populismo y mirada." *Hispamérica* 3, no. 8 (1974): 3–21.

Viteri Gualinga, Carlos. "Biografía." Wordpress. https://carlosviterigualinga. wordpress.com/biografia/.

———. "Visión indígena del desarrollo en Amazonía." *Polis* 3 (2002): 1–6. http://journals.openedition.org/polis/7678.

Vittoria, Francisco de. *De Indis et de Ivre Belli Reflectiones*. Translated by John Pawley Bate. Edited by Ernest Nys. Washington, DC: Carnegie Institute, 1917.

Viveiros de Castro, Eduardo. *Cannibal Metaphysics: For a Post-Structural Anthropology*. Translated by Peter Skafish. Minneapolis: University of Minnesota Press, 2017.

———. "Cosmological Deixis and Amerindian Perspectivism." *The Journal of the Royal Anthropological Institute* 4, no. 3 (1998): 469–88.

———. "Perspectival Anthropology and the Methodology of Controlled Equivocation." *Tipiti* 2, no. 1 (2004): 1–20.

———. *The Relative Native: Essays on Indigenous Conceptual Worlds*. Chicago: Hau, 2015.

Waal, Frans B. M. de, and Peter Tyack, eds. *Animal Social Complexity: Intelligence, Culture, and Individualized Societies*. Cambridge, MA: Harvard University Press, 2005.

Wallerstein, Immanuel. *World Systems Analysis: An Introduction*. Durham, NC: Duke University Press, 2004.

Walsh, Catherine. "Interculturalidad, plurinacionalidad y decolonialidad: Las políticas político-epistémicas de refundar el Estado." *Tabula Rasa* 9 (2008): 131–52.

Wenzel, Jennifer. "Planet vs. Globe." *English Language Notes* 52, no. 1 (2014): 19–30.

Wheeler, A. M. "Animal Imagery as Reflection of Gender Roles in Clarice Lispector's *Family Ties*." *Critique* 28, no. 3 (1987): 125–34.

White, Steven F. *Arando el aire: La ecología en la poesía y la música de Nicaragua*. León, Nicaragua: 400 Elefantes; Alcaldía Municipal de León, 2011.

Whitt, Laurie, Mere Roberts, Waerte Norman, and Vicki Grieves. "Indigenous Perspectives." In *A Companion to Environmental Philosophy*. Edited by Dale Jamieson, 3–20. Malden, MA: Blackwell, 2001.

Whittemore, Mary Elizabeth. ' The Problem of Enforcing Nature's Rights Under Ecuador's Constitution: Why the Environmental Amendments Have No Bite." *Pacific Rim Law and Policy Journal* 20, no. 3 (2011): 659–91.

Whitten, Norman E., Jr., and Dorothea Scott Whitten. "Clashing Concepts of the 'Good Life': Beauty, Knowledge, and Vision versus National Wealth in Amazonian Ecuador." In *Images of Public Wealth or the Anatomy of Well-Being in Indigenous Amazonia*. Edited by Fernando Santos-Granero, 191–215. Tucson: University of Arizona Press, 2015.

Wolfe, Cary. *Before the Law: Humans and Other Animals in a Biopolitical Frame*. Chicago: University of Chicago Press, 2012.

———. *What Is Posthumanism?* Minneapolis: University of Minnesota Press, 2009.

Wylie, Lesley. *Colonial Tropes, Postcolonial Tricks: Rewriting the Tropics in the Novela de la Selva* Liverpool: Liverpool University Press, 2009.

———. *The Poetics of Plants in Spanish American Literature*. Pittsburgh: University of Pittsburgh Press, 2020.

Yúdice, George. "Civil Society, Consumption, and Governmentality in an Age of Global Restructuring: An Introduction." *Social Text* 45 (1995): 1–25.

Zaffaroni, Eugenio Raúl. *La Pachamama y el humano*. Buenos Aires: Colihue, 2012.

INDEX

abjection, 93, 122
Abrams, David, 256
Abya Yala, 29
Acosta, Alberto, 282n2
actants, 60, 70, 246–47, 298n24
actualization, 109, 116, 120, 132–33, 181, 199
Adorno, Theodor, 77, 306n88
aesthetics, 3, 125–26, 152, 181–82
    fantastical, 310n5
    gothic, 92–93, 153
    See also Modernismo, Spanish-American; Romanticism
affects/affectivity, 3–4, 61–63, 69, 81
    and fear, 79, 84
    and hatred, 102–4, 110, 209–10
    and love, 102–4
    and materiality, 61–65, 198
    and shame, 223–24
    See also biosemiotics; body; effects
affiliation/filiation, 76, 102, 127–45, 163, 173
afterlives, 99, 315n36
Agamben, Giorgio, 108, 164, 197, 220, 296n3, 313n19
agency, 65–68, 79–80, 158–59, 232–33, 247–48
    legal, 56–60
    in literature, 232–33
    See also intra-activity

Albert, Bruce, 172, 174–76, 198–206, 343n53. *See also Falling Sky, The* (Kopenawa)
alienation, 90, 101, 276
allegory, 10, 89–90, 109, 309n4–5
alliances, 78–79, 85, 177, 209
altruism, 192, 224
ambivalence, 16, 72, 84, 87, 96
analogy, 88, 114, 213, 219, 229
anarchy, 115, 145–46, 166
    and Zapatista Caracoles, 275
Andermann, Jens, 13
Andrade, Oswald de, 88, 306n79
animism, 256. *See also* shamanism
animot, 17, 94, 133, 220–25
annihilation, 46, 64, 80, 108–9, 246
Anthropocene, 23–24, 44, 72, 0, 231, 236–37
anthropocentrism, 48, 52, 69, 73, 221, 241
anthropomorphism, 8, 88–89, 153–54, 218–19, 223, 248
anthropophagy, 88, 305n79, 308n103, 338n21. *See also* Derrida, Jacques; Viveiros de Castro, Eduardo
arche, 110–11, 116, 159, 169
    of forest, 154–60, 181, 187–88, 194–96
Arguedas, Alcides, 258
"Ariel," (Rodó), 12
Aristotle, 17, 53, 128, 168, 209

www.ingramcontent.com/pod-product-compliance
Lightning Source LLC
Chambersburg PA
CBHW020451270326
41926CB00008B/568